Experiencing
Intercultural
Communication

Experiencing Intercultural Communication

An Introduction

Second Edition

Judith N. Martin

Thomas K. Nakayama

Arizona State University

Boston   Burr Ridge, IL   Dubuque, IA   Madison, WI   New York   San Francisco   St. Louis
Bangkok   Bogotá   Caracas   Kuala Lumpur   Lisbon   London   Madrid   Mexico City
Milan   Montreal   New Delhi   Santiago   Seoul   Singapore   Sydney   Taipei   Toronto

1 2 3 4 5 6 7 8 9 0 DOC/DOC 0 9 8 7 6 5 4

ISBN 0 07 286289 0

Publisher: *Phillip A. Butcher*
Senior sponsoring editor: *Nanette Giles*
Developmental editor: *Josh Hawkins*
Senior marketing manager: *Leslie Oberhuber*
Producer, Media technology: *Jessica Bodie Richards*
Project manager: *Ruth Smith*
Lead production supervisor: *Randy L. Hurst*
Design manager: *Laurie J. Entringer*
Media project manager: *Meghan Durko*
Manager, Photo research: *Brian Pecko*
Cover design: *Laurie Entringer*
Cover image: *Lisa Henderling/Images.com*
Typeface: *10/12 Janson*
Compositor: *G&S Typesetters*
Printer: *R. R. Donnelley and Sons Inc.*

Library of Congress Cataloging-in-Publication Data

Martin, Judith N.
    Experiencing intercultural communication : an introduction / Judith N. Martin,
Thomas K. Nakayama.—2nd ed.
      p. cm.
    Includes bibliographic references and index.
    ISBN 0-07-286289-0 (softcover : alk. paper)
    1. Intercultural communication.   I. Nakayama, Thomas K.   II. Title.
HM1211.M37 2005
303.48′2—dc22

                                                                2004049895

www.mhhe.com

Brief Contents

Contents

PART IV: Intercultural Communication in Applied Settings

Preface

As we continue to teach and write about intercultural communication, we are struck by the continued need for information covering the practical aspects of communicating across cultures. Since we wrote the first edition, the field of intercultural communication has changed at a rapid pace. The events of September 11, 2001, the increasing complexity of global relations, increasing conflicts that are not state sponsored, the increasing diversity of our country, the increasing interconnectedness of nations in a global economy—all mean that our lives and jobs depend more and more on intercultural communication skills. Are there general intercultural communication skills that can be used in a variety of cultural contexts? Is there culture-specific information that can help us become better intercultural communicators? Is there a way to tap into information on the Internet that may provide useful guidelines for intercultural communication?

We wrote this book to address these questions and issues. As in our other books, we have tried to use information from a variety of approaches in the field of intercultural communication, drawing from traditional social psychological approaches as well as from ethnographic studies and more recent critical media studies. However, the emphasis in this book is on the practical, experiential nature of intercultural communication. We attempt to give solid practical guidelines while noting the layers of complexity in communicating across cultural boundaries.

FEATURES OF THE BOOK

This book addresses the core issues and concerns of intercultural communication by introducing a group of general skills in Chapter 1 and by emphasizing the concepts and the skills of communicating interculturally throughout the text. This textbook:

- Includes a balanced treatment of skills and theory. The skills focus is framed by the presentation of the conceptual aspects of culture and communication. Each chapter has a section called "Building Intercultural Skills" that provides guidelines for improving students' intercultural communication skills.

- Provides a framework for understanding intercultural communication by focusing on four building blocks (culture, communication, context, and power) and four barriers (ethnocentrism, stereotyping, prejudice, and discrimination).

- Focuses on personal experiences by including students' narratives and authors' personal experiences throughout the text.
- Presents material in a student-friendly way. There are four types of thoughtful and fun bits of information in the margin provided for student interest. This edition contains new updated examples and websites:

     "What Do You Think?" includes information and questions that challenge students to think about their own culture and communication styles.

     "Surf's Up!" suggests websites that students can visit for more information about culture and communication.

     "Pop Culture Spotlight" presents popular culture examples of culture and communication.

     "Info Bites" provides fun facts and figures that illustrate issues related to intercultural communication.

- Includes separate chapters on history and identity, with sections on Whiteness and assisting European American students in exploring their own cultural issues.
- Focuses on popular culture, both in a separate chapter and in examples woven throughout the book.
- Applies concepts to real-life contexts; the book includes four chapters on how intercultural communication works in everyday settings in tourism, business, education, and health.

NEW TO THE SECOND EDITION

To reflect the increasing importance of religion in global conflicts, particularly in the September 11, 2001, terrorist attacks, we have interwoven a discussion of the role of religion in intercultural communication throughout the text.

For example, in Chapter 1, we explore the intercultural conditions that may have led to these attacks and their relationship to the Peace imperative in the study of intercultural communication. In Chapter 2 we added a discussion of stereotypes that develop based on recent religious struggles. In Chapter 3, we've expanded our discussion of religious identity and in Chapter 8, we explore the role of religion in intercultural conflict.

To acknowledge the increasing role technology plays in human communication, we expanded our discussion of the technology imperative in Chapter 1 to include a discussion of the "digital divide"; we also added a discussion of cyberspace as cultural space in Chapter 6. In Chapter 9, we discuss the role of culture and computer-mediated communication in a new section "Culture and Internet Relationships."

We have also expanded our discussion of cultural variations in communication style and models for effective intercultural communication. For example, in Chapter 5, we added a section on cultural variations in attitudes toward speaking, writing, and silence. There is also a new section on "third culture building" and "intercultural communication as improvised performance."

Finally, to acknowledge the importance of the impact of societal contexts on human communication, we expanded our discussion of the social and political impacts on international business (e.g., terrorism and international business) and tourist (impact of terrorism, SARS scare) encounters.

OVERVIEW OF THE BOOK

Chapter 1 focuses on the changing dynamics of social life and global conditions that provide a rationale for the study of intercultural communication. In this edition, we provide an extensive look at the complexities and possible causes of the 9/11 attacks and how these events impact the lives of everyday communicators. We also incorporate statistics of the 2000 census in our discussion of the demographic imperative.

Chapter 2 outlines a framework for the book and identifies four building blocks of intercultural communication—culture, communication, context, and power—and four attitudinal and behavioral barriers to effective intercultural communication—ethnocentrism, stereotyping, prejudice, and discrimination (including racism and other "isms"). This edition explores how events of 9/11 are related to current stereotyping, prejudice, and discrimination directed at specific cultural groups.

Chapter 3 focuses on helping students see the importance of history in understanding contemporary intercultural communication issues. The edition includes a discussion of global religious histories and their implications for intercultural communication.

Chapter 4 discusses issues of identity and intercultural communication. In this chapter we address a number of identities (gender, age, race and ethnicity, physical ability, religion, class, national and regional identity). We also discuss issues of multicultural identity—and the people who live on the borders—as well as issues of crossing borders and culture shock and adaptation. This edition includes the most recent thinking about white identity and post-ethnicity.

Chapter 5 addresses verbal aspects of intercultural communication, describing the components of language and cultural variations in language and communication style as well as issues of power and language. This edition includes a new section on cultural variations in attitudes toward speaking, writing and silence, and an expanded discussion of models for effective intercultural communication including "third culture building" and "intercultural communication as improvised performance."

Chapter 6 focuses on the role of nonverbal behavior in intercultural interaction, describing universal and culture-specific aspects of nonverbal communication and how nonverbal behavior can provide a basis for stereotyping and prejudice. This chapter also addresses cultural space and its dynamic, changing nature. This edition includes a new discussion of cyberspace as cultural space.

Chapter 7 addresses popular culture and intercultural communication, defining pop culture and discussing the ways in which pop culture forms our images of cultural groups and the ways in which we may consume (or resist) popular culture products. This edition includes a discussion of recent rise in popularity of "reality tv" and its implications for intercultural communication.

Chapter 8 discusses the role of culture and conflict. The chapter identifies characteristics of intercultural conflict, describes both personal and social/political aspects of conflict and how conflict management varies from culture to culture. This edition includes a section on "religion and conflict" and a refined presentation of conflict styles, to reflect recent developments in conflict style scholarship.

Chapter 9 focuses on intercultural relationships in everyday life. It identifies the challenges and benefits of intercultural relationships, examines how relationships may differ across cultures, and explores a variety of relationship types: friendship, gay, dating, and marriage relationships. The edition includes a new section on "culture and Internet relationships."

Chapters 10 through 13 focus on intercultural communication in specific contexts. Chapter 10 addresses issues of intercultural communication in the tourism industry, exploring various ways in which host and tourist may interact, how varying cultural norms may affect tourist encounters, and language issues and communication style. This edition includes an expanded discussion of the sometimes-complex attitudes of hosts toward tourists and a new section on "the social/political contexts of tourism" discussing the impact of terrorism, health risks (e.g., SARS, mad cow disease) on tourism.

Chapter 11 focuses on intercultural communication in business contexts and identifies several communication challenges (work-related values, differences in management styles, language issues, and affirmative action) in both domestic and international contexts. This edition includes a new section on the social and political contexts of business.

Chapter 12 explores intercultural communication and education, discussing different kinds of educational experiences (such as study abroad and culture-specific settings) and communication challenges (such as varying roles for teachers and students and grading and power) and also addressing social concerns and identity issues in educational settings. This edition includes a new section exploring the role of culture in admissions, affirmative action, and standardized tests.

Chapter 13 addresses intercultural communication and health care, focusing on intercultural barriers to effective health care, the historical treatment of cultural groups, and how power dynamics have influenced communication in health care settings. This edition includes a discussion of the role of religion in health care delivery and the implications for intercultural communication.

SUPPLEMENTAL RESOURCES

The Online Learning Center, at www.mhhe.com/experiencing2, provides interactive resources to address the needs of a variety of teaching and learning styles. For every chapter, students and instructors can access chapter outlines, sample quizzes with feedback, crossword puzzles using key terms, and Internet activities. For instructors specifically, the Online Learning Center offers an online Instructor's Resource Manual with sample syllabi, discussion questions, and pedagogical tips designed to help teach the course in general.

ACKNOWLEDGMENTS

As always, we owe a great deal to our colleagues in the Hugh Downs School of Human Communication, College of Liberal Arts, at Arizona State University as well as colleagues outside our school. Our colleagues at ASU helped us work through our ideas and shared insights from their lives and those of their students. In particular, we are grateful for the assistance provided by Dr. Ben Broome, Tamie Kanata, and Etsuko Fujimoto. Our students have contributed a great deal to this book; they willingly shared examples and stories from their lives and enthusiastically supported this project.

Special thanks go to our editorial assistants: To graduate student Elvinet Wilson, who spent hours culling through journals and magazines, surfing the Web and talking with colleagues and students to provide us with lively and relevant material—including the updated margin material. And thanks also to graduate student Hsueh Hua Chen for her patient and competent tracking of copyright permissions. We especially appreciate these students' assistance, given the many demands in their own lives and work.

Many other colleagues contributed including Professor Anneliese Harper (Scottsdale Community College), who gave us the idea of writing this book by pointing out the need for more context-specific and experientially based materials in the intercultural communication curriculum. Professors Shelley Smith (University of Minnesota), Dawn Braithwaite (University of Nebraska) and Denis Leclerc (ASU Department of Recreation Management and Tourism) provided us with resources and suggestions for framing the "context" chapters in the first edition. Thanks also go to Robert Barr, M.S. of Mecklenburg Radiology Associates in Charlotte, North Carolina, for the helpful tips on health communication.

Thanks to the fine team at McGraw-Hill who make it all happen. Thanks to senior sponsoring editor Nanette Kauffman Giles who skillfully guided us through the McGraw Hill publishing process. We also want to acknowledge the fine work of project manager Ruth Smith and development editor Joshua Hawkins, who kept us on track. Thanks also to marketing manager Leslie Oberhuber, designer Laurie Entringer, photo researcher Brian Pecko and media producer Jessica Bodie Richards.

In addition, we want to thank the reviewers, whose thoughtful and insightful comments led to careful revisions and a much improved manuscript: Anneliese Harper, Scottsdale Community College; Mary C. Hopkins, Spokane Falls Community College; Margaret J. O'Connor, Reinhardt College; Peter Ross, Central Michigan University; Curtis L. VanGeison, St. Charles Community College; and Julie Zink, University of Southern Maine.

And to those friends and colleagues who enrich our lives and our scholarship by helping us understand what it means to live interculturally, we are grateful: Dr. Amalia Villegas, Laura Laguna, Cruzita and Aurelio Mori, Lucia Madril and family, as well as many of the faculty, staff, and participants at the Summer Institute for Intercultural Communication in Portland, Oregon, and Jean-Louis Sauvage (Université de Mons-Hainaut). Finally, we thank our partners, Ronald S. Chaldu and David L. Karbonski, for hanging in there with us once again!

About the Authors

Judith Martin grew up in Mennonite communities, primarily in Delaware and Pennsylvania. She has studied at the Université de Grenoble in France and has taught in Algeria. She received her doctorate at the Pennsylvania State University. By background and training, she is a social scientist who has focused on intercultural communication on an interpersonal level and has studied how people's communication is affected as they move or sojourn between international locations. She has taught at the State University of New York at Oswego, the University of Minnesota, the University of New Mexico, and Arizona State University. She enjoys gardening, going to Mexico, and hosting annual Academy Awards parties, and she does not miss the harsh Midwestern winters.

Tom Nakayama grew up mainly in Georgia, at a time when the Asian American presence was much less than it is now. He has studied at the Université de Paris and various universities in the United States. He received his doctorate from the University of Iowa. By background and training, he is a critical rhetorician who views intercultural communication in a social context. He has taught at the California State University at San Bernardino and Arizona State University. He is a voracious reader and owns more books than any other faculty member in his department. He watches TV—especially baseball games—and lifts weights. Living in the West now, he misses springtime in the South.

CHAPTER ONE

Studying Intercultural Communication

CHAPTER OUTLINE

The Peace Imperative

The Economic Imperative
The Workplace
The Global Economy

The Technological Imperative
Technology and Human Communication
Mobility and Its Effect on Communication

The Demographic Imperative
Changing U.S. Demographics
Changing Immigration Patterns

The Self Awareness Imperative

The Ethical Imperative
Ethical Judgments and Cultural Values
Becoming an Ethical Student of Culture

Summary

Building Intercultural Skills

Activities

Endnotes

STUDY OBJECTIVES

After reading this chapter, you should be able to:

1. Describe the peace imperative for studying intercultural communication.

2. Identify and describe the economic and technological imperatives for studying intercultural communication.

3. Describe how the changing demographics in the United States and the changing worldwide immigration patterns affect intercultural communication.

4. Explain how studying intercultural communication can lead to increased self-understanding.

5. Understand the difference between a universalistic and relativist approach to the study of ethics and intercultural communication.

6. Identify and describe characteristics of an ethical student of culture.

KEY TERMS

assimilatable
class structure
cross-cultural trainers
demographics
diversity
enclaves
ethics
global village
globalization

heterogeneity
immigration
maquiladoras
melting pot metaphor
mobility
relativist position
self-awareness
self-reflexivity
universalist position

For many people in the United States, September 11, 2001, was a day that underscored the importance of understanding intercultural relations and the causes of intercultural conflict. Many felt that the attacks on the World Trade Center and Pentagon were a wake-up call to try to understand why people in other countries were so angry at the United States that they would destroy the lives of thousands of innocent civilians representing diverse nationalities, ethnicities, social and economic classes, and occupations.

A newspaper article written by John Jurgensen on the second anniversary of the September 11 tragedy explores American responses to these attacks. According to Jurgensen, in the aftermath of the attacks, emotions made people hungry to learn more about the cultures and religion of the attackers. Community groups, libraries, and churches sought lecturers on Islam and the Middle East. People turned to in-depth news magazines like *The New Yorker* and *The Economist*, which have seen an increase of 100,000 readers since the end of 2000. Some people turned directly to the *Koran* for answers; one publisher sold 250,000 copies in four months after the attacks—more copies than it sells in a typical year.

Another response, Jurgensen believes, was an increased attention to global politics. A research poll at the end of 2002 showed that only 30 percent of Americans thought the United States should mind its own business internationally, compared with 41 percent in 1995.

Some Americans responded by taking very direct personal action, such as changing careers to devote themselves full time to improving intercultural relations and understanding. Jurgensen describes the reaction of one student, Beverly Nemmers, whose two close friends and their children were on the plane that crashed into the Pentagon. For Beverly, reaction to the attacks was instant.

> "I said to myself, 'I have to save the world.'" When she was laid off three weeks after the attacks, Nemmers started looking for ways to act on her impulse. . . . she started in the School for International Training's joint program with the Peace Corps. "I don't know where they are going to send me, but at least I can learn about that country and come back to tell Americans about it," Nemmers says.[1]

Certainly these attacks brought home the complexities of intercultural relations and underscore the need for people to study and understand intercultural communication. It is easy to become overwhelmed by that complexity. However, not knowing everything that you would like to know is very much a part of the learning process, and this inability to know everything is what makes intercultural communication experiences so exciting. Rather than being discouraged by everything that you cannot know, think of all the things you can learn from intercultural communication experiences.

Surf's Up!

Read the "All American Teenager," story to see how intercultural your existence is, even when you are just getting up in the morning (www.founders.howard.edu/cybercamp/allamer.htm).

Why is it important to focus on intercultural communication and to strive to become better at this complex form of interaction? In this chapter, six reasons or imperatives to study intercultural communication are suggested: peace, economics, technology, demographics, self-awareness, and ethics.

THE PEACE IMPERATIVE

The key issue is this: Can individuals of different sexes, ages, ethnicities, races, languages, and religions peacefully coexist on the planet? The history of humankind, as well as recent conflicts in the Middle East, Iraq, North Korea, South Korea, India, Pakistan, and Ireland, are hardly grounds for optimism. Contact among different cultural groups—from the earliest civilizations until today— often leads to disharmony. For example, consider the ethnic struggles in Bosnia and in the former Soviet Union, the conflict between the Indonesians and East Timorese, and the racial and ethnic tensions in various U.S. cities. Some of these conflicts represent a legacy of colonialism around the world, in which European powers forced diverse groups—differing in language, culture, religion, or identity—together to form one state. For example, the union of Bangladesh, Pakistan, and India was imposed by the British; eventually, Pakistan won its independence from India, as did Bangladesh from Pakistan. The tremendous

People are often caught in devastating consequences of conflicts they neither started nor chose. In this photo, Chechnya residents search through the rubble of their house destroyed by war. While communication skills cannot solve all political conflicts, they are vital in dealing with intercultural strife.

diversity—and historical antagonisms—within many former colonies can be better understood in the context of colonialism.

While the reasons for the September 11 attacks are complex and abhorred by the vast majority of Muslims, some analysts believe the sources for the attacks lie in the continuing frustration with lack of attention paid to the Jewish-Palestinian conflict and a perception that Americans turn a blind eye to the suffering of the Palestinian people. As Peter Ford, a writer for the *Christian Science Monitor*, describes it:

> Arab nations have lost three wars against their arch-foe—and America's closest ally—Israel. A sense of failure and injustice is rising in the throats of millions. . . . against the background of that humiliated mood, America's unchallenged military, economic, and cultural policies might be seen as an affront even if its policies in the Middle East were neutral. And nobody voices that view. . . . Over the past year, Arab TV stations have broadcast countless pictures of Israeli soldiers shooting at Palestinian youths, Israeli tanks plowing into Palestinian homes, Israeli helicopters rocketing Palestinian streets. And they know that the US sends more than $3 billion a year in military and economic aid to Israel. . . .
>
> This mood of resentment toward America and its behavior around the world has become so commonplace in their countries that it was bound to breed hostility, and even hatred.[2]

Some of the conflicts are also tied to economic disparities and economic colonialism. The tremendous influence of U.S. technology and media is seen as a positive benefit by some people and as a cause for resistance by others. Communication scholar Fernando Delgado describes these tensions:

> Such cultural dominance, though celebrated at home, can spark intercultural conflicts because it inhibits the development of other nations' indigenous popular culture products, stunts their economic development and foists U.S. values and perspectives on other cultures. These effects, in turn, often lead to resentment and conflict.[3]

He goes on to cite the claim of Canadian leaders that a Canadian cultural identity is almost impossible due to the dominance of American media. Delgado recognizes the complexity of this issue. He recounts noticing anti-American sentiments in graffiti, newspapers, and TV programs during a recent trip to Europe. But U.S. influences also were evident in youth music, television, film, and cars. He observed that locals were amazed and resentful at the same time at the penetration of U.S. popular culture. It would be naive to assume that simply understanding something about intercultural communication would end war and intercultural conflict, but these problems do underscore the need for us to learn more about groups of which we are not members. We need to remember as well that individuals often are born into and are caught up in conflicts that they neither started nor chose and that are impacted by the larger societal forces.

What Do You Think?

A recent book by Brett Dellinger, *Finnish Views of CNN*, points out that the style of news broadcasts in Europe changed once government-run news stations were privatized. Dellinger argues that in Finland people are having to adjust to a new, "punchier," U.S.-inspired news format. Do you think that the U.S. news style is the best for presenting the complexities of events in the world?

THE ECONOMIC IMPERATIVE

You may want to know more about intercultural communication because you foresee tremendous changes in the workplace in the coming years. This is one important reason to know about other cultures and communication patterns. In addition, knowing about intercultural communication is strategically important for U.S. businesses in the emerging transnational economy. Intercultural scholars Bernando Ferdman and Sari Brody observe that "increasing globalization and a more diverse domestic workforce are push factors (organizations that do nothing will lose ground), whereas the benefits to be had from working effectively across differences are pull factors (organizations that take advantage, it is argued, will do better and be more competitive).[4]

The Workplace

Given the growing cultural diversity in the United States, businesses necessarily must be more attentive to diversity issues. As the workforce becomes more diverse, many businesses are seeking to capitalize on these differences: "Once organizations learn to adopt an inclusive orientation in dealing with their members, this will also have a positive impact on how they look at their customer base, how they develop products and assess business opportunities, and how they

What Do You Think?

Why is globalization so controversial? Economic and foreign policy analysts Barry Bosworth and Philip H. Gordon suggest four possible reasons: (1) The generation of open markets and new trading freedoms creates both winners and losers; (2) A significant portion of the world still lives in poverty and has yet to gain anything from the new global marketplace; (3) Globalization has led to new environmental concerns which are a source of conflict; (4) Globalization encourages open national borders to allow the free flow of capital and information but, in turn, potentially risks inviting increased drug trafficking, money laundering, terrorism, and new diseases into individual countries. (Source: *Brookings Review* 19, no. 4, Fall 2001)

Multicultural work environments are becoming increasingly common in the 21st century. In many of these situations, working in small groups is especially important. Given this trend, workers need to learn to deal with cultural differences.

relate to their communities."[5] Benefiting from cultural differences in the workplace involves not only working with diverse employees and employers but also seeing new business markets, developing new products for differing cultural contexts, and marketing products in culturally appropriate and effective ways. From this perspective, diversity is a potentially powerful economic tool for business organizations.

The Global Economy

Businesses all around the world are continually expanding into overseas markets in a process of **globalization.** They sometimes make more money from overseas sales than from domestic sales. For example, in 2003, Nike made $5.1 billion in overseas sales compared to $4.6 billion at home. Signing up big-name athletes like Brazilian soccer star Ronaldo to sell its shoes and clothing has resulted in tremendous sales in Europe, Asia, and Latin America.[6] In addition, U.S. and European banks and construction companies are competing for lucrative contracts in the rebuilding of Iraq, where American officials estimate that the country's annual gross national product totaled at least $29 billion before the war.[7]

Another example of globalization occurred when General Electric (GE) expanded its market to India, hoping to sell products there. While it was not so successful at this enterprise, GE did find lots of low-cost, high-quality talent. The corporation has now hired 17,000 of India's scientists, engineers, and other personnel to manufacture GE's refrigerators and jet engines.[8] And to compete on a global scale, companies like GE and Nike need to understand how business is conducted in other countries. They need to be able to negotiate deals that are advantageous in the U.S. economy. However, U.S. businesses are not always willing to take the time and effort to do this.

However, rampant globalization has many critics who point out the downside of businesses finding cheap labor abroad—U.S. manufacturers have lost more than 2.4 million jobs since 2001, or more than 2,600 jobs a day. Many people blame the Chinese, whose exports to the United States have more than doubled in the past five years, totaling more than $110 billion in 2002. While U.S. exports to China are rising, they are still less than one-fifth of what China shipped to the United States in 2003. After Canada and Mexico, China is the third-largest supplier of goods to the United States.[9]

Opponents say that while globalization is producing great wealth, it is also the cause of growing poverty and inequality on the planet. At the world level, the top 20 percent now has 82 times as much wealth as the bottom 20 percent, compared to a 30-to-1 ratio in the immediate postwar period. Half the world's people live on less than $2 a day, and one-fifth live on less than $1 a day. Also, 800 million are chronically hungry, and new evidence shows that the World Bank (responsible for some of these figures) has, if anything, underestimated the numbers of the destitute. These kinds of inequalities can lead to resentment, despair, and ultimately to intercultural conflict.[10]

International trade is one of the driving forces in interactions between cultures. However, there is some concern that growing poverty and inequality resulting from globalization may lead to intercultural conflict.

In addition, there are other considerations in understanding the global market. Moving operations overseas to take advantage of lower labor costs has far-reaching implications for corporations. One example is the *maquiladoras*—foreign-owned plants that use domestic labor—just across the U.S.-Mexican border. The U.S. companies that relocate their plants there benefit from lower labor costs and lack of environmental and other business regulations, while Mexican laborers benefit from the jobs. But there is a cost in terms of environmental hazards. Because Mexico has less stringent air and water pollution regulations than the United States, many of these *maquiladoras* have a negative environmental impact on the Mexican side of the border. Because the two nations are economically and environmentally interdependent, they share the economic and environmental impact. Thus, these contexts present intercultural challenges for Mexicans and Americans alike.

To help bridge the cultural gap, many companies employ **cross-cultural trainers,** who assist people going abroad by giving them information about and strategies for dealing with cultural differences; such trainers report that Japanese and other business personnel often spend years in the United States studying English and learning about the country before they decide to build a factory or invest money here. By contrast, many U.S. companies provide little or no training before sending their workers overseas and expect business deals to be completed very quickly. They seem to have little regard for cultural idiosyncrasies, which can cause ill will and mistrust, enhance negative stereotypes, and result in lost business opportunities.

In the future, economic development in Japan and other Asian countries (including Singapore, Taiwan, South Korea, and China), as well as in Latin America, will create even more demand for intercultural communication. Economic exchanges will drive intercultural interactions. This development will create not only more jobs but also more consumers to purchase goods from around the world—and to travel in that world.

THE TECHNOLOGICAL IMPERATIVE

In the 1960s, media guru Marshall McLuhan coined the term **global village** to describe a world in which communication technology—TV, radio, news services—brings news and information to the most remote parts of the world.[11] Today, people are connected—via answering machines, faxes, e-mail, electronic bulletin boards, and the Internet—to other people whom they have never met face-to-face. It's possible not only to communicate with other people but also to develop complex relationships with them through such technology.

Technology and Human Communication

These monumental changes have affected how we think of ourselves and how we form intercultural relationships. In his book *The Saturated Self*, psychologist Kenneth Gergen describes the changes that occur as technology alters patterns of communication.[12] In past centuries, social relationships typically were circumscribed by how far one could walk, but they evolved with each technological advance—whether it be the railroad, automobile, telephone, radio, TV, or movies. These relationships have now expanded exponentially. We can be "accessed" in many ways, including e-mail, instant messaging, chatrooms, faxes, phone, and express mail, and be involved simultaneously in many different relationships, all without face-to-face contact.

Most of us cannot imagine life without the Internet, which is now estimated to include one billion websites. The growth of the Internet has tremendous financial implications. By 2004, online commerce will reach $6.8 trillion, includ-

Surf's Up!

What should you know about different cultural practices if you want to become an international business traveler? Check out the International Education Systems's website that highlights a top-ten list of international faux pas (www.marybosrock.com/fauxpas.htm). Monster.com also includes regularly updated feature stories about international cultural misunderstandings submitted by individuals who live, work, or conduct business abroad (http://internazionale.monsteritalia.it/workabroad/articles/falkoff/).

ing business-to-business and business-to-consumer transactions online, with Asian and European nations becoming increasingly active.[13]

What does this have to do with intercultural communication? Through high-tech communication, we come into contact with people who are very different from ourselves, often in ways we don't understand. The people we talk to on e-mail networks may speak languages different from our own, come from different countries, be of different ethnic backgrounds, and have had many different life experiences. America Online, for example, hosts the "Bistro," which brings people in contact via e-mail in various languages. As AOL notes, "The purpose of the Bistro is to bring people of differing cultural and ethnic backgrounds together to speak in their native language, discuss international topics, and learn more about the world we live in." Technology has increased the frequency with which many people encounter multilingual situations and so must decide which language will be used. Contrast this situation with the everyday lives of people 100 years ago, in which they rarely communicated with people outside their own villages, much less people speaking different languages. The use of e-mail for intercultural communication is yet another reason to study this topic.

In the high-tech communication world, the choice of language has itself become an issue. The dominance of English in cyberspace is a sensitive topic. The language we use is very much a part of intercultural communication, and in setting up the Bistro, AOL was sensitive to the issue:

> Literally thousands of dialects are spoken throughout the world. The Bistro Staff recognizes this as a fact and strives to offer as many languages as desired by its members. The languages chosen to be placed on the main screen tabs were the languages *most frequently requested by our members* and do not reflect any bias on the part of the Bistro Staff. (emphasis in the original)

People seek out intercultural communication for many different reasons, including the use of other languages to express their thoughts and feelings.

One of the issues of interest to those who study intercultural communication is the "digital divide" that exists between those who have access to technologies like the Internet and those who do not. When the Internet first became available, there was a large discrepancy between those who had access and those who did not. The majority of users tended to be White, from urban areas in mostly Westernized countries, male, young, and relatively affluent. Great gains have been made in the past five years in narrowing some of these gaps. For example, the gender gap has all but disappeared, but there are gaps between groups of different levels of income and education, old and young, single- and dual-parent families, and those with and without disabilities. For instance, persons with a disability are only half as likely to have access to the Internet as those without a disability. Large gaps also remain among different races and ethnic groups regarding Internet use. Asian Americans and Pacific Islanders have maintained the

Pop Culture Spotlight

In the novel *The Joy Luck Club,* a White American makes several mistakes while eating dinner at the home of his Chinese American girlfriend's mother. He takes all of the best dish for himself, and he adds soy sauce to it after the mother makes negative comments about the dish—not realizing it is a custom for the cook to insult her best recipe. Do you have similar memories of mistakes you've made in intercultural encounters?

highest level of home Internet access at 56.8 percent, while Blacks and Hispanics have the lowest household Internet use at 23.5 percent and 23.6 percent, respectively.[14]

Mobility and Its Effect on Communication

Not only do we come in contact with more people electronically these days, but we come in contact with more people physically. Our society is more mobile than ever before; U.S. families move, on average, five times. Of course, there are still communities in which people are born, live, and die, but this happens far less often than it once did.

Mobility changes the nature of our society, and it also affects the individuals involved. One of the authors of this book, Judith, remembers moving every few years while she was growing up. She was always facing a new group of classmates at a new school. One year, just prior to attending a new high school, she wrote in her diary:

> I know that the worst will be over soon. Always changing schools should make me more at ease. It doesn't. I like to meet strangers and make friends. Once I get to know people, it'll be easier. But I always dread the first day, wondering if I'll fit in, wondering if the other kids'll be nice to me.

Many families move because of divorce. As of 1999, only half of children lived with both birth mother and birth father—down from nearly three-quarters in 1972. Of the other half, some lived with one parent or in stepfamilies or extended families (such as grandparents), or shuttled back and forth between parents' houses.[15] And some children commute between different geographical regions of the United States. For example, they might spend the summer with dad in Chicago and the rest of the year with mom and stepfather in Phoenix. These new family configurations increase intercultural contact as generational, regional, and sometimes cultural differences help frame the cultural notion of what constitutes "family." Increasing mobility also increases the probability of encountering cultural differences related to food (smelt in Chicago versus Sonoran cuisine in Phoenix), languages, and regional ways of life (riding the El in Chicago versus driving to strip malls in Phoenix).

Families also relocate for economic reasons. A U.S. company might expand its operations to Mexico and relocate corporate personnel with the company. The rise of the European Union makes it much easier for Europeans to work in other European countries. For example, Irish citizens can work in Belgium, Belgians can work in France, and the French can work in Ireland. Increasing technology and mobility in a shrinking, interdependent world means that we can no longer afford to be culturally illiterate. Rather, we all need to be more aware of cultural differences and learn to bridge those differences. Even people who never move may increasingly encounter others who are culturally different and so need to learn new strategies to communicate with them.

THE DEMOGRAPHIC IMPERATIVE

The U.S. population has changed radically in recent decades and will continue to do so in the future. The workforce that you enter will differ significantly from the one that your parents entered. These changes come from two sources: changing demographics within the United States and changing immigration patterns.

Changing U.S. Demographics

Demographics refers to the general characteristics of a given population. The U.S. Census Bureau describes how the demographics of the U.S. workforce will continue to change in the near future. Projections are that between 1998 and 2008, about 42 million people are expected to enter the labor force—and give it a new look. The new workers will be younger, more likely to be female, and more ethnically diverse than the current workforce.

Assuming that these trends continue into 2025, the American labor force will become slightly more female (48 percent versus 46 percent in 1998) and noticeably more minority (36 percent versus 26 percent in 1998). However, the aging of the baby boom generation also will make the labor force older in 2025. The integration of the new workers and the current ones will provide both opportunities and challenges for American businesses, as well as for the country as a whole.[16]

Another interesting fact is the increase in multicultural people. The 2000 Census was the first that allowed persons to categorize themselves as "two or more races," and 2.4 percent of respondents did just that. Most of them live in the southern and western regions of the United States, regions with the most ethnic and racial diversity. Based on Census 2000 information, where you live determines to some extent how much opportunity you have to interact with people who are different from you ethnically or racially. According to the 2000 Census, the 10 states with the most ethnically diverse populations are California, Nevada, Arizona, New Mexico, Texas, Louisiana, Mississippi, Georgia, Florida, and Illinois. In fact, in California, the 2000 Census data showed that no single racial or ethnic group, including non-Hispanic Whites, makes up more than 50 percent of the state population. This means that California is officially a "majority-minority" state and presents special challenges and opportunities for intercultural understanding.[17]

Changing Immigration Patterns

The second source of demographic change is **immigration.** There are two contradictory faces to the story of immigration in the United States. The United States often is described as a nation of immigrants, but it is also a nation that established itself by subjugating the original inhabitants of the land and that prospered economically while forcibly importing millions of Africans to perform

Info Bites

U.S. colleges and universities continually market themselves to students from foreign countries. According to the Institute of International Education, educating foreign students has become a billion-dollar industry in the United States. In the year 2000 alone, California earned $1.6 billion, New York $1.3 billion, Massachusetts $804 million, and Texas $614 million in revenue from foreign students. (SOURCE: *Insight on the News,* vol. 17, December 10, 2001)

Info Bites

Since 9/11 there have been many changes to U.S. immigration policies. Some of them affect international students specifically. In fall 2003, the Bureau of Citizenship and Immigration Services (formerly INS) implemented an electronic tracking system known as the Student and Exchange Visitor Information System (SEVIS). Colleges and universities are now required to formally track foreign students and report such information as program start and end dates, field of study, credits completed, student employment, and changes of address.

(Source: *Issues in Science and Technology,* vol. 18, Winter 2001)

slave labor. It is important to recognize the many different experiences that people have had in the United States so that we can better understand what it means to be a U.S. American. We cannot simply think of ourselves as a nation of immigrants if we want to better understand contemporary U.S. society.

Current patterns of immigration are having a significant effect on the social landscape. Prior to the 1960s, most of the immigrants to the United States came from Europe, compared to only 14 percent today. According to the U.S. Census Bureau, the vast majority (about 80 percent) of today's immigrants come from Latin America (52 percent) and Asia (25 percent). These immigrants also tend to settle in particular areas of the country. They are more likely to live in the western part of the United States and are more likely to live in the central locations of metropolitan areas, adding to the diversity of these areas. These immigration changes, along with increasing domestic diversity, clearly show that the United States is becoming more **heterogeneous,** or diverse.[18]

These demographic changes present many opportunities and challenges for students of intercultural communication and for society. The tension among different racial-ethnic groups, as well as fear on the part of politically dominant groups, must be acknowledged. California, for example, is not making the transition to a more diverse society as smoothly as hoped. During the 1990s, the state passed laws eliminating affirmative action, restricting access to medical and social services, and eliminating bilingual education in schools. And there is no guarantee that the new century will bring much more tolerance. On the one hand, many states with the highest percentages of non-White residents are the same states with very contentious racial pasts—for example, Alabama, Mississippi, and South Carolina. On the other hand, Hawaii, a very diverse state in which no one group forms a majority, has largely avoided racial strife. So, you can see that intercultural conflict is not necessarily a consequence of diversity. Culturally speaking, **diversity** can expand our horizons—linguistically, politically, socially—as various lifestyles and ways of thinking come together. We often profit from being exposed to different ways of doing things and incorporate these customs into our own lifestyle. For example, food from many cultures is much more widely available today—from Japanese, to Ethiopian, to Cuban, to Vietnamese.

Historical Overview   To get a better sense of the sociocultural situation in the United States today, let's take a look at our history. As mentioned, the United States has always been a nation of immigrants. When Europeans began arriving on the shores of the New World, an estimated 8 to 10 million Native Americans were already living here. The outcome of the encounters between these groups—the colonizing Europeans and the native peoples—is well known. By 1940, the Native American population of the United States had been reduced to an estimated 250,000. Today, there are about 1.9 million American Indians, from 542 recognized tribes, living in the United States.[19]

African Americans are a special case in the history of U.S. immigration because they were brought to this country involuntarily. Some Europeans and

Asians also arrived in the country as indentured or contract labor. However, by the middle of the 17th century, this system had been dissolved, because it was not economically viable for farmers and did not solve the problem of chronic labor shortage.[20] Landowners needed captive workers who could neither escape servitude nor become competitors. The answer was slavery. Native Americans were not a good choice, given that they could always escape back to their own lands, but Africans were. In fact, Europeans and Africans were already in the slave business, and so America became a prime market. The slave trade lasted about 350 years, during which time 9 to 10 million Africans reached the Americas (the vast majority died in the brutal overseas passage).[21] As James Baldwin has suggested, slavery is what makes U.S. history and current interracial relations different from those in Europe.[22]

Historically, slavery presented a moral dilemma for many Whites, but today a common response is to ignore history. Many Whites say that because not all Whites owned slaves we should simply forget it and move on. For most African Americans, however, this is unacceptable. Rather, as Cornel West, a professor of Afro-American studies and the philosophy of religion at Harvard University, suggests, we should begin by acknowledging the historical flaws in American society and recognizing the historical consequences of slavery.[23] Yet the recent controversy over the Confederate flag flying above the South Carolina state capitol building reflects a desire to remember that past in a different way. It is also interesting to note that there are several Holocaust museums in the United States but no organized, official recognition of the horrors of slavery, such as a national museum of slavery in Washington, DC.

Relationships between residents and immigrants—between old-timers and newcomers—often have been contentious. In the 19th century, Native Americans sometimes were caught in the middle of U.S.-European rivalries. During the War of 1812, for example, Indian allies of the British were severely punished by the United States when the war ended. In 1832, the U.S. Congress recognized Native Americans' right to self-government, but an 1871 congressional act prohibited treaties between the U.S. government and Indian tribes. In 1887, Congress passed the Dawes Severalty Act, terminating Native Americans' special relationship with the U.S. government and paving the way for the removal of Native Americans from their land.

As waves of immigrants continued to roll in from Europe, the more firmly established European—mainly English—immigrants tried to protect their way of life, language, and culture. James Banks has identified various conflicts throughout the nation's history, many of which were not uniquely American but were imported from Europe.[24] In 1729, for example, an English mob prevented a group of Irish immigrants from landing in Boston. A few years later, another mob destroyed a new Scots-Irish Presbyterian church in Worcester, Massachusetts. Subsequently, as immigrants from northern and western Europe came to dominate American culture, immigrants from southern, central, and eastern Europe were expected to assimilate into the so-called mainstream culture—to jump into the "melting pot" and come out "American."

Surf's Up!

Could the slave trade be the first organized system of globalization in world history? Check out one of many *United Nations Educational, Scientific, and Cultural Organization* (UNESCO) websites, focusing on improving global intercultural dialogues (http://www.unesco.org/culture/dialogue/slave/). Here you can read up on a UNESCO project called the Slave Route, launched in 1994 with the goals of maintaining a commitment to peace, historical truth, intercultural dialogue, and human rights and development.

In the late 19th and early 20th centuries, an anti-immigrant, nativistic movement promoted violence against newer immigrants. For example, in 1885, 28 Chinese were killed in an anti-Chinese riot in Wyoming; in 1891, a White mob attacked a Chinese community in Los Angeles and killed 19 people; in 1891, 11 Italian Americans were lynched in New Orleans.

The anti-immigrant, nativistic sentiment was well supported at the government level as well. In 1882, Congress passed the Chinese Exclusion Act, officially prohibiting Chinese from immigrating to this country. In 1924, the Johnson-Reed Act and the Oriental Exclusion Act established strict quotas on immigration and completely barred the immigration of Asians. According to Ronald Takaki, these 1924 laws "provided for immigration based on nationality quotas: the number of immigrants to be admitted annually was limited to 2 percent of

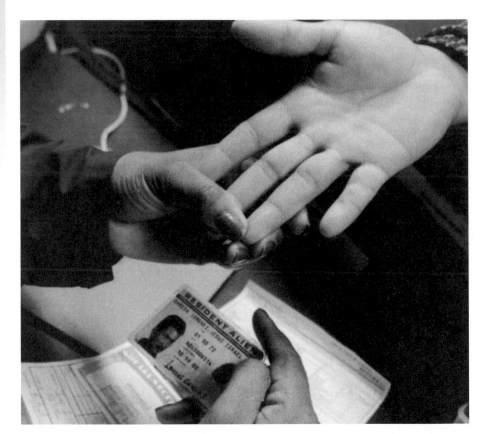

An immigration officer in San Ysidro, California, compares an immigrant's fingerprints against those shown on a green card. Immigration, especially from Asia and Latin America, will only serve to increase the intercultural experiences of many U.S. Americans.

the foreign-born individuals of each nationality residing in the United States in 1890."[25] The underlying rationale was that economic and political opportunities should be reserved for Whites, native-born Americans or not. Thus, the dominance of Whites in the United States is not simply the result of more Europeans wanting to come here; the U.S. government designed our society in this way.

By the 1930s, immigrants from southern and eastern Europe were considered **"assimilatable,"** or able to become members of White American society, and the concept of race assumed new meaning. All of the so-called White races were now considered one, so racial hostilities were directed toward members of non-White ethnic groups, such as Asian Americans, Native Americans, and Mexican Americans;[26] this bias was particularly devastating for African Americans.[27] In the growing but sometimes fragile economy of the first half of the 20th century, only White workers were assured a place. White immigrants may have earned relatively low wages, but they were paid additional "psychological" wages in the form of better schools, increased access to public facilities, and more public deference.

Economic conditions make a big difference in attitudes toward foreign workers and immigration policies. Thus, during the Great Depression of the 1930s, Mexicans and Mexican Americans were forced to return to Mexico to free up jobs for White Americans. When prosperity returned in the 1940s, Mexicans were welcomed back as a source of cheap labor. In fact, this occurs all over the world. For example, Algerian workers are alternately welcomed and rejected in France, depending on the condition of the French economy and the need for imported labor. "Guest workers" from Turkey have been subjected to similar uncertainties in Germany. Indian workers in Kenya, Chinese immigrants in Malaysia, and many other workers toiling outside their native lands have suffered from the vagaries of fluctuating economies and inconsistent immigration policies.

The Current Situation   The tradition of tension and conflict between cultures continues to this day. The conflicts that occurred in Southern California in the 1990s have their roots in the demographic changes in the United States. In fact, the situation in greater Los Angeles is a prime example of the problems associated with intercultural communication in 21st-century America. We often imagine Hollywood and Los Angeles in terms of the California dream as portrayed in TV shows and movies. These unrealistic images sometimes prevent us from recognizing the kinds of intercultural tensions that were manifested in the 1991 Los Angeles riots that followed the acquittal of the police officers who beat Rodney King and the tensions that are fueled by the more recent allegations of widespread police corruption in the L.A. Police Department.

The tensions in Los Angeles among Latinos, African Americans, Korean Americans, and European Americans can be examined on a variety of levels. Some of the conflict is due to different languages, values, and lifestyles. Some African Americans resent the success of recent Korean immigrants—a common

Pop Culture Spotlight

In the John Sayles film *Lone Star,* debates about multiculturalism and immigration are predominant. In the film, the most vigorous opponents of multiculturalism in schools and of immigration are themselves multicultural people and former immigrants. Do such things happen in real life? Why would former immigrants oppose immigration?

reaction throughout history. The conflict may also be due to the pattern of settlement that results in cultural **enclaves**—for example, Blacks in South Central Los Angeles, Latinos in Inglewood and East Los Angeles, Koreans in the "Miracle Mile" section west of downtown Los Angeles, and Whites on the west side of the city. As in other parts of the country, the majority of White suburban Americans live in neighborhoods that are overwhelmingly White.[28]

Some of the conflict may be due to the economic disparity that exists among these different groups. To understand this disparity we need to look at issues of economic class. Most Americans are reluctant to admit that a **class structure** exists, let alone admit how difficult it is to move up in this structure. But the fact is that most people live their lives in the same economic class into which they were born. In addition, the U.S. cultural myth that anyone can move up the class structure through hard work, known as the Horatio Alger myth, is not benign. Rather, it reinforces middle- and upper-class beliefs in their own superiority and perpetuates a false hope among members of the working class that they can get ahead. And there are just enough success stories—for example, Ross Perot, Roseanne, and Madonna—of easy upward mobility to perpetuate the myth.

How have economic conditions changed for the various classes, and what might the future hold? As *Workforce 2020* notes, "more American workers are now paid very well, and more are now paid comparatively poorly."[29] In other words, the number of people at the high and low ends of the pay scale is increasing, but decreasing in the middle. Concurrently, the stable industrial jobs in the cities have been disappearing, as companies move their operations overseas. According to the Center on Budget and Policy Priorities, the gap between the rich and poor in the United States more than doubled from 1979 to 2000. Consider the following:

- The figures show 2000 as the year of the greatest economic disparity between rich and poor for any year since 1979.
- In 2000, the richest 1 percent of Americans had more money to spend after taxes than the bottom 40 percent.
- The higher incomes of the last decade did not lift all people equally. In 2000, the top 1 percent of American taxpayers had, on average, $862,700 each after taxes—more than triple the $286,300 (adjusted for inflation) they had in 1979. The bottom 40 percent in 2000 had $21,118 each, up 13 percent from their $18,695 average in 1979.[30]

The recent economic boom in the United States has made the rich even richer, but this has only increased income disparities between the rich and the poor.

These increasingly diverse groups mostly come in contact during the day in schools, businesses, and hospitals, but they bring different languages, histories, and economic backgrounds to these encounters. This presents a challenge for our society and for us as individuals to look beyond the Hollywood stereotypes, to be aware of this diversity, and to apply what we know about intercultural communication. Perhaps the first step is to realize that the **melting pot metaphor**—

in which all immigrants enter and blend into American society—probably never was viable. That is, not all immigrants could be assimilated into the United States in the same way.

Many Americans believe that they live in the most diverse society on earth. However, the United States is hardly a model of diversity, and many countries are much more ethnically diverse. For example, Nigeria has about two hundred ethnic groups, as does Indonesia. Nigeria was colonized by the British, and national boundaries forced many different groups artificially into one nation-state, which caused many conflicts. Indonesia has also experienced ethnic conflict, recently over East Timor.

Fortunately, most individuals are able to negotiate day-to-day activities in schools, businesses, and other settings in spite of cultural differences. Diversity can even be a positive force. Demographic diversity in the United States has provided us with tremendous linguistic richness and culinary variety, has given us the resources to meet new social challenges, and has created domestic and international business opportunities.

THE SELF-AWARENESS IMPERATIVE

One of the most important reasons for studying intercultural communication is to gain an awareness of one's own cultural identity and background. This **self-awareness** is also one of the least obvious reasons. Peter Adler, a noted social psychologist, observes that the study of intercultural communication begins as a journey into another culture and reality and ends as a journey into one's own culture.[31]

Examples from the authors' own lives come to mind. Judith's earliest experiences in public school made her realize that not everyone wore "coverings" and "bonnets" and "cape dresses," the clothing worn by the females in her Amish/Mennonite family. She realized that her family was different from most of the others she came in contact with. Years later, when she was teaching high school in Algeria, a Muslim country, she realized something about her own religious identity as a Protestant. December 25 came and went, and she taught classes with no mention of Christmas. Judith had never thought about how special the celebration of Christmas was or how important the holiday was to her. She then recognized on a personal level the uniqueness of this particular cultural practice.

When Tom, who is of Japanese descent, first started elementary school, he attended a white school in the segregated American South. By the time he reached the fourth grade, schools were integrated, and some African American students were intrigued by his very straight black hair. At that point, he recognized a connection between himself and the Black students, and he began to develop a kernel of self-awareness about his identity. Living in an increasingly diverse world, we can take the opportunity to learn more about our own cultural

Info Bites

Of the ten tallest buildings in the world in 2000, only four were in the United States. The tallest are the Petronas Towers in Kuala Lumpur, Indonesia. The bridge with the longest span is in Hyogo, Japan; no bridge in the United States is even in the top five. Do these facts surprise you or make you think about the United States in a different way?

backgrounds and identities and about how we are similar to and different from people we interact with.

THE ETHICAL IMPERATIVE

Living in an intercultural world presents challenging ethical issues that can be addressed by the study of intercultural communication. **Ethics** may be thought of as principles of conduct that help govern the behavior of individuals and groups. These principles often arise from communities' views on what is good and bad behavior. Cultural values tell us what is "good" and what "ought" to be.

Ethical Judgments and Cultural Values

Ethical judgments focus more on the degrees of rightness and wrongness in human behavior than do cultural values.[32]

Some judgments are stated very explicitly. For example, the Ten Commandments teach that it is wrong to steal, tell a lie, commit murder, and so on. Many Americans are taught the "Golden Rule"—do unto others as you would have them do unto you. Laws often reflect the cultural values of dominant groups. For instance, in the past, many states had miscegenation laws prohibiting interracial marriage. Contemporary debates about legalizing same-sex marriage reflect the role of cultural values in laws. Many other identifiable principles arise from our cultural experience that may be less explicit—for example, that people should be treated equally and that they should work hard.

Several issues come to mind in any discussion of ethics in intercultural communication. For example, what happens when two ethical systems collide? While "the desire to contribute to the development of a better society by 'doing the right thing' can be an important motivation,"[33] it is not always easy to know what is "right" in more specific situations in intercultural communication. Ethical principles are often culture-bound, and intercultural conflicts arise from varying notions of what constitutes ethical behavior.

Another ethical dilemma involves standards of conducting business in multinational corporations. The U.S. Congress and the Securities and Exchange Commission consider it unethical for corporations to make payments to government officials of other countries to promote trade. Essentially, such payment smacks of bribery. However, in many countries, government officials are paid in this informal way instead of being supported by taxes.[34] What is ethical behavior for personnel in multinational subsidiaries?

This book stresses the relativity of cultural behavior; that is, no cultural pattern is inherently right or wrong. So, is there any universality in ethics? Are any cultural behaviors always right or always wrong?

The answers depend on one's perspective. According to the **universalist position,** we need to identify those rules that apply across cultures. A universalist might try, for example, to identify acts and conditions that most societies think of as wrong, such as murder, treason, and theft. Someone who takes an extreme universalist position would insist that cultural differences are only superficial, that fundamental notions of right and wrong are universal. Some religions take universal positions—for example, that the Ten Commandments are a universal code of behavior. But Christian groups often disagree about the universality of the Bible. For example, are the teachings of the New Testament mainly guidelines for the Christians of Jesus' time, or can they be applied to Christians in the 21st century? These are difficult issues for many people searching for ethical guidelines.[35]

By contrast, according to the **relativist position,** any cultural behavior can be judged only within the cultural context in which it occurs. This means that only a community can truly judge the ethics of its members. Intercultural scholar William S. Howell explains the relativist position:

> Ethical principles in action operate contingently. Circumstances and people exert powerful influences. . . . The environment, the situation, the timing of an interaction, human relationships—all affect the way ethical standards are applied. Operationally, ethics are a function of context. . . . All moral choices flow from the perceptions of the decision maker, and those perceptions are produced by unique experiences in one person's life, in the context in which the choices are made.[36]

These are not easy issues, and philosophers and anthropologists have struggled to develop ethical guidelines that arc universally applicable but that also reflect the tremendous cultural variability in the world.

Scholar David W. Kale has proposed a universal code of ethics for intercultural communicators. This code is based on a universal belief in the sanctity of the human spirit and the desirability of peace. While we may wish to assume that universal ethical principles exist, we must be careful not to assume that our ethical principles are shared by others. When we encounter other ethical principles in various situations, it is often difficult to know if we are imposing our ethical principles on others and whether we should. There are no easy answers to these ethical dilemmas.

The study of intercultural communication should not only provide insights into cultural patterns but also help us address these ethical issues involved in intercultural interaction. First, we should be able to judge what is ethical and unethical behavior given variations in cultural priorities. Second, we should be able to identify guidelines for ethical behavior in intercultural contexts where ethics clash.

Another ethical issue concerns the application of intercultural communication scholarship. Everett Kleinjans, an international educator, stresses that intercultural education differs from some other kinds of education: Although all education may be potentially transformative, learning as a result of intercultural contact is particularly so in that it deals with fundamental aspects of human behavior.[37] Learning about intercultural communication sometimes calls into

Info Bites

How much do you really know about the world? Did you know that in London, it is unlawful to kiss in a movie theater? That in Finland, you must be able to read to get married? That in Athens, you can have your license taken away for driving while unbathed or poorly dressed? (Source: www. kids.infoplease.lycos.com)

question the very core of our assumptive framework and challenges existing beliefs, values, and patterns of behavior.

Becoming an Ethical Student of Culture

Part of learning about intercultural communication is learning about cultural patterns and identities—your own and those of others. Three skills are important here: practicing self-reflexivity, learning about others, and listening to the voices of others.

Practicing Self-Reflexivity   **Self-reflexivity** refers to the process by which we "look in the mirror" to see ourselves. In studying intercultural communication, you must understand yourself and your position in society. When you learn about other cultures and cultural practices, you often learn much about yourself as well. And the knowledge that you gain from experience is an important way to learn about intercultural communication. Intercultural experiences teach you much about how you react and interact in different cultural contexts and help you evaluate situations and deal with uncertainty. Self-reflection about your intercultural experiences will go a long way in helping you learn about intercultural communication. When you consider ethical issues in intercultural communication, you need to recognize the strengths and limitations of your own intercultural experiences. Many immigrants have observed that they never felt so much like someone of their nationality until they left their homeland. As part of the process of self-reflexivity, when you gain more intercultural experiences, your views on ethics may change. For example, you may have thought that arranged marriages were misguided and unethical until you gained more experience with people in successful arranged marriages, which have very low divorce rates in comparison to traditional "romantic" marriages.

Many cultural attitudes and ideas are instilled in you and are difficult to unravel and identify. Discovering who you are is never a simple matter; rather, it is an ongoing process that can never fully capture the ever-emerging person. Not only do you grow older, but your intercultural experiences change who you are and who you think you are. When Judith compares her intercultural experiences in France and in Mexico, she notes that, while the two experiences were similar, her own reactions to these intercultural encounters differed markedly because she was younger and less settled into her identity when she went to France.

It is also important to reflect on your place in society. By knowing what social categories—groups defined by society—you fill and what the implications of those categories are, you will be in a better position to understand how to communicate. For example, your status as a male or female may influence how certain messages are interpreted as sexual harassment. Or your identification as a member of some groups may allow you to use certain words and humor, but using other words or telling some jokes may get you in trouble. Many Belgians, for example, are well aware that French sometimes tell *blagues belges*, or jokes about Belgians. Yet if the same joke is told by a Belgian, it has a different tenor. It is im-

---

Pop Culture Spotlight

Intercultural communication takes place in sometimes unexpected places. For example, a popular computer game called *Starcraft* is often played on the Internet. When the game was released in South Korea in the summer of 1999, the *Starcraft* Internet site, Battle.net, quickly became a site where the majority of the gamers did not speak English. As you might expect, this led to conflict and a number of racist comments.

portant to recognize which social categories you belong to, as well as which ones you are perceived by others to belong to, as it influences how your message may be interpreted.

Learning About Others   It is important to remember that the study of cultures is actually the study of other people. Never lose sight of the humanity of the topic of study. Try not to observe people as if they are zoo animals. Remember that you are studying real people who have real lives, and your conclusions about them may have very real consequences for them and for you.

When Tom was growing up, he was surprised to hear from an older woman that the first time she saw a Japanese or Chinese person was in the circus when she was a little girl. Judith remembers feeling uneasy watching White tourists at the Navajo Nation fair in Window Rock, Arizona, intrusively videotaping the Navajo dancers during their religious ceremonies. In each case, people who were different were viewed and treated as if their cultural practices were for the display and entertainment of others and there was no real attempt to understand them or their culture.

Cultural studies scholar Linda Alcoff discusses the ethical issue involved when students of culture try to describe cultural patterns of others.[38] She acknowledges the difficulty of speaking "for" and "about" people from different cultures. Instead, she claims, students of culture should try to speak "with" and "to" people. Rather than merely describe other people from afar, it's better to listen to and engage them in a dialogue about their cultural realities.

Listening to the Voices of Others   We learn much from real-life experiences. Hearing about the experiences of people who are different from you can lead to different ways of viewing the world. Many differences—based on race, sex, sexual orientation, nationality, ethnicity, age, and so on—deeply affect the everyday lives of people. Listening carefully as people relate their experiences and their knowledge helps us learn about other cultures.

Sometimes communities lose their cultural uniqueness because of intercultural contact. When visiting the Navajo Nation, Judith heard an older Navajo woman lamenting the fact that many of the young people no longer follow the Navajo traditions. By contrast, one reason the Amish have remained culturally intact is that they have resisted contact with outside communities. Other communities, such as some Native American groups, have had contact forced on them. Another example of the transformative power of intercultural contact is international students who come to the United States and do not return, usually acquiring American values and adopting an American lifestyle.

As in other areas of communication, there are ethical issues in the application of our knowledge. What constitutes ethical and unethical applications? One questionable practice concerns people who study intercultural communication in order to proselytize others without their consent. For example, some religious organizations conduct Bible study sessions on college campuses for international students under the guise of English conversation lessons. Another questionable practice involves cross-cultural consultants who misrepresent or exaggerate their ability to deal with complex issues of prejudice and racism in brief, one-shot training sessions.[39]

SUMMARY

In this chapter, we identified six reasons for studying intercultural communication: the peace imperative, the economic imperative, the technological imperative, the demographic imperative, the self-awareness imperative, and the ethical imperative. Perhaps you can think of some other reasons. We stressed that the situations in which intercultural communication takes place are complex and challenging.

BUILDING INTERCULTURAL SKILLS

So what are the skills necessary to communicate effectively across cultures? It isn't easy to come up with specific suggestions that will always work in every situation. Communication is much too complex. However, we can identify several general skills that can be applied to the various aspects of intercultural communication covered in this book: (1) understanding cultural identity and history, (2) improving verbal and nonverbal communication, (3) understanding the role of popular culture in intercultural communication, and (4) building relationships and resolving conflicts.

Throughout the book, we'll focus on cultivating and improving the following communication skills:

1. Become more conscious of your communication. This may sound simple, but how often do you really think about your communication and whether it is working? Much of your communication, including intercultural communication, occurs at an unconscious level. A first step in improving your intercultural communication is to become aware of the messages you send and receive, both verbal and nonverbal. You can't really work on improving your communication until you become aware of it on a conscious level.

2. Become more aware of others' communication. Understanding other people's communication requires the important intercultural skill of empathy—that is, knowing where someone else is coming from, or "walking in their shoes." This is no easy task, but by doing things such as improving your observational skills and learning how to build better intercultural relations you can accomplish it.

3. Expand your own intercultural communication repertoire. This involves experimenting with different ways of looking at the world and of communicating, verbally and nonverbally. Building this skill may require that you step outside your communication comfort zone and look at things in a different light. It may require that you question ideas and assumptions you've not thought about before. All this is part of expanding your communication options.

4. Become more flexible in your communication. Closely related to the previous skill—and perhaps the most important one—this involves avoiding what has been called "hardening of the categories."

5. Be an advocate for others. This is something that isn't often included in lists of communication skills. To improve intercultural communication among groups, however, everybody's voice must be heard. Improving relations among groups of people—whether based on ethnicity, race, sex, physical ability, or whatever difference—is not just about improving individual communication skills; it is also about forming coalitions with others.

It is important to remember that becoming a better intercultural communicator is not achieved quickly, but rather is a lifelong process. So, in each of the following chapters, we invite you to take up the challenge of continuing to build these skills.

ACTIVITIES

1. *Intercultural encounters:* Describe and analyze a recent intercultural encounter with someone of a different age, ethnicity, race, religion, and so on.

    a. Describe the encounter. What made it "intercultural"?

    b. How did you feel after the encounter? Why do you think you felt as you did?

    c. Based on this experience, identify some characteristics that may be important for successful intercultural communication.

2. *Intercultural imperatives:* There are many reasons to study intercultural communication, including the six discussed in this chapter. What other imperatives can you identify?

3. *Household products:* Look at the products in your home. How many different countries do they come from? How might your purchases increase intercultural contact?

THE ONLINE LEARNING CENTER at www.mhhe.com/experiencing2 features self-quizzes, flashcards, and crossword puzzles based on the chapter's key terms and concepts.

www.mhhe.com/experiencing2

ENDNOTES

1. Jurgensen, J. (2003, September 11). Still searching: On the second anniversary of terrorist attacks against America, questions linger about how we got there and where we go from here; 9/11: A changed nation. *The Hartford Courant*, p. A1.

2. Ford, P. (2001, September 27). 'Why do they hate us?' *Christian Science Monitor*, p. 1.

3. Delgado, F. (2002). Mass-mediated communication and intercultural conflict. In J. M. Martin, T. K. Nakayama, & L. A. Flores (Eds.), *Readings in intercultural communication* (pp. 351–360). Boston: McGraw-Hill, p. 353.

4. Ferdman, B. M., & Brody, S. E. (1996). Models of diversity training. In D. Landis & R. Bhagat (Eds.), *Handbook of intercultural training* (2nd ed.). Thousand Oaks, CA: Sage, p. 288.

5. Ferdman, B. M., & Brody, S. E. (1996). Models of diversity training. In Landis & Bhagat, pp. 282–303.

6. Holmes, S. (2003, July 21). The real Nike news is happening abroad. *Business Week*, p. 30.

7. Pacelle, M. (2003, June 12). U.S. banks vie for big postwar roles—Financial reconstruction may include J. P. Morgan, Citigroup, Bank of America. *Wall Street Journal* (Europe), p. A3.

8. Slater, J. (2003, March 26). India's talented research pool lures GE, other firms. *Wall Street Journal*, p. A10.

9. King, N. Jr., Davis, B., & Leggett, K. (2003, July 30). A global journal report: Trade with China is heating up as a business and political issue. *Wall Street Journal*, p. A1.

10. George, S. (no date). Why globalization is pernicious. European Business Forum. http://www.ebfonline.com/at_forum/at_forum.asp?id=292&linked=288

11. McLuhan, M. (1967). *The medium is the message*. New York: Bantam Books.

12. Gergen, K. (1991). *The saturated self: Dilemmas of identity in contemporary life*. New York: HarperCollins-Basic Books.

13. Forrester Research (glreach.com/eng/ed/art/2004.ecommerce.php3)

14. http://www.ntia.doc.gov/ntiahome/digitaldivide/

15. http://www.divorcereform.org/mel/a2parentscarce.html

16. From Ameristats: http://www.prb.org/AmeristatTemplate.cfm?Section=RaceandEthnicity&template=/ContentManagement/ContentDisplay.cfm&ContentID=7884

17. Brewer, C. A., & Suchan, T. A. (2001). *Mapping Census 2000: The geography of U.S. diversity* (U.S. Census Bureau, Census Special Reports, Series CENSR/01-1). Washington, DC: U.S. Government Printing Office.

18. Schmidley, D. (2003). *The foreign born population in the US March 2002, Current Population Reports* (P20-539). Washington, DC: U.S. Census Bureau.

19. U.S. Bureau of the Census. (www.census.gov/population/www/estimates/popest.html).

20. Webster, Y. O. (1992). *The racialization of America*. New York: St. Martin's Press.

21. Curtin, P. D. (1969). *The Atlantic slave trade: A census*. Madison: University of Wisconsin Press.

22. Baldwin, J. (1955). *Notes of a native son*. Boston: Beacon Press.

23. West, C. (1993). *Race matters*. Boston: Beacon Press.

24. Banks, J. (1991). *Teaching strategies for ethnic studies*. Needham, MA: Allyn & Bacon.

25. Takaki, R. (1989). *Strangers from a different shore*. New York: Penguin Books, p. 209.

26. Banks (1991).

27. Roediger, D. (1991). *The wages of Whiteness: Race and the making of the American working class*. New York: Verso.

28. Schmitt, E. (2001, April 3). Analysis of census finds segregation along with diversity. *New York Times* (www.nytimes.com/2001/04/04/national/04CENS.html?ex=987410510&ei=1&en=a2cf77e31f7952)

29. Judy, R. W., & D'Amico, C. (1997). *Workforce 2020: Work and workers in the 21st century*. Indianapolis: Hudson Institute, p. 59.

30. http://www.twincities.com/mld/twincities/business/6853177.htm

31. Adler, P. S. (1975). The transition experience: An alternative view of culture shock. *Journal of Humanistic Psychology*, *15*, 13–23.

32. Johannesen, R. L. (1990). *Ethics in human communication* (3rd ed.). Prospect Heights, IL: Waveland Press.

33. Ferdman & Brody (1996), p. 285.

34. Howell, W. S. (1982). *The empathic communicator*. Belmont, CA: Wadsworth.

35. Johannesen (1990).

36. Howell (1982), pp. 182, 187.

37. Kleinjans, E. (1975). A question of ethics. *International Education and Cultural Exchange*, *10*, 20–25.

38. Alcoff, L. (1991/1992). The problem of speaking for others. *Cultural Critique*, *20*, 5–32.

39. Paige, R. M., & Martin, J. N. (1996). Ethics in intercultural training. In Landis & Bhagat.

CHAPTER TWO

Intercultural Communication

BUILDING BLOCKS AND BARRIERS

STUDY OBJECTIVES

After reading this chapter, you should be able to:
1. Define culture.
2. Define communication.
3. Discuss the relationship between culture and communication.
4. Describe the role that context and power play in intercultural interactions.
5. Identify and define ethnocentrism.
6. Identify and describe stereotyping.
7. Identify and describe prejudice.
8. Identify and describe discrimination.
9. Explain the ways in which ethnocentrism, stereotyping, prejudice, and discrimination act as barriers to effective intercultural communication.

KEY TERMS

communication	perceptions
context	power
culture	power distance
discrimination	prejudice
ethnocentrism	stereotypes
individualism	uncertainty avoidance
intercultural communication	values
masculinity/femininity	worldview

Between 2000 and 2002, several thousand Somalis moved to the small, largely White community of Lewiston, Maine. Many moved from Atlanta, Georgia, but originally had come to the United States in the aftermath of a brutal civil war in their home country. Many found life in the big city of Atlanta difficult and daunting and, like many immigrants to the United States, moved in search of a better life for themselves and their families. The influx of almost 2,000 Muslim Somalis into French-Canadian, Catholic Lewiston has not been easy. According to news reports, there have been culture clashes and economic challenges. Lewiston is a "decaying mill town of 35,000" already facing economic problems. The issue of the Somali immigrants came to a head in fall 2002 when the mayor wrote a letter to the Somali leaders suggesting that they discourage other Somalis from immigrating to Lewiston. According to the mayor, the town was "maxed out, financially, physically, and emotionally." [1]

The letter angered a number of the Somalis and their friends and drew the interest of a self-proclaimed White supremacist group, the World Church of the Creator (WCOC), based in Peoria, Illinois. The WCOC organized a rally in Lewiston to celebrate their cause of promoting Whiteness and in protest of diversity. The local community responded in force, organized a coalition named "Many and One," and held a counterrally in support of their Somali neighbors and other minority groups. Their counterrally drew 4,500 people.

A journalist for the *Lewiston Sun Journal*, Scott Taylor, asked the locals how they felt about the recent events. One resident said that the area had always seemed diverse to him. "He spent his childhood listening to immigrants' tales of dragons flying in China and Jewish children hiding from Cossacks in Russia. . . . Diversity isn't anything new for us. But we need to call attention to that fact every once in a while." And one of the community leaders said, "It's hard to respond to something like this any way but peacefully. We are a community of many different kinds of people, and we are immensely thankful for that. That diversity is wonderful, and it's growing richer, and we want to express that." [2]

This story of Lewiston illustrates the complexity of intercultural interaction, one that is occurring in many places in the world today. Groups of people are coming together, sometimes with enormous differences in cultural backgrounds, beliefs, lifestyles, economic resources, and religions. And it illustrates that intercultural communication does not happen in a vacuum. History, economics, and politics played an important role in how various people and groups reacted—from the mayor, to the hate group in Illinois, to the reaction of many local townspeople. What are some of the specific building blocks and barriers of intercultural communication? The answer to that question is the focus of this chapter.

Intercultural communication may be said to occur when people of different cultural backgrounds interact, but this definition seems simplistic and redundant. To properly define intercultural communication, it's necessary to understand the two root words—*culture and communication*—that represent the first two building blocks. In addition, communication always happens in a particular situation or context—our third building block. Our fourth building block concerns the element of power—something that is part of every intercultural interaction. We first define and describe culture and communication and then discuss how these two interact with issues of context and power to form our understanding of intercultural communication.

BUILDING BLOCK 1: CULTURE

Culture is often considered the core concept in intercultural communication. One characteristic of culture is that we may not think about it very much. Trying to understand one's own culture is like trying to explain to a fish that it lives in water. Often, we cannot identify our own cultural backgrounds and assumptions until we encounter people from other cultures, which gives us a frame of reference. Perhaps the people in Lewiston, Maine, did not think much about their own culture, religion, or being White until they had opportunity to interact with people from a different race and religion. For another example, consider our student, Ann, who participated in a study-abroad program in Mexico. She told us that she thought it was strange that many young Mexicans lived with their parents even after they had graduated from college and were working. Gradually, she recognized that Mexicans tend to have a stronger sense of family responsibilities between children and parents than do Americans. Thus, young people often live at home and contribute to the family income. And older parents rarely go to retirement communities, but are cared for within the family. While volunteering in a senior citizens' home, Ann was impressed by how few people lived in the facility.

Culture has been defined in many ways. For some people, it means the opera or classical music, but for the purposes of this book, we define **culture** as learned patterns of perception, values, and behaviors, shared by a group of people, that is also dynamic and heterogeneous. Let's look at what this definition actually means.

Culture Is Learned

First, culture is learned. While all human beings share some universal habits and tendencies—we all eat, sleep, seek shelter, make love, and share some motivations to be loved and to protect ourselves—these are not aspects of culture. Rather, culture is the unique way we have learned to eat, sleep, and make love because we are American or Japanese, male or female, and so on. For example, most Americans eat holding a fork in one hand, but when they use a knife, they shift the fork to their other hand. Europeans think this is clumsy; they simply eat with fork in one hand and knife in the other. While Americans and Japanese share a need to be loved, Americans tend to express feelings of love more overtly, while

What Do You Think?

Rank-order the following in terms of their importance in defining "American culture": hamburgers, movies, corn, apple pie, pizza, baseball, hot dogs, milkshakes, french fries, and big cars. Did you know that only three of those things actually are indigenous to the United States (corn, baseball, milkshakes), while the other seven are from Europe? What does this say about the ideas and values of U.S. culture?

Many cultural groups value family relationships, but how and how often families interact may depend on the particular cultural norms. How often does your extended family get together and what are the expectations for the interaction?

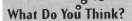

What Do You Think?

What kind of cultural values are embraced by children like multiracial golf star Tiger Woods, who is of Black, Thai, Chinese, and American Indian origins? Can interracial marriages and international or transracial adoptions help us move toward wider intercultural competence? Read about the details of MEPA (Multiethnic Placement Act) passed by the U.S. Congress in 1994 (http://www.acf.hhs. gov/programs/cb/ publications/mepa94/ mepachp1.htm). The bill encourages transracial adoptions and prohibits discrimination in child placement. Another website that discusses the issue is http://transracial. adoption.com.

Japanese are taught to be more restrained. So, when we are born, we don't know how to be a male or female, American or Mexican, and so on. Rather, we are taught. We have to learn how to eat, walk, talk, and love like other members of our cultural groups—and we usually do so slowly and subconsciously, through a process of socialization. Think of how young children learn to be male or female. Young boys imitate their fathers and other grown men, while young girls learn to talk and act like their mothers and other women. The same is true for other groups we belong to. For example, an American child adopted by a Finnish family will embrace Finnish cultural values; likewise, a Korean child raised by a German family will exhibit German cultural values.

Culture Involves Perception and Values

What do cultural groups learn and share? First, they share **perceptions,** or ways of looking at the world. Culture is sometimes described as a sort of lens through which we view the world. All the information we receive in a given day passes through this perceptual lens.[3] We select, evaluate, and organize information (stimuli) from the external environment through perception.

   Thus, all of our prior learning—the information we have already stored in our brains—affects how we interpret new information. Some of this learning and perception is related to the values of cultural groups we belong to. **Values** have to do with what is judged to be good or bad, or right or wrong, in a culture (and we'll talk more about values later). Consider our student, Ann. She saw the young Mexicans' behavior in a particular way because of her cultural upbringing. Whereas an important value for the young Mexicans was to be closely connected to their families, Ann's cultural values emphasized being independent from her family. Like Ann, we all see the world in particular ways because of the cultural groups (based on ethnicity, age, gender, and so on) to which we belong. And each group has a different prescription for its lenses. The difficulty comes in trying to understand our own cultural perceptions, just as it is difficult to look at our own glasses without taking them off.

Another metaphor for culture is a computer program in that culture, in a sense, serves as a "program of the mind" that every individual carries within him- or herself. These programs of the mind, or patterns of thinking, feeling, and potential acting, work just like computer software. That is, they tell people (subconsciously) how to walk, talk, eat, dance, socialize, and otherwise conduct their lives.[4]

Surf's Up!

The Cross-Cultural Communication Table's Questions to Ask About Culture Web site (www.nwrel. org/cnorse/booklets/ ccc/table2.html) lists 19 aspects of culture, with questions for each. Which three aspects do you think are the most important for your culture? What do your classmates think? Do different cultures emphasize different aspects?

Culture Is Shared

Another important part of our definition of culture is that cultural patterns are shared. The idea of a culture implies a group of people. These cultural patterns of perceptions and beliefs are developed through interactions with different groups of individuals—at home, in the neighborhood, at school, in youth groups, at college, and so on. Culture becomes a group experience because it is shared with people who live in and experience the same social environments. So our perceptions are similar to those of other individuals who belong to the same cultural groups. In class, the authors sometimes put students in same-sex groups to highlight how many men share many similar perceptions about being male and similar attitudes toward women; the same seems to hold true for women. For example, men sometimes share a perception that women have power in social situations. Women sometimes share a perception that men think badly of women who go out with a lot of guys. This same pattern of shared perceptions is evident in polls of attitudes of African Americans and Whites. White Americans seem to share a perception that things are getting better for African Americans and that racial attitudes and interactions are improving. By contrast, many African Americans share a perception that, while equality between races has improved, there is still a long way to go.[5]

For example, a recent Gallup poll question asked African Americans and Whites, "Do you feel that racial minorities have equal job opportunities as Whites, or not?" Fifty-five percent of Whites answered yes. In contrast, only 17 percent of Blacks answered affirmatively.[6]

Our membership in cultural groups ranges from involuntary to voluntary. Many of the cultural groups we belong to—specifically, those based on age, race, gender, physical ability, sexual orientation, and family membership—are involuntary associations over which we have little choice. We belong to other cultural

Surf's Up!

Although individualism and collectivism are culture-specific value orientations, some cultures seem to favor one or the other as a barometer for proper living. Check out the websites for the Individualist Research Foundation (home. earthlink.net/~whm/) and Enter Stage Right (www.enterstageright. com/). Do these groups equate individuality with liberty and freedom? How might these groups adapt to life among collectivist cultures like the Navajo or the Thai?

groups—those based on, say, professions, political associations, and hobbies—that are voluntary associations. And some groups may be involuntary at the beginning of our lives—those based on religion, nationality, or socioeconomic status—but become voluntary associations later on.[7]

Culture Is Expressed as Behavior

Our cultural lens or computer program influences not only our perceptions and beliefs but also our behaviors. So, for example, Ann's belief in (or lens on) the importance of individual independence, or simply individualism, is reflected in her behavior. She was expected to become increasingly independent when growing up and to be on her own after college, and she was socialized to make her own decisions about dating, marriage, and career. By contrast, the young people she met in Mexico were socialized to the cultural value of collectivism. That is, they were expected to be more responsible for caring for other family members and to take their wishes into consideration in marriage and career decisions.

It is important to understand that we belong to many different cultural groups and that these groups collectively help determine our perceptions, beliefs, and behavior. Also, these patterns endure over time and are passed on from person to person. Therefore, just as Ann was socialized to be individualistic, she'll probably pass these same beliefs and behaviors on to her own children.

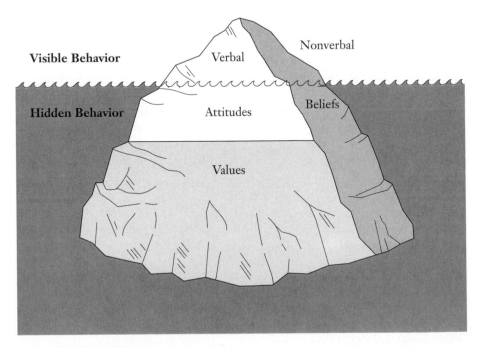

The visible and hidden layers of culture.

Culture Is Dynamic and Heterogeneous

Another crucial feature of culture is that it is dynamic, or changing, and can often be a source of conflict among different groups.[8] It is important to recognize that cultural patterns are not rigid and homogeneous but are dynamic and heterogeneous. And sometimes there is conflict over cultural patterns and meanings. For example, who gets to define what "Native American" means? The government has one definition: a person who has proven Native American ancestry and is enrolled in a particular tribe. But some people feel that a Native American can be anyone who follows Native American cultural and spiritual traditions and practices.

Table 2.1 shows some cultural behaviors that are widely shared in some cultures around the world. Note that these are shared, collective cultural behaviors, rather than individual characteristics.

Viewing culture as dynamic is particularly important for understanding the struggles of various groups—Native Americans, Asian Americans and Pacific Islanders, African Americans, Latinos/as, women, gays and lesbians, working-class people, and so on—as they try to negotiate their relationships and ensure their well-being within U.S. society. By studying the communication that arises from these ongoing struggles, we can better understand several intercultural concerns. Consider, for example, Proposition 227, passed by California voters in 1998, which eliminated public funding for bilingual education. The controversy surrounding the passage of this proposition illustrates the concerns of many different cultural groups. Some Whites and long-term immigrants wanted to eliminate public funding for any programs for more recent immigrants. Others felt

TABLE 2.1 Interesting Cultural Behaviors

Thailand: Thai people greet each other with a wai greeting—hold your hands together at the chest like a prayer and give a light bow.

Egypt: Using the left hand alone to exchange an item with an Egyptian is considered rude.

France: The French expect promptness. They are not accustomed to standing in line.

Germany: Germans often bang their fists on the table to show their appreciation at the end of a meeting.

Japan: When you are offered a gift, you must first refuse it once, modestly and serenely. Then you should accept it using both hands.

Israel: When Israelis invite someone to their home, it is an important gesture. It is appropriate to bring a book as a gift.

Spain: After a meal, you must place your utensils together on the plate. Otherwise, your Spanish host would think that you were not satisfied.

French Polynesia: It is not necessary to tip. People usually give small gifts instead.

Source: M. Mancini. (2003). *Selling destinations: Geography for the travel professional* (4th ed.). Clifton Park, NY: Thomson/Delmar Learning.

Pop Culture Spotlight

We can see the dynamism of changing culture in American movies, especially with remakes. In the original *Father of the Bride* with Spencer Tracy, from the 1950s, his wife is a housewife in high heels. In the Steve Martin version in the 1980s, she has a career. Bela Lugosi's *Dracula* movies from the 1930s only hint at sexuality. In the Christopher Lee films of the 1960s, there are half-naked female vampires in Dracula's castle. And the Gary Oldman version from the 1990s is even more graphic.

that providing bilingual education was a good investment and that failing to do so sent a message of hostility to new immigrants.

Seeing culture as dynamic and heterogeneous opens up new ways of thinking about intercultural communication. After all, the people from a particular culture are not identical, and any culture has many intercultural struggles. For instance, when we speak of Chinese culture or French culture, we ignore the diversity that resides in that culture. That "Chinese culture" may refer to the mainland Chinese; or to the inhabitants of the island of Taiwan, who speak Taiwanese or Mandarin; or to the Chinese from Hong Kong, who speak Cantonese. The label "Chinese" thus obscures incredible diversity. Similarly, "French culture" could refer to the "Pieds Noirs" (North Africans of French descent), or to Vietnamese of French descent, or to the Bretons, who live in northwestern France and speak their own language.

Yet, cultures are not heterogeneous in the same way everywhere. How sexuality, race, gender, and class function in other cultures is not necessarily the same as or even similar to how they do so in the United States. For example, there are poor people in most nations. The poor in the United States are often viewed with disdain, as people to be avoided; in many European countries, by contrast, the poor are seen as a part of society, to be helped by government programs. Likewise, gender issues are not framed the same way in all countries. For example, in the United States, gender equality is defined in terms of equal pay and career opportunities. In some Middle Eastern countries, women may be seen to have equality because they have tremendous power within the home and family but less influence in public arenas. In short, by viewing any culture as heterogeneous, we can understand the complexities of that culture and become more sensitive to how people in that culture live.

BUILDING BLOCK 2: COMMUNICATION

Communication, our second building block, is also complex and may be defined in many ways. For our purposes we define **communication** as a symbolic process whereby meaning is shared and negotiated. In other words, communication occurs whenever someone attributes meaning to another's words or actions. In addition, communication is dynamic, may be unintentional, and is receiver-oriented. Let's look more closely at what this means.

First, communication is symbolic. That is, the words we speak and the gestures we make have no meaning in themselves; rather, they achieve significance only because people agree, at least to some extent, on their meaning. When we use symbols, such as words or gestures, to communicate, we assume that the other person shares our symbol system. If we tell someone to "sit down," we assume that the individual knows what these two words (symbols) mean. Also, these symbolic meanings are conveyed both verbally and nonverbally. Thousands of nonverbal behaviors—gestures, postures, eye movements, facial expressions, and so on—involve shared meaning.

An important U.S. American value revolves around keeping busy and achieving things in life. Unlike people in many cultures, most Americans prefer to work for extra money rather than work less and have more time to spend with family and friends.

Think about the symbolic meaning of some clothing, for example. Why is it that many people value Tommy Hilfiger clothing more than clothes from J. C. Penney's? It has to do with the symbolic meaning associated with the clothing, rather than anything intrinsically special about the clothing. Powerful social symbols—for example, flags, national anthems, and corporate logos—also communicate meaning nonverbally. A good example is the controversial practice of flying the Confederate flag over the South Carolina Statehouse. Obviously, the flag has tremendous symbolic meaning for many people. For some Whites, the flag symbolizes the rich legacy of the South and the gallant fight in the Civil War. For some African Americans, the same flag is a very negative reminder of slavery, oppression, segregation, and prejudice. A more recent example is the lawsuit regarding the placement of the granite Ten Commandment monument in a courthouse in Alabama during the summer of 2003. For those in favor, the monument represented the strength of the Protestant role in U.S. history and politics. For those opposed (who eventually won the lawsuit), the placement violated the First Amendment—separation of church and state. The monument was a powerful symbol for both groups.[9]

Second, communication is a process involving several components: people who are communicating, a message that is being communicated (verbal or nonverbal), a channel through which the communication takes place, and a context. People communicating can be thought of as senders and receivers—they are sending and receiving messages. However, communication does not involve tossing "message balls" back and forth, such that one person sends a single message and the other person receives it. Rather, it is more akin to clicking on a website and being bombarded by many different messages at once.

Surf's Up!

Visit the Deaf Culture website (www.aslinfo .com/deafculture.html). How does deaf culture exemplify the five elements of this textbook's definition of culture?

Third, communication involves sharing and negotiating meaning. People have to agree on the meaning of a particular message, but to make things more complicated, each message often has more than one meaning. For example, the message "I love you" may mean, "I want to have sex with you tonight," "I feel guilty about what I did last night without you," "I need you to do me a favor," "I have a good time when I'm with you," or "I want to spend the rest of my life with you." When we communicate, we assume that the other person takes the meaning that we intend. But for individuals from different cultural backgrounds and experiences, this assumption may be wrong and may lead to misunderstanding and a lack of shared meaning. Often, we have to try harder in intercultural communication to make sure that meaning is truly shared.

Fourth, communication is dynamic. This means that communication is not a single event but is ongoing, so that communicators are at once both senders and receivers. For example, when a teacher walks into the classroom, even before she starts speaking, communication messages are flying all around. The students are looking at her and interpreting her nonverbal messages: Do her attire, her bearing, her facial expressions, and her eye movements suggest that she will be a good teacher? A hard teacher? Someone who is easy to talk with? The teacher in turn is interpreting the nonverbal messages of the students: Are they too quiet? Do they look interested? Disruptive? So, when we are communicating with another person, we take in messages through our senses of sight, smell, and hearing— and these messages do not happen one at a time, but rather simultaneously. When we are communicating, we are creating, maintaining, or sharing meaning. This implies that people are actively involved in the communication process. Technically, then, one person cannot communicate alone—talking to yourself while washing your car in the driveway does not qualify as communication.

Fifth, communication does not have to be intentional. Some of the most important (and sometimes disastrous) communication occurs without the sender knowing a particular message has been sent. During business negotiations, an American businessman in Saudi Arabia sat across from his Saudi host showing the soles of his feet (an insult in Saudi society), inquired about the health of his wife (an inappropriate topic), and turned down the offer of tea (a rude act). Because of this triple insult, the business deal was never completed, although no insult was intended. The American returned home wondering what went wrong.

Finally, communication is receiver-oriented. Ultimately, it is the person who assigns meaning who determines the outcome of the communication situation. That is, the Saudi businessman who misinterpreted the American's messages determined the outcome of the interaction—he never signed the contract. It didn't matter that the American didn't intend this outcome. Similarly, if someone interprets your messages as prejudicial, or sexist, or negative, those interpretations have much more influence over future interactions than does your intended meaning. What can you do when people interpret your communication in ways you don't intend? First, you need to realize that there is a possibility, particularly in intercultural encounters, that you will be misunderstood. To check whether others are understanding you, you can paraphrase or ask questions ("What did

Info Bites

Have you ever wished communication wasn't so complicated and messy? Sometimes simpler is not necessarily better. Researchers in the area of computer-mediated communication (or CMC) have theorized that arguments are more prevalent in online communication because some of the dynamic and unintentional elements of communication, like tone of voice and facial expression, are missing.

you think I meant?"), or you can observe closely to see if others are giving non-verbal cues that they are misinterpreting your messages. We'll address this issue of how to communicate more effectively throughout this textbook.

CULTURE AND COMMUNICATION

Communication, Cultural Worldviews, and Values

As already noted, culture influences communication. All cultural groups influence the ways in which their members experience and perceive the world. Members of a culture create a worldview, which, in turn, influences communication. For Judith, growing up in an Amish/Mennonite culture meant that she thought war was absolutely wrong. Tom, growing up in an Asian American, academic family, did not share that particular perception but learned other values.

Values, you will recall, have to do with what is judged to be good or bad, or right or wrong. They are deeply felt beliefs that are shared by a cultural group and that reflect a perception of what ought to be, not what is. Equality, for example, is a value shared by many people in the United States. It is a belief that all humans are created equal, even though we acknowledge that in reality there are many disparities, such as in talent, looks, and access to material goods. Collectively, the values of a cultural group represent a **worldview**, a particular way of looking at the world. Table 2.2 highlights some interesting cultural patterns from around the world. How do these cultural patterns reflect cultural values? Let's look more closely at specific conceptions of values.

Info Bites

What is your intercultural IQ? To get an idea, name (1) at least three holidays that take place in December (besides New Year's Eve), (2) at least one of the Native American tribes that inhabit or once inhabited the area where you now live, and (3) at least two religions that prohibit the consumption of alcohol.

TABLE 2.2 Interesting Cultural Patterns

Ireland: Irish are very proud of their histories.

Jordan: People are proud of their Arab heritage and are tremendously hospitable to their guests.

Fiji: Time is informal and it may be acceptable to arrive quite late.

Singapore: Punctuality for meetings is expected.

Egypt: Building trust is the most important aspect of any relationship. You should try to engage in extended conversation and coffee before starting a meeting.

Turkey: When you are doing business with Turks, it is important to deal with the person who has the most authority.

Mexico: "Mañana" (putting off a task until tomorrow) is a prevalent norm. This does not indicate Mexicans are lazy, but shows that the pace is more relaxed than other places.

Tahiti: It is polite to taste a little bit of every food offered with your fingers in a Tahitian's home.

Source: M. Mancini. (2003). *Selling destinations: Geography for the travel professional* (4th ed.). Clifton Park, NY: Thomson/Delmar Learning.

What Do You Think?

How do cultural values relate to some of the more horrifying intercultural encounters we have heard about recently in the news? What about Matthew Shepard, a young gay man who was murdered by two homophobes in the rural West? Or James Byrd, a Black man who was dragged to death by several White men in Texas? Or Alex Witmer and Jason Powell, who killed a Black man to earn a spiderweb tattoo from the Aryan Brotherhood?

Kluckhohn and Strodtbeck's Value Orientation   To more fully explain the concept of values, two anthropologists, Fred Strodtbeck and Florence Kluckhohn, studied how the cultural values of Hispanics, Native Americans, and European Americans differ.[10] They suggested that members of all cultural groups must answer these important questions:

- What is human nature?
- What is the relationship between humans and nature?
- What is the relationship between humans?
- What is the preferred form of activity?
- What is the orientation toward time?

There are three possible responses to each question, and each cultural group has one or possibly two preferred responses. The range of answers to these questions is shown in Table 2.3. It is important to remember that value orientations are deeply held beliefs about the way the world should be, and not necessarily the way it is. These questions and responses help us understand broad cultural differences among various cultural groups—national groups, ethnic groups, and groups based on gender, class, and so on.

The Nature of Human Nature   As shown in Table 2.3, there are three "solutions." The solution to the issue of human nature is related to dominant religious and legal practices. One solution is a belief in the basic goodness of human nature. Legal systems in a society holding this orientation would emphasize rehabilitating those who violate the law; jails would be seen as places to train violators to

TABLE 2.3 Value Orientation

	RANGE OF VALUES		
Human Nature	Basically good	Mixture of good and evil	Basically evil
Relationship Between Humans and Nature	Humans dominate	Harmony between the two	Nature dominates
Relationships Between Humans	Individual	Group-oriented	Collateral
Preferred Personality	"Doing": stress on action	"Growing": stress on spiritual growth	"Being": stress on who you are
Time Orientation	Future-oriented	Present-oriented	Past-oriented

Source: Adapted from F. Kluckhohn and F. Strodtbeck (1961), *Variations in value orientations* (Chicago: Row & Peterson).

rejoin society as contributing citizens. Some religions, such as Buddhism and Confucianism, focus on the perceived natural goodness of humans.

A second solution involves a combination of goodness and evil in human nature. We could argue that many groups within the United States hold to this orientation and that there has been a shift in this value orientation in the past 50 years. In terms of religious beliefs, there is less emphasis on the fundamental evil of humanity than in, say, colonial America. However, with regard to the criminal justice system, there seems to be an increasing emphasis on incarceration and punishment ("three strikes" legislation) and less talk about rehabilitation and reform. The United States currently has a higher proportion of citizens incarcerated than any other Western nation.

According to a third solution, humans are essentially evil. Societies holding to this orientation would more likely punish criminals than rehabilitate them. For example, the strict laws and codes of Islam seem to reflect this orientation toward human nature, as do some forms of Christianity. While he lived in Belgium, Tom was particularly struck by the images of punishment and torture on display in the Counts of Flanders Castle in Ghent. He often wondered if he would better understand these cultural practices if he accepted the Christian view of humanity as essentially evil and born with sin.

The Relationship Between Humans and Nature   In most of U.S. society, humans seem to dominate nature. For example, clouds are seeded in an attempt to bring rain. Rivers are rerouted and dammed to make way for human settlement, to form lakes for recreation, and to provide power. Conception is controlled by drugs and birth control devices. Of course, not everyone in the United States agrees that humans should dominate nature. Conflicts between environmentalists and land developers often center on disagreements over this value orientation. For example, there is an ongoing debate in Arizona between astronomers who want to build more telescopes on Mount Lemon (near Tucson) for scientific exploration and environmentalists who want to block construction in order to protect a rare species of squirrel.

By contrast, in a society that emphasizes the domination of nature over humans, families may be more accepting of the number of children that are born naturally. There is less intervention in processes of nature and fewer attempts to control what is seen as the natural order. An example might be people who live in floodplains; they often face floods and devastation, but they accept that relationship with nature. The same can be said of some people in the United States who keep repairing homes built too close to flooding rivers.

Many Native American groups, and also the Japanese, believe in the value of humans living in harmony with nature, rather than one dominating the other. Some Native Americans even consider living animals to be their brothers or sisters. In this value orientation, nature is respected and plays an important role in the spiritual and religious life of the community. Thus, for example, a hawk may be considered a messenger that guides humans in decision making and brings

Surf's Up!

Do you think it's possible for the world to move into the next century with a more universal value system? See what efforts UNESCO is making through their Universal Ethics Project (http://www.unesco.org/opi2/philosophyandethics/pronpro.htm). The website notes, "In a multipolar world of heightened individualism and a possibly unprecedented splintering of perceptions, it is more than ever necessary to look for the acknowledgement, or rather the emergence of a common substratum of values which would make economically, ecologically, socially and culturally viable coexistence possible on a world-scale."

Pop Culture Spotlight

Ever since the popular 1920s documentary *Nanook of the North,* about an Inuit fisherman, movies have often been a place where audiences sought to experience and learn about another culture. Is this a reasonable thing to expect from movies? If so, which movies that you've seen have done the best job of this?

messages from God. And some societies, including many Arab cultural groups, emphasize aspects of both harmony with and domination of nature.

The Relationship Between Humans   As the example of Ann and her Mexican friends showed, some cultural groups value individualism, while others are more group-oriented and so value collectivism. **Individualism,** a key European American (and Canadian and Australian) value, places importance on the individual rather than the family or work team or other group. By contrast, people from more collectivist societies—such as those of Central and South America, many Arab groups, and the Amish and some Chicano and Native American communities in the United States—place a great deal of importance on extended families. For example, someone from a collectivist orientation would be more likely than an individualist to consult extended family members when choosing a spouse or making other life decisions.

Values may also be related to economic class or rural/urban distinctions. In the United States, for example, working-class people may be more collectively oriented than members of the middle or upper classes, given that working-class people reportedly give a higher percentage of their time and money to helping others.

These cultural values may influence how people communicate. For example, people who value individualism tend to value more direct forms of communication and conflict resolution. People in collectivist societies may employ less direct communication and more avoidance-style conflict resolution. It is important to remember that people may belong to cultural groups that hold contradictory values. For example, most work contexts in the United States require highly individualistic behavior, which may conflict with a more collectivist family/ethnic background. Some workers may find it hard to live with these competing values. For example, Phyllencia, a Navajo student, told us that she often feels a conflict between her more family-oriented life at home and the individualistic life expected of college students. And sometimes, she's expected to return home to participate in family and community activities. But she feels torn because she knows she'll be penalized for missing classes and not submitting schoolwork. Many students like Phyllencia, who live "between" two cultures, struggle to meet the demands of both cultures—meeting as many family and cultural obligations as possible while still succeeding in the academic and work worlds. This bicultural existence is akin to swinging on a trapeze. We'll talk more about bicultural identities in Chapter 4.

The Preferred Personality   The most common form of activity in the United States seems to involve a "doing" orientation. Thus, being productive and keeping busy are highly valued in many contexts—for example, in the workplace, where most employees have to document what they "do" (number of sales made, number of clients seen, and so on). The highest status is usually given to those who "do" (sports figures, performers, physicians, lawyers) rather than those who mostly "think" (philosophers, priests, scholars).

By contrast, a "growing" orientation places importance on the spiritual aspects of life. This orientation seems to be less common than the other two; the main practitioners are Zen Buddhists. Some societies, such as Japan, are said to combine a "doing" and a "growing" orientation, emphasizing both action and spiritual growing.

A final orientation revolves around "being." In this process of self-actualization, "peak experiences," in which the individual is fused with the experience, are most important. This orientation can be found in Central and South America, and in Greek and Spanish cultural groups. For example, one of our Spanish students told us that his mother worked for an American company in Spain. The company was behind in production and asked the employees to work overtime, offering a good bonus as an incentive. The company was surprised when all the employees turned them down, saying they would rather have their usual five weeks of summer vacation than the additional money. This illustrates a "being" value orientation, whereby it is more important to spend time interacting with family and friends than to work (doing) for financial gain.

The Orientation to Time   Most U.S. cultural communities—particularly European American and middle-class ones—seem to emphasize the future. This is evident in practices such as depositing money in retirement accounts that can be recovered only in the distant future and having appointment books that can reach several years into the future. A seeming contradiction is the heavy debt load carried by many Americans, indicating a lack of planning and a desire to live in the present. Perhaps this reflects a sense of optimism about the future, an

Surf's Up!

If culture is sometimes about making spaces to resist the dominant culture, Native American cultures are good examples of this. A website that seeks to further this resistance is On This Date in North American Indian History (americanindian. net). What happened on today's date?

This school, attended by Ulysses S. Grant in the early 1800s, was demolished several years ago. The lack of concern for saving "historical" buildings and areas reflects a U.S. American value system that emphasizes newness and innovation rather than preservation of the old.

assumption that things will get better—the future will be "new and improved!" This same optimism about the future can also be seen in the relative lack of concern about saving "historical" buildings and areas. Many old buildings in the United States have been destroyed and replaced with newer—and sometimes less well constructed—buildings, whereas in Europe and South America buildings are constantly being refurbished.

Other societies (Spain, Greece, Mexico) seem to emphasize the importance of the present, recognizing the value of living in the here and now, and the potential of the current moment. Many European societies (France, Germany, Belgium) and Asian societies (Japan, Korea, Indonesia) place a relatively strong emphasis on the past, believing that history has something to contribute to an understanding of contemporary life. And some cultures emphasize the present but also recognize the importance of the past. When Judith was in language school in Mexico, her professors would always answer questions about contemporary society with a story about history. For instance, there were regional elections going on at the time. If students asked about the implications of the campaign platform of one of the candidates, the professors would always answer by describing what had happened in the region 50 or 100 years earlier.

Hofstede's Value Dimensions   Dutch social psychologist Geert Hofstede has identified several additional cultural values that help us understand cultural differences: (1) power distance, (2) masculinity/femininity, (3) uncertainty avoidance, and (4) long-term versus short-term orientation to life.[11] These values also affect communication.

Power distance refers to the extent to which less powerful members of institutions and organizations within a country expect and accept that power is distributed unequally. Societies that value low power distance (Denmark, Israel, New Zealand) believe that less hierarchy is better and that power should be used only for legitimate purposes. So, for example, in organizational settings in the United States, the best bosses are those who play down power differences by telling subordinates to call them by their first name, by accepting subordinates' suggestions as important and worthwhile, and so on. By contrast, in societies that value large power distance (Mexico, Philippines, India), boss-subordinate relationships and decision-making processes are more formalized. Thus, bosses are expected to provide answers and to give orders. For example, an American working in India got into trouble when he tried to use an egalitarian approach and let the workers decide how to sequence their work. The workers thought he was insincere and incompetent because he didn't act the way a boss should act in India and failed to emphasize the status difference between himself and his subordinates.

The **masculinity/femininity** dimension refers to (1) the degree to which gender-specific roles are valued and (2) the degree to which a cultural group values "masculine" (achievement, ambition, acquisition of material goods) or "feminine" (quality of life, service to others, nurturance) values. People in Japan, Aus-

Info Bites

Different approaches toward time are especially important for business issues in intercultural communication. In Carol Turkington's *The Complete Idiot's Guide to Cultural Etiquette,* she focuses on each culture's approach to time, from traditional German punctuality to Indonesia's *jam karet,* or "rubber time." Which of the other cultural elements in this chapter are as important or more important for intercultural communication?

tria, and Mexico seem to prefer a masculine orientation, expressing a general preference for gender-specific roles. In these countries, certain roles (wage-earner) should be filled by men, and other roles (homemaker, teacher) by women. By contrast, many people in northern Europe (Denmark, Norway, Sweden, the Netherlands) seem to prefer a feminine orientation, reflecting more gender equality and a stronger belief in the importance of quality of life for all. In the United States, we tend to prefer gender-specific roles, though not as rigid as in Japan, Austria, or Mexico; but we also tend toward a masculine orientation, with a high value placed on competition and acquisition.

Uncertainty avoidance describes the degree to which people feel threatened by ambiguous situations and try to ensure certainty by establishing more structure. Relatively weak uncertainty-avoidance societies (Great Britain, Sweden, Ireland, Hong Kong, the United States) share a preference for a reduction of rules and an acceptance of dissent, as well as an increased willingness to take risks. By contrast, strong uncertainty-avoidance societies (Greece, Portugal, Japan) usually prefer more extensive rules and regulations in organizational settings and more consensus concerning goals.

The Long-Term Versus Short-Term Orientation

The Long-Term Versus Short-Term Orientation   Hofstede acknowledged and adopted the long-term (Confucian) versus short-term orientation to life, which originally was identified by a group of Asian researchers.[12] This value has to do with a society's search for virtue versus truth. Societies with a short-term orientation (the United States, Canada, Great Britain, the Philippines, Nigeria) are concerned with "possessing" the truth (reflected in Western religions like Judaism, Christianity, and Islam). The emphasis is on quick results in endeavors, and social pressure exists to "keep up with the Joneses" even if it means overspending. Societies with a long-term orientation (China, Hong Kong, Taiwan, Japan, South Korea, Brazil, India) are more concerned with virtue (reflected in Eastern religions like Confucianism, Hinduism, Buddhism, and Shintoism). The emphasis is on perseverance and tenacity in whatever is attempted regardless of how long it takes, as well as on thrift.

Intercultural conflicts often result from differences in value orientations. For example, past-oriented people may feel strongly that it is important to consider how things were done in the past. For them, the past and tradition hold answers. Values often conflict in international assistance projects, such as fertilizing crops or improving infrastructures, in which future-oriented individuals (such as many Americans) may show a lack of respect for traditional ways of doing things. Conflicts may be even more complex when power differentials are factored in. Often, certain values are privileged over others. For example, most U.S. workplaces reward extremely individualistic relationships and "doing" behaviors at the expense of more collaborative, but equally productive, efforts. Individual employees frequently are recognized for achieving the most sales or issuing the most reports, but awards rarely are given for being a good team member or for helping someone else achieve a departmental goal.

Pop Culture Spotlight

Do we learn our values through children's stories? Think of what Kluckhohn and Strodtbeck and Hofstede might say about your favorite characters from the universes of Winnie the Pooh, Bugs Bunny, Mickey Mouse, Scooby Doo, Sesame Street, the Muppets, Marvel superheroes, Teenage Mutant Ninja Turtles, and even the Teletubbies, Pokémon, and the Power Rangers.

Limitations of Value Frameworks   While identifying cultural values helps us understand broad cultural differences, it is important to remember that not everyone in a given society holds the dominant value. We shouldn't merely reduce individuals to stereotypes based on these value orientations. After all, not all Amish or Japanese are group-oriented, and not all Americans and Australians are individualistic. While people in small rural communities may be more collectively oriented, or more willing to help their neighbors, we cannot say that all people in big cities ignore those around them.

One of the problems with these and similar cultural frameworks is that they tend to "essentialize" people. In other words, people tend to assume that a particular group characteristic is the essential characteristic of given group members at all times and in all contexts. But this ignores the heterogeneity within any population. For example, one could characterize the current debate about health care in the United States as a struggle between "masculine" and "feminine" value orientations. Some people believe that each person should be able to take care of him- or herself and should be responsible for paying for his or her own medical care. Others, representing a more feminine position, believe that everyone should sacrifice a little for the good of the whole, that everyone should be assured equal access to health care and hospitalization.

Value heterogeneity may be particularly noticeable in a society that is undergoing rapid change. Japan, for example, was defeated militarily and was in economic ruin only 50 years ago. It now has one of the world's strongest economies. This rapid social and economic change influenced traditional values. While many of the older folk in Japan hold to the traditional values of collectivism, giving undying loyalty to their companies and elders, this is not so true of the younger generation. They are moving toward more individualism, showing less loyalty to their families and companies—causing somewhat of a rift between the generations in contemporary Japanese society.[13] This could be compared to the way that the hippie generation of the 1960s altered some of the traditional values held by previous generations.

While people may differ with respect to specific value orientations, they may hold other value orientations in common. For example, individuals may hold different views on the importance of individual or group loyalty but share a deep belief in the goodness of human nature and in certain religious observances. While these group-related values tend to be relatively consistent, people are dynamic, and their behavior varies contextually. That is, people may be more or less individualistic or group-oriented depending on the context. For example, both Judith and Tom find that they are more individualistic (more competitive, more self-oriented) in work settings than in family settings.

In this sense, there are no easy lists of behaviors that are key to "successful" intercultural interaction. Instead, it's important to understand the contexts when interacting with Asian Americans, or persons with disabilities, or men or women, for that matter. While a trip to the library or Internet research on a particular group may be helpful, always remember that exceptions can and do occur. The value orientations discussed here are general guidelines, not rigid rules, to

What Do You Think?

Culture as lens . . . or film? Media researcher John Fiske has written about Australian aborigines and their reactions to U.S. media products like westerns. He points out that the aborigines often root for the Native Americans so often portrayed as bad guys in the movie because the Native Americans look and act more like they do. In what ways does your culture reinterpret the foreign films you have seen?

help you in your intercultural communication. Your own learning and behavior and experience with others all will make a difference in your intercultural experiences.

Communication and Cultural Rituals

Even as culture influences communication, communication influences and reinforces culture. This means that the way we communicate in cultural contexts often strengthens our sense of cultural identity. For example, participating in communication rituals such as prayers in church or synagogue may strengthen our religious identity and sense of belonging to a religious community. Or even participating in a daily communication greeting ritual ("Hi, how are you?" "Fine, and you?") may strengthen our sense of who we are in our friendship networks.

An example of a communication ritual is the "griping" that takes place among middle-class Israelis. The griping topic in the Israeli ritual usually concerns some event in daily life, such as getting a vehicle emissions test. The purpose of the griping is not to solve the problem but to vent pent-up tensions. By participating in this ritual, Israelis feel more "Israeli"; their communication reinforces their sense of belonging to a cultural group. Like all rituals, the griping ritual follows a predictable sequence: Someone voices a complaint, others comment on the opener, and the griping continues until the end, when everyone sighs and agrees that it is a problem. "It's no joke; things are getting worse all the time," the participants might say. Although individuals belonging to other cultural groups certainly gripe about things, the activity may not be done in this systematic cultural way and may not fill the same function.[14]

Many White, middle-class U.S. residents participate in a similar communication ritual in which people who have a problem often acknowledge the problem and negotiate a solution.[15] These U.S. and Israeli communication rituals are similar in that they both revolve around problems and both provide a means of venting frustrations. However, they are different rituals. Whereas the U.S. ritual holds expectation that some solutions will be presented and discussed, the Israeli ritual focuses more on the venting and complaining. But in its own way, each ritual contributes to a sense of community identity.

There are other examples of how people's communication behavior reinforces their cultural identity and worldviews. For example, in many White working-class communities in the United States, men express their gender roles in many contexts by engaging in conversation with their peers, but not with women or children.[16]

As another example, consider the differences in how people in the United States and Colombia persuade others to do something for them.[17] The pattern in each country reflects and reinforces different value orientations. That is, people in the United States tend to be careful in telling someone what to do in order not to infringe on that person's rights—reflecting a value of individualism. In Bogotá, Colombia, however, with its more collectivistic orientation, giving orders must be negotiated within relationships. There has to be enough *confianza*

What Do You Think?

Why do you think one of the most common pieces of advice people get when learning a foreign language is that they should live in another country for a while?

(respect) or authority (whereby one person is required by the hierarchy to do the other's bidding). So, a close friend or family member may easily persuade someone else to do something, or a boss may easily give a direct order to a secretary. In each case, there is enough respect or authority to make the persuasion successful.

Communication and Resistance to the Dominant Culture

Another way to look at culture and communication is to think about how people may use their own space to resist the dominant culture. For example, we might study the floating bars in New York City—warehouses where people meet, clandestinely and illegally, for a night or two, exchange money, party, and then disappear. Because the "bar" does not obtain a liquor license or pay taxes, the people are circumventing the system. Similarly, workers often find ways to resist the extreme individualism and competition of the workplace. For example, flight attendants sometimes work together to protect each other from the critical gaze of supervisors. We can interpret these behaviors as resistance to the dominant cultural system.

BUILDING BLOCK 3: CONTEXT

A third building block of intercultural communication is **context**—the physical or social situation in which communication occurs. For example, communication may occur in a classroom, a bar, or a church; the physical characteristics of the setting influence the communication. People communicate differently depending on the context. You probably communicate differently when hanging out with friends than you do when talking with one of your instructors.

Context may consist of the physical, social, political, and historical structures in which the communication occurs. Consider the controversy over the Calvin Klein underwear ads that use adolescents as models. The controversy takes place in a social context that says that pedophilia is perverse or immoral. This means that any communication that encourages or feeds that behavior or perspective, including advertising, is deemed wrong by the majority of residents. However, pedophilia has not been considered wrong in all societies in all periods of history. To really understand the Calvin Klein ads, we have to know something about the current attitudes toward and meanings attached to pedophilia wherever the ads are displayed.

The political context in which communication occurs includes those forces that attempt to change or retain existing social structures and relations. For example, to understand the acts of protesters who throw blood or red paint on people who wear fur coats, we must consider the political context. In this case, the political context would be the ongoing informal debates about animal rights and animals farmed for their fur. In other countries or in other times, the protesters' communicative act would not make sense or would be interpreted in other ways.

We also need to examine the historical context of communication. For instance, African Americans and Whites in the United States might have more trouble communicating with one another than Whites and Blacks in Europe because the legacy of slavery influences these interactions even today.

BUILDING BLOCK 4: POWER

Power is always present when we communicate with each other although it is not always evident or obvious. We often think of communication between individuals as being between equals, but this is rarely the case. In every society, a social hierarchy exists that gives some groups more power and privilege than others. The groups with the most power determine, to a great extent, the communication system of the entire society.[18] This is certainly true in intercultural communication. For example, straight people often have more power than gays or lesbians, males more power than females, and the able-bodied more power than those with disabilities. Those in power, consciously or unconsciously, create and maintain communication systems that reflect, reinforce, and promote their own ways of thinking and communicating.

There are two types of group-related power. The first involves membership in involuntary groups based on age, ethnicity, gender, physical ability, race, and sexual orientation and is more permanent in nature. The second involves membership in more voluntary groups based on educational background, geographic location, marital status, and socioeconomic status and is more changeable.[19] The key point is that the dominant communication systems ultimately impede others who do not have the same ways of communicating. Arguably, the communication style most valued in college classrooms is a traditional White, middle-class male style—with emphasis on competition (the first person who raises a hand gets to speak)—a style that is not as comfortable for many women and members of minority groups. By contrast, the call-and-response style of African Americans is not the norm in corporate boardrooms or classrooms. However, some hip-hop cultural norms, such as baggy jeans worn low and caps worn backward, have entered American youth culture.

Power also comes from social institutions and the roles people occupy in those institutions. A college is such an institution. For example, in the classroom, there is temporary inequality, with the instructor having more power. He or she sets the course requirements, gives grades, and determines who speaks. In this case, the power rests not with the individual instructor but with the role that he or she is enacting.

Power is not a simple one-way proposition but is dynamic. Students in a classroom, for example, are not powerless; they may assert and negotiate their power. After all, one cannot be a teacher without students. Also, the typical power relationship between instructor and student often is not perpetuated beyond the classroom. There are, however, also issues of power in broader societal contexts. For example, in contemporary society, cosmetic companies have a

Pop Culture Spotlight

Words have meaning only in our agreement as to that meaning. In the movie *Never Been Kissed*, 20-something journalist Drew Barrymore must learn and adapt to a teen culture. In that film, some of the teenagers make up a new word for "cool": "Rufus." How hip are you? Can you list other examples of words used by teens that seem to mean something only because they say they do?

vested interest in a particular image of female beauty that involves purchasing and using makeup. Advertising encourages women to feel compelled to participate in this cultural definition. But what happens if a woman decides not to buy into this definition? Regardless of her reasons for not participating, other people are likely to interpret her behavior in ways that may not match her own motivation. What her unadorned face communicates is understood against a backdrop of society's definitions—that is, the backdrop developed by the cosmetics industry.

Power in this sense should be thought of in broad terms. Dominant cultural groups attempt to perpetuate their positions of privilege in many ways, but subordinate groups can resist this domination in many ways, too. For example, cultural groups can use political and legal means to maintain or resist domination. But these are not the only means of invoking power relations. Groups can negotiate their various relations to culture through economic boycotts, strikes, and sit-ins. Individuals can subscribe or not subscribe to specific magazines or newspapers, change TV channels, write letters to government officials, or take other action to influence power relations. For example, the European clothing distributor Benetton recently launched an ad campaign showing women with scarred breasts. The purpose was to draw attention to the problem of breast cancer. However, some advertisers found the ads offensive and refused to display them, in this way resisting the advertisements.

The disempowered may negotiate power in many ways. Employees in a large institution, for example, can reposition themselves to gain power. Or students might sign their advisors' signature on their registration schedules if they don't have time to see their advisors or their advisors didn't have time for them.

Power is complex, especially in relation to institutions or the social structure. Some inequities, such as those involving sex, class, or race, are more rigid than those resulting from temporary roles like student or teacher. The power relations between student and teacher, for example, are more complex if the teacher is a woman challenged by male students. In short, we really can't understand intercultural communication without considering the power dynamics in the interaction.

BARRIERS TO INTERCULTURAL COMMUNICATION

Ethnocentrism

Ethnocentrism is the belief that one's own cultural group—usually equated with nationality—is superior to all other cultural groups. Believing that one's own country and culture are good is not bad in itself. After all, it is necessary to believe in one's country and group in order to pass along the values that are seen as important. But ethnocentrism is extreme, to the point that one cannot believe that another culture's values are equally good or worthy. Ethnocentrism becomes a barrier when it prevents people from even trying to see another's point of view, through another's "prescription lens."

Surf's Up!

The Internet has created new and exciting possibilities for communication across cultures. But just as there are barriers to effective cross-cultural communication in "real" life, there are similar constraints in cyberspace. Consider the total number of languages spoken on the Internet (http://www.global-reach.biz/globstats/index.php3). How many groups are potentially excluded from online discourse based on language?

Intercultural communication may involve groups whose members differ in terms of gender, age, ethnicity and physical ability, among other things.

It can be very difficult to see our own ethnocentrism. Often, we see it best when we spend extended time in another cultural group. One of our students, Sara, described her realization of her own ethnocentrism:

> When I was 22 years old, I joined the Peace Corps and lived for two years in a remote, rural part of West Africa. I experienced first-hand a culture that was so entirely different from my own and yet had its own sensible, internal logic, that the complacency and arrogance of my U.S. American ethnocentrism was shaken to its core. I came to realize not only that other societies had valid worldviews and important wisdom but that it would take a special kind of attention to take in and understand these other ways of seeing the world.

Learning to see her own ethnocentrisms helped Sara to be more receptive to learning about other cultures and to be more curious about other people's ways of living and experiencing the world.

Stereotyping

Another barrier to intercultural communication is stereotypes, which develop as part of our everyday thought processes. In order to make sense out of the overwhelming amount of information we receive every day, we categorize and generalize from this information. **Stereotypes** "are widely held beliefs about a

Surf's Up!

Discriminatory practices oftentimes go unnoticed by those who are responsible for them. We tend to perceive ourselves as fair, good-hearted human beings, unaware that there are hidden biases ingrained in us based on our cultural upbringing or socialization. Our cultural biases may be based on such factors as religion, race, class, gender, sexual orientation, age, disability, or even body image. Test yourself to explore your hidden biases, and reflect on what you can do to fight hate and prejudice in society (http://www.tolerance. org/hidden_bias).

group of people" and are a form of generalization—a way of categorizing and processing information we receive about others in our daily life. For example, Tom and Judith hold some generalizations about students. We assume that students don't want to study too much but that they want to know what will be on the tests we give. These generalizations, or mental shortcuts, help us know how to interact with students. However, generalizations become potentially harmful stereotypes when they are held rigidly. Thus, if we thought that all students were lazy or unwilling to study on their own, and we interacted with students based on this belief, we would hold a negative stereotype. Stereotypes also may be positive. For example, some people hold the stereotype that all attractive people are also smart and socially skilled. Even positive stereotypes can cause problems for those stereotyped. Attractive individuals may feel excessive pressure to fit the stereotype that they are competent at something they're not, or they may be hired on the basis of their appearance and then find out they cannot do the job.

Why do we hold stereotypes? One reason is that stereotypes help us know what to expect from and how to react to others. However, stereotypes, once adopted, are not easily discarded. In fact, people tend to remember information that supports a stereotype and to not retain information that contradicts the stereotype.

We pick up stereotypes in different ways. The media, for example, tend to portray cultural groups in stereotypic ways—for example, older people as needing help, or Asian Americans or African Americans as followers or background figures for Whites. Sometimes stereotypes persist because the media choose to not pass along information that would contradict stereotypes. Consider the many recent stereotypes about Muslim people and their religion of Islam. Western portrayals of Islam often omit the fact that Judaism, Christianity, and Islam are closely related—called "the three sisters of Abrahamic religions" by theologians. All three religions are monotheistic and absolutists (in contrast to the Asian religions that have many gods and are more relative in their dictates about right and wrong). Both Islam and Christianity accept Jesus as the messiah, accept the virgin birth, and recognize Jesus's sacred mission on earth—in contrast to Judaism. However in other aspects, Islam and Judaism are closer; for example, they emphasize a God of justice rather than love, hold to dietary laws, and require male circumcision.[20]

Other stereotypes portray Muslims as sexist and violent. The stereotype of Muslim women in Western media is usually drawn from a small minority of Muslim societies and do not represent the vast majority of Muslim people. The media neglect to tell us that when Canada had a first female prime minister, three different Muslim countries already had prime ministers and one also had a woman leader of the opposition. Pakistan, Turkey, and Bangladesh have had women as chief executives, whereas the United States has had no woman president, Germany no woman chancellor, and Russia no woman president.

And what about stereotypes about Islam and violence? It might depend on how we look at peace and violence. Consider Tehran, a city of 10 million people, about the size of New York City. Ali Muzrui writes that in the 1990s he often saw

Pop Culture Spotlight

While cultural studies and critical scholars like Edward Said have emphasized the complexity of East-West cultural and political relations, often the general public garners information about other cultures from the media. Films like *True Lies* (1994), *The Siege* (1998), and *Rules of Engagement* (2000) all depict Middle-Easterners as terrorists or extremists. Could these films in any way influence the way we think of individuals from the Middle East?

women and children picnicking in public parks at 10 P.M. or later. In four different Iranian cities, he observed mothers at night with their children, sometimes without men, walking the streets seemingly without fear of being mugged or sexually assaulted. These are not images we see on American television. The author goes on to explain,

> On the one hand, Iranians are a people capable of collective and purposeful political violence. They have engaged in revolution and war. On the other hand, Iranians seemed to be less prone to petty interpersonal violence such as mugging and rape, than Americans in big cities. . . .Cairo [Egypt] is a city of 15 million people and yet, has only a fraction of the crime rate of Washington, D.C., a much smaller metropolis. Again, much of the explanation is cultural, with Islam playing an important role. By some definitions of *peace*, Islam is a more peaceful tradition than American culture.[21]

We may learn stereotypes in our family. One student, Stephanie, described her parents' stereotypes:

> My parents always explained to me that the Native Americans were the ones who committed the crimes in the city and for me to stay away from them. When I entered junior high school, I started meeting these so-called bad Native Americans. At first, I had a preconceived notion that they were all bad people. But as time went by, I started realizing that they were not bad people. You just had to get to know them first before you could actually judge them. I explained this to my parents, and they understood this concept but said that every Native American that they had ever met before had done something wrong to make my parents not like them. Eventually, I started bringing home some of my Native American friends and proved to my parents that all Native Americans are not bad people and that they do not all commit crimes.

Stereotypes can also develop out of negative experiences. If we have unpleasant contact with certain people, we may generalize that unpleasantness to include all members of that particular group, whatever group characteristic we focus on (race, gender, sexual orientation).

Because stereotypes often operate at an unconscious level and are so persistent, people have to work consciously at rejecting them. This process involves several steps: (1) recognizing the negative stereotypes (we all have them), and (2) obtaining individual information that can counteract the stereotype. For another student, Jenni, an experience working at a homeless shelter helped break some stereotypes. She was amazed at the strength and adaptability of the children who lived there—and then realized that she must have expected something negative. She also realized "that it doesn't matter what race you are, you could end up being down on your luck or homeless. It really broke a stereotype for me personally. As much as I hate to admit it, I always thought of homeless people as lazy and usually not white."

Surf's Up!

There are many barriers to intercultural communication. Read the frequently asked questions page American Misconceptions About Japan (www.faqs.org./faqs/japan/american-misconceptions). How many of these stereotypes do you believe in?

Prejudice

Prejudice is a negative attitude toward a cultural group based on little or no experience. It is a prejudgment of sorts. Whereas stereotypes tell us what a group is like, prejudice tells us how we are likely to feel about that group. Why are people prejudiced? One answer might be that prejudice fills some social functions.[22]

One such function is the adjustment function, whereby people hold certain prejudices because it may lead to social rewards. People want to be accepted and liked by their cultural groups, and if they need to reject members of another group to do so, then prejudice serves a certain function. Another function is the ego-defensive function, whereby people may hold certain prejudices because they don't want to admit certain things about themselves. For example, an instructor who does not feel successful as a teacher may find it easier to blame students and hold prejudices against them than to admit shortcomings as a teacher. Finally, people hold some prejudices because they help to reinforce certain beliefs or values—the value-expressive function. For example, part of belonging to some religious groups might require holding certain prejudices against other religious groups. Our student Ron's family belonged to an evangelical Protestant church. When he was growing up, his parents made disparaging remarks about the Catholic religion. In his family, part of being a good church member meant being prejudiced against Catholics.

Prejudice may also arise from a personal need to feel positive about one's own group and negative about others, or from perceived or real threats.[23] These may be genuine threats that challenge a group's existence or economic/political power, or symbolic threats in the form of intergroup value conflicts and the accompanying anxieties. In addition, if someone has already had negative intercultural contact and is anxious about future contact, particularly if there are inequalities and perceived threats, prejudice likely will develop. This was probably true for the interactions between the residents of Lewiston, Maine, and the Somalis mentioned at the beginning of the chapter. Some of the White residents saw the Somalis as an economic threat (taking jobs in an already economically depressed area), and some saw the Muslim Somalis as presenting a symbolic threat to their Catholic values. These conditions, combined with the White residents' previously held prejudices and lack of experience with racial diversity, probably reinforced some prejudice toward the Somalis. As one Somali student said, "The Somalis are in the limelight in two ways. They're Muslim, and they're black, which is the hardest position for a person to be in the United States today."[24]

It is also helpful to think about different kinds of prejudice. The most blatant prejudice is easy to see but is less common today. It is more difficult, however, to pinpoint less obvious forms of prejudice. For example, "tokenism" is a kind of prejudice shown by people who do not want to admit they are prejudiced. They go out of their way to engage in unimportant but positive intergroup behaviors—showing support for other people's programs or making statements like "I'm not prejudiced" to persuade themselves and others that they are not prejudiced. "Arms-length" prejudice is when people engage in friendly, positive behavior toward members of another group in public and semiformal situations

Pop Culture Spotlight

Bruce Lee was to be the star of the 1970s *Kung Fu* television series. He'd invented that particular martial art and to some extent created the idea for the series. But the producers and network didn't think people would want to see an Asian American hero, so David Carradine got the role. One implication was that the White man knew more about Asian cultures than Asian Americans do.

(casual friendships at work, interactions in large social gatherings or at lectures) but avoid closer contact (dating, attending intimate social gatherings).[25]

Like stereotypes, prejudice, once established, is very difficult to undo. Because it operates at a subconscious level (we often aren't really aware of our prejudice), there has to be a very explicit motivation to change our ways of thinking. One Lewiston resident explained how she had to examine her own reactions as she was tempted to agree with others' prejudicial statements about Somalis, such as, "They don't speak English. They don't work. They're uneducated." She thought about this, noted that most not only speak English but also speak three or four other languages, and wondered, "Now who's uneducated?" And she also recognized that most Somalis worked very hard; they moved to Lewiston because they wanted work and a better life than they had before. Her sister also noted that it took some time and effort to not just unthinkingly adopt the prejudices expressed by those around her. "We were frustrated because we didn't know their culture," she says. "But we asked questions. You have to be able to talk to people."[26]

Discrimination

The behavior that results from stereotyping or prejudice—overt actions to exclude, avoid, or distance oneself from other groups—is called **discrimination.** Discrimination may be based on racism or any of the other "isms" related to belonging to a cultural group (sexism, ageism, elitism). One way of thinking about discrimination is that power plus prejudice equals "ism." That is, if one belongs to a more powerful group and holds prejudices toward another, less powerful, group, resulting actions toward members of that group are based on an "ism" and so can be called discrimination.

Discrimination may range from very subtle nonverbal (lack of eye contact, exclusion of someone from a conversation), to verbal insults and exclusion from job or other economic opportunities, to physical violence and systematic elimination of the group, or genocide. The discrimination toward Somalis in Lewiston ran the gamut. Some was subtle, demonstrating "tokenism" and "arms length" prejudice, like a dirty look toward a Somali speaking her native language or refusing to share a cab with a Somali. Some was crude, such as an obscene hand gesture from a passerby; one Somali college student even endured the taunt "Monkey, go home." But some of the discrimination was even more vicious. A young Somali man was struck by a stranger one evening, and later someone tried to run over two Somali women walking on the side of the road.[27]

And the connection between prejudice and extreme discrimination is closer than you might think. The famous psychologist Gordon Alport showed how, when no one speaks out initially, prejudice against a group of people can develop into scapegoating, which, in turn, can escalate into systematic elimination, or genocide, of a people.[28] This kind of ethnic cleansing has been seen recently in the former Yugoslavia and in Rwanda, as well as in Nazi Germany in the 1930s and 1940s. He makes a powerful case for why it is important to speak up whenever we see prejudice or discrimination.

Surf's Up!

While it is understandable that September 11th was a shocking and unthinkable event for most Americans, many individuals have done little to control their emotions in response to the tragedy. Instead, some individuals have chosen to resort to physical violence and discrimination against Muslims, Arab Americans, mosques, or any person or entity they deem to be connected to the vivid face of terrorism that U.S. media sources have so often highlighted. See the stories of violence that have been documented in and around the United States since the attacks (http://www.adl.org/terrorism_america/adl_responds.asp). What are your feelings about the attacks? How did you respond to the event when you became aware of what happened? What is your reaction to the stories of others' responses? Discuss your feelings with a classmate.

Discrimination may be interpersonal, collective, and/or institutional. In recent years, interpersonal racism seems to be much more subtle and indirect but still persistent.[29] Institutionalized or collective discrimination—whereby individuals are systematically denied equal participation or rights in informal and formal ways—also persists. Sometimes institutional discrimination is very blatant. Consider, for example, the case of supervisors at a hospital outside Philadelphia who violated their antidiscrimination policy when they barred all African American employees from entering a patient's room. The White patient's husband had demanded that no Black employees assist in the delivery of her child.[30]

A more frequent example of discrimination occurs in the hiring process. Consider the following scenario. Two men apply for a low-paying, entry-level job. One man is White and admits to having served 18 months in prison for possession of cocaine with intent to sell. The other is Black and has no criminal record. Which man is more likely to get called back? In a carefully crafted experiment in which college students posed as job applicants visiting 350 employers, the White ex-con was called back 17 percent of the time and the crime-free Black applicant only 14 percent of the time. This shows a graphic example of discrimination in the United States: the disadvantage carried by a young Black man applying for a job as a dishwasher or a driver is equivalent to forcing a White man to carry an 18-month prison record on his back. The researcher, who won an award for his study, concluded:

> In these low-wage, entry-level markets, race remains a huge barrier. Affirmative action pressures aren't operating here . . . Employers don't spend a lot of time screening applicants. They want a quick signal whether the applicant seems suitable. Stereotypes among young black men remain so prevalent and so strong that race continues to serve as a major signal of characteristics of which employers are wary.[31]

In another study, researchers responded in writing to help-wanted ads in Chicago and Boston, using names likely to be identified by employers as White or African American. Applicants named Greg Kelly or Emily Walsh were 50 percent more likely to be called for interviews than those named Jamal Jackson or Lakisha Washington. The researchers concluded that having a White-sounding name on an application is worth as much as an extra eight years of work experience. These examples show how easily stereotypes about race can lead to discrimination.[32]

One of our Latino students, Robert, told us about his experiences with stereotyping, prejudice, and discrimination:

> The lady with the blond hair tells us if we want a drink of water to use the hose in the front yard. In front of the house lay five bikes, three of them brand-new Mongooses, the most desired by kids. The other two not far removed from a scrap heap. Rudy Vargas's, a girl's bike with the frame painted pink and bent at a forty-five-degree angle, and my bike, with mismatched tires and handlebars from an adult ten-speed bike.

The lady with the blond hair sends Rudy and me home. [Her kids] Vincent, Justin, and Keith are going to the movies and to the arcade afterward. She just knows Rudy and I weren't sent any money because my mom is on assistance and Rudy's mom is probably stoned right now.

I went to school and said the pledge of allegiance with those guys on Monday, but I can't say I forgot about the incident. Instead, all those stories I'd heard about from my dad started running through my head. He would tell me not to trust white people because they thought they were better than we were and they would never treat us as equals. How long did that thought last? I don't know. When did I think to myself, "He's right"? I don't know that either. All I know is that I started to pay attention to the times I was treated as second class. It's not okay to be pulled over, detained, and questioned by police. It's not right to be followed by security at the mall. It's definitely not cool to be asked if you're a student here or are with maintenance.

In Robert's account, he understood that the "lady with the blond hair" was operating from stereotypic views when she assumed that Robert and his friend Rudy had no money for the movies. She seemed to show prejudice, a negative attitude, when she told them to use the hose to get a drink of water. Robert may not have known exactly what she intended to communicate. But he understood that she was stereotyping him and communicating prejudice to him, and this formed the foundation of his future interactions with her.

SUMMARY

In this chapter, we identified and described the four building blocks of intercultural communication: culture, communication, context, and power. Culture can be viewed as learned, shared perceptions and values, expressed as behaviors, that are dynamic and heterogeneous. Communication is a symbolic process whereby meaning is shared and negotiated. In addition, communication is dynamic, may be unintentional, and is receiver-oriented. The relationship between culture and communication is complex because (1) culture influences communication, (2) communication reinforces culture, and (3) communication is a way of resisting the dominant culture.

The context—the physical and social setting in which communication occurs, or the larger political, societal, and historical environment—affects that communication. The fourth building block, power, is pervasive and plays an enormous, though often hidden, role in intercultural communication interactions. Power relationships—determined largely by social institutions and roles—influence communication.

We also identified attitudinal and behavioral barriers to intercultural communication. Ethnocentrism is the belief that one's own culture is superior to all others. Stereotyping is the process of rigidly categorizing others; stereotypes may be negative or positive. Prejudice is the negative prejudging of others on the basis of little or no experience. Attitudes like stereotyping and prejudice may lead to behavioral barriers such as discrimination.

Now that we have laid the foundation of our approach to intercultural communication, the next step is to examine the role of history in intercultural communication.

BUILDING INTERCULTURAL SKILLS

1. Become more conscious of the identity groups you belong to, both voluntary and involuntary. Which are most important to you? Also become more conscious of the cultural values of your family. What sayings did your mother and father repeat to you ("Just because so-and-so does something doesn't mean you have to do it too!")? Which values were emphasized and communicated in your family? How do you think these values influenced the way you perceive other cultural groups? How did they influence your communication with others who are different from you?

2. Become more aware of your own communication in intercultural encounters. Think about the message you are sending, verbally and nonverbally. Think about your tone of voice, your posture, your gestures, and your eye contact. Are you sending the messages you want to send?

3. Notice how diverse your friends are. Do you have friends from different age groups? From different ethnic groups? Do you have friends with disabilities? Of both genders? From different socioeconomic classes? Whose first language is not English? Think about why you have/don't have diverse friends and what you can learn from seeing the world through their "prescription lenses."

4. Become more knowledgeable about different cultures by reading local ethnic newspapers and seeing foreign films.

5. Notice how different cultural groups are portrayed in the media. If there are people of color or other minority groups represented, what roles do they play? Major roles? Background? Comic relief?

6. When speaking about other groups, try to use tentative words that don't reflect generalizations—like "generally," or "many times," or "it seems to me," or "in my experience."

7. Practice speaking up when someone tells a joke that is hurtful toward another group. A simple "What do you mean by that?" or "Why is that funny?" or "I really don't think that's very funny" can prod the joketeller into thinking twice about telling racist/sexist jokes around you.

ACTIVITIES

1. *Cultural values:* Look for advertisements in popular newspapers and magazines. Analyze the ads to see if you can identify the societal values that they appeal to.

2. *Cultural groups and communication:* Identify the various cultural groups you belong to, both voluntary and involuntary. Choose two of these groups, and

think about each group and your membership in that group. Then try to describe how belonging to that group influences your perceptions. For example, how is your worldview influenced by belonging to your family? By being a female or male? By being Asian American, or White, or an international student? Finally, describe how your communication with others is influenced by your membership in these two groups.

THE ONLINE LEARNING CENTER at www.mhhe.com/experiencing2 features self-quizzes, flashcards, and crossword puzzles based on the chapter's key terms and concepts.

www.mhhe.com/ experiencing2

ENDNOTES

1. Taylor, S. (2002, November 26). Diverse people stand united against hatred. *Lewiston Sun Journal* (online). (http://www.sunjournal.com/story.asp?slg=112602diversity)
2. Taylor, S. (2002, November 26).
3. Singer, M. R. (1998). *Perception and identity in intercultural communication.* Yarmouth, ME: Intercultural Press.
4. Hofstede, H. (1997). *Cultures and organizations: Software of the mind* (Rev. ed.). New York: McGraw-Hill, p. 3.
5. Morin, R. (2000, July 16). Talking about race. *New York Times Magazine,* pp. 1–48.
6. Wessel, D. (2003, September 4). Studies suggest potent race bias in hiring. *Wall Street Journal,* p. A2.
7. Singer, M. R. (1998).
8. Hall, S. (1992). Cultural studies and its theoretical legacies. In L. Grossberg, C. Nelson, & P. Treichler (Eds.), *Cultural studies* (pp. 277–294). New York: Routledge.
9. WorldNetDaily.Com. (2003, July 31). House rebuffs court on 10 commandments. http://www.worldnetdaily.com/news/article.asp?ARTICLE_ID=33843
10. Kluckhohn, F., & Strodtbeck, F. (1961). *Variations in value orientations.* Chicago: Row, Peterson.
11. Hofstede, H. (1997). *Cultures and organizations: Software of the mind* (Rev. ed.). New York: McGraw-Hill. Note that Hofstede's research can be criticized. He conducted his initial research only in countries where IBM subsidiaries were located, ignoring many African and Middle Eastern countries in developing his value framework. In addition, his masculine/feminine orientation has been criticized for its stereotypical definitions of masculinity and femininity.
12. Chinese Culture Connection. (1987). Chinese values and the search for culture-free dimensions of culture. *Journal of Cross-Cultural Psychology, 18,* 143–164.
13. Matsumoto, D. (2002). *The new Japan: Debunking seven cultural stereotypes.* Yarmouth, ME: Intercultural Press.
14. Katriel, T. (1990). "Griping" as a verbal ritual in some Israeli discourse. In D. Carbaugh (Ed.), *Cultural communication and intercultural contact* (pp. 99–112). Hillsdale, NJ: Lawrence Erlbaum.
15. Katriel, T., & Philipsen, G. (1990). What we need is communication: "Communication" as a cultural category in some American speech. In Carbaugh, pp. 77–94.
16. Philipsen, G. (1990). Speaking like a man in "Teamsterville": Culture patterns of role enactment in an urban neighborhood. In Carbaugh, pp. 11–12.
17. Fitch, K. L. (1994). A cross-cultural study of directive sequences and some implications for compliance-gaining research. *Communication Monographs, 61,* 185–209.
18. Orbe, M. O. (1998). *Constructing co-cultural theory: An explication of culture, power, and communication.* Thousand Oaks, CA: Sage.
19. Loden, M., & Rosener, J. B. (1991). *Workforce America! Managing employee diversity as a vital resource.* Homewood, IL: Business One Irwin.

20. Muzrui, A. A. (2001). Historical struggles between Islamic and Christian worldviews: An interpretation. In V. H. Milhouse, M. K. Asante, & P. O. Nwosu (Eds.), *Transcultural realities* (pp. 109–119). Thousand Oaks, CA: Sage.

21. Muzrui, A. A. (2001). p. 114.

22. Brislin, R. (1999). *Understanding culture's influence on behavior* (2nd ed). Belmont, CA: Wadsworth.

23. Hecht, M. L. (1998). Introduction. In M. L. Hecht (Ed.), *Communicating prejudice* (pp. 3–23). Thousand Oaks, CA: Sage.

24. Jones, C. (2003, February 7). Newcomers give old city a look at itself. *USA Today*, p. A13.

25. Brislin, R. (1999).

26. Jones, C. (2003, February 7).

27. Jones, C. (2003, February 7).

28. Alport, G. (1970). *The nature of prejudice*. Reading, MA: Addison-Wesley.

29. Maluso, D. (1995). Shaking hands with a clenched fist: Interpersonal racism. In B. Lott & D. Maluso (Eds.), *The social psychology of interpersonal discrimination* (pp. 50–79). New York: Guilford Press.

30. Pritchard, O. (2003, October 5). NAACP wants hospital supervisers punished. *The Philadelphia Inquirer* (online). http://www.philly.com/mld/inquirer/news/local/6928671.htm

31. Wessel, D. (2003, September 4).

32. Wessel, D. (2003, September 4).

CHAPTER THREE

History and Intercultural Communication

CHAPTER OUTLINE

From History to Histories
Political, Intellectual, and Social Histories
Family Histories
National Histories
Cultural Group Histories
The Power of Other Histories

History and Identity
Histories as Stories
Nonmainstream Histories

Intercultural Communication and History
Historical Legacies

Summary

Building Intercultural Skills

Activities

Endnotes

STUDY OBJECTIVES

After reading this chapter, you should be able to:

1. Understand the role of history in intercultural communication interactions. Describe some of the histories that influence our communication.

2. Explain the importance of nonmainstream histories and their relation to cultural identities. Explain why it is necessary to recover "nonmainstream" histories.

3. Understand the role of narratives in understanding various histories.

4. Understand the importance of history in contemporary intercultural relations.

5. Explain how diasporic histories influence intercultural interactions.

6. Explain how we can negotiate histories in interactions.

KEY TERMS

colonial histories
cultural group histories
diaspora
diasporic histories
ethnic histories
family histories
gender histories
grand narrative
Homo narrans
intellectual histories

national histories
political histories
postcolonialism
racial histories
religious histories
sexual orientation
  histories
social histories
socioeconomic class
  histories

57

I, Liliuokalani of Hawaii, *by the Will of God named heir-apparent on the tenth day of April, A.D. 1877, and by the grace of God Queen of the Hawaiian Islands on the seventeenth day of January, A.D. 1893, do hereby protest against the ratification of a certain treaty, which, so I am informed, has been signed at Washington by Messrs, Hatch, Thurston, and Kinney, purporting to cede those Islands to the territory and dominion of the United States. I declare such a treaty to be an act of wrong toward the native and part-native people of Hawaii, an invasion of the rights of the ruling chiefs, in violation of international rights both toward my people and toward friendly nations with whom they have made treaties, the perpetuation of the fraud whereby the constitutional government was overthrown, and, finally, an act of gross injustice to me.*
—Letter from Queen Liliuokalani to
President William McKinley, June 17, 1897[1]

Surf's Up!

What do you know about Harlem? Check out some of the cultural history of the Harlem Renaissance, and think again (www.si. umich.edu/CHICO/ Harlem/).

This is part of a letter written by the Queen of the Kingdom of Hawaii to the President of the United States in which she implores him not to allow ratification of a treaty that annexes Hawaii against the will of the native people and the monarchy. We know what happened in this situation. Hawaii today is one of the 50 states. But what does this history have to do with intercultural communication? How does this history play an important role in the cultural identities of those living in Hawaii today? How does this history give rise to a number of groups seeking Hawaiian sovereignty? Different perspectives on this history can sometimes come into conflict, as they have over the legality of the annexation of the Hawaiian islands.

It is not always immediately apparent what history has to do with culture, communication, or intercultural communication. In this chapter, we hope to show you the significance of history in forming cultural identities and in forming intercultural interactions.

The history that we know and our feelings about that history are strongly influenced by our culture. When people from differing cultural backgrounds encounter one another, these differences can form hidden barriers to communication. However, people often overlook this set of dynamics in intercultural communication. Although we typically think of "history" as something contained in history books, an awareness of history is important in understanding intercultural interaction.

History, of course, spans a long, long time. Many events have happened in the past that have created differences among cultural groups and then maintained those differences. It is not always easy to look back and deal with some of these events. Some people ask, "Why do we have to dwell on the past? Can't we all move on?" Other people say that it is impossible to understand them without understanding the history of their cultural group. These different viewpoints certainly can affect the intercultural communication among these people.

On a larger scale, we can see how history influences intercultural interaction in many different contexts. For example, Australia used to have what is often called a "White Australia" policy that guided their immigration restrictions. Australian immigration policy restricted non-Europeans from immigrating until the last of the racial restrictions was lifted in the 1970s.[2] When you imagine an "Australian" today, what do you envision? There are historical reasons why Australia is populated largely by people with European origins. History helps us understand why Australia looks the way it does today. In reaction to this history, in 1989, Australia launched its "National Agenda for a Multicultural Australia." As a part of this national policy, Australia's history is reflected in its language policy, which reads, "English is our national language and it is critical—for the individual, for society and for our collective prosperity—that every Australian be given the opportunity to master it."[3] Does your imaginary Australian speak English? Not one of the aboriginal languages?

How we view the past directly influences how we view ourselves and others even here in the United States. Think about where you are from and what that might signify. What does it mean to be a midwesterner? A southerner? A Californian? A New Yorker? How do you know what these other regional identities mean, given that people's identities are rooted in different histories? In fact, this is the main theme of this chapter—that history is an important element in the experience of intercultural communication.

As you will see, culture and cultural identities are intimately tied to history, as they have no meaning without history. Yet there is no single version of history; the past has been recorded in many different ways. For example, your family has its own version of its history. Is it important to you to feel positively about who your forebears were and where they came from? We often feel a strong need to identify in positive ways with our past even if we are not interested in history. The stories of the past, accurate or inaccurate, help us understand why our families live where they do, why they own or lost land there, and so on. It helps us understand who we are and why we live and communicate in the ways we do.

In this chapter, we discuss the various histories that provide the contexts in which we communicate: political, intellectual, social, family, national, and cultural group. We then describe how these histories are intertwined with our various identities, based on gender, sexual orientation, ethnicity, race, and so on. Two identities have strong historical bases—diasporic and colonial. We pay particular attention to the role of narrating our personal histories. Finally, we explore how history influences intercultural communication. Throughout this chapter, you should think about the importance of history in constructing your own identity and how the relationship between the past and the present helps us understand different identities for others in different cultural groups.

FROM HISTORY TO HISTORIES

Many different kinds of history influence our understanding of who we are—as individuals, as family members, as members of cultural groups, as citizens of a nation. These histories necessarily overlap and influence one another. For example, think about the history of your family. How has your family history been influenced by your family's membership in certain cultural groups but not others? How has members' nationality been an important part of this history? How does your family history tie into the larger story of U.S. history? Identifying the various historical contexts is the first step in understanding how history affects communication.

Political, Intellectual, and Social Histories

Some people view "history" as only that information contained in documented events. When these types of history focus on political events, we call them **political histories.** When they focus on the transmission and development of ideas or ways of thinking, we call them **intellectual histories.** And when they provide insight into the everyday life experiences of various groups in the past, we call them **social histories.**

This way of organizing and thinking about history may seem more manageable than the broad notion of history as "everything that has happened before now." But many different kinds of history influence our views of and knowledge about the past, and many historical events never get documented. For example, the strict laws that forbade teaching slaves in the United States to read kept many of their stories from being documented. The lack of a written record, of course, does not mean that the people did not exist, that their experiences do not matter, or that their history has no bearing on us. To consider such absent histories requires that we think in more complex ways about the past and the ways it influences the present and the future.

Family Histories

Family histories occur at the same time as other histories but on a more personal level. Often, they are not written down but are passed along orally from one generation to the next. Perhaps surprisingly, some people do not know which countries or cities their families emigrated from, or what tribes they belonged to, or where they lived in the United States. But other people place great emphasis on knowing that, say, their ancestors arrived in the Mayflower, or migrated to Utah with Brigham Young, or survived the Holocaust. Many of these family histories are deeply intertwined with ethnic group histories and religious histories, but the family histories identify the family's actual participation in

What Do You Think?

How reliable is history? Edmund Morris, Ronald Reagan's biographer, was roundly criticized for inserting himself as a fictional character in Reagan's life in his book. He argued that it gave a unique perspective: It made it easier for us to imagine we were there and thus made the history more meaningful. Do you agree?

these events. A key issue is whether it is possible or even desirable to escape from the history of one's family.

National Histories

Obviously, the **national history** of any nation—its great events and figures—is important to the people of that nation. U.S. national history typically begins with the arrival of Europeans in North America. U.S. citizens are expected to recognize the great events and the so-called great people (mostly men of European ancestry) who were influential in the development of the country. Thus, students are told stories, verging on myths, that give life to these events and people. For example, they learn about the Founding Fathers—George Washington, Benjamin Franklin, Thomas Jefferson, James Madison, and so on. They learn about Patrick Henry's "Give me liberty or give me death" speech, although the text of the speech was collected by a biographer who "pieced together twelve hundred words from scattered fragments that earwitnesses remembered from twenty years before."[4] And they learn about George Washington chopping down a cherry tree and then confessing his guilt, and about Abraham Lincoln helping to bind the nation's wounds with his stirring Gettysburg Address.

Yet, as you probably already know, U.S. history textbooks "leave out anything that might reflect badly upon our national character."[5] They are written for White Americans. In his review of textbooks, James Loewen points to the importance of studying Native American Indian history since it "is the antidote to the pious ethnocentrism of American exceptionalism, the notion that European Americans are God's chosen people. Indian history reveals that the United States and its predecessor British colonies have wrought great harm in the world. We must not forget this—not to wallow in our wrongdoing, but to understand and to learn, that we might not wreak harm again."[6]

National history gives us a shared notion of who we are and solidifies our sense of nationhood. Although we may not personally fit into the national narrative, we are expected to know this particular telling of U.S. history so we can understand the many references used in communication. For example, when people talk about the "13 colonies," we are expected to know that the speaker is not referring to colonies in Africa or Asia. National history simply represents one way of constructing cultural discourses and cultural identities.

Yet U.S. students do not often learn much about the histories of other nations and cultures unless they are studying their languages. As any student of another language knows, it is part of the curriculum to study not only the grammar and vocabulary of the language but also the culture and history of the people who speak that language. Table 3.1 shows some of the name changes that some places have undergone. Understanding the history of these places would help you understand why their names have changed.

Judith and Tom both studied French. Because we learned a great deal about French history, we were taught the French national narrative. The French have their own national history, centering on the evolution of France from a

Info Bites

George Washington never chopped down that cherry tree, and he also didn't really use wooden dentures. Abe Lincoln had a high-pitched, squeaky voice, and his Gettysburg Address was generally considered an embarrassment when he delivered it. How much of what you think you know about history is real, and how much is fiction? The more interesting question is, How can you be sure of the difference?

TABLE 3.1 Dynamic Country Names

PRESENT NAME	PREVIOUS NAME
Benin	Dahomey
Burkina Faso	Upper Volta
Cambodia	Kampuchea Republic
Ghana	Gold Coast
Hawaii	Sandwich Islands
Iran	Persia
Myanmar	Burma
Québec	New France
Sri Lanka	Ceylon
Taiwan	Formosa

Surf's Up!

How do we investigate cultural history? What motivates us to explore historical ruins? Read the account of an early 1900s American expedition to Europe and the Near East. The mission of the lead scientist was to find early Christian manuscripts and photograph historical sites (http://www.si.umich.edu/chico/kelsey/descrip/html). Read the history and evaluate the photographs that are archived there. What does this example of a scientist's work tell us about culture and the recording of history? What kinds of things does this work leave out?

monarchy, to a dictatorship, to a republic. For example, French people know that they live in the Cinquième République (or Fifth Republic), and they know what this means within the grand narrative of French history. This history helps French citizens comprehend what it means to be French, as well as their country's relationships with other nations.

Cultural Group Histories

Although people may share a single national history, each cultural group within the nation may have its own history. The history may be hidden, but it also is related to the national history. These **cultural group histories** help us understand the identity of the group.

Consider, for example, the expulsion in the 1750s of many French-speaking Acadians from eastern Canada and their migration to Louisiana. These historical events are central to understanding the cultural traits of the Cajuns. For example, the popular saying "Laissez les bons temps roulez!" (Let the good times roll!) is spoken in French because of this history. The forced removal in 1838 of the Cherokees from their former nation, New Echota (located mostly in Georgia), to settlements in what eventually became the state of Oklahoma resulted in the death of one fifth of the Cherokee population. This event, known as the Trail of Tears, explains much about the Cherokee Nation, including the split between the eastern and western Cherokees. The northward migration of African Americans in the early 20th century helps us understand the settlement patterns and working conditions in northern cities like Cleveland, Detroit, Chicago, and New York. These cultural histories are not typically included in our national history, but they are important in the development of group identities, family histories, and the contemporary lives of individual members of these cocultures.

In this sense, history represents the many stories we tell about the past, rather than one ongoing story on a singular time continuum. Certainly, the

IN THIS TEMPLE
AS IN THE HEARTS OF THE PEOPLE
FOR WHOM HE SAVED THE UNION
THE MEMORY OF ABRAHAM LINCOLN
IS ENSHRINED FOREVER

The Lincoln Memorial in Washington, DC, attests to the historical legacy of Lincoln and his contribution to our national identity. He is often portrayed as extremely honest ("Honest Abe") and as the man who freed the slaves. What cultural myths do we tell ourselves about Lincoln?

events of families, cultural groups, and nations are related; even world events are related. Ignorance of the histories of other groups makes intercultural communication more difficult and fraught with potential misunderstandings.

The Power of Other Histories

We live in a time of rapid change, and this change causes us to rethink cultural struggles and identities. It may be difficult for you to envision, but at one time a unified story of humankind—the **"grand narrative"**—dominated how people thought of the past, present, and future. This is no longer the case, as there are now many competing stories of the past.[7]

In place of the grand narrative are revised and restored histories that had been suppressed, hidden, or erased. The cultural movements that make this shift possible empower other cultural identities and enable the rewriting of the history of U.S. colonialism, slavery, immigration laws, and so on. Recovering various histories is necessary to rethinking what some cultural identities mean. It also helps us rethink the dominant cultural identity—what it means to be an "American."

Regardless of whether we choose to recognize the foundations for many of our differences, these inequalities influence how we think about others and how we interact. They also influence how we think about ourselves—our identities. These are important aspects of intercultural communication. It may seem daunting to confront the history of the world, and, indeed, there are many histories of the world. Nevertheless, the more you know, the better you will be positioned to engage in successful intercultural interactions.

HISTORY AND IDENTITY

Surf's Up!

Visit the History Channel website (www. historychannel.com/). What happened today in history?

In the previous chapter, we saw how individual identities develop. Here, we discuss the development of cultural identities, which is strongly influenced by history.

Histories as Stories

Faced with these many levels of history, you might wonder how we make sense of them in our everyday lives. Although it might be tempting to ignore them all and just pretend to be "ourselves," this belies the substantial influence that history has on our own identities.

According to communication scholar Walter Fisher, telling stories is fundamental to the human experience.[8] Instead of referring to humans as Homo sapiens, Fisher prefers to call them **Homo narrans,** because that label underscores the importance of narratives in human life. Histories are stories we use to make sense of who we are and who we think others are. However, it is important to recognize that a strong cultural element sometimes encourages us to try to forget history. As French writer Jean Baudrillard observes, "America was created in the hope of escaping from history, of building a utopia sheltered from history. . . . [It] has in part succeeded in that project, a project it is still pursuing today."[9]

The desire to escape history is significant in what it tells us about how our own culture negotiates its relation to the past and how we view the relation of other nations and cultures to their pasts. By ignoring history, we sometimes come to wrongheaded conclusions about others that reinforce particular stereotypes—for example, that "everybody loves Americans" in spite of many historical reasons they would not. The paradox is that we really cannot escape history even if we fail to recognize it or try to suppress it.

Nonmainstream Histories

For people whose histories are hidden from the mainstream, speaking out is an important step in the construction of personal and cultural identities. Telling our personal narratives offers us an entry into history and an opportunity to reconcile with the events of history. These stories help us understand how others negotiated the cultural attitudes of the past that have relevance for the present. Here, we identify some kinds of history that have the most influence on intercultural interaction.

Religious Histories   Different religious groups have had very different experiences throughout history. **Religious histories** emphasize the role of religions in understanding the past. Religious conflicts between Muslims and Christians have a very long history. This history, even if it is unimportant to some U.S. Americans, can be the cause of intercultural conflict. For example, when President George W. Bush was about to go to war in Iraq, he referred to this war as a "crusade." The use of this term evoked strong negative reactions in the Islamic world, due to the history of the Crusades nearly 1,000 years ago. Even if the Crusades carry little or no historical weight in the United States, this may not be true

What Do You Think?

Are the labels *Muslim* and *Arab* synonymous? Are most Arabs in the United States Christian or Muslim? Take a look at the essay "Islam in America" located on the Foreign Policy Research Institute website (http://www.fpri.org/ ww/0404.200307. jenkins.islaminamerica. html). How would you answer these questions after reading the essay?

When Brigham Young, who led the Mormons to Utah, first crossed the Wasatch Mountains and saw the Salt Lake Valley, he proclaimed, "This is the place." Today, a state park and monument mark "the place." This historic site is a significant part of Mormon identity.

among other cultural groups around the world. The Crusades are a very important historical event in the religious identity of Muslims. The *Boston Globe* noted the following: "President Bush calls it a 'crusade,' a war against a new kind of evil. But using such a term, loaded with historical baggage about religious wars, could alienate moderate Muslims that the United States needs, some experts caution."[10] While President Bush may not have knowingly wanted to frame the Iraq invasion as a religious war against Muslims, the history of the Crusades may make others feel that it is.

For Jewish people, remembering the Holocaust is crucial to their identity. A Jewish colleague recalls growing up in New York City in the 1950s and 1960s and hearing stories of Nazi atrocities. Survivors warned that such atrocities could happen again, that persecution and victimization were always a possibility. Recent attempts by revisionists to deny that the Holocaust happened have been met with fierce opposition and a renewed effort to document that tragedy in grim detail. The Holocaust Museum in Washington, DC, is a memorial to that history for all of us.

Mormons also have experienced a turbulent history. In the early 19th century, Mormons were not welcomed in many U.S. communities, moving from New York to Ohio to Illinois, where they founded the town of Nauvoo (Hebrew for "beautiful place"). After the murder of Mormon leader Joseph Smith in 1844, however, Brigham Young decided to take the Mormons west, on what today is known as the Mormon Trek. Eventually, after crossing the pass into the Salt Lake Basin, Young is purported to have claimed, "This is the place!" Without understanding this history, you may not understand why so many Mormons today live in Salt Lake City and elsewhere in Utah.

Religious histories are never isolated; rather, they crisscross other cultural trajectories. Thus, we may feel placed in the role of victim or victimizer by historical events, or even both roles at the same time. Consider, for example, the position of German American Mennonites during World War II. They were punished as pacifists and yet also were seen as aggressors by Jewish Americans. It is often important to see the various ways that these histories make religious differences significant.

Gender Histories   Feminist scholars have long insisted that much of the history of women has been obliterated, marginalized, or erased. **Gender histories** emphasize the importance of gender in understanding the past, particularly the role of women. These histories are important in understanding how we live today, but they are often ignored. Historian Mei Nakano notes:

> The history of women, told by women, is a recent phenomenon. It has called for a fundamental reevaluation of assumptions and principles that govern traditional history. It challenges us to have a more inclusive view of history, not merely the chronicling of events of the past, not dominated by the record of men marching forward through time, their paths strewn with the detritus of war and politics and industry and labor.[11]

Pop Culture Spotlight

In Octavia Butler's *Kindred*, a modern African American woman is mysteriously sent back in time to the 1850s South, where she must learn to adapt to the horrid conditions of slavery to survive. She makes it back to her own time with a new sense of her people's history and struggle. What movies or books have caused you to rethink who you are and where you come from?

Although contemporary scholars are very much interested in women's history, they find it difficult to write that history due to the historical restrictions on women's access to public forums, public documents, and public records. For example, in the United States, women did not obtain the right to vote until 1920, so their participation in the nation's political history was restricted. And the attainment of women's suffrage has not followed the same pattern around the world, as the history of gender has been different in other cultures. For example, in 1893, New Zealand became the first nation to grant women the right to vote. Some nations recognized women's right to vote earlier in the 20th century, such as Poland (1918), Mongolia (1924), Turkey (1930), Thailand (1932), Brazil (1934), and France (1944); others were slower to do so, such as Switzerland (1971), Jordan (1974), Iraq (1980), Liechtenstein (1984), and Samoa (1990). Yet women have played significant roles throughout history, even if it is difficult to recover that history.

It is important to note that contemporary life continues to be influenced by gender histories. Traditionally, many women were encouraged to focus on the home and on domestic concerns. Even today, many women in dual-career couples feel tremendous pressure to do the bulk of the housework, reflecting the influence of the past on the present. However, many people are working to overcome these historical legacies.

Sexual Orientation Histories   Interest in the history of sexuality is a fairly recent phenomenon that is beginning to challenge the ways that we think about the past. **Sexual orientation histories** emphasize the significance of sexuality in understanding the past and the present, yet these histories are often overlooked or silenced. If we do not listen to or cannot hear the voices of others, we will miss important historical lessons and create enormous misunderstandings about who we are. For example, Martin Duberman notes that "until recently the official image of the typical American was hysterically suburban: Anglo-Saxon, monogamous, heterosexual parents pair-bonded with two children and two cars—an image as narrow and propagandist as the smiling workers of China saluting the rice fields." [12] To correct this narrow view of the past, he wrote a partial history of gays and lesbians in the United States.

The late Guy Hocquenghem, a gay French philosopher, lamented the letting go of the past because that made it difficult to avoid the lessons of history. He once observed: "I am struck by the ignorance among gay people about the past—no, more even than ignorance: the 'will to forget' the German gay holocaust. . . . But we aren't even the only ones who remember, we don't remember! So we find ourselves beginning at zero in each generation." [13]

How we think and what we know about the past contribute to building and maintaining communities and cultural identities. For example, stories of the treatment of gays and lesbians during World War II promote a common history and influence intercultural communication among gays and lesbians in France, Germany, the Netherlands, and other nations. Today, a monument in Amsterdam

Surf's Up!

If you were going to collect objects in a museum to preserve a society's "cultural history," what would you include? Examine the website for the Fowler Museum (www .fmch.ucla.edu/), and see what they included.

marks that history, helping to ensure that we remember that gays and lesbians were victims of the Nazi Holocaust as well.

Racial and Ethnic Histories   People from nonmainstream cultural groups often struggle to retain their histories. Theirs are not the histories that everyone learns about in school, yet these histories are vital to understanding how others perceive us, and why. Mainstream history has neither the time nor the space to include all **ethnic** and **racial histories,** which focus on the significance of race and ethnicity in understanding the past. Sometimes, the histories of such cultural groups seem to question, and even undermine, the celebratory nature of a national history.

The injustices done by any nation are often swept under the carpet. For example, in her book *The Rape of Nanking,* Iris Chang attempts to recover the history of the atrocities that occurred in the 1937 Japanese attack on Nanking, China—what she calls the "forgotten holocaust."[14] The millions killed in Kampuchea (Cambodia) after the Vietnam War, as well as the millions of Africans killed by European colonists in Africa and South America, are all reminders of the silencing of these histories. For example, the Royal Museum of Central Africa has little to say about the atrocities committed by the Belgians in the Congo.

In the United States, other histories have also been overlooked. In an attempt to bring attention to an understanding of the internment of Japanese Americans during World War II, former English professor John Tateishi collected the stories of some of the internees. He notes at the outset of his book that it "makes no attempt to be a definitive academic history of Japanese American internment. Rather it tries to present for the first time in human and personal terms the experience of the only group of American citizens ever to be confined in concentration camps in the United States."[15]

Although this collection of oral histories is not an academic history, it offers valuable insights into the experience of many Japanese Americans. Because this historical event demonstrates the fragility of the constitutional system and its guarantees in the face of rampant prejudice, it is not often discussed as a significant event in U.S. history. For Japanese Americans, however, it has been the most defining event in the development of their communities.

When Tom's parents meet other Japanese Americans of their generation, they are often asked, "What camp were you in?" This question makes little sense outside of its historical context. We can see how this question is embedded in understanding a particular moment in history, a moment that is not widely understood. In the aftermath of that experience of internment, the use of that history as a marker has been important in maintaining cultural identity.

Diasporic Histories   The international relationships that many racial and ethnic groups have with others who share their heritage and history often are overlooked in intercultural communication. These international ties may have been created by transnational migrations, slavery, religious crusades, or other histori-

What Do You Think?

What kind of history classes should be required in college? Should you take Western Civilization, or should you have the option of learning the history of other regions of the world? What might be the arguments on both sides?

This photo shows a gallery within the National Museum of the American Indian in New York City. How could understanding American Indian history improve intercultural interactions in the United States today?

cal events and forces. Because most people do not think about the diverse ways that people have connections to other nations and cultures, we consider these histories to be hidden. In his book *The Black Atlantic*, scholar Paul Gilroy emphasizes that, to understand the identities, cultures, and experiences of African descendants in Britain and the United States, we must examine the connections between Africa, North America, and Europe.[16]

A massive migration, often caused by war, famine, enslavement, or persecution, that results in the dispersal of a unified group is called a **diaspora.** A cultural group (or even an individual) that flees its homeland is likely to bring along some old customs and practices to its new homeland. In fact, diasporic migrations often cause people to cling more strongly to their group's identity. Over the years, though, people become acculturated to some degree in their new homelands.

Consider, for example, the dispersal of eastern European Jews who migrated during or after World War II to the United States, Australia, Argentina, Israel, and other parts of the world. They brought with them their Jewish culture and their eastern European culture. But they also adopted new cultural patterns as they became U.S. Americans, Argentinians, Israelis, and so on. Imagine the communication differences among these people that have evolved over time. Imagine the differences between these groups and the dominant culture of their new homelands.

Info Bites

The Constitution and the Declaration of Independence are preserved in the National Archives in Washington, DC. Would you feel differently about your culture and history if someone came and took them away? What do you think happened to the history and cultures of the societies in Africa that had their artifacts taken by the British Museum?

Diasporic histories help us understand the important cultural connections among people affected by diasporas and other transnational migrations. Yet we must be careful to distinguish between the ways that these connections are helpful or hurtful to intercultural communication. For example, some cultures tend to regard negatively those who have left the homeland. Many Japanese tend to look down on Japanese Canadians, Japanese Americans, Japanese Brazilians, Japanese Mexicans, and Japanese Peruvians. By contrast, the Irish tend not to look down on Irish Americans or Irish Canadians. Of course, we must remember as well that many other intervening factors might influence diasporic relationships on an interpersonal level.

Colonial Histories   As you probably know from history, many nations did not confine themselves within their own borders. Due to overpopulation, limited resources, notions of grandeur, or other factors, many people in recent centuries left their homelands to colonize other lands. It is important to recognize these **colonial histories,** which emphasize the important role of colonialism in understanding the past and its influence on the present, so we can better understand the dynamics of intercultural communication today.

Let's look at the significance of colonialism in determining language. Three of the most important colonizers were Britain, France, and Spain. As a result of colonialism, English is spoken in Canada, Australia, New Zealand, Belize, Nigeria, South Africa, India, Pakistan, Bangladesh, Zimbabwe, Hong Kong, Singapore, and the United States, among other places. French is spoken in Canada, Senegal, Tahiti, Haiti, Benin, Côte d'Ivoire, Niger, Rwanda, Mali, Chad, and the Central African Republic, among other places. And Spanish is spoken in most of the Western Hemisphere, from Mexico to Chile and Argentina, including Cuba, Venezuela, Colombia, and Panama.

Many foreign language textbooks proudly display maps that show the many places around the world where that language is commonly spoken. But the maps don't reveal why those languages are widely spoken in those regions, and they don't reveal the legacies of colonialism in those regions. For example, the United Kingdom maintains close relations with many of its former colonies through the Commonwealth of Britain—an organization of 54 nations, including Britain and its former colonies. The queen of England is also the queen of Canada, Australia, New Zealand, and the Bahamas.

Other languages have been spread through colonialism, including Portuguese in Brazil, Macao, and Angola; Dutch in Angola, Suriname, and Mozambique; and a related Dutch language, Afrikaans, in South Africa. Russian is spoken in the breakaway republics of Kazakhstan, Azerbaijan, and Tajikistan. But many nations have reclaimed their own languages in an effort to resist the influences of colonialism. For example, Arabic is spoken in Algeria, and Vietnamese is spoken in Vietnam; at one time, French was widely spoken in both countries. Today, in the newly independent Latvia, the ability to speak Latvian is a requirement for citizenship.

The reality is, we do not freely choose the languages we speak. Rather, we must learn the languages of the societies into which we are born. Judith and Tom, for example, both speak English, although their ancestors came to the United States from non-English-speaking countries. We did not choose to learn English among all of the languages of the world. Although we don't resent our native tongue, we recognize why many individuals might resent a language imposed on them. Think about the historical forces that led you to speak some language(s) and not others. Understanding history is crucial to understanding the linguistic worlds we inhabit.

The imposition of language is but one aspect of cultural invasion. Much colonial history is a history of oppression and brutality. To cast off the legacy, many people have looked toward **postcolonialism**—an intellectual, political, and cultural movement that calls for the independence of colonized states and for liberation from colonialist ways of thinking. In many ways, we continue to privilege European literature and music as worthy of study in our universities, but not the music and literature of other places around the world. The legacy of this latter invasion, the cultural invasion, often lasts much longer than the political relationship.

Socioeconomic Class Histories   Many U.S. Americans prefer to ignore class differences, but socioeconomic class has been a significant factor in the way people experienced the past. **Socioeconomic class histories** focus on the role of class in understanding these experiences. While we often overlook the importance of socioeconomic class as a factor in history, socioeconomic class helps explain why many people have immigrated to the United States. The poverty in 19th-century Ireland did much to fuel the flight of the Irish to the United States, so that today there are more Irish Americans than Irish.

Yet it is not always the socioeconomically disadvantaged who immigrate. After the Russian Revolution in 1917, a large number of fairly wealthy Russians moved to Paris. Similarly, after the Cuban Revolution in 1959, a large number of fairly wealthy Cubans fled Cuba. Today, Canada's sale of Canadian citizenship to those who can afford the fairly substantial price tag ensures that socioeconomic class will continue to inspire some migrations.

The point here is that these socioeconomic class distinctions often are overlooked in understanding the historical migrations and acculturation of groups around the world. The kinds of locations these migrants settled and the employment they found often were marked by the kinds of capital—cultural and financial—that they were or were not able to bring with them. These class distinctions also influence the kinds of interaction and politics of differing groups; for example, Mexican Americans and Cuban Americans, as groups, frequently are at odds over Latino politics. Arguments over whether Elian González should have been allowed to stay with his relatives in Florida or returned to his father in Cuba reflected continuing differences. Interestingly, arguments about the economic opportunities that were available to Elian are not similarly made to allow Mexicans into the United States.

What Do You Think?

There are a range of attitudes that exist in approaching the ideas of culture and conflict and the ways in which they are recorded throughout history. In recognizing this range of attitudes, consider *convivencia*, a term used in Spain during the Middle Ages that translates to English as "living side by side." It refers to the coexistence of communities of different cultures or origins. The practice of coexistence has been marked throughout history by tense relations that often erupt into destabilizing forms of violence. Yet we have seen individuals and groups in history continually take a stance against violence and conflict. When you consider *convivencia*, where would you stand?

INTERCULTURAL COMMUNICATION AND HISTORY

So far, we have examined some interesting ways of thinking about the past and of viewing history. We are often uncomfortable in dealing with the past because we do not know how we should feel about or deal with many of the ugly things that have happened. Think, for example, about the history of the indigenous peoples in the United States. Native peoples throughout most of the United States were exterminated or removed to settlements in other regions, and many states now have few Native Americans and few, if any, reservations. The current residents had nothing to do with the events in their state's history, but they are the beneficiaries through the ownership of farms and other land. So, although

Not all history is hidden. Here we see family members of the Oklahoma City bombing gathering silently around a memorial chair. How might this memorial influence the way Oklahomans and other U.S. Americans think about terrorism?

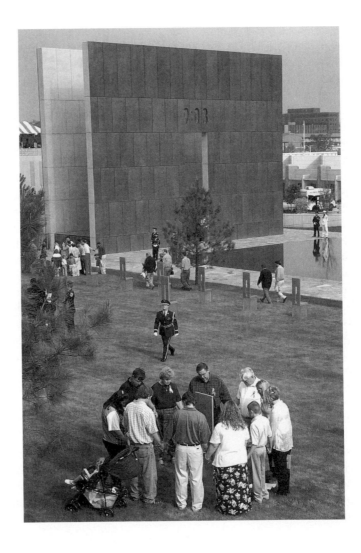

contemporary U.S. Americans are not in a position of fault, they are, through these benefits, in a position of responsibility. In *Writing the Disaster*, Maurice Blanchot makes this important distinction between the position of fault and the position of responsibility.[17] Dealing with this past is not easy, but it is even more problematic simply to ignore it, because ignoring the past erases other cultural identities by pretending that we are all the same.

Our lives are entangled in the web of history from which there is no escape, only denial and silence. How should this influence the ways we think about intercultural communication? What does all of this have to do with intercultural interaction? There are various ways that we might think about history and intercultural communication. First, we can think about the ways that history helps us understand who we are—with all of our identities—and how we may feel constrained by those identities. Second, we can examine how various histories are negotiated in intercultural interaction.

Think about how history has determined, for example, what languages you do and do not speak. Many U.S. Americans no longer speak the language(s) of their forebears. Yet, languages may be an attraction or a repellent in intercultural interactions. Many U.S. Americans, for example, enjoy traveling to Britain, Australia, and Canada, where English is spoken. Many U.S. Americans also are hesitant to travel to non-English-speaking countries because of language differences, and popular movies may reinforce these fears. For instance, in *Red Corner*, Richard Gere's character is arrested in China and becomes dependent upon his interpreter because he does not speak Chinese.

Also consider what your identity positions mean to you. How do you feel about being an "American," if this is your national identity? How might non-Americans feel about "Americans" based on their historical knowledge of what U.S. Americans have and have not done to them and for them? Why do some people dislike U.S. Americans? Can you offer the same reflexive analyses of your other identities?

It is important to recognize that your identities—as a member of a racial/ethnic group, a nationality, a socioeconomic class, and so on—do not have the same meanings for you as they might for someone with differing identities. If you are "White," how might your racial identity have a different meaning for you than for someone who is not White? Is there a history to "Whiteness" that gives it different meanings for different groups of people? Conversely, what their identities mean to you may not be the same as what they mean for them. For example, your notion of "Hawaiian" may differ significantly from that of Hawaiians. Questions about the legality of the overthrow of the Hawaiian monarchy, the Hawaiian sovereignty movement, and the history of the United States in Hawaii may create enormous differences in how these identities function in intercultural interactions.

Second, how can we balance the past and the present in our everyday intercultural interactions? Initially, it is important to recognize that each of us brings our histories (some known, some hidden) to interactions. We can try to evaluate

Info Bites

Are you U.S. American? What does that mean to you? Would it change your ideas about what that means if you knew that there is evidence that Viking sailors settled briefly on the east coast or that Japanese fishermen and Chinese explorers landed on the west coast of North America centuries before Columbus set sail?

the role that history plays for those with whom we interact. (Many tourist guide-books offer a brief history of other countries to help tourists prepare for their trip there.)

Also, we should understand the role that histories play in our identities, in what we bring to the interaction. Communication scholar Marsha Houston says there are three things that White people who want to be her friends should never say: "I don't notice you're black," "You're not like the others," and "I know how you feel." In her opinion, each of these denies or rejects a part of her identity that is deeply rooted in history.[18]

Sometimes, it is unwise to ask people where they are "really from." Such questions assume that they cannot be from where they said they were, due to racial characteristics or other apparent features. Although she was born and raised in New York City, Geetha Kothari is often asked where she is from. She writes:

> "Where are you from?" The bartender asks this as I get up from my table. It's quiet at the Bloomfield Bridge Tavern, home of the best pirogies in Pittsburgh. . . . The man has no reason to ask me that question. We are not having a conversation, I am not his friend. Out of the blue, having said no other words to me, he feels that it is okay for him, a white man, to ask me where I am from. The only context for this question is my skin color and his need to classify me. I am sure he doesn't expect me to say New York. I look different, therefore it's assumed that I must be from some-where, somewhere that isn't here, America. It would never occur to him to ask my boyfriend, who is white—and Canadian—where he's from.[19]

Although it may seem innocent to ask her where she is from, the question implies differences based on racial characteristics between those assumed to be "American" and those assumed to be from somewhere else. Recognizing a person's history and its link to his or her identity, as well as your own histori-cal blinders and assumptions, is a first step toward establishing intercultural relationships.

Historical Legacies

Given these different histories—histories that we have been exposed to and his-tories that have remained hidden from us—what are the consequences of this past? How have they changed how we live, who we are, and what we hope for the future? We have already discussed how these different histories influence what languages we speak and what languages we do not speak.

At the outset of this chapter, we began with a look at the U.S. annexation of the Hawaiian islands. How does this history influence how we think about Hawaiians and their place in U.S. society? How does this history influence the ways U.S. Americans think about Hawaii and possibly spending a vacation there? In 1978, the State of Hawaii reestablished the Hawaiian language as an official language of Hawaii. How did the Hawaiian language become marginalized on

Iolani Palace in Honolulu, Hawaii, is the only palace on U.S. soil. Although the kingdom of Hawaii is now the state of Hawaii, debates about the historical events that led to the U.S. annexation of Hawaii continue today. The rise of the Hawaiian sovereignty movement reflects the unhappiness of many Hawaiians with this annexation.

the Hawaiian islands? Can it regain its dominant position again? In 1993, on the 100th anniversary of the overthrow of the Hawaiian monarchy, President Clinton signed a formal apology on behalf of the United States which, in part, "apologizes to Native Hawaiians on behalf of the people of the United States for the overthrow of the Kingdom of Hawaii on January 17, 1893 with the participation of agents and citizens of the United States, and the deprivation of the rights of Native Hawaiians to self-determination."[20] Given the historical legacy that led to statehood for Hawaii, how can the United States correct its past mistakes in taking Hawaii? Should the United States grant independence to Hawaii? Would that solve the historical problems, or is it impossible to return Hawaii to how it might have been without U.S. intervention?

You can probably speculate on these and many more aspects of the legacy of the annexation of Hawaii by the United States. What is important to understand is that the past is not simply over; rather, we should consider all of the ways that the past has constructed how we live in the present and what we think should happen in the future. These are all influences in intercultural interaction and how we think about ourselves and others.

SUMMARY

In this chapter, we explored some of the dimensions of history in intercultural communication. Multiple histories are important for empowering different cultural identities. These include political, intellectual, social, family, national, religious, and cultural group histories.

History is constructed through narrative. Our understanding of the events that occur comes to us through our "telling" of the events. Histories that typically are not conveyed in a widespread manner are considered to be hidden. These include histories based on gender, sexual orientation, race and ethnicity, migration, colonialism, and socioeconomic class. All kinds of histories contribute to the success or failure of intercultural interaction.

We also looked at how history plays a role in intercultural interaction. The key is to balance the past and the present in intercultural encounters. As the controversy over the relationship between the United States and Hawaii shows, history certainly plays a central role in intercultural conflict.

BUILDING INTERCULTURAL SKILLS

1. Reflect on the limitations of your understanding of the past and how some of those histories have been marketed to you. What kinds of history would you want to include in a tourist guidebook for non-Americans who are visiting your state? What would you not include? Why? Whose histories would you include? Think about how history might shape people's understanding of a destination and what they want to see.

2. Think about how some of these histories are important to different people in different ways. Some tourist destinations are marketed based on their historical importance. How might you connect this history with what you expect to see, say, in Tombstone, Arizona; at the Magnolia Plantation in South Carolina; or in Williamsburg, Virginia? Why might some people want to visit the old slave auction block in Fayetteville, North Carolina, or German concentration camps, such as Auschwitz in Poland or Dachau in Germany?

3. Reflect on the history of your family. In what ways does this history connect you with members of some cultural groups and distance you from members of other cultural groups? How has your family history determined your culture—what language(s) you speak, what foods you eat, what holidays you celebrate, and so on?

4. Understand the relationship between identity and history. How does history help you understand who you are? Which kinds of history are most important in your identity? National? Family? Sexual orientation?

5. Develop sensitivity to other people's histories. Aside from "Where are you from?" what questions might strangers ask that can be irritating to some people? Should you know about how history has shaped other cultural group identities? Think about how their histories are intertwined with your histories.

ACTIVITIES

1. *Family history:* Talk to members of your own family to see how they feel about your family's history. Find out, for example, how the family history influences the way they think about who they are. Do they wish they knew more about your family? What things has your family continued to do that your forebears probably also did? Do you eat some of the same foods? Practice the same religion? Celebrate birthdays or weddings in the same way? Often, the continuity between past and present is taken for granted.

2. *Cultural group history:* Individually or in groups, choose a cultural group in the United States that is unfamiliar to you. Study the history of this group, answering the following questions:

   a. What is the historical relationship between this group and other groups (particularly the dominant cultural groups)?

   b. What are some significant events in the group's history?

   c. Are there any historical incidents of discrimination?

   d. What are common stereotypes about the group, and how did they originate?

   e. Who are important leaders and heroes of the group?

   f. What are some notable achievements of the group?

   g. In what ways does the history of this group influence the identity of group members today?

THE ONLINE LEARNING CENTER at www.mhhe.com/experiencing2 features self-quizzes, flashcards, and crossword puzzles based on the chapter's key terms and concepts.

**www.mhhe.com/
experiencing2**

ENDNOTES

1. Queen Lilioukalani. (1897). Letter to President McKinley. http://libweb.hawaii.edu/libdept/hawaiian/annexation/protest/liliu5.html

2. Department of Immigration & Multicultural & Indigenous Affairs, Public Affairs Section, Fact Sheet No. 8, "Abolition of the 'White Australia' Policy," November 6, 2002. http://www.immi.gov.au/facts/08abolition.htm

3. Department of Immigration & Multicultural & Indigenous Affairs, Public Affairs Section, "National Agenda for a Multicultural Australia," 1989. http://www.immi.gov.au/multicultural/_inc/publications/agenda/agenda89/toc.htm

4. Thonssen, L., Baird, A. C., & Braden, W. W. (1970). *Speech criticism* (2nd ed.). New York: Ronald Press, p. 335.
5. Loewen, J. W. (1995). *Lies my teacher told me: Everything your American history textbook got wrong.* New York: Touchstone, p. 13.
6. Loewen (1995), p. 136.
7. Lyotard, J.-F. (1984). *The postmodern condition: A report on knowledge* (G. Bennington & B. Massumi, Trans.). Minneapolis: University of Minnesota Press, p. 37.
8. Fisher, W. (1984). Narration as a human communication paradigm: The case of public moral argument. *Communication Monographs, 51,* 1–22; Fisher, W. (1985). The narrative paradigm: An elaboration. *Communication Monographs, 52,* 347–367.
9. Baudrillard, J. (1988). *America* (C. Turner, Trans.). New York: Verso, p. 80.
10. Buzbee, S. (2001, September 17). Muslims fret over Bush's use of term 'crusade.' *Boston Globe* (online). http://www.boston.com/news/daily/17/bush_crusade.htm
11. Nakano, M. (1990). *Japanese American women: Three generations, 1890–1990.* Berkeley and San Francisco: Mina Press and National Japanese American Historical Society, p. xiii.
12. Duberman, M. B. (1991). Introduction to first edition (1986). *About time: Exploring the gay past.* New York: Penguin Books, p. xiii.
13. Hocquenghem, G., & Blasius, M. (1980, April). Interview. *Christopher Street, 8*(4), 40.
14. Chang, I. (1997). *The rape of Nanking: The forgotten holocaust of World War II.* New York: Basic Books.
15. Tateishi, J. (1984). *And justice for all: An oral history of the Japanese American detention camps.* New York: Random House, p. vii.
16. Gilroy, P. (1993). *The Black Atlantic: Modernity and double consciousness.* New York: Verso.
17. Blanchot, M. (1986). *The writing of the disaster* (A. Smock, Trans.). Lincoln: University of Nebraska Press.
18. Houston, M. (1997). When Black women talk with White women: Why dialogues are difficult. In A. González, M. Houston, & V. Chen (Eds.), *Our voices: Essays in ethnicity, culture, and communication* (2nd ed.) (pp. 187–194). Los Angeles: Roxbury.
19. Kothari, G. (1995). Where are you from? In G. Hongo (Ed.), *Under Western eyes: Personal essays from Asian America* (p. 153). New York: Anchor/Doubleday.
20. U.S. Public Law 103-150, 103rd Congress, Joint Resolution 19, November 23, 1993.

CHAPTER FOUR

Identity and Intercultural Communication

STUDY OBJECTIVES

After reading this chapter, you should be able to:

1. Explain how identities are developed through our communicative interaction with others.

2. Identify some of the ways in which people communicate their identity.

3. Explain how the context of the larger society contributes to the formation of identity.

4. Identify some of the major social and cultural identities that are manifest in our communication.

5. Explain differences in how identities are developed for minority versus majority group members in the United States.

6. Explain identity development of multiracial people.

7. Describe the relationship between identity and language.

KEY TERMS

age identity
class identity
constructive identity
core symbols
culture shock
encapsulated identity
ethnic identity
gender identity
global nomads
hyphenated Americans
identity
labels
majority identity development

minority identity
   development
multicultural identity
national identity
norms
personal identity
physical ability identity
racial identity
regional identity
religious identity
sexual identity
U-curve theory
Whiteness

The year I studied abroad in France was crucial to developing my identity. Not only was I interacting among French people, but I also dealt with other international students and American exchange students. I developed a new identity and achieved a complete transformation of self. All my intercultural experiences have helped me to become a more competent and understanding person.

—*Maggie*

What does it mean to be Dutch? Before I came to America I thought it meant little to me that I was Dutch. I have never been nationalistic or overproud of my country when I was in Holland, but now that I am here, I realize it definitely does matter to me. I like telling people that I am from Holland, and I like to explain some things about my country to other people. Furthermore, I brought some typically Dutch things like the wooden shoes on our keychains to show to the people we meet.

—*Marina*

Identity plays a key role in intercultural communication, serving as a bridge between culture and communication. As Maggie and Marina tell us, it is through communication with our family, friends, and others (sometimes people from different cultures) that we come to understand ourselves and our identity. And it is through communication that we express our identity to others. Knowing about our identity is particularly important in intercultural interactions.

Conflicts may arise when there are sharp differences between who we think we are and who others think we are. For example, Mario, one of our students, has been living on his own since he was a freshman and considers himself an independent adult. But when he goes home, he says, his parents still treat him like he's a child, imposing curfews and questioning his lifestyle choices. Cassandra, a student with disabilities who is often in a wheelchair, tells us that she gets irritated when people ignore her in conversations and talk with other people she's with. And Sam, a fourth-generation Chinese American, informs us that he's not sure how to answer when people ask him, "Where are you really from?" He is American and has never been to China. In each case, the person's identity is not confirmed but is questioned or challenged in the interaction.

In this chapter, we examine the relationship between communication and identity, and the role of identity in intercultural communication. After we define identity, we focus on the development of specific aspects of our social and cultural identity including those related to gender, age, race or ethnicity, physical

Surf's Up!

What do you consider to be your identity? Look at what other students said in response to the question "Who are you? Please describe your cultural identity" (www-learning. berkeley.edu/AC/ archive/other/identities/ identities01.html).

ability, religion, class, and nationality. We then turn our attention to culture shock and cultural adaptation, and to multicultural identity, which refers to individuals who live on the borders between several identities and cultures. Finally, we discuss the relationship between identity, language, and communication.

UNDERSTANDING IDENTITY

How do we come to understand who we are? What are the characteristics of identity? Essentially, **identity** is our self-concept, who we think we are as a person. Identities are created through communication, and they develop not smoothly but in spurts, over a long period of time. Further, we have not merely one identity but multiple identities, which are influenced by society and are dynamic. And the way identities develop depends on one's cultural background. Let's look more closely at these five aspects of identities.

Identities Are Created Through Communication

Identities emerge when communication messages are exchanged between persons; they are negotiated, cocreated, reinforced, and challenged through communication.[1] This means that presenting our identities is not a simple process. Does everyone see you as you see yourself? Probably not. Janice, a student of ours from Canada, is proud to be Canadian and gets tired of students in the United States always assuming she is U.S. American.

Different identities are emphasized depending on whom we are communicating with and what the conversation is about. In a social conversation with someone we are attracted to, our gender or sexual orientation identity is probably more important to us than, say, our ethnic or national identities. And our communication is probably most successful when the person we are talking with confirms the identity we think is most important at the moment. For example, if you are talking with a professor about a research project, the interaction will be most successful if it confirms the relevant identities of professor and student rather than other identities—for example, those based on gender, religion, or ethnicity.

Identities Are Created in Spurts

Identities are created not in a smooth, orderly process but in spurts. Certain events provide insights into who we are, but these are framed by long periods during which we may not think much about ourselves or our identities. Thus, we sometimes may feel that we know exactly who we are and our place in the world and at other times may be rather confused.

Communication is crucial to the development of identity. For instance, our student Amanda felt confident of her religious identity until she married into another faith. Following long discussions with her in-laws about issues of spirituality, she began to question this aspect of her identity. As this example suggests, we may occasionally need to take some time to think through identity issues. And during difficult times, we may internalize negative identities as we try to answer the question of who we are. For example, Judith didn't tell any of her friends in high school that she had an Amish background, because she was embarrassed and thought that her friends would look down on her if they knew. Not until she became an adult would she disclose her religious background. Similarly, our student Shawna didn't want her friends to know that her mother was White and her father was Black, because she was afraid it would affect the way they felt about her.

Identities Are Multiple

It makes more sense to talk about our identities than our identity. Because we belong to various groups, we develop multiple identities that come into play at different times, depending on the context. Thus, in going to church or temple, we may highlight our religious identity. In going to clubs or bars, we may highlight our sexual orientation identity. Women who join social groups exclusive to women, or men who attend social functions just for men, are highlighting their gender identity.

Identities Are Influenced by Society

Our identities are formed through communication with others, but societal forces related to history, economics, and politics also have a strong influence. To grasp this notion, think about how and why people identify with particular groups and not others. What choices are available to them? The reality is, we are all pigeonholed into identity categories, or contexts, even before we are born. Many parents give a great deal of thought to a name for their unborn child, who is already part of society through his or her relationship to the parents. Some children have a good start at being, say, Jewish or Chicana before they are even born. It is very difficult to change involuntary identities rooted in ethnicity, gender, or physical ability, so we cannot ignore the ethnic, socioeconomic, or racial positions from which we start our identity journeys.

To illustrate, imagine two children on a train that stops at a station. Each child looks out a window and identifies their location. One child says that they are in front of the door for the women's room; the other says that they are in front of the door for the men's room. Both children see and use labels from their seating position to describe where they are; both are on the same train but describe where they are differently. And like the two children, where we are positioned—by our background and by society—influences how and what we see, and, most important, what it means.[2]

For example, many White students, when asked what it means to be an American, talk about the many freedoms they experience, but members of minority groups and international visitors may not have the same experience. As one of our Dutch students said, "I think that Americans think that being an

---

What Do You Think?

Sherry Turkle argues that computers are making our identities more fluid and fragmented. She points out how people take on multiple fictional identities while interacting with others on the Internet. Have you ever done this? Microsoft's latest version of Outlook Express, their e-mail program, has a system for managing multiple identities so you don't accidentally send an e-mail from the wrong self.

American means having a lot of freedom. I must disagree with that. Measuring it with my own experiences, I found America not so free at all. There are all those little rules I don't understand the meaning of." By "rules," she meant all those regulations that U.S. Americans accept as normal but Europeans are surprised at—for example, enforced drinking ages, leash laws, prohibitions against topless bathing on most beaches, and no-smoking ordinances.

The identities that others assign to us are socially and politically determined. But how are certain identities created by popular culture? For example, the label "heterosexual" is a relatively recent invention, less than a hundred years old.[3] The word originally referred to someone who engaged in sexual activity with a person of either sex; only relatively recently has it come to mean someone who engages in sexual activity only with members of the opposite sex. And the term has had different social and political meanings over the years. In earlier times, the rules governing heterosexual behavior emphasized procreation and female submissiveness and passivity. There were even rules about when sex could happen; it was a sin for a man to "love" his wife too much. In World War II, the military devised a series of tests to determine the "true" sexuality of men, and those who failed the test were rejected from service. In this way, sex became a fixed identity, like race, with political implications.

When we think about how society or other people create ideas about our identity, we might try to resist those attempts to pigeonhole us and thus try to assign other identities to ourselves. Agusia, a Polish student of ours, counters "Polish jokes" by educating joke-tellers about the origination of the term *Polack*, which simply means "Polish man." The negative connotation came about during a period of U.S. history when there was intense hostility toward immigrants from southern and eastern Europe. By educating people about Polish immigration history, Agusia "resists" the negative, stereotypic identity that society places on her.

Similarly, people with disabilities often have the experience of being stereotyped as helpless. Many people with disabilities view themselves as public educators—determined to redefine people's perceptions concerning disabilities and resisting stereotypes. For example, they sometimes humorously refer to nondisabled persons as "TABs" (temporarily able-bodied), reminding people that no one is immune from disability, or they may redefine an assisting device, such as by calling a cane a "portable railing."[4]

How do societal influences relate to intercultural communication? Basically, they establish the foundation from which the interaction occurs. Recall Sam, a Chinese American student of ours, who is occasionally asked where he is from or whether he is Chinese. The question puts him in an awkward position. He does not hold Chinese citizenship, nor has he ever lived in China. Yet the questioner probably doesn't mean to address these issues. It sometimes seems to Sam that the person who is asking the question is challenging Sam's right to his identity as an American. In this sense, the questioner seems to imply that Sam holds some negative identity.

Pop Culture Spotlight

In one scene from *Dragon: The Bruce Lee Story,* Bruce Lee is attacked by White youths who mistake him for a Korean. One youth's father was killed in the Korean War. After he wins the fight, Lee says, "Sorry about your father. But that was Koreans. I'm an American." If someone were to ask you about who you are, what would you say first? What is the most important part of your identity to you?

Identities Are Dynamic

The social forces that give rise to particular identities are always changing. For example, the identity of "woman" has changed considerably in recent years in the United States. Historically, being a woman has variously meant working outside the home to contribute to the family income or to help out the country when men were fighting wars, or staying at home and raising a family. Today, there are many different ideas about what being a woman means—from wife and mother to feminist and professional. Similarly, the emergence of the European Union has given new meaning to the notion of being "European." Some Europeans are embracing the idea of a European identity, while others are rejecting the notion; the idea is dynamic and changing. For example, some Europeans prefer to be identified as "French," "Italian," or "German," instead of "European" since "European" does not communicate their strongest feelings of identification. In the future, do you think that "European" may become more important than these national identities?

As another example, think about how identity labels have changed from "colored," to "Negro," to "Black," to "Afro-American," to "African American," with a significant number of people still preferring the label "Black." Although the labels seem to refer to the same group of people, the political and cultural identities associated with these labels are different.

Identities Are Developed in Different Ways in Different Cultures

In the United States, young people often are encouraged to develop a strong sense of identity, to "know who they are," to be independent and self-reliant. This stems from the value of individualism, discussed in Chapter 2. However, this individualistic emphasis on developing identity is not shared by all societies. In many African, Asian, and Latino societies, the experience of childhood and adolescence revolves around the family. In these societies, then, educational, occupational, and even marital choices are made with extensive family guidance. As Andrea, a Mexican American student, explains, "Family is the sole source behind what it means to be Hispanic. The role parents play in our lives is an ongoing process that never ends. It is the complete opposite of America where the child turns 18 and is free of restriction and authority. Family is the number-one priority and the basis of all that is to come." Thus, identity development does not occur in the same way in every society. Many African, Asian, and Latino societies emphasize dependency and interdependency among family members. So, in some cultural contexts, it makes more sense to speak of a familial or relational self than the self-creation of one's personal identity.[5]

However, if the dominant idea of individual identity development is presented as the only alternative, it can make members of some cultural groups in the United States feel inferior or even question their psychological health. For example, Manoj, an Indian medical student in New York, attended a lecture on adolescent development by a very well known scholar. In his lecture, the professor said that unless a person went through a rebellious stage as an adolescent, it

Surf's Up!

Choose "MUDs, MUSHes, and MOOs," from the Yahoo! menu of Internet games (dir.yahoo.com/recreation/games/computer_games/internet_games). These are Internet-based role-playing games like Dungeons and Dragons. In these games, you create an identity, or an "avatar," and then play the game as that character. Thus, if your character is an elf, you must try to act and talk like an elf. While that may seem strange to many of us, how different is it from, say, sitting in a classroom and acting like a student?

was impossible to achieve a healthy identity. Manoj searched within himself for any sign of rebellion he had felt against either of his parents when he was growing up in India or against any other parent figure. When he couldn't recall any such experience, he concluded that he must be abnormal.[6]

SOCIAL AND CULTURAL IDENTITIES

People can identify with a multitude of groups based on such things as gender, age, and ethnicity, as well as on occupational interests, sports (as spectators or participants), leisure activities, and special abilities. One of our friends belongs to a special car club—all owners of 1960s and 1970s "muscle cars." And all these groups help shape our identities and affect our communication to some degree. In this section, we identify those identities that most affect our cultural perceptions and influence how we communicate cross-culturally.

Gender Identity

We often begin life with gendered identities. When newborns arrive, they may be greeted with clothes and blankets in either blue or pink. To establish a **gender identity** for a baby, visitors may ask if it's a boy or a girl. But gender is not the same as biological sex. This distinction is important in understanding how our views on biological sex influence gender identities.

We communicate our gender identity, and popular culture tells us what it means to be a man or a woman. For example, some activities are considered more masculine or more feminine. Similarly, the programs that people watch on television—soap operas, football games, and so on—affect how they socialize with others and come to understand what it means to be a man or a woman.

As a culture changes, so do notions of what is masculine or feminine. Even the popular image of the perfect male body changes. In the 1860s, the middle-class view of the ideal male body type was lean and wiry. By the 1890s, however, the ideal male body type was bulky with well-defined muscles.[7] These popular notions of the ideal male (or female) body are largely determined by commercial interests, advertising, and other cultural forces. This is especially true for women. Advertisements in magazines and commercials on television tell us what it means, and how much it will cost, to be a beautiful woman. As one of our students explained, "I must compete with my fellow Americans for external beauty. As an American, I am expected to project a beautiful appearance. Perfection is portrayed at every stage in life—whether it is a beautiful doll little girls are given to play with or perfect-looking supermodels in fashion magazines. It is no secret what is expected and accepted." Our expression of gender identity not only communicates who we think we are but also constructs a sense of who we want to be. We learn what masculinity and femininity mean in our culture, and we negotiate how we communicate our gender identity to others.

Consider, for example, the contemporary trend against body hair on men. Today, the ideal male body type is sleek, with little body hair. Many men view their own bodies in relation to this ideal and decide to change themselves accordingly. Of course, at one time, a hairy body was considered more masculine, not less.

Or think about the controversy over whether certain actresses, like Calista Flockhart, are too thin. The female models appearing in magazine advertisements and TV commercials are very thin—leading young girls to feel ashamed of any body fat. It was not always so. In the mid-1700s, a robust woman was considered attractive. And in many societies today, in the Middle East and in Africa, full-figured women are much more desirable than thin women. This shows how the idea of gender identity is both dynamic and closely connected to culture. Society has many images of masculinity and femininity; we do not all seek to look and act according to a single ideal. At the same time, we do seek to communicate our gendered identities as part of who we are.

There are implications for intercultural communication as well. Gender means different things in different cultures. U.S. students who travel abroad often find that their movements are more restricted. For example, single women cannot travel freely in many Muslim countries. And gender identity for many Muslim women means that the sphere of activity and power is primarily in the home and not in public.

Sexual Identity

Our **sexual identities** should not be confused with our gender identities. Sexual identity is complex, particularly since different cultures organize sexualities in different ways. While many cultures have similar categories for male/female and masculine/feminine, many cultures have very different definitions of sexualities. For example, in the United States today, we often think of the categories heterosexual, gay, lesbian, and bisexual; yet the development of these categories is largely a late-19th-century invention.[8]

The difficulty that researchers have had with sexual identity across cultures is reflected in their own difficulties categorizing and understanding other ways of organizing sexualities. Rudi Bleys has attempted to demonstrate the ways that Western researchers have attempted to understand sexualities across cultures and how those understandings have shifted over time. It is important to understand that the ways we categorize sexualities today may not be the same as other cultures in other times may have organized sexualities.[9]

The way we organize sexuality, however, is central to the development of sexual identities. If nobody identifies as "gay," then there can be no "gay rights" movement. If nobody identifies as "heterosexual," then there can be no assumption that anyone is only attracted to members of the opposite sex.

The language we use to self-identify can also complicate sexual identity. For example, someone who has not yet engaged in any sexual activities with anyone might identify as "gay," while someone else may identify as "heterosexual" but occasionally sleeps with members of the same sex. How might these categories be more complex than they first appear?

Sexual attraction, of course, makes sexual identities even less categorizable. Not only are sexual desires quite complex, but they are also influenced by attraction to those of other cultures, racial/ethnic backgrounds, ages, and cultural identities. Our language is full of terms for people who desire others who are quite different from themselves. How do these terms communicate meaning about sexual identities? How do they communicate value judgments about other sexual identities?

As you encounter people from around the world, do not assume that your framework for sexual categories is universal. Nor should you assume that the ways that sexuality is handled in public is the same as in your hometown. Sometimes people from other countries are shocked that U.S. Americans speak so openly to strangers about being in their second marriage. Others do not understand the public interest and uproar over President Clinton's activities with Monica Lewinsky, which they may see as part of private—not public—life.

Age Identity

As we age, we tap into cultural notions of how someone our age should act, look, and behave; that is, we establish an **age identity.** And even as we communicate how we feel about our age to others, we receive messages from the media telling us how we should feel. Thus, as we grow older, we sometimes feel that we are either too old or too young for a certain "look." These feelings stem from an understanding of what age means and how we identify with that age.

Some people feel old at 30; others feel young at 40. There is nothing inherent in age that tells you that you are young or old. Our notions of age and youth are all based on cultural conventions—the same cultural conventions which suggest that it is inappropriate to engage in a romantic relationship with someone who is far older or younger.

Our notions of age often change as we grow older ourselves. When we are quite young, a college student seems old. But when we are in college, we do not feel so old. The relative nature of age is only one part of the age identity process; social constructions of age are another. The meanings that our society holds for different ages is an important influence in age identity. Often these are intimately connected to gender identity. A recent study of U.S. Americans shows that almost "a third of unmarried American women in their 40s through 60s who date are going out with younger men."[10] Traditionally, men were expected to be the same age or older than the women they dated. Does age play a role in your dating experiences? Gender and age also work together as we age. A male colleague of ours who is in his late 40s recently purchased a new silver convertible. A female colleague in her 40s colors her hair. How do these purchasing decisions help both of them negotiate their age identities? What do they communicate about their identities?

Age identity, however, is not simply about how you feel about your age. It is also about how others treat you based on your age. Due to the practice of discrimination against older workers, the U.S. government enacted the Age

Discrimination in Employment Act of 1967, which protects people who are 40 and older from employment discrimination. Aside from employment, are there other areas in society where people are treated differently based on their age? [11]

Moreover, while in the United States old age is demeaned, in other societies it is revered. An example of this is in East Africa, where words for old persons are used endearingly to refer to any respected person in the community. These different views on aging have implications for intercultural communication. For example, in one cultural exchange program between the People's Republic of China and the United States, Chinese administrators were offended because the United States sent young adults as the first exchangees. The Chinese, wanting to include some of their best and most revered citizens, sent scholars in their 50s and 60s.

Racial And Ethnic Identity

Racial Identity   In the United States today, the issue of race seems to be pervasive. It is the topic of many public discussions, from television talk shows to talk radio. Yet many people feel uncomfortable discussing racial issues. Perhaps we can better understand the contemporary issues if we look at how the notion of race has developed historically in the United States.

Cultural traditions like the celebration of Kwanzaa often strengthen groups' sense of ethnic and/or religious identity. Kwanzaa, a December holiday observed by many African Americans, promotes group solidarity, cooperation, and unity, and harmony with nature.

The roots of current debates about race can be located in the 15th century, when European explorers encountered people who looked different from themselves. The debates centered on the religious question of whether there was "one family of man." If so, what rights were to be accorded to those who were different? Arguments about which groups were "human" and which were "animal" pervaded popular and legal discourse and provided a rationale for slavery. Later, in the 18th and 19th centuries, the scientific community tried to establish a classification system of race based on genetics and brain size. However, these efforts were largely unsuccessful.

Most scientists now agree that there are more physical similarities than differences among so-called races and have abandoned a strict biological basis for classifying racial groups. Instead, taking a more social scientific approach to understanding race, they recognize that racial categories like White and Black are constructed in social and historical contexts.[12]

Several arguments have been advanced to refute the physiological basis for classifying racial groups. First, racial categories vary widely throughout the world. In general, distinctions between White and Black are fairly rigid in the United States, and many people become uneasy when they are unable to categorize individuals. By contrast, Brazil recognizes a wide variety of intermediate racial categories in addition to White and Black. This indicates a cultural, rather than a biological, basis for racial classification.

Second, U.S. law uses a variety of definitions in determining racial categories. The 1982 Susie Phipps case in Louisiana reopened debates about race as socially created rather than biologically determined. When Susie Phipps applied for a passport, she discovered that under Louisiana law she was Black because she was one thirty-second African. (Her great-grandmother had been a slave.) She then sued to be reclassified as White. Not only did she consider herself White, as she grew up among Whites and attended White schools, but she also was married to a White man. Because her children were one sixty-fourth African, however, they were legally White. Although she lost her lawsuit, the ensuing political and popular discussions persuaded Louisiana lawmakers to change the way the state classified people racially. This legal situation does not obscure the fact that social definitions of race continue to exist.[13]

Third, as their fluid nature indicates, racial categories are socially constructed. As more and more southern Europeans immigrated to the United States in the 19th century, the established Anglo and German society initially tried to classify some of them (Greeks, Italians, Jews) as non-White. However, members of this group realized that according to the narrower definition they might no longer form a majority and therefore would lose some power. So the notion of who was White was expanded to include all Europeans, while non-Europeans were designated as non-White.[14]

Racial identities, then, are based to some extent on physical characteristics, but they are also constructed in fluid social contexts. The important thing to remember is that the way people construct these identities and think about race influences how they communicate with others.

What Do You Think?

What ethnic label do you prefer for yourself? In an essay in the collection *Our Voices,* Dolores Tanno describes what the labels "Spanish," "Mexican American," "Latina," and "Chicana" mean to her. She concludes by saying that each of these terms, with its own unique meaning, describes a part of her. Which aspects of yourself do your preferred terms describe?

Ethnic Identity   One's **ethnic identity** reflects a set of ideas about one's own ethnic group membership. It typically includes several dimensions: self-identification, knowledge about the ethnic culture (traditions, customs, values, behaviors), and feelings about belonging to a particular ethnic group. Ethnic identity often involves a common sense of origin and history, which may link members of ethnic groups to distant cultures in Asia, Europe, Latin America, or other locations.[15]

Ethnic identity thus means having a sense of belonging to a particular group and knowing something about the shared experiences of group members. For example, Judith grew up in an ethnic community; her parents and relatives spoke German, and her grandparents made several trips back to Germany and often talked about their German roots. This experience contributed to her own ethnic identity.

For some Americans, ethnicity is a specific and relevant concept. These people define themselves in part in relation to their roots outside the United States—as "**hyphenated Americans**" (Mexican-American, Japanese-American, Welsh-American—although the hyphen often is dropped)—or to some region prior to its being part of the United States (Navajo, Hopi, Cherokee). For others, ethnicity is a vague concept; they see themselves as "American" and reject the notion of hyphenated Americans. (We'll discuss the issues of ethnicity for White people later in the chapter.)

The question remains, What does "American" mean? And who defines it? It is important to determine what definition is being used by those who insist that we should all just be "Americans." If one's identity is "just American," how is this identity formed, and how does it influence communication with others who see themselves as hyphenated Americans?[16]

Racial Versus Ethnic Identity   Scholars dispute whether racial and ethnic identities are similar or different. Some scholars emphasize ethnic identity to avoid any racism inherent in a race-centered approach; others reject this interpretation. On the one hand, discussions about ethnicity tend to assume a "melting pot" perspective on U.S. society. On the other hand, discussions about race as shaped by U.S. history allow for racism. If we talk not about race but only about ethnicity, we cannot fully consider the effects and influences of racism.

For most White people, it is easy to comprehend the sense of belonging in an ethnic group. Clearly, for example, being Amish means following the *Ordnung* (community rules). Growing up in a German American home, Judith's identity was characterized by seriousness and a lack of expressiveness. This identity differed from that of her Italian American friends at college, who were much more expressive.

However, what it means to belong to the dominant, White culture is more elusive. It can be difficult to identify the cultural practices that link White people together. For example, we should think of Thanksgiving and the Fourth of July as primarily White holidays.

Our sense of racial or ethnic identity develops over time, in stages, and through communication with others. These stages seem to reflect phases in the development of our self-understanding. They also depend to some extent on the types of groups we belong to. For example, members of many ethnic or racial groups experience common forces of oppression and so adopt attitudes, and behaviors consistent with the effort to develop a strong sense of self—and group—identity. For many groups, these strong identities have served to ensure their survival.

Physical Ability Identity

We all have a **physical ability identity** because we all have varying degrees of physical capabilities. We are all handicapped in one way or another—by our height, weight, sex, or age—and we all need to work to overcome these conditions. And our physical ability, like our age, changes over a lifetime. For example, some people experience a temporary disability, such as breaking a bone or experiencing limited mobility after surgery. Others are born with disabilities, or experience incremental disability, or have a sudden-onset disability (waking up quadriplegic).

The number of people with physical disabilities is growing, constituting as much as 19 percent of the population and forming the largest minority group in some states.[17] In fact, people with disabilities see themselves as a cultural group and share many perceptions and communication patterns.[18] Part of this identity involves changing how they see themselves and how others see them. For people who become disabled, there are predictable stages in coming to grips with this new identity. The first stage involves a focus on rehabilitation and physical changes. The second stage involves adjusting to the disability and the effects that it has on relationships; some friendships will not survive the disability. The final stage is "stigma incorporation," when the individual begins to integrate being disabled into his or her own definition of self. As one woman said, "I find myself telling people that this has been the worst thing that has happened to me. It has also been one of the best things. It forced me to examine what I felt about myself. . . . confidence is grounded in me, not in other people."[19]

Communication related to issues of identity often is difficult between the able-bodied and those with disabilities. Able-bodied people may not make eye contact and otherwise restrict their communication with people with disabilities. For their part, people with disabilities struggle to convey a positive identity, to communicate that their physical ability (as is true for everyone) is only one of their many identities. As one young man said, "We need friends who won't treat us as weirdo asexual second-class children or expect us to be 'Supercrips'. . . . We want to be accepted the way we are."[20]

Religious Identity

Religious identity is an important dimension of many people's identities, as well as a common source of intercultural conflict. Often, religious identity gets confused with racial/ethnic identity, which means it can be problematic to view religious identity simply in terms of belonging to a particular religion. For example, when someone says, "I am Jewish," does this mean that this person practices

What Do You Think?

In August 2002, the University of North Carolina at Chapel Hill was in the midst of controversy over a religious text assigned to incoming freshmen and transfer students enrolled in their summer reading program. The book *Approaching the Qu'ran: The Early Revelations* included excerpts called suras, which are poetic forms of scripture often compared to the Psalms of David in the Christian Bible. The university, having made the reading of the text a requirement, was promptly sued by three students who were identified as Jewish, Evangelical Christian, and Catholic. They were represented by a conservative Christian law firm, known as the American Family Association for Law and Policy. The plaintiffs alleged in part of the suit that the reading requirement violated their First Amendment rights to freedom of religion. Read more about the case at the website— http://www.pbs.org/wnet/religionandethics/week551/news.html. How do you think the courts should have decided this case? What would you have done if you were a student in this situation?

Judaism or views Jewishness as an ethnic identity? When someone says, "That person has a Jewish last name," does this confer a Jewish religious identity? Historically, Jews have been viewed as a racial group, an ethnic group, and a religious group. Drawing distinct lines between various identities—racial, ethnic, religious, class, national, regional—can lead to stereotyping. For example, Italians and Irish are often assumed to be Catholic, while Episcopalians are frequently seen as belonging to the upper classes.

Intercultural communication among religious groups also can be problematic. Religious differences have been at the root of conflicts from the Middle East, to Northern Ireland, to India/Pakistan, to Bosnia-Herzegovina. In the United States as well, religious conflict forced the Mormons to migrate from New York to Ohio and Illinois and then to Utah. The traditional belief is that everyone should be free to practice whatever religion they want to, but conflict can result from the imposition of one religion's beliefs on others who may not share those beliefs. Recently, Alabama Supreme Court Justice Roy Moore was found in violation of separation of church and state for his refusal to remove a monument to the Ten Commandments from the Alabama Supreme Court Building. When one religion is acknowledged over other religions in public places, controversy can ensue.[21] Religion traditionally is considered a private issue, and there is a stated separation of church and state. However, in some countries, religion and the state are inseparable, and religion is publicly practiced. Some religions communicate and mark their religious differences through their dress—for example, Hassidic Jews. Other religions do not mark their members through their clothes; for example, you may not know if someone is Buddhist, Catholic, Lutheran, or atheist based upon their dress. Because these religious identities are less obvious, everyday interactions may not invoke them.

Even though religious convictions (or the lack thereof) are viewed as private matters in the United States, they have implications for intercultural communication. One of our students described his experience in a discussion group made up of people of faith and those (like him) who considered themselves spiritual but had no particular religious convictions:

> It became very clear that many of the beliefs held were strong ones. It is as if two different cultures were meeting. The two groups act very differently and run their lives in very different ways. I have learned that many of the stereotypes that I have labeled religious people with are false, and I would hope that this group eliminated any stereotypes that religious people may have labeled someone like me with.

Class Identity

We seldom think about socioeconomic class as an important part of our identity—especially those in the middle class. As with race, there is invisibility associated with this dominant or normative **class identity.** Whereas members of the middle class rarely think about class, those in the working class are often reminded that they do not belong to the middle class. Class plays an important role in shaping our reactions to and interpretations of culture.

In our everyday language, terms like "trailer park trash" and "White trash" mark these class differences. Given their negative associations with members of the working class, not surprisingly, many Americans identify themselves as "middle class." But many people do not like to discuss class distinctions, as these conversations can range dangerously close to discussions of money—a topic to be avoided in "polite society."

Yet class identities are an important aspect of our identities in the United States, and even more so in some other societies. People use various strategies to locate individuals in the class hierarchy, as directly asking someone may be seen as impolite and may yield inaccurate information. Certain foods, for example, are viewed as "rich folks' food": lamb, white asparagus, brie, artichokes, goose, caviar. A lack of familiarity with these foods may reveal something about one's class background. People might ask where you went to college as a clue to your class background. Other signs of your class background include the words you use, the magazines you read, and the drinks you consume.[22]

This lack of overt recognition of social class in the United States has several consequences. Despite evidence to the contrary, a popular belief is that, with hard work and persistence, individuals can improve their class standing.[23] One result of this myth is that when poverty persists the poor are blamed. That is, they are poor because of something they did or didn't do, or were lazy, or didn't try hard enough, or were unlucky—a classic case of "blaming the victim." The media often reinforce these notions.

Working-class individuals who aren't upwardly mobile are often portrayed on TV shows (*The King of Queens, Everybody Loves Raymond, The Simpsons*) and in the movies as happy but unintelligent or unwilling to do what they have to do to better their lot in life. And members of the real working class, showing up increasingly as guests on talk shows like *Jerry Springer*, are urged to be contentious—verbally and sometimes even physically aggressive toward each other. Thus, the images of working-class people that are served up to the mass viewing audience are hardly positive.[24]

Race and class, and sometimes gender, identities are interrelated. For example, being born African American, poor, and female increases one's chances of remaining in poverty. At the same time, however, race and class are not synonymous; there are many poor Whites and increasing numbers of wealthy African Americans. So it is important to see these multiple identities as interrelated but not identical. In any event, the lack of understanding about class differences and the stereotypes perpetuated in the media often makes meaningful communication between classes difficult.

National Identity

Among our many identities is a national identity, which should not be confused with racial or ethnic identity. **National identity,** or nationality, refers to one's legal status in relation to a nation. Many U.S. citizens trace their family history to Latin America, Asia, Europe, or Africa, but their nationality, or citizenship, is with the United States.

What Do You Think?

Benedict Anderson has written a book called *Imagined Communities,* in which he argues that nations are fictions. That is, they are imaginary constructs not directly linked to the land that supposedly contains them. Thus, we base parts of our identities on these fictions. What parts of your identity may be based on fiction?

What does it mean to be an American? When we ask our students this question, they respond in many ways. Some mention only positive things: freedom, the ability to do what one wants (within reason), economic opportunity, entertainment, and sports. Others mention unhealthy eating habits, obsession with diets, pressure to make lots of money, media determination of what is glamorous or accepted, more tax dollars spent on prisons and sports facilities than on education, and random violence on the highway and in the neighborhoods and schools. And yet, almost every student is proud of his or her national identity.

Our national identity certainly influences how we look at the world and communicate with people of other nationalities. As one of our students observed:

> The more I do to expand my cultural horizons, the more amazed I am at the way I look at life as a result of being American. There are so many things we take for granted as the only way of doing something or thinking. Like the whole individualism thing and all the behaviors and values associated with it. And there are types of people and personalities that I just never imagined before.

National identity may be especially complicated when a nation's status is in doubt. For example, the Civil War erupted over the attempted secession in the mid-1800s of the Confederate States of America from the United States. More recently, bloody conflicts resulted when Eritrea tried to separate from Ethiopia, and Chechnya from Russia. Less bloody conflicts also involving nationhood led to the separation of Slovakia and the Czech Republic.

Contemporary nationhood struggles are being played out as Quebec attempts to separate from Canada, Corsica and Tahiti from France, Scotland from Great Britain, and Oaxaca from Mexico. Sometimes, nations disappear from the political map but persist in the social imagination and reemerge later; examples include Korea, Poland, the Ukraine, and Norway. In all of these cases, people identify with various ways of thinking about nationality.

Regional Identity

Closely related to national identity is the notion of **regional identity.** Many regions of the world have separate but vital and important cultural identities. For example, the Scottish Highlands region of northern Scotland is distinctly different from the Lowlands to the south, and regional identity remains strong in the Highlands.

Here in the United States, regional identities remain important. Southerners, for example, often view themselves and are viewed by others as a distinct cultural group. Texas advertises itself as "A Whole Other Country," promoting its regional identity. And people from New York are often stereotyped as brash and aggressive. These stereotypes based on regional identities often lead to difficult intercultural interactions. Our colleague Joyce's college roommate, Linda, was from southern Virginia. She told Joyce she had no desire to visit New York City because she had heard how unfriendly and aggressive people were there. After

People in the United States are often proud of where they live—whether town, city, state, or region. As this sign advertising "bewitching" Salem, Massachusetts, shows, these regional identities often are promoted in tourist publicity.

the two roommates got to know each other better, Joyce persuaded Linda to accompany her to the city. While the visit didn't dispel all her stereotypes, Linda did come to appreciate the energy and vitality of New York and New Yorkers.

Some regional identities can lead to national independence movements, but more often they are cultural identities that affirm distinctive cuisines, dress, manners, and sometimes language. These identities may become important in intercultural communication situations. For example, suppose you meet someone who is Chinese. Whether that person is from Beijing, Hong Kong, or elsewhere in China may raise important communication issues, because there are many dialects of the Chinese language, including Mandarin and Cantonese.

Personal Identity

Many issues of identity are closely tied to one's notion of self. Each of us has a **personal identity,** but it may not be unified or coherent. While we are who we think we are, we are also who others think we are. In other words, if you think you are incredibly attractive, but others do not, are you attractive? Sometimes our personal identity is largely defined by outside forces.

At other times, how we behave and communicate to others helps construct our personal identity. If you are trustworthy and reliable, others may come to see you as trustworthy and reliable, which reinforces your personal identity.

Sometimes, however, our personal identity can come into conflict with other identities. For example, not all gay men are sharp dressers and knowledgeable about fine foods, yet they often feel as if they should be. Television shows like *Queer Eye for the Straight Guy* often reinforce these stereotypes. As another

What Do You Think?

According to Alan Watts, "Trying to define yourself is like trying to bite your own teeth." Stuart Hall says, "You know firmly who you are only by leaving out three-quarters of the most interesting parts of the story." What do you leave out when you tell the story of your identity?

example, some people raised in very religious families may not feel similarly about their religious identity. They may feel caught between their family's traditional religious beliefs and their own personal identities. They may feel obligated to uphold their family's traditional ways, yet not feel comfortable with those beliefs. Along the Arizona-Utah border, a number of families belong to the Fundamentalist Church of Jesus Christ of Latter Day Saints. When members' personal identities do not match religious identities, conflicts often result:

> David Bateman, 19, said he had been in hot water with the church leadership since he stopped attending services two years ago. Word got out that he was going to movies in nearby St. George and listening to rock groups like Creed at home. "They really treat you bad if you don't conform to their way of thinking," Bateman said. "People drive by your house and flip you off. Others give you stares and dirty looks. I had two young kids on bicycles ride by me on the street. One of them yelled, 'Hey, faggot, what are you doing here?' The other one called me an SOB."[25]

The solution is often to be forced to choose.

Who we think we are is important to us, and often to those close to us, and we try to communicate that to others. We are more or less successful depending on how others respond to us. Sometimes those responses can be harsh. We use the various ways that identity is constructed to portray ourselves as we want others to see us.

IDENTITY DEVELOPMENT

Minority Identity Development

As mentioned previously, minority group members in the United States tend to develop a stronger sense of racial and ethnic identity than do majority group members. Whites tend to take their culture for granted; although they may develop a strong ethnic identity, they often do not really think about their racial identity.

In its four stages, **minority identity development** focuses on racial and ethnic identities but may also apply to other identities such as class, gender, or sexual orientation.[26] It is important to remember that, as with any model, this one represents the experiences of many people, but not everyone moves through these stages in exactly the same way. Some may spend more time in one stage, may experience a stage in different ways, or remain stuck in one of the early stages.

Stage 1: Unexamined Identity   This stage is characterized by the lack of exploration of ethnicity. Minority members may initially accept the values and attitudes of the majority culture, including negative views of their own group. They may have a strong desire to assimilate into the dominant culture, and they may express positive attitudes toward the dominant group. In this stage, their

Info Bites

Who do you have to be to participate in the "Latin music explosion"? Does it matter that Marc Anthony's first albums were all in English? If he is from New York and his native language is English, does he have the right kind of "identity" to be a Latino movie star?

ideas about identity may come from parents or friends—if they have any interest in ethnicity. As one writer put it, "We were all color-blind in our relationships and remained so until our parents assigned the colors that were supposed to have meaning and made them ugly."[27]

Stage 2: Conformity   In this stage, individuals have a strong desire to assimilate into the dominant culture and so internalize the values and norms of the dominant group. These individuals may have negative, self-deprecating attitudes toward themselves, as well as toward their group in general. One Jewish woman recalls that in college she had a real aversion to associating with Jewish women whom she believed fit the negative social stereotype of a "materialistic, whiny people."[28] Later she came to see this as her own buying into racism. People who criticize other members of their own group may be given negative labels such as "Uncle Toms" or "oreos" for African Americans, "bananas" for Asian Americans, "apples" for Native Americans, and "Tio Tacos" for Chicanos. Such labels condemn attitudes and behaviors that support the dominant White culture. This stage often continues until the person encounters a situation that causes him or her to question the dominant culture attitudes, which then starts the movement to the next stage: an ethnic identity search.

Stage 3: Resistance and Separatism   Many kinds of events can trigger the move to the third stage, including negative events, such as encountering discrimination or name calling. Sometimes, a growing awareness that not all the values of the dominant group are beneficial to minorities may lead to this stage. Suppose, for example, that someone who has been denying his or her racial heritage meets another person from that racial group who exhibits a strong cultural identity. A student of ours, Amalia, recounted her experience of going to college and meeting other Chicano students for the first time who had strong ethnic identities and were proud to be Mexican American. She hadn't thought about her heritage very much up to that point, so this was an important experience for her. She became interested in learning about the history of Mexican Americans in the United States, and she developed a stronger sense of her own identity. For Max, an African American, this awareness happened suddenly. He describes his awareness that the Cinderella in his childhood coloring books was White. He was also deprived a part in a school play because of his color and was forced into pre-algebra class despite exceptional talent in math. This caused a rage and fury, and he became certain he was "destined for failure."[29]

This stage may be characterized by a blanket endorsement of one's group and all the values and attitudes attributed to it. At the same time, the person may reject the values and norms associated with the dominant group. For example, at this stage, individuals may find it important to join ethnic clubs like MEChA (*Movimiento Estudiante de Chicanos d'Aztlan*), the Black Students Union, or other groups where they can discuss common interests and experiences and find support.

Info Bites

"Chicano" was once considered a derogatory term referring to immigrant farm workers. But due to the efforts of people like Cesar Chavez and other members of the farm workers' movement, the word has been redefined. Now, Mexican Americans use the term to help define their political struggle to participate fully in American society.

Group identities are often expressed and strengthened through communication. Which identities are being expressed and affirmed by these students' being together?

Stage 4: Integration   According to this model, the ideal outcome of the minority identity development process is the last stage, an achieved identity. People who reach this stage have a strong sense of their own group identity (based on gender, race, ethnicity, sexual orientation, and so on) and an appreciation for other cultural groups. In this stage, individuals realize that racism and other forms of oppression occur but try to redirect any anger from the previous stage in more positive ways. A Latino writer describes how he entered this stage. It happened when he shared a college apartment with students from Taipei— persons who were foreign to the United States and its prejudices and who were interested in his background. "As I spoke to them of the history of my people— something I'd always known but never before thought about—I began to internalize that history. In a sense their curiosity sparked my own. Never again could I deny it, never again would I care to." [30] The end result is a confident and secure identity for a person who wants to eliminate all forms of injustice, not just oppression aimed at his or her own group.

Majority Identity Development

Two influential educators/scholars describe **majority identity development** for members of the dominant group. The following model differs somewhat from the minority identity model in that it is more prescriptive. That is, it doesn't represent exactly how White people's identities develop, but rather how they might move in unlearning the racism (and other isms) that we unconsciously acquire as we grow up. [31]

Stage 1: Unexamined Identity   The first stage is the same as for minority individuals. People may be aware of some physical and cultural differences, but they do not fear other racial or ethnic groups or feel a sense of superiority. As our student Jenny said, "I remember in kindergarten my best friend was African American. We did everything together at school. We never even thought about the fact that we were of different races." Communication (and relationships) at this stage is not based on racial differences.

Stage 2: Acceptance   The second stage represents the internalization and acceptance of the basic racial inequities in society. This acceptance is largely unconscious, and individuals have no conscious identification with the dominant White culture. However, some assumptions, based on an acceptance of inequities in the larger society, are subtly racist (minority groups are culturally deprived and need help to assimilate; White culture—music, art, and literature—is "classical"; works of art by people of color are folk art or "crafts"). There is also an assumption at this stage that people of color are culturally different, whereas Whites are individuals with no group identity, culture, or shared experience of racial privilege.

At this stage, communication with minorities is either avoided or patronizing—or both. As one of our White students, Kortni, said, "I never thought about it until I took this class how I don't have any friends who aren't White. I came from a small town, and I just never really felt comfortable around people who weren't White."

Some people never move beyond this stage. If they do, it is usually the cumulative result of a number of events. Perhaps they become good friends with people of color, or they participate in a class or workshop that deals with issues of White privilege or racism. For our student Jenny, it was an undergraduate course in ethnic relations: "The professor had us read really interesting authors who talked about their experiences of growing up as people of color in the United States. I realized how little I knew about the experiences of those who aren't White." She described it as an eye-opening experience that prodded her to the next stage.

Stage 3: Resistance   This stage represents a major shift, from blaming minority members for their conditions to blaming the social system as the source of racial or ethnic problems. Resistance may be passive, with little behavioral change, or active—an ownership of racism. Individuals may feel embarrassed and ashamed at this stage, avoiding or minimizing their communication with other Whites and seeking out interactions with persons of color. This is what happened with Rina, a White student of ours who started dating an African American. According to one of her friends, "as she got to know this man she started to really reject the White culture that she was from. She criticized her family and any White person. She got an attitude that her Black friends had an exclusive right to anything that related to style or music or dance. She rejected her own culture and immersed herself in the culture she had discovered." She also started to speak up about racism when she saw it. Whites who resist are often criticized by other Whites, who may call them "race traitors" or "reverse oreos"; they may jokingly warn other Whites about dating African Americans, since "once you go Black, you never go back." This type of communication condemns attitudes and behaviors that resist dominant White culture.

Stage 4: Redefinition and Reintegration   In the fourth stage, as in minority identity development, people begin to refocus their energy to redefining Whiteness in nonracist terms and are finally able to integrate their Whiteness into all other facets of their identity. It is not clear why some Whites achieve this stage while others do not. Whites in this stage realize they don't have to accept the definition of White that society imposed on them. They can move beyond the connection to racism to see positive aspects of being European American and to feel more comfortable being White. They not only recognize their own identity as White but also appreciate other groups. Interestingly, at this stage, there is no defensiveness about racism; individuals don't say, "I'm not prejudiced." Rather, there is the recognition that prejudice and racism exist and that blame, guilt, or denial won't help solve the problem. There is also a recognition of the importance of understanding Whiteness and White identity. However, it is a big challenge to identify what White identity is for several reasons. First, because Whiteness has been the norm in U.S. society, it is often difficult to see. Next, what it means to be White in the United States is changing. As the U.S. population becomes more diverse, Whites are becoming more aware of their race and express this awareness in a variety of ways—from affinity for White supremacy groups to Wiggers (White youth adopting or co-opting Black culture) to those rejecting White privilege. These recent changes demonstrate that one single model of White identity development probably does not exist and presents a number of challenges for Whites in the United States.[32]

Characteristics of Whiteness

What does it mean to be White in the United States? What are the characteristics of a White identity? Does some unique set of characteristics define Whiteness, just like other racial identities? Consider the following dialogue between Victor, who is African American, and David, who is White, in the film *The Color of Fear*, produced in the early 1990s:

> VICTOR: What I hear from White people is, they talk about being human. They don't talk about themselves as White people. What I want to know is what it means to be White.

> DAVID: We don't look at ourselves as part of an ethnic group. I think that's what you're looking for, and you're not going to find it.

> VICTOR: Do you know that that means something? The fact that you have no answer to that?

It may be difficult for most White people to describe exactly what cultural patterns are uniquely White. However, there are at least three common characteristics of **Whiteness** in the United States: (1) an advantage of race privilege, (2) a standpoint from which White people view themselves, others, and society, and (3) a set of cultural practices, largely unrecognized by White people.[33]

The Advantage of Race Privilege   White people in the United States enjoy many benefits of race privilege. Some are economic in that Whites, on average, still have higher incomes than members of minority groups; others are more social.[34] For example, Whites can wander through stores and be fairly sure no store employees will track their movements; they are rarely asked to speak for their entire race; and they see people who look like themselves most places they go.[35]

At the same time, while being White in the United States is linked with privilege, the two are not synonymous. All Whites do not have power and do not have equal access to power. At times during U.S. history, some White communities were not privileged and were viewed as inferior—for example, the Irish in the early 20th century and German Americans during World War II. There are also many poor White people in the United States who have no economic power.

There is an emerging perception that Whiteness is not equated with privilege, particularly as demographics change in the United States and as some Whites perceive themselves to be in the minority. For example, when White students at Temple University in Philadelphia were asked to estimate the ratio of Whites to Blacks on campus, many reported that they thought the ratio was 30 percent White and 70 percent Black; they perceived themselves as in the minority. The actual ratio was 70 percent White and 30 percent Black. These students' perceptions affected their sense of identity, which, in turn, influenced intercultural communication.[36] And when they were asked what they thought about being White, many of the students, mostly from working-class families, said they were very aware of their Whiteness. Further, they felt that being White was a liability, that they were being prejudged as racist and blamed for social conditions that they did not cause and were denied opportunities that were unfairly given to minority students.

In addition, as U.S. corporations downsize and more U.S. jobs are located overseas, increasing numbers of middle-aged White men fail to achieve the economic or professional success they had hoped for. They sometimes attribute their lack of success to immigrants who will work for less or to the increasing numbers of women and minorities in the workplace. In these cases, Whiteness is not invisible; it is an important aspect of the White individuals' identities.

The point is not whether these perceptions are accurate—and, indeed, many are not accurate. The reality is that most of the wealth, leadership, and power remains in the hands of Whites in the United States. Given that identities are negotiated and challenged through communication, and that people act on their perceptions and not on some external reality, perceptions related to racial identity make it difficult for Whites and Blacks to communicate effectively.

Pop Culture Spotlight

What is the ethnic identity of white rap artists like Eminem and Kid Rock? Are they simply confused? Or are they, as some critics have argued, merely the latest in a line of musicians, from Pat Boone, to Elvis Presley, to the Backstreet Boys, who have copied African American musical styles and movements? If ethnicity is not the same as race, how should we categorize these musicians?

A Standpoint from Which to View Society   Some viewpoints are shared by many Whites, and opinion polls frequently reveal significant differences in how Whites and Blacks see many issues. According to one poll, 24 percent of Whites think "about the right amount" of attention is paid to race and racial issues today, compared to only 14 percent of Blacks.[37] How can the perception of race relations be so different for Whites and Blacks? Something about being White, and something about being African American, influences how people view the world and, ultimately, how they communicate.

In one research study, women were asked about their Whiteness and about White culture. Some reported that they viewed the culture as less than positive—as artificial and dominant, bland and sterile, homogeneous, and less interesting and rich than non-White culture. Others, however, viewed it as positive—as representing what was "civilized," as in classical music and fine art.[38] White identity often includes some ambivalence about being White. As these women note, there may be some elements of White culture to be proud of and others that are more problematic.

A Set of Cultural Practices   Is there a specific, unique "White" way of viewing the world? As noted, some views held consistently by Whites are not necessarily shared by other groups. And some cultural practices and values, such as individualism, are expressed primarily by Whites and significantly less by members of minority groups. These cultural practices are most clearly visible to those who are not White, to those groups that do not share in the privileges enjoyed by Whites.[39] For example, the celebration of Snow White's beauty—emphasizing her pure white skin—is often seen as problematic by people who are not White. Perhaps it is easier to see why Snow White is offensive if one is not White.

MULTICULTURAL IDENTITY

Today, a growing number of people do not have clear racial, ethnic, or national identities. These are people who live "on the borders" between various cultural groups. While they may feel torn between different cultural traditions, they also may develop a **multicultural identity**—an identity that transcends one particular culture—and feel equally at home in several cultures. Sometimes, this multicultural identity develops as a result of being born or raised in a multiracial home. Table 4.1 shows the U.S. states with the highest percentage of multiracial people. Why might these states have the highest percentages? Which states might have the lowest percentages? At other times, it develops as a result of living in different cultures for extended periods of time.

Multiracial People

According to the U.S. Census Bureau, in 2000, the United States had an estimated 6.8 million multiracial people—that is, people whose ancestry includes two or more races—and this number is increasing.[40] The development of racial

TABLE 4.1 Mixed Race: States with the Highest Percentage of People Who Self-identified as More Than One Race

1. Hawaii	6. Texas
2. Alaska	7. Florida
3. California	8. Illinois
4. Oklahoma	9. New Jersey
5. New York	10. Washington

Source: U.S. Census Bureau (http://www.census.gov/Press-Release/www/releases/archives/population/000441.html)

identity for multiracial children seems to be different from either majority or minority development.[41] These children learn early on that they are different from other people and that they don't fit into a neat racial category—an awareness-of-differentness stage.[42] Take our student Maureen, for example. Her mother is Korean and her father is African American. When she was 5, her family moved to a small town in northern New Mexico that was predominantly White. She recalled:

> I soon realized that I wasn't the only person who was different; the town had a large population of Hispanic and Native Americans. Yet, I also realized that I was still different from the rest of the children. It seemed that Hispanic children stayed with Hispanic children, White children with White children, Native American children with Native American children, and Asian children with Asian children. There weren't any Black children, and there definitely weren't any Black and Asian mixed children. The grouping of these children helped me realize that I was very different from all the children I went to school with. This realization left me confused and depressed.

Maureen's experience is typical of the first stage in the identity development of multiracial children.

The second stage involves a struggle for acceptance, in which these children experiment with and explore both cultures. They may feel as if they live on the cultural fringe, struggling with two sets of cultural realities and sometimes being asked to choose one racial identity over the other. This happened to Maureen. She was frustrated by the forms she had to fill out at school that asked her to indicate her ethnicity, because there was no space for multiracial ethnicity. She recalled, "It was explained to me that I needed to choose. I asked them if there was a possibility I could represent both, but I was firmly told that it would be a nuisance to try to identify with two different cultures for the rest of my life." As happens with some multiracial children in this stage, she chose one: "It was on this day that I officially became an African-American."

There are increasing numbers of multicultural families in the United States and other countries. The children in these families may feel torn between various cultural patterns and traditions, but they also may develop a multicultural identity and feel equally at home in several different cultures.

Whereas monoracial identity usually progresses toward one end state—one either resolves or doesn't resolve identity issues—biracial adolescents may resolve their identity status in several ways: they may identify with one group, both groups, or a new group (for example, biracial people). In the final stage, self-acceptance and assertion, these children find a more secure sense of self. This exposure to more than one culture's norms and values often makes difficulty for biracial children—they may find themselves rejected alternately by both groups (not Black enough or White enough). The family and neighborhood play a huge role in biracial children's identity development. Strong family role models and a supportive neighborhood can lead to a flexible and adaptable sense of identity—a multicultural identity. Table 4.2 summarizes the stages of minority, majority, and multiracial development.[43]

Identity and Adaptation

Other people may develop multicultural identities for other reasons. Examples include **global nomads,** who grow up in many different cultural contexts because their parents moved around a lot. The families of missionaries, international business employees, diplomats, and military personnel often are global nomads. People who maintain long-term romantic relationships with members of another ethnic or racial culture also tend to develop multicultural identities.

TABLE 4.2 Stages in Minority, Majority, and Multiracial Identity Development

| | STAGE | |
Minority	*Majority*	*Multiracial*
Unexamined identity	Unexamined identity	Awareness of difference
Conformity	Acceptance	Struggle for acceptance
Resistance and separatism	Resistance	Self-acceptance and assertion
Integration	Redefinition and reintegration	

There seem to be some common patterns of adaptation to a new culture, described as the **U-curve theory** of adaptation. In this model, migrants go through three fairly predictable phases in adapting to a new cultural situation. In the first phase, they experience excitement and anticipation, especially if they moved to the new culture voluntarily (study-abroad students, missionaries).

The second phase, culture shock (the bottom of the U-curve), happens to almost everyone in intercultural transitions. **Culture shock** is a relatively short-term feeling of disorientation, of discomfort due to the unfamiliarity of surroundings and the lack of familiar cues in the environment. However, people who are isolated from the new cultural context may experience culture shock minimally. For example, U.S. military personnel and diplomatic personnel often live in compounds overseas where they interact mainly with other Americans and have little contact with the indigenous cultures. Similarly, spouses of international students in the United States may have little contact with Americans. By contrast, corporate spouses may experience more culture shock, because they often have more contact with the host culture: placing children in schools, setting up a household, shopping, and so on.

During the culture shock phase, individuals experience disorientation and perhaps an identity crisis. Because our identities are shaped and maintained by our cultural contexts, experiences in new cultural contexts often raise questions about identities. One student in a study-abroad program in Mexico described her feelings of culture shock:

> I want to be at home—nothing feels familiar here—I'd like to be on a bus—in a theater—on a street—in a house—on the phone— ANYWHERE AND UNDERSTAND everything that's being said. I love my family and miss my friends. I'm lonely here—I'm unable to be me—conversations either elude me or make me sound like I'm 3 years old—I'm so different without my language. . . . I just ask for something simple—TO SPEAK—TO BE ME. Yet, as I think now, as I write, I see how much more than language it is—it's history—what's familiar—a lifetime—my lifetime—my home—and now I'm here—SO FAR AWAY.[44]

Info Bites

"The sun never set on the British Empire" because at one time Britain controlled enough colonies that it was always day somewhere in the Empire. How important is your national identity to you? Are you patriotic? Would your answer change if your nation was not a nation but a colony of another country?

Notice that the challenge of language is often a big part of culture shock. The problem is the feeling that one can't really be oneself in another language—which is part of the identity crisis in cultural adaptation.

The third phase is adaptation, in which individuals gradually learn the rules and customs of the new cultural context. They may learn the language, figure out how much of themselves to change in response to the new context, and decide to change some aspects of their behavior. But they may also want to retain a sense of their previous cultural identities; each sojourner has to decide to what degree he or she wants to adapt. The student who wrote about her culture shock experiences later wrote, "Perhaps it was the rain—the downpour and the thunderstorm that preceded it. I feel good about Mexico now. The rainslick streets, the *torta Cubana* [a pastry]—the windy busride in the pitch-dark night. It's a peaceful beauty—I've regained a sense of self and space."

Although the U-curve seems to represent the experiences of many short-term sojourners, it may be too simplistic.[45] It might be more accurate to think of long-term cultural adaptation as a series of U-curves, where one alternates between feeling relatively adjusted and experiencing culture shock. Over time, the feeling of culture shock diminishes.

Culture shock occurs to almost all people who cross cultural boundaries, whether they have done so voluntarily or not. Most individuals then experience a long-term process of more or less adapting to the new culture. However, for many individuals, the long-term adaptation is not easy. Some actively resist assimilation in the short term, as is the case with many immigrants. Others resist assimilation in the long term, as is the case with religious groups like the Amish and Hutterites. Some would like to assimilate but are not welcome in the new culture, as is the case with many Latin American immigrants to the United States. And some adapt to certain aspects of the new culture but not others. In short, many people who adapt to new cultural contexts also develop multicultural identities.

Living "On the Border"

The multicultural person is someone who comes to grips with multiple cultural realities, whether from being raised in a multiracial home or through adaptation to a new culture. This multicultural identity is defined not by a sense of belonging but by a new sense of self.[46] Multicultural individuals may become "culture brokers" who facilitate intercultural interaction. However, it is important to recognize that there are stresses and tensions associated with being multicultural. These people may confuse the profound with the insignificant, lose sight of what is really important, feel fragmented, or feel a lack of authenticity.[47] Lucia, a Yaqui college student, described some of the challenges of living "on the border" between her Yaqui community and the college community:

> I get caught in the in-between. This is who I am: I'm Native American, and my belief system is to follow my Creator, walk the walk of the red road, and be aware of all things in nature around me. And then I look at

What Do You Think?

Gloria Anzaldua argues from what she calls the borderlands between two cultures. She also links this with racial issues involved in being *mestiza*, or of mixed heritage, as many Latinos and Latinas are. Other theorists have seized upon this notion of hybridity as something to be proud of; it also represents a rejection of years of denigration of biracial people. Do you experience living on cultural borderlands?

the other—that is, going to school, which is geared more to the fast lane, a school of achievers. . . . When I go back to my village, I'm very special in one sense. In another sense, it makes me too smart. They still love me, but I notice I'm not like them anymore. I get sad, and it closes off communication; they don't talk to me. They think, "Now she's too intellectual."

Some people, trapped by their own multiculturalness, become "encapsulated"; others who seem to thrive on living on the border could be labeled "constructive."[48] Multicultural people with an **encapsulated identity** feel torn between different cultural identities. They have difficulty making decisions, are troubled by ambiguity, and feel pressure from both groups. They try to assimilate but never feel comfortable or "at home." As one multiracial student of ours said:

> In high school, I was the only Black student and was often left out, and when I got to college, I was thrilled that I was no longer the only Black girl, but I was different. I couldn't understand why they would want to exclude me. College has left me even more confused than elementary, junior high, or high school. I don't know if I will ever understand my culture since I am often left out of it, whatever it may be.

By contrast, multicultural people with a **constructive identity** thrive in their lives on the margins of two cultures. They see themselves, rather than others, as choice makers. They recognize the significance of being "in between," as many multicultural people do. April, a Korean American student of ours, explained:

> I still believe that I am, for lack of a better phrase, a hyphenated American because I grew up Korean in America. I am not truly Korean or American; I am somewhere in between. Yet I cannot deny that my beliefs about life stem from both my cultures. I hold many Korean notions very near my heart. Yet I am also very American.

Even so, this identity is constantly being negotiated and explored; it is never completely easy. April went on to say, "My American selfishness fights with my Korean selflessness, my boisterous nature with my quiet contentment, my freedoms with my respect. I have had to find a way to mix those two very different cultures in my life."

Post-Ethnicity

Recently, a new approach to racial/ethnic identity called post-ethnicity has emerged. In the post-ethnic United States, identities are very fluid and driven by personal identity preferences. As two writers for the *Washington Post* recently observed, "Post-ethnicity reflects not only a growing willingness—and ability—to cross cultures, but also the evolution of a nation in which personal identity is shaped more by cultural preferences than by skin color or ethnic heritage."[49] The freedom to cross cultures is a relatively recent phenomenon. As shown in

What Do You Think?

The debate about whether the Confederate flag should fly over the South Carolina Statehouse has been raging for years. For the supporters of the flag, it is a symbol of regional identity, a symbol of the spirit of Confederate rebellion. For African Americans, it is a symbol of a slave system enthusiastically supported by the South under that flag. What does the Confederate flag mean to you?

Chapter 3, enormous social and legal barriers that prevent post-ethnicity are a part of everyday life in the United States. As these same two writers noted, however, "We aren't quite there yet." [50] What might be some reasons that we are not living in a post-ethnic society?

On October 7, 2003, California held an election in which most of the media coverage focused on the recall of then-California governor Gray Davis and the many candidates running to replace him. In that same election, however, voters had to decide on Proposition 54; if passed, it would forbid California cities, counties, and state agencies from collecting data on race and ethnicity. Opponents argued that the lack of data on racial/ethnic disparity would prevent schools, for example, from addressing financial inequities and disparities in performance. Two UCLA professors offered some examples of the value of collecting these data:

> [I]n 2002–03, high schools with predominately Latino and African American students had four times as many uncertified teachers and twice the proportion of new teachers as schools with the lowest concentration of these students. . . . Schools with majority Latino and African American students had greater shortages of textbooks and instructional materials. [51]

Why does race continue to reflect disparities in the allocation of resources? How far are we from really reaching a post-ethnic society?

IDENTITY, LANGUAGE, AND INTERCULTURAL COMMUNICATION

We express our identities to others through communication—in core symbols, labels, and norms. **Core symbols** tell us about the fundamental beliefs and central concepts that define a particular identity. For example, core symbols of African American identity might be positivity, sharing, uniqueness, realism, and assertiveness. [52] Individualism is often cited as a core symbol of European American identity.

Labels are a category of core symbols. They are the terms we use to refer to particular aspects of our own and others' identities (African American, Latina/o, White, European American). The labels that refer to particular identities are an important part of intercultural communication. Communication scholar Dolores Tanno describes her own multiple identities reflected in the various labels (Spanish, Mexican American, Latina, Chicana) applied to her. [53] The label "Spanish" was applied by her family and designates her ancestral origins in Spain. "Mexican American" reflects two important cultures that make up her identity. "Latina" reflects cultural and historical connectedness with others of Spanish descent, such as Puerto Ricans and South Americans, while "Chicana" promotes political and cultural assertiveness in representing her identity. She stresses that she is all of these, that each reveals a different facet of her identity: symbolic, historical, cultural, and political.

Stuart Hall, a West Indian writer, describes the variety of labels he's been given: "coloured," "West Indian," "Negro," "Black," "immigrant"—sometimes spoken in a friendly manner and sometimes in an abusive way. But he reminds us that, in fact, he is not one or another of these ways of representing himself but is all of them at different times and to varying degrees.[54] These and other terms construct relational meanings in communication situations. The interpersonal relationships between people are important, but so are such terms' social meanings. So there is no set, easy-to-understand identity that is "you." We have multiple identities that are dynamic and complex and that can only be understood in relation to the contexts and cultures in which we live.

Finally, some behavioral **norms,** or common patterns of behavior, are associated with particular identities. For example, women may express their gender identity by being more concerned about safety than men. They may take more precautions when they go out at night, such as walking in groups. People might express their religious identity by participating in activities such as church services or Bible study meetings.

Identity has a profound influence on intercultural communication processes. Sometimes, we assume knowledge about another person's identity, based on his or her membership in a particular cultural group. We may ignore the individual, but we need to recognize and balance both the individual and the cultural aspects of another's identity. As Tom put it: "The question here is one of identity: Who am I perceived to be when I communicate with others? . . . My identity is very much tied to the ways in which others speak to me and the ways in which society represents my interests."[55]

Think about the assumptions you might make about others based on their physical appearance. What do you "know" about people if you know they are from the South, or Mexico, or Australia, or Pakistan? Or think about the times that people have made erroneous assumptions about you based on limited information—assumptions that you became aware of in the process of communication. Focusing only on someone's nationality, birthplace, education, religion, and so on can lead to mistaken conclusions about the person's identity.

Given the many identities that each of us negotiates for ourselves in our everyday interactions, it is clear how our identities and those of others make intercultural communication problematic. It is important to remember that while identities are somewhat fixed they are also very dynamic. For example, the wide array of communication media available multiply the identities we must negotiate. Consider the relationships that develop by e-mail, for example. Some people even create new identities as a result of online interactions. We change who we are depending on the people we communicate with and the manner of our communication.

SUMMARY

In this chapter, we explored some of the facets of identity and the importance of identities in intercultural communication. Identities do not develop as a smooth process and are created through communication with others. Also, they are multiple and develop in different ways in different cultures. They are dynamic and may be created for us by existing social contexts and structures and in relation to group membership. When these created identities conflict with our sense of our own identity, we need to challenge, resist, and renegotiate those identities.

We also examined how identities are multiple and reflect gender, age, race, ethnicity, physical ability, religion, class, nationality, and other aspects of our society and culture. Identities develop in several stages in relation to minority and majority group membership as well.

Finally, we discussed multicultural identities, emphasizing both the benefits and the challenges of living on the border between two or more cultural realities. Identity is expressed through core symbols, labels, and norms of behavior. It is important to try to minimize making faulty assumptions about other people's identities in intercultural interactions. We need to remember that identities are complex and subject to negotiation.

BUILDING INTERCULTURAL SKILLS

1. Become more conscious of your own identities and how they relate to your intercultural communication. In what contexts and in which relationships do you feel most comfortable? Which aspects of your identity are most confirmed? Which identities do you most resist? Practice resisting those identities people assign to you that you're not comfortable with. Also practice communication strategies to tell people which identities are important to you and which are not.

2. Become more aware of how you assign identities to other people. What assumptions do you make about others' identities? About poor people? Older people? White people? People with disabilities? How do these assumptions influence your communication? Notice how you communicate with them based on your assumptions.

3. Practice communicating with others in ways that affirm their identities.

4. Talk about identities with your friends. Which identities are most important to them? Which identities do they resist? Which identities do they affirm?

ACTIVITIES

1. *Stereotypes:* List some of the stereotypes that foreigners have about Americans.
   a. Where do you think these stereotypes come from?
   b. How do these stereotypes develop?
   c. How do these stereotypes influence communication between Americans and people from other countries?

2. *Stereotypes and prime-time TV:* Watch four hours of television during the next week, preferably during evening hours when there are more commercials. During the commercials, record the number of representatives from different identity groups (ethnic, racial, gender, age, class, and so on) that are in-

cluded and the roles they are playing. Report on this assignment to the class, answering the following questions:

a. How many different groups were represented?

b. What groups were most represented? Why do you think this is so?

c. What groups were least represented? Why do you think this is so?

d. Were there any differences in the roles that members of the cultural groups played? Did one group play more sophisticated/glamorous roles than others?

e. In how many cases were people depicted in stereotypical roles, such as African Americans as athletes or women as homemakers?

f. What stereotypes were reinforced in the commercials?

g. What do your findings suggest about the power of the media and their effect on identity formation and intercultural communication?

THE ONLINE LEARNING CENTER at www.mhhe.com/experiencing2 features self-quizzes, flashcards, and crossword puzzles based on the chapter's key terms and concepts.

www.mhhe.com/ experiencing2

ENDNOTES

1. Hecht, M. L., Collier, M. J., & Ribeau, S. A. (1993). *African American communication: Ethnic identity and cultural interpretation.* Newbury Park, CA: Sage.

2. Lacan, J. (1977). The agency of the letter in the unconscious or reason since Freud. In *Ecrits: A selection* (A. Sheridan, Trans.) (pp. 146–178). New York: Norton. (Original work published 1957.)

3. Katz, J. (1995). *The invention of heterosexuality.* New York: Dutton.

4. Braithwaite, D. O., & Braithwaite, C. A. (2000). Understanding communication of persons with disabilities as cultural communication. In L. A. Samovar & R. E. Porter (Eds.), *Intercultural communication: A reader* (pp. 136–145). Belmont, CA: Wadsworth.

5. Roland, A. (2003). Identity, self, and individualism in a multicultural perspective. In E. P. Salett & D. R. Koslow (Eds.), *Race, ethnicity and self: Identity in multicultural perspective* (2nd ed.) (pp. 3–16). Washington, DC: National Multicultural Institute.

6. Roland (2003), p. 8. http://www.vindy.com/print/296810619099445.shtml

7. Bederman, G. (1995). *Manliness and civilization: A cultural history of gender and race in the United States, 1880–1917.* Chicago: University of Chicago Press.

8. Miller, N. (1995). *Out of the past: Gay and lesbian history from 1869 to the present.* New York: Vintage.

9. Bleys, R. (1996). *The geography of perversion: Male-to-male sexual behavior outside the West and the ethnographic imagination, 1750–1918.* New York: New York University Press.

10. Crary, D. (2003, September 29). "Generation gap? Older women dating younger men." *Chicago Sun Times.* www.suntimes.com/output/lifestyles/cst-nws-young29.html

11. U.S. Equal Employment Opportunity Commission. (1997, January 15). Facts about Age Discrimination. http://www.eeoc.gov/facts/age.html

12. Omi, M., & Winant, H. (2001). Racial formation. In P. S. Rothenberg (Ed.), *Race, class and gender in the United States* (5th ed.) (pp. 11–21). New York: Worth.

13. Hasian, M., Jr., & Nakayama, T. K. (1999). Racial fictions and cultural identity. In J. Sloop & J. McDaniels (Eds.), *Treading judgment.* Boulder, CO: Westview Press.

14. Omi, M., & Winant, H. (2001). Racial formation. In P. S. Rothenberg (Ed.), *Race, class and gender in the United States* (5th ed.) (pp. 11–21). New York: Worth.

15. Bernal, M. E., & Knight, G. (Eds.). (1993). *Ethnic identity*. Albany: State University of New York Press. See also Spindler, G., & Spindler, L. (1990). *The American cultural dialogue*. London: Falmer Press.

16. Alba, R. D. (1990). *Ethnic identity: The transformation of White America*. New Haven, CT: Yale University Press. See also Carbaugh, D. (1989). *Talking American: Cultural discourse on Donahue*. Norwood, NJ: Ablex.

17. http://www.census.gov/hhes/www/disable/disabstat2k/table1.html

18. Siple, L. A. (2000). Cultural patterns of deaf people. In Samovar & Porter, pp. 146–157.

19. Braithwaite & Braithwaite (2000), p. 141.

20. Pogrebin, L. C. (1992). The same and different: Crossing boundaries of color, culture, sexual preference, disability and age. In W. B. Gudykunst & Y. Y. Kim (Eds.), *Readings on communicating with strangers* (pp. 318–332). New York: McGraw-Hill.

21. Gettleman, J. (2003, August 23). Alabama judge's colleagues order Ten Commandments removed. *International Herald Tribune*. http://www.iht.com/articles/107476.html

22. Fussell, P. (1992). *Class: A guide through the American status system*. New York: Touchstone Books. (Original work published 1983).

23. Ehrenreich, B. (2001). Nickel and dimed: *On (not) getting by in America*. New York: Metropolitan Books (Henry Holt).

24. Moon, D. G., & Rolison, G. L. (1998). Communication of classism. In M. L. Hecht (Ed.), *Communication of prejudice* (pp. 122–135). Thousand Oaks, CA: Sage.

25. Shaffer, M., & Reeves, J. A. (2003, September 28). "Foreigners in their own country.'" *The Arizona Republic*. http://www.azcentral.com/news/articles/0928polyg-males28.html

26. Ferguson, R. (1990). Introduction: Invisible center. In R. Ferguson, M. Gever, T. M. Trinh, & C. West (Eds.), *Out there: Marginalization and contemporary cultures* (pp. 9–14). New York and Cambridge, MA: New Museum of Contemporary Art and MIT Press.

27. Manjarrez, C. A. (1991). Mis palabras [my words]. In D. Schoem (Ed.), *Inside separate worlds*. Ann Arbor: University of Michigan Press, p. 51.

28. Hoare, C. H. (2003). Psychosocial identity development in the United States society: Its role in fostering exclusion of cultural others. In E. P. Salett & D. R. Koslow (Eds.), *Race, ethnicity and self* (2nd ed.) (p. 28). Washington, DC: National MultiCultural Institute.

29. Hoare, p. 28.

30. Manjarrez, p. 61.

31. Hardiman, R. (2003). White racial identity development in the United States. In E. P. Salett & D. R. Koslow (Eds.), *Race, ethnicity and self* (2nd ed.) (pp. 117–136). Washington, DC: National MultiCultural Institute, p. 28. See also Helms, J. G. (1995). An update of the Helm's White and people of color racial identity models. In J. G. Ponterotto, J. M. Casas, L. A. Suzuki, & C. M. Alexander (Eds.), *Handbook of multicultural counseling* (pp. 181–198). Thousand Oaks, CA: Sage.

32. Hardiman.

33. Frankenburg, R. (1993). *White women, race matters: The social construction of Whiteness*. Minneapolis: University of Minnesota Press.

34. Altonji, J., Doraszelskil, U., & Segal, L. (2000). Black/White differences in wealth. *Economic Perspectives, 24*, 38–50.

35. For lists of White privileges, see McIntosh, P. (1995). White privilege and male privilege: A personal account of coming to see correspondences through work in Women's Studies. In M. L. Andersen & P. H. Collins (Eds.), *Race, class, and gender: An anthology* (2nd ed.) (pp. 76–87). Belmont, CA: Wadsworth. See also Kivel, P. (1996). White benefits, middle class privilege. In *Uprooting racism: How White people can work for racial justice* (pp. 28–35). Gabriola Island, BC: New Society.

36. Gallagher, C. A. (1994). White construction in the university. *Socialist Review, 1/2*, 167–187.

37. Morin, R. (2001, July 11). Misperceptions cloud whites view of Blacks. *Washington Post*, p. A01.

38. Frankenburg (1993).

39. Helms, J. (1994). *A race is a nice thing to have: A guide to being a White person*. Topeka, KS: Content Communication.

40. Jones, N. A., & Smith, A. S. (2001). The two or more races population. Census 2000 Brief (U.S. Census Bureau Publication No. C2KBR/01-6). Washington, DC: US. Gov't Printing Office.

41. See Miller, R. L., Watling, J. R., Staggs, S. L., & Rotheram-Borus, M. J. (2003). Growing up biracial in the United States. In Salett & Koslow, pp. 139–167.

42. Kich, G. K. (1992). The developmental process of asserting a biracial, bicultural identity. In M. P. P. Root (Ed.), *Racially mixed people in America* (pp. 304–317). Newbury Park, CA: Sage.

43. Miller, Watling, Staggs, & Rotheram-Borus (2003).

44. From a student journal compiled by Jackson, R. M. (1992). *In Mexico: The autobiography of a program abroad.* Queretaro, Mexico: Comcen Ediciones, p. 49.

45. Berry, J. W. (1992). Psychology of acculturation: Understanding individuals moving between two cultures. In R. W. Brislin (Ed.), *Applied cross cultural psychology* (pp. 232–253). Newbury Park, CA: Sage.

46. Bennett, M. J. (1993). Towards ethnorelativism: A developmental model of intercultural sensitivity. In M. Paige (Ed.), *Education for the intercultural experience* (pp. 21–72). Yarmouth, ME: Intercultural Press. See also Kim, Y. Y. (2001). *Becoming intercultural.* Thousand Oaks, CA: Sage.

47. Adler, P. (1974). Beyond cultural identity: Reflections on cultural and multicultural man. *Topics in Culture Learning, 2,* 23–40.

48. Bennett, J. M. (1993). Cultural marginality: Identity issues in intercultural training. In Paige, pp. 109–136.

49. Kotkin, J., & Tseng, T. (2003, June 16–22). All mixed up: For young Americans, old ethnic labels no longer apply. *The Washington Post National Weekly Edition,* pp. 22–23.

50. Kotkin, J., & Tseng, T., p. 23.

51. Oakes, J., & Rogers, J. (2003, October 5). Who needs data on race? The schools for one. *Los Angeles Times.* http://www.latimes.com/news/opinion/sunday/commentary/la-op-oakes5oct05,1,7281774.story?coll=la-sunday-commentary

52. Hecht, M. L., Collier, M. J., & Ribeau, S. A. (1993). *African American communication: Ethnic identity and cultural interpretation.* Newbury Park, CA: Sage.

53. Tanno, D. (2000). Names, narratives, and the evolution of ethnic identity. In A. González, M. Houston, & V. Chen (Eds.), *Our voices: Essays in ethnicity, culture, and communication* (pp. 25–28). Los Angeles: Roxbury.

54. Hall, S. (1985). Signification, representation, ideology: Althusser and the post-structuralist debates. *Critical Studies in Mass Communication, 2,* 91–114.

55. Nakayama, T. K. (2000). Dis/orienting identities: Asian Americans, history, and intercultural communication. In González, Houston, & Chen, p. 14.

CHAPTER FIVE

Verbal Issues in Intercultural Communication

STUDY OBJECTIVES

After reading this chapter, you should be able to:
1. Identify and define the components of language.
2. Discuss the role that language plays within different cultures.
3. Describe ways that people deal with language and communication style differences.
4. Explain how language is related to power.
5. Discuss multilingualism and the process of moving between languages.

KEY TERMS

bilingual	low-context
bilingualism	communication
cocultural groups	multilingual
code switching	phonology
communication style	pragmatics
equivalency	semantics
high-context communication	social positions
interpretation	source text
improvised performance	syntactics
language	target text
language acquisition	third-culture style
language policies	translation

Life Is Not a Bowl of Cherries

I went to Europe on a senior trip right after I graduated high school for one month. We visited nine countries and had an amazing time. Since I was born in Yugoslavia, I considered myself to be very culturally knowledgeable and thought I would have no problems. The first part of the trip was fine because we were in English-speaking countries. We then went to Germany, and in Munich is where I discovered that life is not a bowl of cherries. We had a free day so our group decided to go shopping in the local market. I saw a cherry vendor, and since cherries are my favorite fruit I decided to pick some up. I went up and asked the guy for four pounds of cherries. My naïve self of course asked the man in English, which frustrated him to no end. After me getting petrified from him yelling at me, I took the bag of cherries, which was more like eight pounds (four kilos!), paid for them and made my way sweating and confused. I was acting like the ethnocentric American. My advice, learn some of the language before you visit a country!

Iva, U.S. college student

As our student Iva discovered, intercultural communication involves more than just language skills, but language clearly cannot be overlooked as a central element in communication. Sometimes a very small misunderstanding of one simple sound or word can change the meaning in an interaction and present challenges for intercultural communicators. For example, consider our student Pat's experience in his job selling motorcycles. One day he received a call from a Japanese man looking for parts for his motorcycle:

> He told me the brand, which was a Honda, and the type. He asked if we had any "changes." I then proceeded to talk about the changes to that particular motorcycle. He politely said, after I spoke for a minute without interruption, "chains." I said "motorcycle chains?" He politely said "yes." I was embarrassed but apologized. He was very receptive to my apology. I told myself that I should have asked twice since I wasn't sure. We continued our conversation and I was able to get the parts he needed.

How can we begin to understand the important role of **language** in intercultural communication? The sheer number of languages spoken in the world today, about 6,000, is staggering. The top 10 languages (Chinese-Mandarin,

Info Bites

It is projected that in a hundred years half of the world's currently spoken 6,000 languages will disappear. Ken Hale is quoted as saying that "when we lose a language, it is like dropping a bomb on the Louvre." When we lose languages, we lose cultures. (Source: *National Geographic*, August 1999, p. 65)

Language is an important aspect of intercultural communication, particularly when we travel internationally. We sometimes rely on universal symbols or meanings as represented by a passport or identity card when we cross national borders.

Surf's Up!

Aside from the official languages of any country, many languages and dialects are spoken. Explore this website to see all of the languages that are spoken around the world: http://www.ethnologue.com/country_index.asp. Be sure to look at how many languages are spoken in the United States.

English, Spanish, Bengali, Hindi, Portuguese, Russian, Japanese, German, and Chinese-Wu) are spoken by nearly half of the world's population.[1] How can people possibly communicate given all these different languages? What are some of the difficulties in translating and interpreting? How can we use language to become better intercultural communicators? Is it possible for two people to communicate effectively if they don't speak the same language? Should everyone learn a second or third language? These are some of the questions we explore in this chapter.

First we identify the components of language and explore the dynamic relationship between language, meaning, and perception. Next, we explore cultural variations of language and how people successfully communicate across these cultural variations. In the fourth section, we discuss the relationship between language and power. Finally, we examine multilingualism.

THE STUDY OF LANGUAGE

The Components of Language

Are there any universal aspects shared by all languages? Can the same concept be expressed in any language? Or are there ideas that can only be expressed in particular languages? For answers to these questions, we turn to the discipline of linguistics. Linguistics usually divide the study of language into four parts:

Learning another language, as these students are doing, is never easy, but there are rewards. People have varying reasons for studying a language, including adapting to a new cultural context, getting a job, and traveling abroad.

phonology, semantics, syntactics, and pragmatics. Let's look at each of these components.

Phonology **Phonology** is the study of the sound system of language—how words are pronounced, which units of sounds (phonemes) are meaningful for a specific language, and which sounds are universal. Because different languages use different sounds, it is often difficult for nonnative speakers to learn how to pronounce some sounds.

French, for example, has no equivalent for the voiced "th" sound (as in *mother*) or the unvoiced "th" sound (as in *think*) in English. French speakers often substitute similar sounds to pronounce English words with "th." By contrast, English speakers often have a difficult time pronouncing the French "r" (as in *la fourrure*), which is produced further back in the mouth than in English. English speakers also have trouble pronouncing some Japanese words that contain a sound that is between the English "r" and "l" sounds—for example, the words *ramen* and *karaoke*. Also, in some African languages, sounds like "mba" and "njo" give English speakers problems because they are unfamiliar.

Semantics **Semantics** is the study of meaning—that is, how words communicate the meaning we intend to get across in our communication. For example, an international student ordered a cheeseburger at a fast food restaurant, and the

Surf's Up!

Languages often adopt words from other languages. France, in fact, has a special division of the cultural ministry designed to monitor the French language for the pollution of English words. Look at the list of "Foreign Words and Phrases" (infoplease. lycos.com/ipa/A0001619. html). Perhaps the most amazing thing is how short it is. Now look at the etymologies of words in your dictionary; notice how many words have roots in another language.

worker behind the counter asked him, "Is this for here or to go?" The international student understood the individual words—"for-here-or-to-go"—but not the meaning of the words strung together in that fashion.

Sometimes semantics focuses on the meaning of a single word. For example, what is a chair? Do we define a chair by its shape? Does a throne count as a chair? Do we define it by its function? If I sit on a table, does that make it a chair? Different languages have different words for the same object. Thus, the object that is called *a chair* in English is called *une chaise* in French and *la silla* in Spanish. Even different cultures that share a language, such as Great Britain and the United States, may have different words for the same object. The following list shows some differences between U.S. and British English:[2]

British	*U.S.*
jersey	sweater
pants	underwear
pumps	tennis shoes
trousers	pants
biscuit	cookie, cracker
chips	french fries
crisps	potato chips
twigs	pretzels
cooker	stove
rubber	eraser
loo	toilet
carrier bag	grocery sack

Similarly, in Mexico, a swimming pool is an *alberca*, but in Spain it is a *piscina*. Even within the United States there are semantic differences. For example, a *cabinet* in Rhode Island is often called a *milkshake* elsewhere. A *gumband* in Pittsburgh is called a *rubber band* in Phoenix.

Syntactics **Syntactics** is the study of the structure of a language—the rules for combining words into meaningful sentences. One way to think of this is to consider how the order of the words in a sentence creates a particular meaning. For example, the word order in the sentence "The red car smashed into the blue car" makes a big difference in the meaning of the sentence. "The blue car smashed into the red car" means something else entirely.

In French, there is a difference between "Qu'est-ce que c'est?" and "Qu'est-ce que c'est que ça?" and "C'est quoi, ça?" Although all three questions mean "What is that?" they each emphasize something different. (Roughly translated, they mean "What's that?" "What is that?" and "That is what?") This illustrates that in French, meaning depends more on syntax than on the emphasis of single words in a sentence. This is often the case in English as well.

Each language has particular rules concerning the structure and expression of plurals, possessives, gender forms, subject-verb-object arrangement, and so on. For example, to express possession in English, we add an *'s* ("John's hat" or "the man's hat"). Other languages, such as Spanish, express possession through word sequence ("the hat of John" or "the hat of the man"). In English, the subject or actor is usually placed at the beginning of the sentence ("The girl ran"). By contrast, in Spanish, the subject is sometimes placed at the end of the sentence ("ran the girl"). Thus, learning a new language involves not only learning new words and their meaning but also the particular rules that govern that language. We'll give more examples of different syntactic rules in the next section.

Pragmatics   **Pragmatics** is the study of how language is actually used in particular contexts; the focus is on the specific purposes of language use. What are the main functions or purposes for language use in everyday interaction?

Let's look more closely at five specific functions of language. First, we use language to give information, as when a child explains an illness to his parents (maybe when he doesn't want to go to school!) or when a teacher explains assignments to a class of students. Second, we use language to control others' behavior, as when a student persuades a teacher to give a higher grade. Third, we use language to communicate feeling, as when we tell our loved ones how much we care about them. Fourth, we use language for participating in rituals, as when someone gives a eulogy. Finally, we also use language to execute plans, as when a person plans a shopping trip.

Of course, these are only some of the ways in which we use language, and we can employ more than one purpose for the same words. For example, if someone says, "That's a lovely outfit," you might interpret it in different ways depending upon the way the speaker said it, your relationship with the speaker, and so on. The person might be making fun of your outfit, flirting with you, or simply giving you a compliment. So the meaning does not come from the words or the word order alone but depends on other things like nonverbal cues (facial expressions, vocal intonation), which we'll explore further in the next chapter.

Language and Perception

How much of our perception is shaped by the particular language we speak? Do English speakers see the world differently from Arabic speakers? As a writer for *National Geographic* says, "More than a cluster of words or a set of grammatical rules, a language is a flash of the human spirit by which the soul of a culture reaches into the material world."[3] The idea that the particular language we speak determines our perception of reality is best represented by the Sapir-Whorf hypothesis. The hypothesis was developed by Edward Sapir and Benjamin Whorf, based on research they conducted on Native American languages. They proposed that language not only expresses ideas but also *shapes* ideas about and perceptions of the world.[4]

What Do You Think?

In some cultures, honorifics are very important. In the Spanish language, as a mark of respect, someone is referred to as "usted," which is a bit like "sir" in English. With familiarity, people may begin to use the "tu" form. When Americans learn Spanish in school, though, they often are taught to use the "tu" form unless they are speaking to the elderly, communicating in a business situation, or traveling in another country. Why do you think this is the case in this country?

Figure 5.1 Linguistic maps show where different languages are spoken. This linguistic map shows where different dialects of Chinese are spoken in China. What might a linguistic map of other parts of the world look like?

Source: University of Texas at Austin Library http://www.lib.utexas.edu/maps/middle_east_and_asia/china_ling_90.jpg

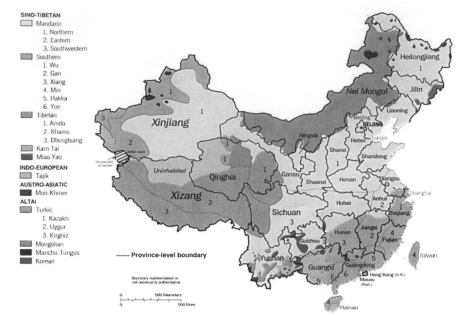

According to the Sapir-Whorf hypothesis, language defines our experience. For example, there are no possessives (his/her/our/your) in the Navajo language; we might conclude, therefore, that Navajos think in a particular way about the concept of possession. In contrast to English speakers, Navajos may think that it's less important for individuals to own things; they may take a more communal approach to possession. The Penan people in Borneo have only one word for "he," "she," and "it," but they have six different words to express "we." This might suggest that social cooperation or collectivism is an important value for the Penan.[5]

A final example demonstrates the different ways various languages express formality and informality. English speakers do not distinguish between a formal and informal "you" (as in German, with *du* and *Sie*, and in Spanish, with *tu* and *usted*). This may mean that English speakers think about formality and informality differently than do German or Spanish speakers. And, indeed, people from outside the United States often comment on the informality of U.S. Americans, in social life, education, and business. As Geraldo, an exchange student of ours from Spain, observed, "It just amazes me how informal everyone is here—saying 'help yourself' to a guest in your home and meaning it! And everyone calling each other by first names, including teachers and students. This would never happen in my country."

How close is the relationship between language and perception? Probably not as close as suggested by the Sapir-Whorf hypothesis. For example, even though cultural groups may have different words for different colors, most can identify a particular color when asked. This means that we can "see" the same colors even if we have different words to describe them.[6] Thus, a more moderate view, in which language is a tool to communicate rather than a mirror of perception, is probably more accurate. As these examples show, however, the language we speak has a tremendous impact on what and how we communicate every day.[7] And this has important implications for intercultural communication. Perhaps it's not just languages that are different; rather, it may mean that members of cultural groups really experience the world very differently and, in a sense, live in very different perceptual worlds.

CULTURAL VARIATIONS IN LANGUAGE

Which is more important, being a good speaker or a good listener? Is it preferable to be effective at communicating verbally or nonverbally? Is it better to be direct and to the point in communicating, or is it better to take some time getting to the point? Is it more important to tell the truth or to make others feel good, even if it means being deceptive? As we'll see, different cultural groups have different answers to these questions. There are cultural variations in how language is used: differences in attitudes toward speech and silence, differences in whether meaning is more in the verbal or nonverbal communication, and differences in communication style. Let's look at each.

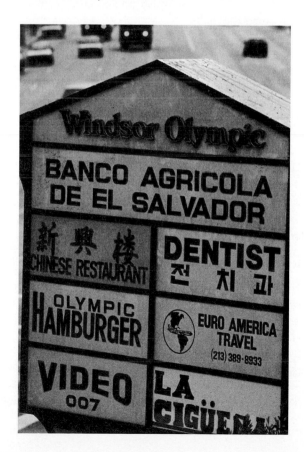

In our increasingly diverse world, many languages may be represented in a given area. This sign suggests that people from many cultural backgrounds live, work, and shop in the same neighborhood.

Attitudes Toward Speaking, Writing, and Silence

In some cultural groups, including many U.S. speech communities, speaking is highly valued. It's also important to be articulate in many contexts (interpersonal, small-group, public speaking). For example, being a good political, business, or religious leader often depends on the ability to express oneself well, or to be "quick on one's feet." In these cultural groups, a secondary, or less important, mode of communication is listening. Silence is sometimes viewed negatively. For example, people may feel bad or embarrassed if there are too many pauses or quiet moments in conversations, or they may feel that they aren't really connecting with people. Silence also can be interpreted as a sign of hostility or rejection, as when people are given "the silent treatment." It may even be interpreted as reflecting a lack of knowledge or a lack of verbal skills.[8]

By contrast, many cultural groups place a primary emphasis on silence and harmony and a secondary emphasis on speech. These groups may actually distrust speech, particularly public speech. The Amish, for example, are sometimes referred to as "the Quiet in the Land" due to their preference for silence, especially in public settings. Judith remembers being struck by the difference between her Amish friends and the non-Amish adolescents she saw in the malls in Lancaster, Pennsylvania. The non-Amish adolescents seemed so free and expressive as they roamed the malls.

The same is true for some Native American groups. Leon Rising Wolf, a member of the Blackfeet Indian Nation, describes the group's primary communication style as a "deeply communicative silence—active silence in which people share a communal silence."[9] Speaking is a secondary communication mode and is important for some Blackfeet people such as tribal leaders. But speaking is also seen as somewhat risky, because it might serve to undermine the communal connectedness.

Many East Asians not only distrust speech but also see the skillful use of silence as an important aspect of competent conversation; it shows the ability to read another person's mind intuitively, and it may even be a powerful way of controlling conversation. This emphasis on silence is based partly on religious

TABLE 5.1 Attitudes Toward Speech and Silence

Often, common phrases reveal cultural attitudes toward speaking and silence. Note the following examples:

It is what people say that gets them into trouble. (Japanese)

A loud voice shows an empty head. (Finland)

To be always talking is against nature. (Taoist saying)

One who speaks does not know. (Taoist saying)

The cat that does not mew catches rats. (Japanese)

Source: Min-Sun Kim (2002). *Non-Western perspectives on human communication: Implications for theory and practice.* Thousand Oaks, CA: Sage, pp. 135, 137.

teachings (Confucius rejected eloquent speaking and instead advocated hesitancy and humble talk in his philosophy of the ideal person) and partly on other cultural beliefs:

> Since ancient times, Japanese people have believed in *kotodama*, which literally means "the spirit living in words." This folk belief creates the superstition that a soul dwelling in words has a supernatural power to make anything happen simply by verbalizing it. Even in modern Japan, meaningless or careless utterance is not respected and valued.[10]

Other Asian cultures share this distrust of speech. As one of our Taiwanese students told us, "In America, sometimes students talk about half the class time. Compared to my classes in Taiwan, if a student asked too many questions or expressed his/or opinions that much, we would consider the person a show-off or insincere. Consequently, this is one of the difficulties I have experienced because of differences in culture."

Thus, it is clear that different views on silence can cause misunderstandings and even conflict in intercultural communication and that silence should be viewed as a legitimate conversational strategy. Since silence is a way of saying "no" for many cultural groups, knowing when *not* to talk in a particular cultural situation and knowing the meanings of silence is as important as knowing when and how to talk. For example, if European Americans, who think that a primary way to connect with people is through verbal communication, try to befriend Native Americans, who use silence as a way to "get to know someone" and reserve talk for more intimate relationships, misunderstanding between the two groups is likely. See Table 5.1 for examples of attitudes toward speech and silence. We'll talk more about silence in the next chapter, on nonverbal communication issues.

The relationship between writing and speaking differs across cultures. In the United States (and other Western cultures), we often emphasize writing over speaking. Having something in writing, such as a written contract, is far more powerful than a verbal promise. We often ask, "Did you get that in writing?" to emphasize the importance of any agreement. Writing is clearly valued over speaking in these cultural contexts. In some cultures, however, oral communication is valued more highly than written communication. Publicly saying that you make a commitment is highly valued and seen as more significant than signing a paper. In the United States, remnants of valuing oral communication can be seen in the importance of saying "I do" when getting married, as opposed to signing a marriage license.

Variations in Communication Style

Communication style combines verbal and nonverbal elements. It refers to the way people use language, and it helps listeners understand how to interpret verbal messages. Recognizing different communication styles helps us understand cultural differences that extend beyond the words we speak. There are at least three distinct dimensions of communication style: high-/low-context, direct/indirect, and elaborated/understated.

High-/Low-Context Styles   A primary way in which cultural groups differ in communication style is a preference for **high-context** or **low-context communication.** Consider this conversation:

> ROBERT: What's for dinner?
>
> PATRICIA: There's a great movie playing, and Barbara told me about this new Thai restaurant that's next to the Scottsdale 24-plex.
>
> ROBERT: We could have the burritos we got the other night from Chili's.
>
> PATRICIA: Whatever.

Patricia is using a high-context communication style. In this rather indirect style, most of the information is not in the verbal message; rather, the meaning is in the context or is internalized in the speaker.[11] This style emphasizes understanding messages without direct verbal communication. Often people in long-term relationships communicate in this style. For example, one partner may send a meaningful glance across the room at a party, and the other knows that it is time to go home.

In contrast, Robert's style is low-context communication, with most of the meaning contained in the spoken word. Low-context communication emphasizes explicit verbal statements ("What's for dinner?" "We could have the burritos . . ."). In most contexts in the United States, this style of communication is highly valued. For example, in business contexts, people are encouraged to value verbal communication, to make words "mean what they say." Interpersonal communication textbooks often stress that we should not rely on nonverbal, contextual information. It is better to be explicit than ambiguous.

By contrast, cultural groups around the world value high-context communication. In these groups, children and adolescents are encouraged to pay close attention to contextual cues (body language, environment), and not just the words spoken in a conversation. For example, a Japanese student told us how his mother encouraged him to try to understand what a neighbor was really saying when making a comment that they (the neighbors) would be going away for a while.[12] As the student recalled, he eventually understood that the neighbor actually was indirectly asking for help in caring for the yard while they would be away. The meaning was not in the words expressed, but in the context—the relationship between the two families, who had been neighbors for a long time.

Direct/Indirect Styles   The indirect/direct dimension is closely related to high-/low-context communication. A direct communication style, like Robert's, is one in which verbal messages reveal the speaker's true intentions, needs, wants, and desires; the emphasis is on low-context communication. An indirect style, like Patricia's, is one in which verbal messages may obscure or minimize the speaker's true intentions, needs, wants, and desires; the emphasis is on high-

---

Pop Culture Spotlight

We don't usually look to action movies starring the likes of Arnold Schwarzenegger or Bruce Willis to provide culturally diverse communication styles. But the quips and puns they use are similar to high-context kinds of communication. Arnold's "I let him go" in *Commando* or "See you at the party, Richter" in *Total Recall* makes sense only if you bring your own memories of what happened to these characters to the dialogue.

context communication. For example, Patricia didn't directly tell Robert that she preferred to go out for dinner, but the implication was evident.

Many English speakers in the United States view the direct speech style as the most appropriate in most contexts. Although "white lies" may be permitted in some situations, the preference is for honesty, openness, individualism, and forthrightness, especially in business contexts:

> White male business executives tend to be clear, specific, and direct in their verbal communication, even if it means dealing with unpleasant realities. As they like to say: "Let's lay our cards on the table, shall we?" Or, "Let's stop beating around the bush and get to the point." (They) generally do not place a high value upon indirection or ambiguity, certainly not as much as some Asian Americans. Even in personal discussion, let alone a more impersonal business conversation, directness frequently is chosen over sensitivity toward feelings.[13]

By contrast, some cultural groups prefer a more indirect style, with an emphasis on high-context communication. Preserving the harmony of relationships has a higher priority than complete honesty. A speaker might look for a "soft" way to communicate that there is a problem in the relationship, perhaps providing contextual cues. For example, three Indonesian students living in the United States were invited by their advisor to participate in a cross-cultural training workshop. They did not want to participate, nor did they have the time. But they did not want to offend their professor, whom they held in high regard. Rather than tell him that they couldn't attend, they simply didn't return his calls and didn't show up for the workshop.

Fekri, a student of ours from Tunisia, had been in the United States for several months before he realized that if one was asked directions and didn't know the location of the place, one should tell the truth instead of making up an answer. He explained that he had been taught that it was better to engage in conversation, to give a person some response, than to disappoint the person by revealing that he didn't know.

Differing communication styles are responsible for many problems that arise between men and women and between persons from different ethnic groups. Many problems are caused by different priorities with regard to truth, honesty, harmony, and conflict avoidance in relationships. Perhaps you can think of times when you tried to protect someone's feelings by communicating indirectly but that person preferred a more direct style. Or perhaps you tend to be more direct, valuing honesty over relationship harmony. For example, our student Janelle has two roommates who both preferred a more indirect style of communicating. When there are conflicts among the three, Janelle tended to "tell it like it is," even if it meant saying negative things. It took her a while to realize that her roommates were offended by her direct, low-context way of speaking. And, of course, they didn't tell her they were offended because that would have required more direct communication, which they were uncomfortable with. They eventually solved their communication problem when Janelle learned to be more

Surf's Up!

The history of the English language is very complex, and there are many different kinds of English. Explore some varieties of English on the following website: http://ebbs. english.vt.edu/hel/ hel.html. Should we consider these forms of English as the same language?

Info Bites

Language is often the source of misunderstandings in cross-cultural encounters. We recall a story about a group of people from the United States who lived in Turkey for two years. One of the women in the group's name was Kim. But in Turkish, the word *kim* means "who?" So, when Turks asked Kim her name, it sounded as if she was uncertain of whom they were asking this.

indirect and began to ask them if things were going OK, and her roommates learned to be a bit more direct with Janelle. We'll talk later about the importance of flexibility and adaptability in communicating effectively across cultures.

Elaborate/Understated Styles   This dimension refers to the quantity of talk that people value and is related to attitudes toward speech and silence. The elaborate style involves the use of rich, expressive language in everyday conversation. For example, Arabic speakers use many metaphorical expressions in everyday speech. In this style, a simple, assertive statement means little, and the listener might believe the opposite. Thus, if my host asks me if I've had enough to eat and I simply respond, "Yes," the host may not believe me; I need to elaborate.

By contrast, in the understated style, simple assertions and silence are valued. Amish people often use this style of communication. A common refrain is, "If you can't say anything good, don't say anything at all." Free self-expression is not encouraged. Silence is especially appropriate in ambiguous situations; that is, if one is unsure of what is going on, it is better to remain silent.

In international negotiations, visible differences in style can highlight these cultural variations. At the outset of the 2003 invasion of Iraq, or "Operation Iraqi Freedom," Saddam Hussein and George W. Bush each gave speeches to their own citizens that demonstrate these differences in communication styles. In his speech on March 20, 2003, George W. Bush used directness and succinctness:

> My fellow citizens. At this hour, American and coalition forces are in the early stages of military operations to disarm Iraq, to free its people, and to defend the world from grave danger.
>
> On my orders, coalition forces have begun striking selected targets of military importance to undermine Saddam Hussein's ability to wage war. These are the opening stages of what will be a broad and concerted campaign.[14]

Bush's speech stands in stark contrast to Hussein's:

> Oh great mojahed people.
> Oh sons of our glorious nation.
> Oh men, bearers of arms and the honor of resistance. God's peace be upon you as you confront the invaders, the enemies of God and humanity, the transient blasphemers with chests brimming with faith and the love of God. . . .
> Seize the opportunity, the pride of Iraq and the nation. It is the opportunity to become eternal and a long life for the living and glory unparalleled.
> Strike at them, fight them. They are aggressors, evil, accursed by God, the exalted. You shall be victorious and they shall be vanquished. . . .
> Fight them everywhere the way you are fighting them today and don't give them a chance to catch their breath until they declare it and withdraw

from the lands of the Muslims, defeated and cursed in this life and the afterlife.[15]

These different uses of language communicate different things to their culturally different audiences. The same thing can happen in interpersonal communication. A Pakistani friend used the elaborate style when he thanked Judith for accompanying his young daughter to the doctor. He told Judith that she was "his angel of mercy to whom he was forever indebted." She remembers thinking (before she studied intercultural communication!) that the thanks seemed out of proportion and a bit insincere for a simple favor. It is not always easy to interpret language use from other people's perspectives.

Variations in Contextual Rules

While recognizing that there are differences in communication styles, we need to avoid stereotyping specific groups (such as Japanese or English speakers) in terms of style. No group uses a particular communication style all the time. It is also important to realize that the particular style we use may vary from context to context. Think of the contexts in which you communicate during the day—classroom, family, work, and so on—and about how you alter your communication to suit these contexts. For example, you may be more direct in your family contexts and less direct in classroom settings.

Let's look more closely at how different communication styles vary from context to context and may reflect the values of cultural groups. One example is the communication dynamics in many traditional Black churches in the United States. Many such congregations employ the call-response communication form, in which the minister proclaims and the audience gives a response. We can also see this call-response form in secular contexts, in the form of banter between the rapper and others in the social group. This form of call and response arises from the values or priorities identified in many African American communities: the importance of religion; the participatory, interrelatedness of people; the connectedness of spiritual and secular life. Also, public speaking is viewed as a communal event in which speakers are supported and reinforced.

Intercultural problems related to communication style can occur in Black-White communication. For example, when the Black person is speaking, the White person, because call-response is not part of his/her cultural heritage, likely will not engage in the response process. Instead, the White person might remain relatively passive, perhaps voicing an occasional, subdued, "uh-huh." Judging from the White person's seeming lack of involvement, the Black communicator might get the feeling that the White person isn't listening to him. And the White person might get the feeling that the Black person isn't listening because he keeps interrupting.[16]

Another example of different contextual rules for communication can be found in the classroom with Blackfeet students and White students. As we already explained, the primary mode of communication for Blackfeet is silence,

What Do You Think?

As the use of e-mail and Internet chat rooms increases, certain communication styles will probably become more important because of the unique kind of communication involved in such text-based media. Of the three styles, what is the preferred one for e-mail and computer-mediated communication?

TABLE 5.2 Summary of Blackfeet and "Whiteman's" Models of Communication in a Classroom Setting

	BLACKFEET	"WHITEMAN"
Primary Mode	Silence →	Speaking →
Cultural Premise	Listener-active, interconnected	Speaker-active, constructive
Secondary Mode	Verbal speaking →	Silence →
Cultural Premise	Risky, rupture	Division
Social Position	Differences by gender and age	Commonality, equality
Typical Speaker	Elder male	Citizen
Cultural Persona	Relational connection	Unique individual
Values	Nature, heritage, modesty, stability	Upward mobility, change, progress

Source: D. Carbaugh (1995), "I can't do that!" but I "can actually see around corners": American Indian students and the study of public "communication." In J. Lehtonen & L. Lahtinen (Eds.), *Critical perspectives on communication research and pedagogy.* St. Ingbert, Germany: Rährig Universitätsverlag, pp. 215–234. With permission from the publisher and author.

whereas a White person's primary mode is speaking. In this case, a young female Blackfeet student was caught between several conflicting sets of contextual rules: (1) the Blackfeet primary mode, which called for proper connective silence, and the Whiteman's primary mode, which seemed to her a presumptuous verbal performance; (2) her Blackfeet heritage, which taught her to respect differences in people based on age and gender and to remain observant, and the White citizen's role, which called for her to speak out; and (3) the Blackfeet preference for a learning environment in which she could be a respectful listening student and the White people's expectation that she be a verbally active student. Table 5.2 summarizes the two modes of communication in this classroom setting.

As we've seen, people communicate differently in different cultural communities. Thus, the context in which the communication occurs is a significant part of the meaning. And while we might communicate in one way in one culture, we might change our communication style for another culture. People who live "on the border" between two different cultures often do this with ease. It's called **code switching.** A colleague of ours can always tell whether her daughter Shaquina is talking to her African American or White friends on the phone, because she uses a different language code. Many Spanish-speaking students do the same thing, speaking "Spanglish" among themselves and then code-switching to Standard English when speaking to their professors in class. Native American students who travel between their nations and university campuses may also code switch, being more direct and personal in their university context and then being more indirect and contextual at home. Understanding the dynamics of various speech communities helps us see the range of communication styles.

COMMUNICATING ACROSS DIFFERENCES

Given all these differences in language use and communication styles, how can people successfully communicate with people from different cultures? Sometimes fear can get in our way. One of our students, Emily, described her nervousness in trying to communicate in French:

> Before leaving for France, I thought I was fully prepared for what to expect. I had, at that point, taken four years of French. When I was out to dinner with my "host" sister, one of her friends asked me in French, "What is your name?" I was so nervous and trying so hard to understand her native accent, but I couldn't make out her sentence. After asking me multiple times, slowly, she ended up asking me in English. Needless to say, it was embarrassing because it was one of the most elementary sentences and I couldn't understand!

Even when people speak the same language, there can be differences in communication style and language use. In this situation, which style should dominate? It probably depends on the context. In situations like Emily's, a foreigner is generally expected to adapt to the language and communication style of the host country. Usually both persons try to adapt somewhat to the language and style of the other—creating together what is sometimes called a **third culture style.** That is, when two people try to adapt to each other, they sometimes end up constructing a style that is not exactly like either of their styles![17]

Another way of thinking about intercultural interaction is as two people putting together an **"improvised performance."** In intercultural interaction, we don't have a ready-made conversation script (like we do in our familiar cultural contexts), and we might feel like we are just making up the performance as we go. As we become more skillful at intercultural communication, we can better "sense" where one person is going, and we try to follow and adapt, like a dance or an improvised performance. As we mentioned previously, this improvisation involves being flexible and adapting to the situation.

Mary Catherine Bateson, a famous anthropologist, gives an example of an intercultural improvisation when meeting her Armenian husband's extended family for the first time. She was uncertain about whom she should and should not kiss in greeting them. She assumed she should probably kiss the mother, the brother, and the sister, so she did. But should she kiss the sister's husband? the sister's husband's brother? She wasn't sure. She describes how they improvised:

> So I kissed the sister's husband, and I could feel in the set of his shoulder muscles that I had done the wrong thing, and at least I knew better than to kiss his brother. I was only a little off in this particular improvisation and there was good will to spare.[18]

We improvise verbally in similar ways. For example, if we are speaking to someone whose native language is not English, we might follow that person's lead and speak a little slower, using less slang. We might adapt to the speaker's

Info Bites

Naming or labeling someone can have important implications. In fairy tales, when you named someone or knew their real name, you had power over them. Perhaps this is why many nations in the world are called by something other than their own preferred name in most languages in the world. For example, the Japanese call their nation *Nippon;* the Greeks, *Ellas;* Greenlanders, *Kalatdlit-Nunat; Nunat;* and Germans, *Deutschland.*

use of gestures and eye contact (or lack of both), which might not exactly follow our own set of cultural rules.

LANGUAGE AND POWER

All language is social and powerful and complicates the view of intercultural interaction as third-culture building or an improvised performance. The language that is used, the words and the meanings that are communicated, depends not only on the context but also on the social relations that are part of that interaction. For example, bosses and workers may use the same words, but the meanings that are communicated may differ. A boss and a worker may both refer to the company personnel as a "family." To the boss, this may mean "one big happy family," while to a disgruntled employee, it may mean a "dysfunctional family." To some extent, the difference is due to the power differential between boss and worker.

Language is powerful and can have tremendous implications for people's lives. For example, saying the words "I do" can influence lives dramatically. Being called names can be hurtful, despite the old adage "sticks and stones may break my bones, but words will never hurt me." In this section, we show how language is related to social position and is used by **cocultural groups**—groups that are not dominant within society's social structure.

Language and Social Position

Just as organizations have particular structures and specific job positions within them, societies are structured so that individuals occupy **social positions**—social constructs embedded with assumptions about gender, race, class, age, sexuality, and so on. Differences in social positions are central to understanding communication. For one thing, not all positions within society are equivalent; everyone is not the same. Thus, for example, when men whistle at a woman walking by, it has a different force and meaning than if women were to whistle at a man walking by.

Power is a central element, by extension, of this focus on differences in social position. When a judge in court says what he or she thinks freedom of speech means, it carries much greater force than when your neighbor who is not a judge gives an opinion about what this phrase means. When we communicate, we tend to note, however unconsciously, the group membership and positions of others.

Groups also hold different positions of power in society. Groups with the most power (Whites, men, heterosexuals)—consciously or unconsciously—use a communication system that supports their perception of the world. This means that cocultural groups (ethnic minorities, women, gays) have to function within communication systems that may not represent their lived experience. These nondominant groups find themselves in struggles: Do they try to adapt to dominant communication, or do they maintain their own styles? Women in large,

TABLE 5.3 Cocultural Communication Orientations

	SEPARATION	ACCOMMODATION	ASSIMILATION
Nonassertive	Avoiding	Increasing visibility	Emphasizing commonalities
	Maintaining interpersonal barriers	Dispelling stereotypes	Developing positive face
			Censoring self
			Averting controversy
Assertive	Communicating self	Communicating self	Extensive preparation
	Intragroup networking	Intragroup networking	Overcompensating
	Exemplifying strengths	Using liaisons	Manipulating stereotypes
	Embracing stereotypes	Educating others	Bargaining
Aggressive	Attacking	Confronting	Dissociating
	Sabotaging others	Gaining advantage	Mirroring
			Strategic distancing
			Ridiculing self

Source: M. P. Orbe (1998). *Constructing co-cultural theory.* Thousand Oaks, CA: Sage, p. 110.

male-dominated corporations often struggle with the same issue: Should they adopt a male, corporate style of speaking or assert their own style?

There seem to be three general answers to this question of how cocultural groups can relate to the more powerful (dominant) groups. They can communicate nonassertively, assertively, or agressively. Within each of these communication postures, cocultural individuals may emphasize assimilation—trying to become like the dominant group—or they can try to accommodate or adapt to the dominant group. They can also try to remain separate from the dominant groups as much as possible.[19]

These three sets of orientations result in nine types of communication strategies. Which strategy is chosen depends on many things, including the desired outcome, perceived costs and rewards, and the context. Let's look at each of these orientations; Table 5.3 gives a summary.

Assimilation Strategies

Some cocultural individuals may use nonassertive assimilation strategies. These communication strategies emphasize trying to fit into and be accepted by the dominant group. Such strategies might emphasize commonalities ("I'm not that

Pop Culture Spotlight

If you are a *Star Trek* fan, you know that "assimilation" is what the Borg do to people. The Borg are cyborg villains who share a collective intelligence. They assimilate captives into the collective, stripping them of all individual thought and turning them into drones. How is that similar and different from the process of assimilation into the dominant culture?

different"), be self-monitoring ("I'd better be careful about what I say in this or-ganization to make sure I don't offend those in power"), and, above all, avoid controversy.

There are both costs and benefits for cocultural members who use these strategies. For example, women and members of ethnic minorities may use these strategies at work if they feel that their job success depends on not "making waves"—so they may benefit by keeping their job. For instance, they may keep quiet when they hear offensive or noninclusive remarks, such as a boss's use of "girls" to refer to female staff members. However, there are potential costs as well, for both cocultural members and the dominant group. The cocultural per-son may experience a lowering of self-esteem due to the feeling that he or she cannot be authentic. In addition, these kinds of strategies can foster an unhealthy communication climate that reinforces the dominant group's social and political power. For example, African Americans may believe that Whites do not really know or care how they feel.

Assertive assimilation strategies also seek to downplay cocultural differences and promote a convergence into existing structures. But they do so more force-fully than the nonassertive strategies, not giving priority to others' needs ("I'll try to fit in, but I have to let people know how I feel from time to time"). How-ever, these strategies may promote an us-versus-them mentality, and many people find it difficult to sustain them for long. Eventually, the cocultural mem-ber experiences burnout.

Aggressive assimilation strategies emphasize fitting in; cocultural members using these strategies go to great lengths to prove that they are like members of the dominant group. Some strategies are dissociating (showing that one is *not* like other cocultural group members), mirroring (dressing and behaving like the dominant group), or self-ridiculing. The benefits of these kinds of strategies are that the dominant group does not see the cocultural group members as "typical," but the costs sometimes involve ridicule from other cocultural members ("She's trying so hard to be White" or "male" or "straight"). So these individuals may find themselves constantly negotiating their position with the dominant group while being isolated from their own cocultural group.

Accommodation Strategies

Nonassertive accommodation strategies emphasize blending in with the domi-nant group but also tactfully challenging the dominant structure to recognize co-cultural practices. Strategies include increasing visibility and dispelling stereo-types. For example, an African American manager might point out that she isn't particularly good friends with the one other African American in the organiza-tion; just because both workers are minorities doesn't mean they'll be good friends. The potential benefits for both dominant and cocultural groups are ob-vious. In this case the cocultural member is gently educating her colleagues and helping to change stereotypes of the cocultural group.

Also, using this strategy, the cocultural member may be able to influence group decision making while still showing loyalty to larger organizational goals.

Surf's Up!

How much of assimila-tion is linguistic, and how much has to do with other cultural norms, such as issues of hygiene? Read Raimonda Mika-tavage's discussion of fitting in (www.dcpages. com/Commentary/ rmikatavage/ rmikatavage0298a.html). To what extent do eco-nomics determine the meanings of words like *soap*?

For example, a female business executive who shows that she's willing to work long hours, head up committees, and travel influences decision making while showing that she doesn't fulfill the stereotype of a working mother, for whom family always comes first. However, there are costs as well. Individuals with this orientation may be criticized by others for not being more aggressive in trying to change the dominant structures. Also, these communication strategies don't really promote major change in organizations to make them more inclusive and reflective of larger society.

Assertive accommodation strategies involve trying to strike a balance between the concerns of cocultural and dominant group members. These strategies involve communicating self, doing intragroup networking, using liaisons, and educating others. For example, using these strategies, African Americans may share information about themselves with their coworkers and educate others about phrases that are offensive, such as "working like a slave." Or gay colleagues may educate coworkers about how they feel excluded when so much of straight people's conversation focuses on heterosexual relationships and assumes that everyone is straight.

Aggressive accommodation strategies involve becoming a part of dominant structures and then working from within to promote significant changes, no matter how high the personal cost. Cocultural members who use these types of communication strategies may be seen as confrontational and self-promoting. However, they also reflect a genuine desire to work with and not against the dominant group members. For example, a Chicana colleague of ours uses this strategy in consistently reminding our department that affirmative action goals have to be integrated into the mission of the department and not seen as a separate goal—in which case people could compartmentalize their actions and only sometimes work for affirmative action. Similarly, a colleague with a disability consistently reminds the office staff that the facilities need to be more accessible—mailboxes that can't be reached, doors that do not open automatically, bathrooms that do not accommodate wheel chairs, and so on.

Cocultural members with this orientation may periodically use assertive as well as aggressive accommodation strategies and so may be perceived as genuinely committed to the larger group's good. In this way, they reap the benefits of being perceived positively by the dominant group and also have an impact on the organization. However, cocultural members who consistently use aggressive accommodating strategies may find themselves alienated from both other cocultural members and dominant group colleagues for being too confrontational.

Separation Strategies

Nonassertive separation strategies are employed by individuals who assume that some segregation is part of everyday life in the United States. Generally, people live, work, learn, play, and pray with people who resemble themselves. This is generally easier for the dominant group than for cocultural members. Some cocultural individuals regard segregation as a natural phenomenon but also use subtle communication practices to maintain separation from the dominant group. Perhaps the most common strategy is simply avoiding interaction with dominant group members whenever possible. Thus, gay people using this orientation may spend their social time with other gay people. Or women may prefer to use professional women's services (having a female doctor, dentist, and attorney) and socialize with other women.

Assertive separation strategies reflect a conscious choice to maintain space between dominant and cocultural group members. Typical strategies include communication practices such as stressing strengths and embracing stereotypes. Some assertive separation strategies, such as communicating self and intragroup networking, might also be employed by those wanting to assert separation. One of the benefits of assertive separation strategies, like the nonassertive strategies, is that they promote cocultural unity and self-determination. However, individuals might implement the strategies without having access to resources controlled by the dominant group.

Aggressive separation strategies are used by those for whom cocultural segregation is an important priority. These strategies include attacking and sabotaging others. Individuals using these strategies often criticize those who use assimilation or accommodation strategies. While cocultural members do not have the power base that members of the dominant group have, these strategies do enable cocultural members to confront pervasive discriminatory structures. However, they also risk retaliatory attacks by the dominant group.

It is useful to think about when it is effective to use these various strategies given that each may have some benefits and costs associated with it. For example, suppose Luis, the only minority group member, thinks that he is consistently "cut out of the loop" at work. He has just discovered that there was a meeting that impacts his projects that he was not told about. There are a number of ways that he might handle this situation. He could use an aggressive assimilation strategy and simply try as hard as he can to fit in and to be included. But this may not give him the outcome he wants and may lead to a perception that he doesn't have a strong ethnic identity. He could use an assertive accommodation strategy, reminding his coworkers that he needs to be included and explicitly pointing out when he is not included. This could produce the desired outcome and help the organization become more aware of its need for increased inclusiveness. Or he could adopt an aggressive accommodation strategy and march into the director's office, demanding to be included.

The "Power" Effects of Labels

Another way of looking at power and language is to think about the labels we use to refer to other people and ourselves. Labels acknowledge and communicate particular aspects of our social identity, as discussed in Chapter 4. For example, we might label ourselves or others as "male" or "female" to indicate gender identity. Or we might say we are "Canadian" or "midwestern," indicating a national or regional identity. The context in which a label is used may determine how strongly we feel about the label. On St. Patrick's Day, for example, someone may

Pop Culture Spotlight

In the film *The Wedding Banquet*, an Asian American is trying to figure out how to tell his traditional Chinese parents that he is gay, while his White lover to trying to learn Mandarin. In one very funny scene, the lover gives his partner's mother some beauty cream, but his Mandarin is so bad he describes it as cream for "old ladies." Are there things we can do to prepare for those inevitable mistakes?

feel more strongly about being an Irish American than about being a woman or a student or a midwesterner.

Sometimes people feel trapped or misrepresented by labels. They might complain, "Why do we have to have labels? Why can't I just be me?" But the reality is that it would be nearly impossible to communicate without labels. We rarely have problems with nonjudgmental labels such as "man," "student," "Minnesotan," or "Venezuelan." Trouble arises, however, from the use of labels that we don't like or that we feel inaccurately describe us. Think about how you feel when someone describes you by terms that you do not like.

Labels communicate many levels of meaning and establish specific relationships between speaker and listener. Sometimes people use labels to communicate a sense of equality with and closeness and affection for another—for example, "friend," "lover," or "partner." At other times, people intentionally invoke labels to establish a hostile, unequal relationship—for example, "dumb bitch," "White trash," "camel jockey," or "gook." And people sometimes use labels that are unintentionally offensive to others, which merely reflects the speaker's ignorance, lack of cultural sensitivity, and real connection to the other group. For instance, the use of terms such as "Oriental" and "homosexual" communicates negative characteristics about the speaker and establishes distance between speaker and listener. "Oriental" is viewed as negative because it does not refer to any real place and has negative connotations of things exotic and strange. It is better to use the term "Asian." And "homosexual" is seen as negative because it emphasizes sexuality; many prefer the term "gay."

What Do You Think?

What kinds of personal power do you invoke with your labels? When people talk about their "husband" or "wife," it is a signal that they are heterosexual, and in many situations that is a kind of privilege. Some straight married people refuse this privilege, though, preferring to talk about their "partners." How do most of your friends refer to their significant others?

STUDENT VOICE

Labels and Heritage: Describing the Fix

By Elvinet S. Wilson

> *The following essay illustrates, through one Afro-Caribbean woman's struggle with identity, the importance of identity "labels." It highlights a particular standpoint that may be described as a "fix"—the awkward position of negotiating race and still taking pride in African heritage.*

My name is Ellie, at least that's what my family calls me. I am a woman who was born in The Commonwealth of the Bahamas on an island called New Providence. I came to the United States when I was 18. I had no prior knowledge of the US racial system before I came here. By knowledge, I don't mean information, I mean experience. Other than hearing stories of civil rights abuses like that of the Rodney King incident on world news, I had no knowledge of the true depth and context of racial thought.

I've lived in the United States for eight years now, and sometimes I still wonder why people call me or think of me as African American. African Americans in the United States have made remarkable contributions to their country's history and have set precedents for marginal groups' social and political struggles. However, few people discuss differences within the racial category "Black," or within the group "African American." The two categories are also often used synonymously.

I understand the term "Black" because Bahamian politicians used it to talk about our struggles against "White" and foreign business owners when I was growing up. I remember my History teacher, Mr. Mulai (a Guyanese man) referring to the term "Black" as being used predominantly after word spread of the successes of U.S. Civil Rights legislation and as the Pan African Movement further developed. While I was taught about my own people's history and recognize my African heritage, I never really thought of myself as keenly African. An African to me is a person who was born on the continent.

I have many African friends; some from Kenya, Nigeria and Zimbabwe, others from the Ivory Coast and Botswana. I remember many gatherings when we would talk about how similar we all were and yet how different. I grew up in the West, but there are many things about me that are Eastern, like my history, my love for spicy foods, and possibly my aesthetic sensibility. They grew up in the East, but there are many things about them that are Western, like their dress (sometimes), the fact that many of them speak European languages, their schooling and other things. All of us are a part of a post-colonial history that has affected how we see ourselves.

My friend Ben from Kenya said that he could look at me and make an educated guess about where my people originated just based on my facial and bodily features. He claimed he was sure I would fit perfectly into a local tribe in his country called the Luo, from the Lake Victoria region of Kenya. One of my other Kenyan friends, John, when we first met, told me he knew that I was not African American when he met me, because of how I introduced myself, smiled at him and answered "good night" in our greeting of each other. He said African American women seemed much more distrustful of him and many of them on campus did not respond to his greetings.

Many of my African American friends when I first met them often knew right away that I was not African American. A number of them were always interested in finding out more about my country, especially about the beaches and the food. But often, they would make the mistake of calling me Jamaican or Haitian. Jamaica and Haiti are different countries in the Caribbean, south of our islands on a map. While our cultures are similar, we are very different in a number of ways—one of those ways is the variety in our regional accents, but many Americans cannot tell the difference. Jamaicans often speak a much deeper English patios (note that there are variations in thickness) and Haitians of course often speak a French creole. Jamaicans make up the majority of the English-speaking Caribbean population in the U.S. though, and have been migrating longer and in larger numbers than other English-speaking Caribbean groups. That would make the likelihood that people would meet a Jamaican, higher than that of meeting someone like me, from The Bahamas or from the Cayman Islands.

Many of my White American friends on the other hand, usually think I am African American when they first meet me. They are often surprised when I say I am from The Bahamas or the Caribbean. Many of them note that I do not speak with an accent and I usually explain that I do have an accent, but I use it only when I'm talking to people from my region. I was taught: "proper English" is to be used outside the home, and you only use dialect with friends or family. Intercultural scholars call this "code-switching." Some Caribbean people were not taught the same thing though. Many of them would never consider code-switching, even after moving to another country.

So I don't call myself African even though I identify with that heritage. And I never really thought I was American either; although I may entertain using the label if I were naturalized. I prefer to use the term Bahamian (my national identity) because of my experiences growing up, but I've also learned how to function under the labels, "Black" and "African American," because I am aware that people think of me that way. Whenever I have to fill out things like medical forms or admissions forms, I use "Black" if there is no space for "Other" or I write in "Bahamian" if there is. But sometimes, I'm not really sure what either of them means anymore.

Language use is closely linked to social structure, so the messages communicated through the use of labels depend greatly on the social position of the speaker. If the speaker and listener are close friends, then the use of certain labels may not be offensive or cause a rift in the relationship. But if the speaker and listener are strangers, then these same labels might invoke anger or close the lines of communication.

Furthermore, if the speaker occupies a powerful social position, he or she can have an even greater influence. For example, when Edith Cresson was the prime minister of France, she made several controversial statements. Her claims that the "Japanese are like ants" and that "25% of all English and Americans are homosexual" did not promote the kinds of relations with Japan, the United Kingdom, or the United States that France desired. Because of Cresson's powerful position in the social structure, her use of language created international and domestic controversies.

The authors of this book conducted a study about reactions to labeling.[20] We asked White students which of the following ethnic terms they preferred to be called: White, Caucasian, White American, Euro-American, European American, Anglo, or WASP. The majority expressed a preference for the more general label "White" rather than the more specific label "WASP" or "European American." We concluded that they probably had never thought about what labels they preferred to be called. This preference may also be related to issues of power. The more powerful aspects of identity seem to go unnoticed; for many

What Do You Think?

Do you know how many language groups were represented in your high school? How about in your college? How many would you guess for each one? Hollywood High School in California has over 30 language groups, while Arizona State University has over 400.

White people, Whiteness simply "is," and the preferred label is a general one that does not specify origin or history. Individuals from the more powerful groups do the labeling of others; they themselves do not get labeled. For example, when men are asked to describe their identities, they often forget to include gender. By contrast, women often specify gender as a key element in their identity. This may mean that men are the defining norm and that women exist in relation to this norm. We can see this in the labels we use for men and women and for people of color. We rarely refer to a "male physician" or a "White physician," but we do refer to a "female doctor" or a "Black doctor."

As discussed in Chapter 4, this "invisibility" of Whiteness may be changing. It seems that Whites are becoming increasingly more conscious of their White identity, which may change the practice of labeling. Perhaps as the norm of being White is challenged by changing demographics, by increased interaction in a more diverse United States, and by racial politics, more Whites will think about the meaning of labels for their own group.

MOVING BETWEEN LANGUAGES

Multilingualism

People who speak two languages are considered **bilingual**; people who speak more than two languages are considered **multilingual**. Rarely, however, do bilinguals speak both languages with the same level of fluency. More commonly, they prefer to use one language over another, depending on the context and the topic.

Sometimes, entire nations are officially bilingual or multilingual. Belgium, for example, has three national languages: Dutch, German, and French. Canada recognizes English and French. Switzerland is a multilingual nation that has four official languages: French, German, Italian, and Romansh. And the United States has a growing number of speakers of English and Spanish as well as many other languages. Table 5.4 lists the ten most commonly spoken languages (other than English) that are spoken in U.S. homes. Laura, a college student, describes how it feels to be bilingual:

> Growing up bilingual, one must think before the words come out. If I am communicating with my boss at work, English is the common language. In a restaurant, depending on the person or friend, the language is determined: Is he or she English-speaking, Spanish-speaking, or bilingual? At home with family, it is natural to talk to them in Spanish. Growing up bilingual sometimes feels like a job. A job to be proud of.
>
> English I learned at school was second to Spanish. Growing up, it was normal to talk English to teachers and schoolmates at school, but at home, my grandmother and family spoke Spanish, and so did I. Spanish is what I heard and learned first growing up and raised by my grandmother. I feel comfortable and happy talking in Spanish. I feel I am the Spanish words that come out of my mouth.

TABLE 5.4 Top Ten Non-English Languages Most Commonly Spoken at Home in the United States

1. Spanish	6. Vietnamese
2. Chinese	7. Italian
3. French	8. Korean
4. German	9. Russian
5. Tagalog	10. Polish

Source: U.S. Census Bureau (http://www.census.gov/prod/2003pubs/c2kbr-29.pdf).

I am proud to be bilingual. I talk like who I am, mestiza, mixed in my blood and in my language. There are many people who grew up like me, knowing two languages. A lot of the times as we talk we mix both Spanish and English together and come up with Spanglish, un mestizo. Spanglish is not a language on its own, it is a mix of two languages, English and Spanish, like our lives. I can communicate well with my boss and English-speaking friends. I can talk to my family and friends in Spanish. I can also combine both Spanish and English languages, and still others will understand me.

On either the individual or the national level, multilinguals must engage in language negotiation. That is, they need to work out, whether explicitly or implicitly, which language to use in a given situation. These decisions are sometimes clearly embedded in power-relations. For example, French was the court language during the reign of Catherine the Great, in 18th-century Russia. French was considered the language of culture, the language of the élite, whereas Russian was considered a vulgar language, the language of the uneducated.

Sometimes, a language is chosen as a courtesy to others. When Judith is with her bilingual friends (Spanish-English), they often speak English, because Judith's Spanish proficiency is low. Tom joined a small group going to see the fireworks display at the Eiffel Tower on Bastille Day one year. (Bastille Day is a French national holiday, celebrated on July 14, commemorating the storming of the Bastille prison and the beginning of the French Revolution.) One person in the group asked, "Alors, on parle français ou anglais?" ["Are we speaking French or English?"] Because one member was quite weak in English, French was chosen as the language of the evening.

The reasons people become bilingual reflect the trends we identified in Chapter 1 that drive the need for intercultural communication. **Bilingualism** results from these imperatives, as people move from one country to another, as businesses expand into international markets, and so on. More personal imperatives also drive people to become bilingual. Alice Kaplan, a French professor at Duke University, notes, "Speaking a foreign language is, for me and my students, a chance for growth, for freedom, a liberation from the ugliness of our received ideas and mentalities."[21] Many people use foreign languages to escape from the history of oppression in their own languages.

Perhaps it is easier to think of language as a "prisonhouse," since all of the semantic, syntactic, pragmatic, and phonetic systems are enmeshed in a social system from which there is no escape, except through the learning of another language. Consider the case of Sam Sue, a Chinese American born and raised in Mississippi, who explained his own need to negotiate these social systems—often riddled by stigmatizing stereotypes—by changing the way he speaks:

> Northerners see a Southern accent as a signal that you're a racist, you're stupid, or you're a hick. Regardless of what your real situation is. So I reacted to that by adapting the way I speak. If you talked to my brother, you would definitely know he was from the South. But as for myself, I remember customers telling my dad, "Your son sounds like a Yankee."[22]

Among the variations in U.S. English, the southern accent unintentionally communicates many negative stereotypes. Developing another accent is, for some, the only way to escape the stereotypes. When you hear different accents, what kinds of stereotypes do these accents invoke?

Learning another language is never easy, but the rewards of knowing another language are immense. The reasons for studying intercultural communication that we discussed in Chapter 1 can also be applied to learning a second language. The demographic and economic imperatives are especially relevant, particularly in regions of the country where there is increasing ethnic and linguistic diversity. Our student Laura recently moved from Michigan to Arizona, where she works with many individuals who have recently moved there from Mexico. She comments, "It is sometimes hard, because you want to communicate, but do not always have the words. I do not speak much Spanish, so conversations can be difficult. However, where there's a will, there's a way. My friends and I make an effort to get our meanings across, and I have met some wonderful people as a result."

Language acquisition simply refers to the process of learning another language. Language acquisition studies have shown that it is nearly impossible for someone to learn the language of a group of people they dislike. And learning another language can lead to respect for another culture. Our student Karla describes such an experience:

> As soon as I entered the seventh grade, I began to learn Spanish. It was very difficult and after speaking Spanish for many years I have a greater respect for bilingual people. (In fact, when I was little I always assumed that Mexicans were smarter than Americans because many of them spoke English and Spanish!). Once I began to advance in my Spanish classes, we learned more in depth about different cultures including Mexican and Spanish cultures. I had one teacher who realized that reading about other people was a hard way to relate to them. She designed an after-school group of teens that spoke English as their second language. As a class we

Surf's Up!

There are many artificial languages in the world. Check out the website about the Elfish language from Tolkien's *Lord of the Rings* trilogy (www.elvish.org/resources.html). Also look at the information about Klingon from *Star Trek* (www.kli.org/). Why might someone be attracted to these languages—enough to write books on them?

would get together and talk with these students. This was a good opportunity to become friends with people I would never have met otherwise.

People react differently to living in a multicultural world. Some work hard to learn other languages and other ways of communicating, even if they make a number of errors along the way. Others retreat into their familiar languages and customs. The tensions that arise over different languages and different meaning systems are played out around the world. And these tensions will never disappear but will always provide new challenges for intercultural communicators.

Translation and Interpretation

Intercultural communication scholars are also concerned with the role of translation and interpretation—that is, how people understand each other when they speak different languages. Because it is impossible to learn all of the languages in the world, we must rely on translation and interpretation—two distinct but important means of communicating across languages. The European Union (EU), for example, has a strict policy of recognizing all of the languages of its constituent members. Hence, a large number of translators and interpreters are hired to work by the EU to bridge linguistic differences.

Translation generally refers to the process of producing a written text that refers to something said or written in another language. The original-language text of a translation is called the **source text;** the text into which it is translated is called the **target text.** So, when *Gone with the Wind* is translated into Hungarian, the original text written by the author is the source text. The result of the translation, the Hungarian version, is the target text.

Interpretation refers to the process of verbally expressing what is said or written in another language. Interpretation can either be simultaneous, with the interpreter speaking at the same time as the original speaker, or consecutive, with the interpreter speaking only during the breaks provided by the original speaker.

Languages are entire systems of meaning and consciousness that are not easily translated into other languages word for word. The ways in which different languages convey views of the world are not equivalent, as we noted earlier. Remember the dilemma regarding color? The English word *brown* might be translated as any of these French words, depending on how the word is used: *roux, brun, bistre, bis, marron, jaune,* and *gris.*[23] For example, *brun* is used to describe brown hair, while *bis* is used to describe a brown pencil.

Issues of Equivalency and Accuracy.   Some languages have tremendous flexibility in expression; others have a limited range of words. The reverse may be true, however, for some topics. This variation between languages is both aggravating and thrilling for translators and interpreters. The tradition of translation studies has tended to emphasize issues of accuracy and **equivalency**—the condition of being equal in meaning, value, quantity, and so on. That is, the focus,

Surf's Up!

The practice of subtitling films is not easy. This website highlights some important practices to follow in doing a good job: http://www.titel bild.de/en/TITELBILD/ About_Us/Info_for _Subtitlers/Good _Subtitling_Practice/ body_good_subtitling _practice.html. How might this information benefit those of us who rely on subtitles to see films in another language?

Surf's Up!

There are many different ways of speaking English. Some of them may invoke stereotypes or images to you. Check out this website to listen to many different ways of speaking English: http://www.ku.edu/~idea/.

largely from linguistics, has been on comparing the translated meaning to the original meaning. For those interested in the intercultural communication process, the emphasis is not so much on equivalence but on the bridges that people construct to "cross" from one language to another.

Once when Tom was in Normandy, in northern France, a French policeman asked him to tell an English-speaking woman to get down from a wall that was high above the street. Tom called out to her that the policeman wanted her to get down. She refused. The police officer became angry and began speaking louder and faster, repeating his request. Tom, too, began speaking louder and faster, giving the same request in English. The situation escalated until the woman hollered, "Tell him to go to hell!" At this point, Tom felt trapped, so he turned to the police officer and said, "Je ne comprends pas. Je ne parle pas français" ["I don't understand. I don't speak French"].

Tom tried to apologize and escape the situation. But the police officer interrupted him immediately and retorted, "Mais oui, tu peux parler français!" ["Oh yes, you can speak French!"]. He continued barking angry commands at the woman. Throughout this situation, Tom never really expressed the nuances of the statements on either side. The officer, unless he understood English and refused to speak it, did not know the obscenities that were being hurled his way. Nor did the woman understand the demeaning familiar forms of language used by the officer, or the significance of his demands as a police officer, a position of much more authority than in the United States.

The Role of the Translator or Interpreter   We often assume that translators and interpreters are "invisible," that they simply render into the target language whatever they hear. The roles that they play as intermediaries, however, often regulate how they render what is said. Consider the previous example again. Because of the French police officer's position, it was nearly impossible for Tom to tell him what the woman was saying—even apart from the linguistic difficulty of translating profanity.

It is important that you acknowledge the role of an interpreter if you find yourself in that situation. Tom recently met with some journalists from China, and an interpreter who spoke Mandarin Chinese and English was brought along. Tom was sure to acknowledge her presence and asked her when and how he should stop speaking so she could interpret. He also ensured that she felt free to ask questions to clarify anything that might be interpreted in different ways. By doing this, the interpreter was given more flexibility and authority in interpretation, which hopefully assisted in the interpretation process.

We often assume that anyone who knows two languages can be a translator or an interpreter. Research shows, however, that a high level of fluency in two languages does not necessarily make someone a good translator or interpreter. The task obviously requires the knowledge of two languages. But that's not enough. Think about all the people you know who are native English speakers. What might explain why some of them are better writers than others? Knowing English, for example, is a necessity for writing in English, but this knowledge does not necessarily make a person a good writer. Because of the complex relationships between people, particularly in intercultural situations, translation and interpretation involve far more than linguistic equivalence, which traditionally has been the focus.

Language Politics and Policies

Some nations have multiple official languages. Here in the United States, there is no official, legal national language, although English is the de facto national language. There were discussions about language policy during the writing of the Constitution, as a number of languages were spoken by Europeans in the Americas at that time, including English, French, German, and Spanish. Ultimately, however, the Founding Fathers decided to not say anything in the Constitution with regard to language. Today, special-interest groups in many states, especially Arizona and California, have pushed for laws declaring English the official language. In contrast, Hawaii has two official languages—English and Hawaiian—and New Mexico recognizes both English and Spanish as its official languages. Many nations have even more official languages.

Laws or customs that emerge to determine which language is to be spoken where and when are referred to as **language policies.** These policies often emerge from the politics of language use. Historically, for example, European aristocrats spoke French. Recall that, in the court of Catherine the Great of Russia, one heard and spoke French, not Russian. According to the language policies of the period, speaking Russian was seen as vulgar, or as they might have said, declassé. The French language, within those language policies, was closely tied

Surf's Up!

Experiment with www. Freetranslation.com. When the idiomatic expression "Eat your heart out" was translated into Spanish, out came "Coma el corazón fuera," which does not quite get the intended meaning and doesn't quite make sense. When it was then translated back into English, it turned into "Eat the heart went," which doesn't make sense on any level. And a translation back into Spanish gives "Coma el corazón fue."

Languages are entire systems of meaning and consciousness that are not easily translated into another language. This is also true for spoken language and sign language.

TABLE 5.5 Top Ten Non-English Languages Most Commonly Spoken in the World

1. Mandarin	6. Arabic
2. Spanish	7. Portuguese
3. Russian	8. Bengali
4. French	9. Japanese
5. Hindi	10. German

Surf's Up!

Did you know that most of the world's population is bilingual or multilingual? Check out this website to find more information on bilingualism and multilingualism: http://www.lsadc.org/web2/multiling.htm. Note how difficult it can be to count bilinguals and multilinguals.

to the politics of social and economic class. To illustrate, think about how you would feel if in the United States speaking English was a sign that you were "vulgar," while speaking French was a sign of high status.

It is important to remember that language policies are connected to politics of class, culture, ethnicity, and economics and do not really say anything about the supposed "quality" of the language itself. The following is an example from Belgium, a country with three official languages. After gaining its independence from the Netherlands in 1830, Belgium chose French as its national language, perhaps as a reaction to years of Dutch rule. However, after the Flemish protested, Dutch was added as a national language in 1898, and Belgium became bilingual. Then in 1962, a linguistic border was drawn across the country to mark the new language policies, indicating which language would be the official language of what region.

As a result, Belgium's oldest university, the Catholic University of Leuven—bilingual at the time—found itself at the center of a linguistic conflict. Leuven is in Flanders. In 1968, the Flemish people demanded that the French-speaking part of the university get out of Flanders. As a consequence, the government split the university and built a new city and new campus for the French-speaking part across the linguistic border, in a city now called Louvain-la-Neuve (New Leuven).

But the story doesn't end there. In 1980, Belgians divided their country into three language communities (Dutch, French, German) and into three regions (Brussels, Flanders, Wallonia). As a result of these language policies, Dutch is the official language in Flanders, and French is the official language in Wallonia (except in the Eastern Cantons, where German is spoken). When riding the trains in Belgium, the train conductor makes all announcements in French in Wallonia, but as soon as the linguistic border is crossed, the train conductor make all announcements in Dutch (except in Brussels, which is the only officially bilingual part of the nation). Switching languages is a matter of law, not simply linguistic ability.

While many Belgians may speak Dutch and French, the decision to speak one language or another in particular contexts communicates more than linguistic ability. Some Belgians believe it is rude not to speak the official language of the region one is in at the moment. Others believe that one should always try to speak the language of the other person to be accommodating and polite. Still others insist on speaking "their" language. Each of these communication decisions in a multilingual context reflects a range of political and social issues.

While some predict the end of the Belgian state due to these language "battles," others don't see it as that much of a problem. Some Belgians embrace bilingualism; others embrace monolingualism.[24] While not all multilingual nations are discussing dissolution, the language politics and policies of Belgium show how the history of language groups, economics relations, and political power are all interrelated. And not all multilingual nations create language territories, as Belgium has recently done. The majority of Belgians are Flemish, and Flanders is currently doing better economically; but the French-speaking Walloons previously were numerically larger and economically stronger. These differences make intercultural communication more difficult in Belgium.

SUMMARY

In this chapter, we explored many dimensions of language in intercultural communication. Linguists study four basic components of language as they investigate how language works: (1) phonology, the study of the sound system, (2) semantics, the study of meaning, (3) syntax, the study of structure, and (4) pragmatics, the study of the purposes and contexts of language in use.

We also discussed the Sapir-Whorf hypothesis and how the particular language we speak influences our perception. Language is powerful, but it does not totally determine our perception. Languages exhibit many cultural variations, both in communication style and in the rules of context. Cultural groups may emphasize speech or silence, as well as the importance of verbal (low-context) or nonverbal (high-context) communication. Two types of communication styles are indirect/direct and elaborate/understated. The context in which the communication occurs is a significant part of the meaning. People bridge these different communication styles in intercultural interactions by together creating a "third culture style" and improvising a communication performance.

We also examined the role of power in language. Dominant groups, consciously or unconsciously, develop communication systems that require nondominant groups to use communication that doesn't fit their lived experience. We identified nine strategies that cocultural group members may use in communication with dominant group members. The effects of power are also revealed in the use of labels, with the more powerful people in a society labeling the less powerful. Individuals who occupy powerful positions in a society often don't think about the way their positions are revealed in their communication.

Next, we discussed multilingualism. Individuals learn languages for different reasons, and the process is often a rewarding one. The complexities of moving between languages is facilitated by interpretation and translation, in which issues of equivalency and accuracy are crucial. Being a good translator or interpreter requires more than just fluency in two languages.

Finally, we looked at the situation in Belgium to explore some issues surrounding language policies and intercultural communication. The issue of what language should be spoken when, to whom, and why becomes quite complex.

BUILDING INTERCULTURAL SKILLS

1. Become more conscious of how you use language. Are you sending the messages you think you are sending? Sharpen your own skills by checking to see if people are interpreting messages the way you intend, particularly in intercultural situations. One way to do this is by asking others what they understood. If they didn't get your point, try paraphrasing.

2. Become more aware of others' verbal messages in intercultural encounters. Be aware of your own assumptions about others' language skills. For example, what kind of assumptions do you make when you hear accented English? Or a southern accent? Or an elaborated style? Or a succinct style? Practice your decoding skills. Check to see if others really meant to say what you understood. One way to do this is by asking others directly. However, remember that not everyone is comfortable with direct questions and answers. Practice other ways of trying to understand messages, such as observing or asking indirect questions.

3. Practice expanding your language repertoire in intercultural situations. When you speak with others whose first language is different from yours, speak more slowly, use easy-to-understand words and simple sentences, and avoid slang. If English isn't your first language, practice asking questions when you don't understand. And try to vary your own language patterns. If you tend to speak a lot, try listening. If you are often quiet, try speaking up.

4. Practice being flexible and adapting to others language style in intercultural encounters. In formal situations, use more formal language. Or if someone uses a more indirect style, try using a more indirect style.

5. Practice using labels that are preferred by group members. Gay or homosexual? African American or Black? White or Caucasian? If you aren't sure, investigate using appropriate communication strategies—after making sure that you have the kind of relationship where you can ask freely.

ACTIVITIES

1. *Regional language variations:* Meet in small groups with other class members and discuss variations in language use in different regions of the United States (accent, vocabulary, and so on). Identify perceptions that are associated with these variations.

2. *"Foreigner" labels:* Meet in small groups with other class members, and come up with a list of general labels used to refer to people from other countries who come to the United States (such as immigrants, aliens, or foreigners). For each label, identify a general connotation (positive, negative, mixed). Discuss how the connotations of these words may influence our perceptions of people from other countries. Would it make a difference if we referred to them as *guests* or *visitors?*

THE ONLINE LEARNING CENTER at www.mhhe.com/experiencing2 features self-quizzes, flashcards, and crossword puzzles based on the chapter's key terms and concepts.

www.mhhe.com/ experiencing2

ENDNOTES

1. Davis, W. (1999). Vanishing cultures. *National Geographic, 196*, pp. 62–89.
2. Genzer, D. *The disorientation manual 1987–88*. (A guide for American students studying at the University of St. Andrews, Scotland). St. Andrews, Scotland: University of St. Andrews.
3. Davis (1999), p. 65.
4. Hoijer, H. (1994). The Sapir-Whorf hypothesis. In L. Samovar & R. E. Porter (Eds.), *Intercultural communication: A reader* (pp. 194–200). Belmont, CA: Wadsworth.
5. Davis (1999), pp. 62–89.
6. Davies, I. R. L., & Sowden, P. T. (1998). A cross-cultural study of English and Setswana speakers on a colour triads task: A test of the Sapir-Whorf hypothesis. *British Journal of Psychology, 89*, 1–15.
7. Steinfatt, T. M. (1989). Linguistic relativity: Toward a broader view. In S. Ting-Toomey & F. Korzenny (Eds.), *Language, communication and culture* (pp. 35–78). Newbury Park, CA: Sage.
8. Giles, H., Coupland, N., & Wiemann, J. (1992). Talk is cheap . . . but "My word is my bond": Beliefs about talk. In K. Bolton & H. Kwok (Eds.), *Sociolinguistics today* (pp. 218–243). New York: Routledge.
9. Carbaugh, D. (1995). "I can't do that!" But I "can actually see around corners": American Indian students and the study of public "communication." In J. Lahtonen & L. Lahtinen (Eds.), *Critical perspectives on communication research and pedagogy* (pp. 215–234). St. Ingbert, Germany: Rohrig Universitätsverlag.
10. Kim, M.-S. (2002). *Non-Western perspectives on human communication*. Thousand Oaks, CA: Sage, p. 135.
11. Hall, E. T. (1976). *Beyond culture*. Garden City, NY: Doubleday, p. 79.
12. Gudykunst, W. B., & Ting-Toomey, S. (1988). *Culture and interpersonal communication*. Newbury Park, CA: Sage.
13. Kikoski, J. F., & Kikoski, C. K. (1999). *Reflexive communication in the culturally diverse workplace*. Westport, CT: Praeger, p. 67.
14. Bush, G. (2003, March 20). George Bush's address on the start of war. *The Guardian* (online). (www.guardian.co.uk/Iraq/Story/0,2763,918031,00.html)
15. Hussein, S. (2003, April 1). Strike at them, fight them. *The Guardian* (online). (www.guardian.co.uk/Iraq/Story/0,2763,927647,00.html)
16. Daniel, J. L., & Smitherman, G. (1990). How I got over: Communication dynamics in the Black community. In D. Carbaugh (Ed.), *Cultural communication and intercultural contact* (pp. 27–40). Hillsdale, NJ: Lawrence Erlbaum.
17. Casmir, F. L. (1999). Foundations for the study of intercultural communication based on a third culture building model. *International Journal of Intercultural Relations, 23*, 91–116.
18. Bateson, M. C. (1993). Joint performance across cultures: Improvisation in a Persian garden. *Text and Performance Quarterly, 13*, 119.
19. Orbe, M. P. (1998). *Constructing co-cultural theory: An explication of culture, power, and communication*. Thousand Oaks, CA: Sage.
20. Martin, J. N., Krizek, R. L., Nakayama, T. K., & Bradford, L. (1996). Exploring Whiteness: A study of self-labels for White Americans. *Communication Quarterly, 44*, 125–144.
21. Kaplan, A. (1993). *French lessons: A memoir*. Chicago: University of Chicago Press, p. 211.
22. Sue, S. (1992). Growing up in Mississippi. In J. F. J. Lee (Ed.), *Asian Americans* (pp. 3–9). New York: New Press.
23. Vinay, J. P., & Darbelnet, J. (1977). *Stylistique comparée du français et de l'anglais: Méthode de traduction*. Paris: Marcel Didier, p. 261.
24. Engels, P. (1998, April 24–30). La frontière à saute-mouton. *Le Vif/L'Express, 242*, 40–45.

CHAPTER SIX

Nonverbal Communication Issues

STUDY OBJECTIVES

After reading this chapter, you should be able to:
1. Define nonverbal communication.
2. Understand the difference between verbal and nonverbal communication.
3. Describe what nonverbal behavior communicates.
4. Identify cultural differences in nonverbal behavior.
5. Understand how nonverbal communication can reinforce cultural stereotypes.
6. Define and give examples of cultural space.
7. Describe the relationship between cultural identity and cultural space.
8. Describe the dynamic nature of cultural spaces.

KEY TERMS

adaptors
contact cultures
cultural spaces
deception
emblems
eye contact
facial expressions
gestures
home
illustrators
migration
monochronic

neighborhood
noncontact cultures
nonverbal
   communication
personal space
polychronic
regionalism
regulators
relational messages
silence
status
traveling

A police officer trainee is riding around in the squad car with her supervisor. It's her first day on the job, and she's trying to pay attention to all the things going on around them—messages coming across the police radio, sights and sounds in the street, languages she's never heard before, things she's never seen before. She's feeling very confused and scared. Suddenly, the supervisor stops the squad car, jumps out, shoves a guy against a wall, and takes a gun from him. The trainee wonders, "How did he know that?"[1]

In this case, the supervisor saw some nonverbal behavior that led him to believe the man was a threat to the public order. His skill at reading nonverbal behavior on the streets was perhaps critical to his and others' survival. Of course, examples of the importance of correctly understanding nonverbal behavior in intercultural communication are not usually so dramatic. Sometimes we use nonverbal behavior simply to help us get our messages across or to interpret the messages of others. For example, our student Yadira was camping with friends in Greece and wanted to ask permission to pitch their tent in a local farmer's meadow, but she didn't speak Greek. By drawing a picture of a tent and using lots of hand gestures, she was able to obtain permission. At other times, however, nonverbal communication can be problematic. For instance, David, an international student from Uruguay, thought his host family was angry with him because they never touched or hugged him. He was used to a lot of physical contact in greetings. It took him a while to realize that most people in the United States do not kiss or shake hands in everyday greetings.

You may never become a police officer or be an international student, but you certainly will find yourself in many intercultural communication situations. In this chapter, we discuss the importance of understanding nonverbal aspects of intercultural communication. We also explore specific nonverbal communication codes (personal space, gestures, facial expressions, and so on) and expressions of power in intercultural contexts. Finally, we investigate the concept of cultural space and the way people's cultural identities are shaped by the spaces (home, neighborhood, and so on) they occupy.

What Do You Think?

How would you categorize gang signs in terms of nonverbal communication? What kinds of things do they communicate? Do they mean different things to different kinds of people? To new gang members? To rival gang members? To teachers and parents? To police officers?

DEFINING NONVERBAL COMMUNICATION

What is not said is often as important as what is said. **Nonverbal communication** is communication through means other than language—for example, facial expression, personal space, eye contact, use of time, and conversational silence. Nonverbal communication also involves the notion of cultural space. **Cultural spaces** are the contexts that form our identity—where we grow up and where we live (not necessarily the actual homes and neighborhoods, but the cultural meanings created in these places).

Comparing Verbal and Nonverbal Communication

Both verbal and nonverbal communication are symbolic, both communicate meaning, and both are patterned—that is, are governed by rules that are determined by particular contexts and situations. And just as different societies have different spoken languages, so they have different nonverbal languages. However, there are some important differences between nonverbal and verbal communication in any culture. Let's look at some examples of these differences.

The following incident happened to Judith when she was teaching public speaking to a group of Japanese teachers of English. She explained how to write a speech and gave some tips for presenting the speech. The teachers seemed attentive, smiling and occasionally nodding. But when the time came for them to present their own speeches, she realized that they had many questions about how to prepare a speech and had not really understood her explanations. What she learned was that it is customary for students in Japan to not speak up in class unless they are called upon. In Japan, a nod means that one is listening—but not necessarily that one understands. As this example illustrates, rules for nonverbal communication vary among cultures and contexts.

Let's consider another example. Two U.S. American students attending school in France were hitchhiking to the university in Grenoble for the first day of classes. A French motorist picked them up and immediately started speaking English to them. They wondered how he knew they spoke English. Later, they took a train to Germany. The conductor walked into their compartment and scolded them in English for putting their feet on the opposite seat. Again, they wondered how he had known that they spoke English. As these examples show, nonverbal communication includes more than gestures. Even our appearance can communicate loudly; in fact, the students' very appearance no doubt was a good clue to their national identity. As these examples also show, nonverbal behavior operates at a subconscious level. We rarely think about how we stand, what hand gestures we use, what facial expressions we're using, and so on. Occasionally, someone points out such behaviors, which brings them to a conscious level.

When misunderstandings arise, we are more likely to question our verbal communication than our nonverbal communication. We can use different words to explain what we mean, or look up words in a dictionary, or ask someone to explain unfamiliar words. But it is more difficult to identify and correct nonverbal miscommunications or misperceptions.

Learning Nonverbal Behavior   Whereas we learn rules and meanings for language behavior in grammar and spelling lessons, we learn nonverbal meanings and behaviors more unconsciously. No one explains, "When you talk with someone you like, lean forward, smile, and touch the person frequently, because that will communicate that you really care about him or her." In the United States, these behaviors often communicate positive meanings.[2] But if someone does not display these behaviors, we are likely to react quite differently.

Sometimes we learn strategies for nonverbal communication. For example, you may have been taught to shake hands firmly when you meet someone, or you

Surf's Up!

John Bulwer was one of the first people to study nonverbal communication, way back in 1649. He is quoted as arguing that facial expressions are important to understand because "they are the neerest and immediate organs of the voluntaire or impetuous motions of the mind." Check out the website mambo.ucsc.edu/ps1/bulwer.html to see some of Bulwer's early explorations into nonverbal communication. Do you agree that nonverbal communication reflects internal feelings? Are his ideas relevant in cross-cultural situations?

may have learned that a limp handshake indicates a person with a weak character. Likewise, many young women learn to cross their legs at the ankles and to keep their legs together when they sit. In this sense, we learn nonverbal behaviors as part of being socialized about appropriate behavior.

Coordinating Nonverbal and Verbal Behaviors   Nonverbal behaviors can reinforce, substitute for, or contradict verbal behaviors. When we shake our heads and say "no," we are reinforcing verbal behavior. When we point instead of saying "over there," we are substituting nonverbal behavior for verbal communication. In the example of Yadira and the tent, Yadira's drawing and gestures substituted for verbal communication. And when we tell a friend, "I can't wait to see you," and then don't show up at the friend's house, the nonverbal behavior is contradicting the verbal behavior.

Because nonverbal communication operates at a more subconscious level, we tend to think that people have less control over their nonverbal behavior. Therefore, we often think of nonverbal behaviors as containing the "real" message. Have you ever received a compliment from someone you thought was not being sincere? You may have thought the person insincere because her nonverbal communication contradicted the spoken words. Perhaps she did not speak very forcefully or was not smiling very much. Perhaps she was giving other nonverbal clues indicating that she did not really mean what she was saying.

What Nonverbal Behavior Communicates

Nonverbal behavior sends relational messages and communicates status and deception.[3] Although language is effective at communicating specific information, nonverbal communication often communicates **relational messages** about how we really feel about the person, and so on. For example, when you first meet someone, he may say, "Glad to meet you," but he also communicates nonverbally how he feels about you. He may smile, make direct eye contact, and mirror your body language—all very positive messages in U.S. culture. Or perhaps he does not make direct eye contact, does not smile, and does not give any other nonverbal cues that indicate enthusiasm. One difficulty is that nonverbal clues are not always easy to interpret. And it is dangerous to assume that, every time someone doesn't smile or make direct eye contact, he is communicating lack of interest. It may be that he is preoccupied, and his nonverbal message is not meant the way you interpret it.

There are three guidelines to prevent hasty interpretations of nonverbal behaviors. The first is to think about the context. What is going on in the situation that might help you interpret someone's nonverbal message? For example, if someone has her arms folded and does not make eye contact after meeting you, it may mean that she is not enthusiastic about meeting you. But it also may mean that the room is cold or that she is focusing on something else at the moment. So always remember to think about the context.

The second guideline is to consider the person's other nonverbal behaviors. Don't interpret nonverbal behaviors in isolation. If the person has her arms

Info Bites

Did you know that the way a teacher looks may be just as important as how she or he teaches? According to one research study, good looks play an important role in how teachers are evaluated by students. In this study, better-looking professors got consistently higher ratings on their students' course evaluations. This leads some researchers to call into question the practice of using student evaluations as a factor in setting teacher pay scales and promotion. Others acknowledge that this is a fact of life—attractive people often receive more social and economic rewards than their less attractive counterparts. (SOURCE: Golab, A. (2003, October 23) Why good-looking profs get better grades from students, *Chicago Sun-Times*, p. 4.)

Tattoos and body piercing communicate different meanings to different audiences. Think about the inferences people can draw from these nonverbal communication markers about social status. For example, most of us would be shocked if the president was tattooed and pierced.

folded but is also smiling, making direct eye contact, and leaning toward you, then she probably is sending a positive message. So, while each message carries some relational meaning, we must be cautious about being too hasty in interpreting this message.

A third guideline is to remember to consider the verbal messages along with the nonverbal messages. If a person is talking in a pleasant voice and standing with arms folded, the overall relationship message is likely positive. On the other hand, if the person is saying negative things to you, standing with arms folded, and averting eye gaze, then it is likely that the overall message is a more negative one. Thus, you really have to read the whole message and not just part of it.[4]

Nonverbal behavior also communicates **status**—the relative position a person occupies in an organizational or social setting. For example, a supervisor may be able to touch subordinates, but it usually is unacceptable for subordinates to touch a supervisor. Expansive gestures and control over space are associated with high status; conversely, holding one's body in a tight, clenched position communicates low status. For example, in meetings in most U.S. American business contexts, the people who make the grandest gestures and who take up the most space generally are the ones who have the highest status. This might be one reason women generally carry books close to their bodies and sit with their feet and legs together; by contrast, men generally carry books under their arms and tend to sprawl when sitting.

Nonverbal behavior also communicates **deception.** Early researchers believed that some nonverbal behaviors—such as avoiding eye contact and touching or rubbing the face—indicated lying. But more recent research shows that deception is usually communicated verbally. Only a few nonverbal behaviors, such as dilated pupils, rapid blinking, and higher voice pitch, are consistently related to deception. And each person has his or her own distinct way of communicating deception.[5] It is important to remember that most nonverbal communication about relational messages, status, and deception happens at a subconscious level. For this reason, it plays an important role in intercultural interactions. We may communicate messages that we aren't even aware of—as in the examples at the beginning of this section.

CULTURAL VARIATIONS IN NONVERBAL BEHAVIOR

How do culture, ethnicity, and gender influence nonverbal communication patterns? How universal is most nonverbal communication? Do people in most countries communicate in the same way nonverbally? In this section, we look for cultural variations in nonverbal behavior that may serve as tentative guidelines to help us communicate better with others.

There is something very basic, and perhaps universal, about much of our nonverbal behavior—particularly our **facial expressions,** facial gestures that convey emotions and attitudes. For example, the more researchers learn about animal behavior, particularly that of nonhuman primates like chimps and gorillas, the more similarities they find between them and humans, although animal communication appears to be less complex.[6] That is, humans are capable of many more gestures and facial expressions than are animals. Apparently, there are also some nonverbal behaviors that are innate, that we don't have to learn. For example, children who are blind usually make the same facial expressions as sighted children—even though they can't see to learn how to make these expressions.[7]

There are many universal facial gestures, including the eyebrow flash (raising the eyebrow to communicate recognition), the nose wrinkle (indicating slight social distancing), and the "disgust face" (sending a strong signal of social repulsion). In fact, at least six basic emotions—happiness, sadness, disgust, fear, anger, and surprise—are communicated by facial expressions in much the same way in most societies. The fact that facial expressions for these emotions are recognized by most cultural groups as having the same meaning seems to suggest some innate, universal basis for these behaviors.[8]

However, nonverbal communication also varies in many ways from culture to culture. The evoking stimuli, or that which causes the nonverbal behavior, may vary from one culture to another. Smiling, for example, is universal. But

Surf's Up!

Take a look at the Automated Face Analysis website (www.cs.cmu.edu/ ~face/home.htm). Do you believe that these kinds of facial expressions not only are similar across cultures but can be accurately deciphered by a computer?

what prompts a person to smile may be culture-specific. In some cultures, seeing a baby may cause people to smile; in other cultures, one is not supposed to smile a lot at babies. Judith's Navajo friend told her that in the Navajo Nation the first person to cause a baby to smile has to throw a party for baby and family, so people don't always want to cause a baby to smile!

There are variations in the rules for nonverbal communication and the contexts in which it takes place. For example, people kiss in most cultures, but there is variation in who kisses whom and in what contexts. When French friends greet each other, they often kiss each other on both cheeks but never on the mouth. Friends in the United States usually kiss each other on greeting only after a long absence, and this is usually accompanied by a hug. The rules for kissing also vary along gender lines. In this section, we examine how nonverbal communication varies from culture to culture.

Nonverbal Codes

Personal Space   **Personal space** is the "bubble" around each of us that marks the territory between ourselves and others. How big your bubble is depends on your cultural background. In some cultures, people stand very close together to talk, while in others, they feel a need to be farther apart when talking. This difference in personal space rules can cause misunderstandings and even some discomfort in intercultural interactions. For example, in one university, there were reports of miscommunication between Arab and U.S. American students. The Arab students complained that the American students were distant and rude, while the U.S. American students characterized the Arab students as pushy, arrogant, and impolite. The problem was that the two groups were operating with different rules concerning personal space. The Arab students were accustomed to standing closer together when talking, while the U.S. American students had been raised to do just the opposite.

In fact, some cultural groups are identified as contact cultures, and others as noncontact cultures. **Contact cultures** are those in which people stand closer together while talking, make more direct eye contact, touch frequently, and speak in louder voices. Societies in South America and southern Europe are identified as contact cultures. By contrast, those in northern Europe, North America, East Asia, and the Far East are **noncontact cultures,** in which people tend to stand farther apart when conversing, maintain less eye contact, and touch less often.[9] Jolanta, a Polish student of ours, talked about her first experience abroad, as the guest of an Italian family, and being overwhelmed by the close physical contact and intense nonverbal behavior: "Almost every aspect of this family's interactions made me anxious and insecure. This included the extreme close personal distance, touching and speaking loudly, all of which was quite overwhelming." Figure 6.1 shows the "immediacy orientations" of selected countries and regions.

Is it possible that the degree of contact is affected by geography and climate? It is interesting that many high-contact cultures are in warmer places, located

Pop Culture Spotlight

Anthropologist E. T. Hall argues that art helps us order our cultural universe, and this includes our sense of space, or proxemics. A recent exhibit at the art museum in Phoenix focused on uses and depictions of the American flag. There were flags in toilets and flags treated with respect. To write comments about the exhibit in the book, visitors had to step on a giant American flag on the floor. That is a very literal version of the way art affects our use of personal space.

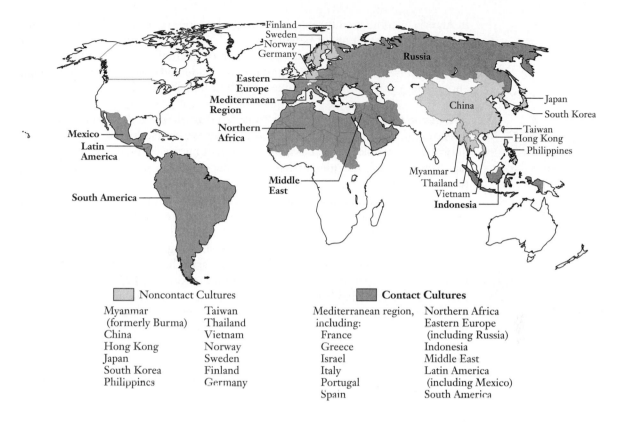

Figure 6.1   Immediacy orientations of selected countries and regions.

closer to the equator. In contrast, most low-contact cultures are in cooler climates. And even within many Northern countries, Southerners are more nonverbally expressive and interpersonally oriented than northerners. Think of the
general impression of U.S. Southerners as being warmer, hospitable and open,
whereas New Englanders have the reputation for being more reserved and less
demonstrative. The same is true for people in the south and north of France.
One explanation might be that where it's colder, people spend more time dressing, storing food, and planning for winter (being task oriented), whereas people
in warmer climates have access to each other all year round.[10]

Of course, we cannot say categorically that these patterns are found everywhere. Many countries in Asia, for example, have warm climates and are considered low contact. Here, the influence of Confucianism with emphasis on self-
control and proper behavior may be a greater influence.

Of course, many other factors besides culture determine how close together
or far apart people stand. Gender, age, ethnicity, the context of the interaction,
and the topic of discussion all influence the use of personal space. For example,

in Algeria (a contact culture), gender might be more important than nationality in determining amounts of personal space. Unmarried young women and men rarely stand close together, touch each other, or maintain direct eye contact with each other. However, young men commonly hold hands with their male friends, and young women will do the same with their female friends.

Eye Contact   **Eye contact** is often considered an element of personal space because it regulates interpersonal distance. Direct eye contact shortens the distance between two people, while a lack of eye contact increases the distance. Eye contact communicates meanings related to respect and status, and it often regulates turn taking in conversations.

Patterns of eye contact vary from culture to culture. In many societies, avoiding eye contact communicates respect and deference, although this may vary from context to context. For many Americans, maintaining eye contact communicates that one is paying attention or showing respect. But a Navajo student told us that the hardest thing for her to learn when she left the Navajo Nation to study at Arizona State was to remember to look her professors in the eye. Her whole life, she had been taught to show respect by avoiding eye contact.

When they speak with others, most U.S. Americans look away from their listeners most of the time. They might look at their listeners every 10 or 15 seconds. And when a speaker is finished taking a turn, he or she looks directly at the listener to signal completion. However, some cultural groups within the United States use even less eye contact while they speak. For example, some Native Americans tend to avert their eyes during conversation.

Facial Expression   As noted previously, some facial expressions seem to express the same emotions all over the world. However, it's important to recognize that there is variation in many aspects of facial expressions. A smile may universally indicate pleasure and happiness, and a frown may indicate sadness, but there is a lot of variation in what causes someone to smile or frown. For example, in the United States, meeting someone for the first time may call for a smile, while in other cultures, it is better to look serious. By contrast, a snake may call for a facial expression of disgust in some cultural contexts, and in others may call for a smile at the prospect of a delicious meal.

The rules that regulate facial expressions also may vary. Thus, a greeting may call for a wide smile in some cultures and a much more subdued or less expressive smile in others. Europeans often remark that U.S. Americans seem to smile too much. For instance, a Polish student of ours observed that "Polish facial expressions are almost always neutral when communicating with strangers. For example, strangers are not expected to smile or to express any emotion; otherwise, they would be perceived as interfering or even dangerous."

Gestures   **Gestures** are simply arm and hand movements that communicate nonverbally. There are at least four different kinds of gestures: emblems, illustrators, regulators, and adaptors.[11] **Emblems** are those gestures that have a

What Do You Think?

If you like someone in an Internet chatroom, how might you let that person know? In cyberspace we have adapted to a lack of visual cues by creating nonverbal codes that act as facial expressions for such things as kissing and showing other forms of affection. Many of us are beginning to recognize signs such as :-) and :-(), which can be read as "I'm smiling right now" and "I'm sending you a kiss." Do you recognize or interpret these signs similarly? What about (()):**, which is often interpreted as "Sending you lots of hugs and kisses." Do you know of any special kinds of emoticons only used in some online communities, or are facial expressions on the Internet universal?

specific verbal translation. For example, when you wave your hand as someone is leaving, it means good-bye. Or when you give "the finger," it is interpreted as an insult. There are at least a hundred identifiable gestures in our culture. Of course, other cultures have their own emblems. For example, in India, a slow shaking of the head means "yes" (not "no"). And in some ways, these are the easiest gestures to understand cross-culturally, because they are easy to reproduce. When people are in a foreign country and do not know the language, they often resort to emblems. For example, our student Dave was visiting in Mexico with some friends, none of whom spoke much Spanish. They were trying to find a hotel. "We were trying to communicate that we needed somewhere to stay and the man couldn't understand us and started acting very frustrated. We started using nonverbal gestures—showing signs of sleep—and he understood and showed us a place to stay. Everything turned out okay."

More difficult types of gesture to understand in intercultural communication are the illustrators and regulators. **Illustrators** are all those gestures that go along with our speech. Have you ever noticed that there seems to be a "flow" to people's verbal communication—when they are talking, their gestures are usually very synchronized? For example, when emphasizing a point by shaking a finger, the speaker stops shaking the finger at the end of the sentence. And it all seems very natural. In fact, symptoms of mental illness are sometimes revealed in people's gesturing behavior; their gestures may seem "jerky" or seem not to go with their speech.

Of course, different cultural groups use different types and amounts of illustrators. Italians are often characterized as "talking a lot with their hands," or using a lot of illustrators. Another student, Marjorie, who traveled to Italy, noticed this: "In watching people in the streets, it always seemed like they must be angry at each other—all the waving of hands and gesturing." Actually, it is merely the custom there to use a lot of illustrating gestures. Other cultural groups, like the Chinese, may use fewer illustrators. Of course, the number of illustrators used may also be related to a person's family background or individual preferences. The important thing to remember is that, if you encounter someone who uses many illustrators, it doesn't mean that he's angry; and if someone uses few illustrators, it doesn't mean that she's not into the conversation.

We rarely think about it, but much of our conversation is regulated by nonverbal gestures, called **regulators.** Thus, when someone tries to interrupt while we are talking, we may put out our hand, indicating that we aren't finished speaking. Greeting and leave-taking are usually indicated by regulating gestures. For example, when we greet someone, we may shake their hands or hug them. When we get ready to leave, we often gather our stuff together. It is important to remember that each language has a somewhat unique set of regulators. For example, in Japan, turn taking is regulated more by pauses than by gestures, so that a brief pause in the conversation indicates that the next person may talk. In fact, Japanese people remark that it is sometimes difficult to jump into an American conversation because they are waiting for the regulating "pause" that never comes.

Info Bites

Did you know that in Mexico it is considered a challenge when you put your hands on your hips? That in France, when you kiss someone's cheeks, you should start on the right side? That in Britain and Thailand people point with their heads? That in Poland it is acceptable for a stranger to join you at your restaurant table for dinner? That winking has no meaning in Japan? Or that yawning is considered rude in Argentina? (SOURCE: *The Complete Idiot's Guide to Cultural Etiquette*)

Surf's Up!

Do your gestures have legal status? Read the short paper about legal gestures to find out (www.law.pitt.edu/ hibbitts/re_mem.htm).

The final type of gesture is **adaptors,** which are related to managing our emotions. For example, we may tap our feet or fingers when we're nervous, or rub our eyes when we feel like crying, or clench our fists when we're angry. Again, from a cultural perspective, it's important to recognize that the adaptors we use are part of our particular cultural upbringing, and that other people may use other types of adaptors to manage or reflect their emotions.

Time Orientation There are many cultural variations regarding how people understand and use time. One way to understand these variations is to look at the differences between monochronic and polychronic time orientations.[12] People who have a **monochronic** concept of time, like most people in the United States,

Holidays are often filled with nonverbal symbols that communicate important meanings to the participants. The objects in this Latino family's *offrenda* or altar are an important part of their "Dia de los Muertos" (All Souls Day) holiday and help them remember family members who have died. How does your family remember those who have died?

regard time as a commodity: Time can be gained, lost, spent, wasted, or saved. In this orientation, time is linear, with events happening one after another. In general, monochronic cultures value punctuality, completion of tasks, and adherence to schedules. For instance, most college staff and faculty in the United States maintain a monochronic orientation to time. Classes, meetings, and office appointments start when scheduled. Faculty members see one student at a time, hold one meeting at a time, and keep appointments except when faced with an emergency. Typical family problems are considered poor reasons for not fulfilling academic obligations—for both faculty and students.

By contrast, people with a **polychronic** orientation conceptualize time as more holistic, perhaps more circular: Many events can happen at once. U.S. American businesspeople often complain that meetings in the Middle East do not start "on time," that people socialize during meetings, and that meetings may be canceled because of personal obligations. Often, tasks are accomplished because of personal relationships, not in spite of them.

Many international business negotiations, technical assistance projects, and team projects fail because of differences in time orientation. One of our students, Rachel, told us that she was in a chemistry study group in high school, and one of the group members, who was from Spain, continually showed up late for meetings and would never apologize. Rachel became annoyed and eventually said something concerning the issue. As Rachel recounts it, "She then apologized and explained to me what 'time' meant to her in her culture. I know now that she was operating under a polychronic time frame while mine was monochronic."

International students and business personnel often complain that U.S. Americans seem too busy and too tied to their schedules; they suggest that U.S. Americans do not care enough about relationships and about the personal aspects of living. An international student of ours complained, "It is so hard to get used to the fast pace of college life here. It seems that people are too busy to enjoy other people and relationships; they are just anxious and always worried about being on time and getting thing done."

Some ethnic groups in the United States may also have a polychronic time orientation. Chicano college students often find that their family and social obligations, viewed as very important at home, are not as important at the university. As one student, Lucia, said, "It's hard to make sure everyone in my family is taken care of and to get my school work done at the same time. Sometimes I have to take my grandmother to the doctor, go grocery shopping with my mom, help my aunt with her Medicare problems, and still somehow find the time to attend class and get my homework done."

The implications for intercultural misunderstandings between people with these different time orientations are significant. In technical assistance projects overseas, for example, coworkers with different time orientations can become very frustrated with one another, as revealed in this summary of how monochronic Western workers and polychronic workers from Madagascar (Africa) viewed each other.[13]

Surf's Up!

What are acceptable and unacceptable nonverbals among cocultures in the United States? One website on cross-cultural communication (www. nwrel.org/cnorse/ booklets/ccc/table4. html) lists some differences between African Americans and Anglo Americans. For which group is touching another's hair offensive? For which group are hats and sunglasses appropriate to be worn indoors? For which group is interruption rude? What other cocultural nonverbal communication differences can you think of?

Monochronics on Polychronics	Polychronics on Monochronics
They never plan for the future.	They are always in a hurry.
They are losing time and money.	They don't give priority to the art of living.
They fail to plan and so cause problems.	They are obsessed with money.
	They do not give priority to people.

It takes a great deal of patience and cross-cultural understanding to work together in these situations.

Silence   As we noted in Chapter 5, cultural groups may vary in the relative emphasis placed on speaking and on **silence**. In most U.S. American contexts, silence is not highly valued. Particularly in developing relationships, silence communicates awkwardness and can make people feel uncomfortable. One of the major reasons for communicating verbally in initial interactions with people is to reduce uncertainty. In U.S. American contexts, people employ active uncertainty reduction strategies, such as asking questions.

However, in many other cultural contexts, people reduce uncertainty by more passive strategies, such as remaining silent, observing, and perhaps asking a third party about someone's behavior. And silences can be as meaningful as language. For example, silence in Japan is not simply the absence of sound or a pause in the conversation that must be filled. Silence can convey respect for the person who has spoken, or it can be a way of unifying people. Silence in Japan has been compared to the white space in brush paintings or calligraphy scrolls: "A picture is not richer, more accurate or more complete if such spaces are filled in. To do so would be to confuse and detract from what is presented."[14]

And silences can have many meanings in various contexts. In a classic study on the rules for silence among the Western Apache in Arizona, researcher Keith Basso identified five contexts in which silence was appropriate: meeting strangers, courting, seeing friends after a long absence, being with people who are grieving, and getting cursed out. Some of these patterns hold true for other Native American groups, like the Navajo and the Yaqui, as well. Being shy around strangers is directly related to the belief that forming social relationships is a serious matter that calls for caution, careful judgment, and plenty of time.[15]

In courting among Western Apache, individuals can go without speaking for a very long time. Similarly, encounters between individuals who have been apart for a long time may call for silence. For example, after a child has returned from boarding school, the parents may remain silent for a while to see if the returning child has changed for the worse.

The Western Apache also believe that silence is an appropriate response to an individual who becomes enraged and starts shouting insults and criticisms. The silence acknowledges that the angry person is not really him- or herself—that the person has temporarily taken leave of his or her senses, is not responsible, and therefore may be dangerous. In this instance, silence is a safe way to

Info Bites

If you are standing in the doorway to a home or office, are you inside or outside? Germans consider the doorway part of the interior space, so an intrusion into these areas will cause problems. By contrast, in an Arab country, it is perfectly acceptable to push and elbow someone out of a desired spot in a public place. How do you think a typical German tourist would fare in Egypt?

TABLE 6.1   Interesting Nonverbal Behaviors

Brazil: The Brazilian considers the OK sign in the United States (made with the thumb and forefinger) as obscene.

China: Chinese always use both hands when passing a gift or food.

Kenya: Pointing with an index finger is very insulting.

Samoa: It is rude for a person standing to sway while having a conversation.

Fiji: Crossed arms is a sign of respect when talking.

Italy: The American gesture for one (raising the index finger) means two in Italy.

Greece and Turkey: When saying "no," it is expressed with a small nod of the head upward.

Japan: Laughter may signify embarrassment instead of amusement in certain situations.

Thailand: Thais believe a spirit lives at the doorsill of a house, so one never pauses on the doorsill.

Source: M. Mancini (2003). *Selling destinations: Geography for the travel professional*, 4th ed. Clifton Park, NY: Thomson/Delmar Learning.

deal with the individual. Being with people who are sad or bereaved also calls for silence, for several reasons. First, talking is unnecessary because everyone knows how it feels to be sad. Second, intense grief, like intense rage, produces temporary personality changes and personal instability, so it is better to remain silent until the emotion subsides. Otherwise, the individual is likely to project a negative self-image. Table 6.1 lists some cultural variations in nonverbal behaviors, but we must be careful not to assume that every member of that cultural group exhibits the same nonverbal behaviors, nor that we don't have to consider the context in which these nonverbal behaviors may be used.

Basso hypothesizes that the underlying commonality in all these social situations is that participants see their relationships in these contexts as ambiguous and/or unpredictable, and silence is an appropriate response to uncertainty and unpredictability. He also hypothesizes that this same contextual rule may apply to other cultural groups. It is also possible that in many communities silence is associated not just with uncertainty, but also with social situations in which a known and unequal distribution of power exists among participants.[16] For example, in work contexts in Japan, being silent and listening very respectfully to one's boss would be the appropriate response, whereas a U.S. American supervisor might admire the subordinate who "speaks right up."

Cultural Variation or Stereotype?

As noted previously, one of the problems with identifying cultural variations in nonverbal codes is that it is tempting to overgeneralize these variations and to stereotype groups of people. For example, we have to be very careful when comparing Japanese and Western attitudes toward silence. Those familiar with life in

Info Bites

The Nazis believed that different races had different genetically determined gestural repertoires. For example, they thought that they could ferret out persons with some Jewish blood simply by observing their gestures. In response, Franz Boaz and his colleagues at Columbia University began to study gestural patterns to combat the Nazi idea. This was the beginning of serious work on nonverbal communication in the United States. (Source: Randall Harrison, *Beyond Words*)

Japan have observed that the television is on nonstop in many Japanese homes, and Zen gardens offer tape-recorded messages about the beauty to be seen. So, although silence might be a cultural ideal, things may differ in practice. In specific situations, such as mother-daughter relationships, there may be more emphasis on silence than in comparable U.S. American situations. Still, we should take these warnings about the dangers of overgeneralizations seriously.[17]

Cultural variations are tentative guidelines that we can use in intercultural interaction. They should serve as examples, to help us understand that there is a great deal of variation in nonverbal behavior. Even if we can't anticipate how someone's behavior may differ from our own, we can be flexible when we do encounter differences in, say, how close a person positions him- or herself, uses eye contact, or conceptualizes time.

Prejudice is often based on nonverbal aspects of behavior. That is, the negative prejudgment is triggered by physical appearances or physical behavior. For example, even college students' evaluations of professors' teaching may be subtly influenced by their professors' physical appearances. A recent research study showed that college students consistently rate less attractive professors as less skilled in teaching. Perhaps more interesting was that students rated both female and minority professors lower overall than their White, male peers. As one psychologist explained, "It just shows that white, native-speaking males are still the norm for professors in students' eyes."[18]

Teachers also may be influenced by the physical appearance of their students. Some educators suggest that decisions to place African American students in special education classes may be partially related to administrators' negative evaluations of their posture and walk. When African American high school students don't walk the typical "White walk" (erect posture and steady stride), and instead deliberately swagger with bent posture, head tilted to one side, and one foot dragging, White teachers tend to perceive them as aggressive, low achievers and potential candidates for special education programs. In fact, 21 percent of African Americans are in special education even though they represent only 16.8 percent of the U.S. public school population.[19] Similarly, immigrant Asian children and some Asian Americans are sometimes negatively evaluated and discriminated against because of their cultural practice of remaining quiet in the classroom to show respect for the teacher.[20]

An even more extreme example of the importance of physical appearances in expressions of prejudice is the tragic killing of a Sikh in Arizona four days after the World Trade Center attack in September 2001. Balbir Singh Sodhi owned a gas station in Mesa, Arizona. He was shot and killed by a 44-year-old White man, Frank Silva Roque, who took him to be an Arab because he wore a turban and beard as part of his Sikh faith. After shooting Sodhi, Roque shot at another gas station, where the clerk was a man of Lebanese descent. Continuing his rampage, Roque then shot at the home of an Afghan family.[21]

Two years later, again in Arizona, Avtar (Singh) Chiera, a Sikh and small-business owner, was waiting for his son to pick him up after parking his semi in North Phoenix. While he was waiting, two White men pulled up in a small, red pickup truck and started yelling at him. They then opened fire, wounding him.

Cultures differ widely in the systems of nonverbal symbols that they use. This woman has a bindra—a dot on her forehead. People use many other nonverbal symbols to mark their cultural identities, including attire, hairstyles, jewelry, and tattoos.

His son found him bleeding in the parking lot. "Sikhs were targeted soon after the September 11, 2001 terror attacks because ignorant White vigilantes identified them with Osama bin Laden because of their turbans and flowing beard," Guru Roop Kaur Khalsa, a spokeswoman for the Sikh community in Arizona, said. "Many Arizonans have stood up for the Sikh community since Sodhi's killing but Sikhs will need to continue to educate people."[22]

As in many other instances of hate crimes, the victim's appearance was more significant than his specific cultural heritage. From these kinds of experiences with prejudice, people start to develop "a map" that tells them where they belong and where they are likely to be rejected. They may even start to avoid places where and situations in which they do not feel welcome.[23]

DEFINING CULTURAL SPACE

What are cultural spaces, and what do they have to do with intercultural communication? Cultural space relates to the way communication constructs meanings of various places. For example, at the beginning of this book, we provided some background information about ourselves and the cultural places where we grew up. These particular cultural spaces are important in understanding our identities. There is nothing in the rolling hills of Delaware and Pennsylvania or the red clay of Georgia that has biologically determined who Judith and Tom are. However, our identities and our views of ourselves are formed, in part, in relation to cultural places—the mid-Atlantic region for Judith and the South for Tom. Each region has its own histories and ways of life that help us understand who we are. Our decision to tell you something about the cultural spaces we grew up in was meant to communicate something about who we think we are.

The meanings of cultural spaces are dynamic and ever-changing. Therefore, the Delaware that Judith left behind and the Georgia that Tom left behind are no doubt much different now. In addition, the relations between people's cultural spaces and identities are negotiated in complex ways. Thus, because someone is from India does not mean that his or her identity and communication practices are always and only "Indian." Let's look at some specific cultural spaces that we can all identify with—our homes and our neighborhoods.

Cultural Identity and Cultural Space

Home   Cultural spaces are important influences on how we think about ourselves and others. One of the earliest cultural spaces we experience is our **home**—the immediate cultural context for our upbringing. As noted previously, nonverbal communication involves issues of status, and the home is not exempt from issues of status. For example, the social class of an American home is often expressed nonverbally—from the way the lawn is cared for, to the kinds of cars in the driveway, to the way the television is situated, to the kinds of furniture in the home. These signs of social class are not always so obvious for all social class positions, but they often provide important clues about social class.[24]

Even if our home does not reflect the social class we wish to be in, we often identify with it strongly. We often model our own lives on the way things were done in our childhood homes. Although this is not always the case, the home can be a place of safety and security. African American writer bell hooks remembers:

> When I was a young girl the journey across town to my grandmother's house was one of the most intriguing experiences. . . . I remember this journey not just because of the stories I would hear. It was a movement away from the segregated blackness of our community into a poor white neighborhood [where] we would have to pass that terrifying whiteness—those white faces on porches staring down on us with hate. . . . Oh! that feeling of safety, of arrival, of homecoming when we finally reached the edges of her yard.[25]

"Home," of course, is not the same as the physical location it occupies, nor the building (the house) on that location. Home is variously defined as specific addresses, cities, states, regions, and even nations. Although we might have historical ties to a particular place, not everyone feels the same relationship between those places and their own identities.

Some people have feelings of fondness for the region of the country where they grew up. Another writer talks about his relationship to his hometown in South Carolina:

> Now that I no longer live there, I often think longingly of my hometown of Charleston. My heart beats faster and color rushes to my cheek whenever I hear someone mentioning her; I lean over and listen, for even hearing the name casts a spell. Mirages rise up, and I am as overcome and drenched in images as a runner just come from running. I see the steeples, the streets, the lush setting.[26]

But others feel less positive about where they come from. A writer who grew up in Texas expresses his ambiguous feelings about the state: "What I feel when I fly from California to Texas must be what an expatriate from any country feels returning to his childhood home. . . . Texas is home, but Texas is also a country whose citizenship I voluntarily renounced."[27] The meanings of Texas no longer "fit" this writer's sense of who he is or who he wants to be.

The relationships between various places and our identities are complex. These three writers have different feelings about their "home," which highlights the complexity that exists between identity and location. Where you come from and where you grew up contributes to how you see yourself, to your current identity. Many people experience ambivalence about the regions of the country where they grew up. They may have fond memories, but they may now also see the area in a new way—as perhaps provincial, or conservative, or segregated.

Neighborhood   One significant type of cultural space that emerged in U.S. cities is the **neighborhood,** a living area defined by its own cultural identity, especially an ethnic or racial one. Cities typically developed segregated neighborhoods, reflecting common attitudes of prejudice and discrimination, as well as people's desire to live among people like themselves. Malcolm X, in his autobiography, tells of the strict laws that governed where his family could live after their house burned down: "My father prevailed on some friends to clothe and house us temporarily; then he moved us into another house on the outskirts of East Lansing. In those days Negroes weren't allowed after dark in East Lansing proper . . . where Michigan State University is located."[28]

The phenomenon of "Whites-only" areas has been very common in U.S. history. These types of neighborhoods are good examples of how power influences intercultural contact. In these segregated neighborhoods, certain cultural groups defined who got to live where and dictated the rules by which other groups had to live. These rules were enforced through legal means and by harassment. For Malcolm X and bell hooks, these lines of segregation were clear and unmistakable. One of our older students also recalls these times:

> I lived 9 of my first 12 years in Miami, Florida, where segregation and discrimination were a way of life. Schools and housing were segregated, and "colored" people had to ride at the back of the bus. . . . When I was about 7 or 8, I saw a man get hit by a car as he was crossing the street.

Surf's Up!
Explore the Hand-speak website (www.handspeak.com). Take the tour and find out how to say "Hello," "Good-bye," and "Friend" in ASL. How is sign language similar to and different from other forms of nonverbal communication?

Many neighborhoods are marked by their ethnic and religious character. While there may have been laws that created these kinds of neighborhoods in the past, what are the advantages and disadvantages of sustaining these neighborhoods today?

They called an ambulance, but when it came they wouldn't take the man to the hospital because they had sent the wrong "color" of ambulance. I don't remember if the man was Black or White; I only recall how angry I was. . . . Later we moved to California, where segregation of Whites and Blacks was accomplished covertly by "White flight"—when African Americans moved into a neighborhood, most of the Whites moved out.

In San Francisco, different racial politics constructed and isolated Chinatown. Until racial covenants were lifted in 1947, Chinese Americans were forced to live in Chinatown. The boundaries that marked the acceptable place for Chinese Americans were clear and were carefully guarded through violence:

> The sense of being physically sealed within the boundaries of Chinatown was impressed on the few immigrants coming into the settlement by frequent stonings which occurred as they came up Washington or Clay Street from the piers. It was perpetuated by attacks of white toughs in the adjacent North Beach area and downtown around Union Square, who amused themselves by beating Chinese who came into these areas. "In those days, the boundaries were from Kearny to Powell, and from California to Broadway. If you ever passed them and went out there, the white kids would throw stones at you," Wei Bat Liu told us.[29]

In contrast to Malcolm X's family being excluded from living in East Lansing, the Chinese of San Francisco were forced to live in a marked-off territory. Yet another system of segregation developed in Savannah, Georgia, around 1900. There, Chinese immigrants were advised by other Chinese Americans to live apart from each other, rather than settle in ethnic enclaves, because of the negative experiences of residents of Chinatowns in San Francisco and New York.[30] They felt that creating a Chinatown would increase anti-Chinese sentiment, as well as make them easier targets for anti-Chinese discrimination.

Historical forces and power relations have led to different settlement patterns of other cultural groups in ethnic enclaves across the U.S. landscape. Many small towns across the Midwest were settled by particular European groups— for example, in Iowa, Germans in Amana, Dutch in Pella, and Czechs and Slovaks in Cedar Rapids. Cities, too, have their neighborhoods, based on settlement patterns. For instance, South Philadelphia is largely Italian American, South Boston is largely Irish American, and Overtown in Miami is largely African American. Although it is no longer legal to mandate that people live in particular districts or neighborhoods based on their racial or ethnic backgrounds, the continued existence of such neighborhoods underscores the importance of historical influence.

Regionalism   Ongoing regional conflicts, expressions of nationalism, ethnic revivals, and religious strife point to the continuing struggle over who gets to define whom. Such conflicts are hardly new, though. In fact, some cultural spaces, such as Jerusalem, have been ongoing sites of struggle for many centuries. Similarly, during the 20th century, Germany and France fought over Alsace-Lorraine, and both the Germans and the Czechs claimed the Sudetenland region. Other areas have retained their regional identities despite being engulfed by a larger nation—for example, Scotland and Wales in Britain, the Basque region in both Spain and France, Catalonia in Spain, Brittany and Corsica in France, and the Kurdish region in both Turkey and Iraq. Although regions may not always be clearly marked on maps of the world, many people identify quite strongly with particular regions.

Regionalism—loyalty to some area that holds cultural meaning—can take many different forms, from symbolic expressions of identification to armed conflict. Within the United States, people may identify themselves or others as southerners or midwesterners. People from Montreal might identify more strongly with the province of Quebec than with their country, Canada. Similarly, some Corsicans might feel a need to negotiate their identity with France. Sometimes people fly regional flags, wear particular kinds of clothes, celebrate regional holidays, and participate in other cultural activities to communicate their regional identification. But these expressions of regionalism are not always simply celebratory, as the violent conflicts in Kosovo, Chechnya, Eritrea, Tibet, and East Timor indicate. The idea of national borders may seem simple enough, but they often ignore or obscure conflicting regional identities. To understand how intercultural communications may be affected by national borders, we must consider how issues of history, power, identity, culture, and context come into play.

Changing Cultural Space

Traveling   What happens when people change cultural spaces? Traveling is frequently viewed as simply a leisure activity, but it is more than that. In terms of intercultural communication, **traveling** changes cultural spaces in a way that

Info Bites

Research reports that deaf babies "babble" with hand gestures in the same way that hearing babies babble with vocal sounds. Why do you think nonverbal communication is so necessary before (and after) we have the ability to communicate verbally? If nonverbal communication is universal, why are there cultural variations? (SOURCE: *The Nonverbal Communication Reader*, p. 54)

often transforms the traveler. Changing cultural spaces means changing who you are and how you interact with others. Perhaps the old saying "When in Rome, do as the Romans do" holds true today as we cross cultural spaces more frequently than ever. However, this is not always easy to do. After traveling to Morocco, our student Jessica described the nonverbal behavior of some of the U.S. American students she was with:

> We were informed before the trip that women in Morocco dress differently, that they cover practically every inch of their bodies. We were not expected to do that, but we were told to dress appropriately, in pants or a skirt that covered our legs and a shirt with sleeves. It felt like a slap in the face when I saw two girls on the trip in cut-off jean shorts and tight tank tops that showed their midriffs. They even had the nerve to ask our tour guide why the Moroccan women were shouting "shame" and casting evil looks.

Should people alter their communication style when they encounter travelers who are not in their traditional cultural space? Do they assume that the travelers should interact in the ways prescribed by their own cultural space? These are some of the issues that travel raises; we address these issues in Chapter 10.

Migration   People also change cultural spaces through **migration** from a primary cultural context to a new one. Migration, of course, involves a different kind of change in cultural spaces than traveling. With traveling, the change is temporary and, usually, desirable. It is something people seek out. By contrast, people who migrate do not always seek out this change. For example, many people were forced from their homelands of Rwanda and Bosnia and had to settle elsewhere. Many immigrants leave their homelands simply to survive. But they often find it difficult to adjust to the change, especially if the language and customs of the new cultural space are unfamiliar. That is, they may suffer culture shock, as described in Chapter 4. As one recent immigrant to the United States describes it, "I myself experienced such shock after arriving in the United States. The people's language and behavior were the first aspects that made me feel insecure and disoriented. The stress I experienced caused sleeplessness and a feeling of being lost."

Even within the United States, people often find it difficult to adapt to new surroundings when they move. Tom remembers how northerners who moved to the South often were unfamiliar with the custom of banks closing early on Wednesday or with the traditional New Year's Day foods. And ridiculing or ignoring the customs of their new cultural space simply led to further intercultural communication problems.

The Dynamic Nature of Cultural Spaces

The dynamic nature of cultural space stands in sharp contrast to more traditional Western notions of space, which promoted land ownership, surveys, borders, colonies, and territories. No passport is needed to travel in the current dynamic

What Do You Think?

Are salespeople a cocultural group? When it comes to nonverbal communication, we might think so. Salespeople tell stories of negotiation sessions in which a prolonged stare must be maintained for a surprisingly long time between adversaries. The first person to blink or look away loses the initiative and is then on the defensive.

cultural space, because there are no border guards. The dynamic nature of current cultural spaces underscores their relationship to changing cultural needs. The space exists only as long as it is needed in its present form.

Phoenix, Arizona, for example, which became a city only in the past few decades, has no Chinatown, no Japantown, no Koreatown, no Irish district, no Polish neighborhood, and no Italian area. Instead, for example, people of Polish descent might live anywhere in the metropolitan area but congregate for special occasions or for specific reasons. On Sundays, the Polish Catholic mass draws worshipers from throughout Phoenix. When people want to buy Polish breads and pastries, they can go to the Polish bakery and also speak Polish there. Ethnic identity is only one of several identities important to these people. When they desire recognition and interaction based on their Polish heritage, they can fulfill these desires. When they seek other forms of identification, they may go to places where they can be, say, Phoenix Suns fans or art lovers. Ethnic identity is neither the sole factor nor necessarily the most important factor at all times in their lives. The markers of ethnic life in Phoenix are the urban sites where people congregate when they desire ethnic cultural contact. At other times, they may frequent other locations to express other aspects of their identities. In this sense, this contemporary urban space is dynamic and allows people to participate in the communication of identity in new ways.[31]

The rise of the Internet has added a new dimension to the creation of cultural spaces. We can now enter (virtually) a number of spaces where we can communicate in ways that express different aspects of our cultural identities. Our physical space or location is no longer the most significant barrier to communicating with others who share our cultural identities. For example, at http://www.islamicity.com/ people can engage in discussions about issues important in the Islamic world. Others may go to http://www.africana.com/ to read about and participate in discussions on issues relevant to African Americans. Because we are communicating in cyberspace, we are no longer bound by our physical bodies. We can "pass" as men or women, members of many different religious and ethnic communities, or people with different political perspectives or sexualities. While it is still difficult to communicate in languages we do not speak, the Internet even makes some rudimentary translation sites available. Many people, however, have no interest in enacting identities with which they do not identify. Why communicate about lacrosse, for example, if you would prefer to spend time communicating about your auto that reflects your identity? Cyberspace pushes the boundaries of what cultural space is, how quickly cultural spaces can shift, and how quickly we can take control over whom we are and where we are, whenever we wish.[32]

SUMMARY

In this chapter, we examined both nonverbal communication principles and cultural spaces. Nonverbal communication, which operates at a subconscious level, is learned implicitly and can reinforce, substitute for, or contradict verbal behaviors.

What Do You Think?

Online message boards have become popular as they create new kinds of cultural spaces for various groups in society. From support groups for illnesses, to groups that participate in online gaming, to boards that feature discussions about ancient philosophers, cyberspace communities reflect the diversity of the real world and often attempt to meet the needs of people who have something in common. But are these spaces safe? Check out the online community at WWWomen.com, which you can access at http://talk.wwwomen.com. Go to *New Members—Introduce Yourself!* Read the community guidelines for new members. Consider the notion that in the "real" world, individuals may be pushed in and out of cultural spaces. In cyberspace, web moderators and administrators try to create safe and accessible environments for the groups they wish to attract. How difficult do you think this might be?

Nonverbal behaviors can communicate relational meaning, status, and deception. Nonverbal communication is influenced by culture, although many cultures share some nonverbal behaviors. Methods of nonverbal communication include eye contact, facial expressions, gestures, time orientation, and silence. Sometimes cultural differences in nonverbal behaviors can lead to stereotyping of other cultures.

Cultural space influences cultural identity. Cultural spaces relate to issues of power and intercultural communication. Homes, neighborhoods, regions, and nations are all examples of cultural spaces. Two ways of changing cultural spaces are travel and migration. Current cultural spaces are dynamic, accommodating people of different cultural identities who coexist.

BUILDING INTERCULTURAL SKILLS

1. Become more conscious of your nonverbal behavior in intercultural encounters. Practice your encoding skills. You can do this by noting the nonverbal behaviors of others—their facial expressions, gestures, eye contact, and so on. Check to see if their nonverbal communication is telling you that they understand or misunderstand you.

2. Become more aware of others' nonverbal communication. What messages are they sending? And how do you react to those messages? Think about when you are uncomfortable in intercultural encounters. Is your discomfort due to the nonverbal messages others are sending? Are they violating the rules you're used to? Standing too close, or too far away? Touching too much, or not enough? Talking too loudly, or too softly?

3. Practice your decoding skills. Check out your perceptions of others' nonverbal behavior. Are you accurate, or do you misread their nonverbal cues? Are they misunderstanding when you think they are understanding? Are they happy when you think they are upset?

4. Expand your nonverbal communication repertoire. Practice new nonverbal behaviors. Try varying your posture, facial expressions, and eye contact.

5. Be flexible and adaptable in your nonverbal communication in intercultural encounters. Try synchronizing your behavior to that of others, which usually communicates that you feel good about your relationship. If others stand with their arms folded, do the same. If they stand closer than you're used to, don't move away. If they use more eye contact, try to do the same.

6. Become more aware of your prejudicial assumptions based on nonverbal behavior. When you have a very negative reaction to someone, check out the basis for these assumptions. Is it simply because of the way they look? Give them another chance.

ACTIVITY

Nonverbal rules: Choose a cultural space that you are interested in studying. Visit this space on four different occasions to observe how people there interact. Focus on one aspect of nonverbal communication, such as eye contact or personal space. List some rules that seem to govern this aspect of nonverbal communication. For example, if you are focusing on personal space, you might describe, among other things, how far apart people tend to stand when conversing. Based on your observations, list some rules about proper (expected) nonverbal behavior in this cultural space. Share your conclusions with the class. To what extent do other students share your conclusions? Can we generalize about nonverbal rules in cultural spaces? What factors influence whether an individual follows unspoken rules of behavior?

THE ONLINE LEARNING CENTER at www.mhhe.com/experiencing2 features self-quizzes, flashcards, and crossword puzzles based on the chapter's key terms and concepts.

www.mhhe.com/ experiencing2

ENDNOTES

1. Fletcher, C. (1992). The semiotics of survival: Street cops read the street. *The Howard Journal of Communications, 4* (1, 2), 133–142.
2. Knapp, M. L., & Hall, J. A. (2001). *Nonverbal communication in human interaction.* Belmont, CA: Wadsworth.
3. Knapp & Hall (2001).
4. Jones, S. E., & LeBaron, C. D. (2002). Research on the relationship between verbal and nonverbal communication: Emerging integration. *Journal of Communication, 52,* 499–521.
5. Henningsen, D. D., Cruz, M. G., & Morr, M. C. (2000). Pattern violations and perceptions of deception. *Communication Reports, 13,* 1–9. See also Nance, J. (2001). *Conquering deception.* Irvin-Benham Group.
6. Ekman, P., & Friesen, W. V. (1987). Universals and cultural differences in the judgments of facial expressions of emotion. *Journal of Personality and Social Psychology, 53,* 712–717. See also Preuschoft, S. (2000). Primate faces and facial expressions. *Social Research, 67,* 245–271.
7. Ekman, P., & Keltner, D. (1997). Universal facial expressions of emotion: An old controversy and new findings. In Segerstråle & Molnár, pp. 27–46. See also Galati, et. al. (2003, July). Spontaneous facial expressions in congenitally blind and sighted children aged 8–11. *Journal of Visual Impairment and Blindness, 97,* 418–428.
8. Watson, O. M. (1970). *Proxemic behavior: A cross cultural study.* The Hague: Mouton. See also Hall, E. T. (1966). *The hidden dimension.* New York: Doubleday.
9. Andersen, P. A., Hecht, M. L., Hoobler, G. D., & Smallwood, M. (2002). Nonverbal communication across cultures. In W. B. Gudykunst & B. Mody (Eds.), *Handbook of international and intercultural communication* (2nd ed.) (pp. 89–106). Thousand Oaks, CA: Sage.
10. Andersen, Hecht, Hoobler, & Smallwood (2002).
11. Knapp, M. L. & Hall, J. A. (2001). *Nonverbal communication in human interaction.* Belmont, CA: Wadsworth.
12. Hall, E. T. (1959). *The silent language.* New York: Doubleday. See also Hall, E. T. (1976). *Beyond culture.* New York: Doubleday.
13. Dahl, O. (1993). *Malagasy meanings: An interpretive approach to intercultural communication in Madagascar.* Stavanger, Norway: Center for Intercultural Communication, p. 66.
14. Condon, J. (1984). *With respect to the Japanese.* Yarmouth, ME: Intercultural Press, p. 41.
15. Basso, K. (1970). "To give up on words": Silence in Western Apache culture. *Southwestern Journal of Anthropology, 26,* 213–230.
16. Braithwaite, C. A. (1990). Communicative silence: A cross-cultural study of Basso's hypothesis. In D. Carbaugh (Ed.), *Cultural communication and intercultural contact* (pp. 321–327). Hillsdale, NJ: Lawrence Erlbaum.

17. Mosbach, H. (1988). The importance of silence and stillness in Japanese nonverbal communication: A cross cultural approach. In F. Poyatos (Ed.), *Cross cultural perspectives in nonverbal communication* (pp. 201–215). Lewiston, NY: Hogrefe.

18. Montell, G. (2003, October 15). Do good looks equal good evaluations? *Chronicle of Higher Education* (online). (http://chronicle.com/jobs/2003/10/2003101501c.htm)

19. Neal, L. V. I., McCray, A. D., & Webb-Johnson, G. (2001). Teachers' reactions to African American students' movement styles. *Intervention in School and Clinic, 36,* 168–174.

20. Matthews, R. (2000). Culture patterns of South Asian and S.E. Asian Americans. *Interventions in School and Clinic, 36,* 101–105.

21. Associated Press (2003, October 15). Man sentenced to die for Sikh's killing gets more time. (http://www.cnn.com/2003/LAW/10/15/sikh.shooting.ap/)

22. Parasuram, T. V. (2003, October 23). Sikh shot and injured in Arizona hate crime. *The Sikh Times* (online). (http://www.sikhtimes.com/news_052103a.html)

23. Marsiglia, F. F., & Hecht, M. L. (1998). Personal and interpersonal interventions. In M. L. Hecht (Ed.), *Communicating prejudice* (pp. 287–301). Thousand Oaks, CA: Sage.

24. Fussell, P. (1983). *Class.* New York: Summit Books.

25. hooks, b. (1990). *Yearning: Race, gender, and cultural politics.* Boston: South End Press, p. 41.

26. Greene, H. (1991). Charleston, South Carolina. In J. Preston (Ed.), *Hometowns: Gay men write about where they belong* (pp. 55–67). New York: Dutton.

27. Saylor, S. (1991). Amethyst, Texas. In J. Preston (Ed.), *Hometowns: Gay men write about where they belong* (pp. 119–135). New York: Dutton.

28. X, Malcolm, & Haley, A. (1964). *The autobiography of Malcolm X.* New York: Grove Press, pp. 3–4.

29. Nee, V. G., and Nee, B. D. B. (1974). *Longtime Californ': A documentary study of an American Chinatown.* Boston: Houghton Mifflin, p. 60.

30. Pruden, G. B., Jr. (1990). History of the Chinese in Savannah, Georgia. In J. Goldstein (Ed.), *Georgia's East Asian connection: Into the twenty-first century: Vol. 27. West Georgia College studies in the social sciences* (pp. 17–34). Carrollton: West Georgia College.

31. Drzewiecka, J. A., & Nakayama, T. K. (1998). City sites: Postmodern urban space and the communication of identity. *Southern Communication Journal, 64,* 20–31.

32. Strate, L., Jacobson, R. L., & Gibson, S. L. (Eds.). *Communication and cyberspace: Social interaction in an electronic environment.* Creskill, NJ: Hampton Press.

CHAPTER SEVEN

Popular Culture and Intercultural Communication

STUDY OBJECTIVES

After reading this chapter, you should be able to:

1. Define popular culture.
2. Identify some types of popular culture.
3. Describe characteristics of popular culture.
4. Explain why it is important to understand popular culture in intercultural communication.
5. Discuss why people consume or resist specific cultural texts.
6. Understand how cultural texts influence cultural identities.
7. Discuss how cultural group portrayals in popular culture forms influence intercultural communication.
8. Suggest effects of the global domination of U.S. popular culture.

KEY TERMS

cultural identities	high culture
cultural imperialism	low culture
culture industries	media imperialism
cultural texts	popular culture
electronic colonialism	reader profiles

There is an old joke that says, "There's more culture in a pint of yogurt than in all of Southern California." This joke, of course, plays off of two different meanings of *culture*. Yogurt culture is a bacterial culture, but the point of the joke is that Southern California lacks the elite kinds of "culture" often associated with Western high culture—for example, first-rate symphonies, operas, theater, and museums—as found in New York, Paris, and London.

Culture is central to intercultural communication, but we often overlook some of the meanings of culture in everyday life. One kind of culture that is often overlooked by intercultural communication scholars is popular culture. But popular culture plays a very important role in how we understand the world, helping us reinforce our sense of who we are and confirming our worldviews.

Neither Tom nor Judith has ever been to Cuba, Kenya, Brazil, Nigeria, India, Russia, or China. Yet all of these places, and many more, evoke images of what it is "really" like to be there. We derive images about these places from the news, movies, television shows, advertisements, and other kinds of popular culture. Sometimes we feel as if we've been somewhere when we watch the Travel Channel. And when people actually visit Paris, or Honolulu, or Tokyo, they might exclaim that it looks just like it does on television! Obviously, not all of this "information" in popular culture is up-to-date and accurate. Some popular culture images reinforce stereotypes of other cultures, while other images challenge those stereotypes. In this chapter, we examine the role that popular culture plays in building bridges in, as well as barriers to, intercultural communication.

POPULAR CULTURE AND INTERCULTURAL COMMUNICATION

We can experience new places by traveling and by migrating. But there will always be places around the world that we have not visited and where we have not lived. Most of us do not even make it around the globe.

So what do we know about places we have never been, and how do we acquire this "knowledge"? Much of what we know about these places probably comes from popular culture—the media outlets of television, music, videos, and magazines that most of us know and share. And how does this experience of places traveled to only through popular culture affect intercultural communication?

The complexity of popular culture is often overlooked in our society. People express concerns about the social effects of popular culture—for example, the effects of television violence on children or the relationship between heterosexual pornography and violence against women. Yet most people look down on the study of popular culture, as if there is nothing of significance to learn there. This attitude can make it difficult to investigate and discuss popular culture.

As U.S. Americans, we are in a unique position in relationship to popular culture. Products of U.S. popular culture are well known and widely circulated around the globe. Many U.S. film, music, and television stars, such as Tom Cruise, Julia Roberts, and Madonna, are also popular outside the United States, creating an uneven flow of **cultural texts**—cultural artifacts that convey norms, values, and beliefs—between the United States and other nations. Scholars Elihu Katz and Tamar Liebes note the "apparent ease with which American television programs cross cultural and linguistic frontiers. Indeed, the phenomenon is so taken for granted that hardly any systematic research has been done to explain the reasons why these programs are so successful."[1]

By contrast, U.S. Americans are rarely exposed to popular culture from outside the United States. Exceptions to this largely one-way movement of popular culture include foreign performers who sing in English, such as Abba, Björk, Golden Earring, and Celine Dion. Consider how difficult it is to find foreign films or television programs throughout most of the United States. The apparent imbalance of cultural texts globally not only makes U.S. Americans more dependent on U.S.-produced popular culture but also can lead to cultural imperialism, a topic we will discuss later in this chapter.

The study of popular culture has become increasingly important in the communication field. Although intercultural communication scholars traditionally have overlooked popular culture, we believe that these forms of culture are significant influences in intercultural interaction. In this chapter, we explore some of these influences.

WHAT IS "POPULAR CULTURE"?

In Chapter 2, we discussed notions of "culture" and distinguished between **high culture** (ballet, theater, opera, and so on) and **low culture,** which has been reconceptualized as **popular culture.** Barry Brummett, a contemporary rhetorician, offers the following definition: "Popular culture refers to those systems or artifacts that most people share and that most people know about."[2] According to this definition, television, music videos, and popular magazines are systems of popular culture. By contrast, the symphony and the ballet do not qualify as popular culture because most people would not be able to identify much about them. Thus, popular culture often is seen as populist, in that it includes forms of contemporary culture that are made popular by and for the people. As John Fiske, professor of communication arts, observes:

> To be made into popular culture, a commodity must also bear the interests of the people. Popular culture is not consumption, it is culture—the active process of generating and circulating meanings and pleasures within a social system: culture, however industrialized, can never be adequately described in terms of the buying and selling of commodities.[3]

In his study of popular Mexican American music in Los Angeles, ethnic studies professor George Lipsitz highlights the ways that marginalized social groups are able to express themselves in innovative, nonmainstream ways. In this study, he demonstrates how the "popular" can arise from a mixing and borrowing from

What Do You Think?

According to the U.S. Census Bureau's March 2000 official statistical estimates, there are 32.8 million Hispanics residing in the United States. The media continue to insist that there has been a "Latin cultural explosion" in the popular music industry, which is evident in the success of artists such as Ricky Martin, Marc Anthony, Christina Aguilera, and Jennifer Lopez. What aspects of Latino culture are apparent in the works of these individual entertainers? Are they becoming more mainstream than in previous years?

U.S. American pop stars, like Janet Jackson, often enjoy worldwide popularity. The global popularity of U.S. popular culture products has important implications for both individuals and cultures worldwide.

other cultures. He suggests that "the ability of musicians to learn from other cultures played a key role in their success as rock-and-roll artists."[4] Here, as elsewhere, the popular speaks to—and resonates with—the people, but it speaks to them through many cultural voices. Lipsitz continues:

> The marginality of Chicano rock-and-roll musicians has provided them with a constant source of inspiration and a constant spur toward innovation that gained them the attention of mainstream audiences. But this marginal sensibility amounts to more than novelty or personal eccentricity; it holds legitimacy and power as the product of a real historical community's struggle with oppression. . . . As Chicano musicians demonstrate in their comments about their work, their music reflects a quite conscious cultural politics that seeks inclusion in the American mainstream by transforming it.[5]

Intercultural contact and intercultural communication play a central role in the creation and maintenance of popular culture. Yet, as Lipsitz also points out, the popular is political and pleasurable, which opens new arenas for complicating the ways we might think about popular culture.

Thus, popular culture can be said to have four significant characteristics: (1) It is produced by culture industries, (2) it is different from folk culture, (3) it is everywhere, and (4) it fills a social function. As Fiske points out, popular culture is nearly always produced by what are called **culture industries** within a

TABLE 7.1   U.S. Television Shows Imported from Other Countries

While many television shows from the United States are popular in other countries, sometimes U.S. television shows borrow ideas from other countries. Here are some examples of that borrowing:

"The Weakest Link"—Great Britain
"Big Brother"—The Netherlands
"The Naked Chef"—Great Britain
"Most Extreme Elimination"—Japan
"Mr. Bean"—Great Britain

---

capitalist system that sees the products of popular culture as commodities to be sold for profit. The Disney Corporation is a noteworthy example of a culture industry because it produces amusement parks, movies, cartoons, and a plethora of associated merchandise. As shown in Table 7.1, culture products can be imported from other countries.

Folk culture refers to the traditional rituals and traditions that maintain cultural group identity. Unlike popular culture, folk culture is typically not controlled by any industry and is not driven by a profit motive. For example, the celebration of Oktoberfest in Germany is laden with rituals that vary from one region to another. While these rituals may be open to outsiders, they express and confirm cultural identity and group membership.

Popular culture also is ubiquitous. We are bombarded with it, every day and everywhere. On average, U.S. Americans watch more than 40 hours of television per week. Movie theaters beckon us with the latest multimillion-dollar extravaganzas, nearly all U.S.-made. Radio stations and TV music stations blast us with the hottest music groups performing their latest hits. And we are inundated with a staggering number of advertisements and commercials daily.

It is difficult to avoid popular culture. Not only is it ubiquitous, but it also serves an important social function. How many times have friends and family members asked about your reactions to recent movies or television programs? What kind of reaction would you get if you said, "I don't watch television"? Communication scholars Horace Newcomb and Paul Hirsch suggest that television serves as a cultural forum for discussing and working out our ideas on a variety of topics, including those that emerge from television programs.[6] We see how others feel about various issues—from divorce, to immigration, to school shootings—and how we feel about them as they are discussed on television. These forums include daytime and late-night talk shows, news programs, and situation comedies, among many others. Television, then, has a powerful social function—to serve as a forum for social issues.

The ways in which people negotiate their relationships to popular culture are complex. And it is this complexity that makes understanding the role of popular culture in intercultural communication so difficult. Clearly, we are not

Info Bites

Scholar Raymond Williams argued that popular culture is important to study because in one week we are exposed to more stories and dramas in the media than Europeans a thousand years ago would have been exposed to in their entire lives.

passive receivers of this deluge of popular culture. We are, in fact, quite active in our consumption of or resistance to popular culture, a notion that we turn to next.

CONSUMING AND RESISTING POPULAR CULTURE

We navigate our ways through the numerous popular culture choices. After all, as Australian scholar Nadine Dolby notes, "Popular culture, at the end of the 20th century, is a key site for the formation of identities, for the ways in which we make sense of the world, and locate ourselves within it."[7] In order to maintain our identities, as well as to reshape them, we often turn to popular culture. At times, we seek out cultural texts; at other times, we try to avoid certain texts.

Consuming Popular Culture

Faced with such an onslaught of cultural texts, people navigate their ways through popular culture in quite different ways. Popular culture texts do not have to win over the majority of people to be "popular." In fact, people often seek out or avoid specific forms of popular culture. For example, romance novels are the best-selling form of literature, but many people are not interested in reading these novels. Likewise, whereas you may enjoy watching soap operas or professional wrestling, many people find no pleasure in those forms of popular culture. We are bombarded every day with a myriad of popular culture texts. We actively

"Queer Eye for the Straight Guy" is currently a very popular show. Why might some viewers be attracted to such a show and others resist it? How might consuming or resisting such a show be related to one's cultural identity?

seek out and choose those texts that serve our needs. Often people in our social groups participate in particular forms of popular culture, and so we feel that we should participate as well.

Although there is unpredictability in the ways in which people navigate popular culture, certain patterns are evident. Advertising departments of popular magazines even make their **reader profiles** available to potential advertisers. These portrayals of readership demographics indicate what the magazine believes its readership "looks" like. Although reader profiles do not follow a set format, they generally give the average age, gender, individual and household incomes, and other pertinent data about their readers. Thus, the reader profile for *Vogue* would not look like the reader profile for *Esquire* or *Vibe*, for example.

Other popular culture industries likewise attempt to market their products to particular audiences. The advertisements you see during the Super Bowl are not always the same ones you will see on MTV or during beauty pageants. While demographic information alone will not predict which forms of popular culture a particular person will consume, certain trends in popular culture consumption usually can be identified. For example, the type of consumers who might be interested in *Blue's Clues*, as opposed to MTV's *Road Rules*, should be fairly evident.

The recent rise of reality television shows has again sparked debates about the consumption of these cultural texts and the type of cultural identity they reinforce. The enormous popularity of some of these shows, including *Joe Millionaire*, *Survivor*, and *American Idol*, point to their importance in our society. But what is it about these shows that we enjoy? Why do we consume them? A writer for *Time* magazine asks, "Isn't there something simply wrong with people who enjoy entertainment that depends on ordinary people getting their heart broken, being told they can't sing or getting played for fools?"[8] There are no easy answers, of course, and we do not know what meanings people are drawing from reality TV. But perhaps, we do enjoy a critique of our mainstream cultural values: "Companies value team spirit; *Survivor* says the team will screw you in the end. The cult of self-esteem says everybody is talented; *American Idol*'s Simon Cowell says to sit down and shut your pie hole. Romance and feminism say a man's money shouldn't matter; *Joe Millionaire* wagers $50 million that they're wrong."[9] The popularity of these shows points to some cultural needs that are being fulfilled. Why do you think so many reality TV shows are popular? What kind of cultural identity might be served by these shows?

The important point here is that popular culture serves important cultural functions that are connected to our **cultural identities**—our view of ourselves in relation to the cultures we belong to. We participate in those cultural texts that address issues that are relevant to our cultural groups, for example, by offering information and points of view that are unavailable in other cultural forums. They also tend to affirm, by their very existence, these other cultural identities that sometimes are invisible or are silenced in the mainstream culture. Some cultural texts focus on issues relevant to people in particular religious, ethnic, regional, political, and other contexts.

For example, many non-English-language products circulate in the United States that serve the same functions as other popular culture texts. Newspapers

What Do You Think?

Music videos have emerged to play an important part in identifying aspects of American culture. MTV has captured the attention of a particularly young audience and can now be viewed in countries from Russia to the United States. Although its programming is often regarded as alternative or at times radical in comparison to standard network television, MTV's primary lineup of music videos and urban-centered shows tends to illustrate diverse lifestyles, activities, and forms of social and artistic expression. What kinds of intercultural matters have you seen discussed on MTV? What impact do you think this might have on the current generation?

printed in Spanish, Vietnamese, Japanese, French, Korean, Arabic, Polish, Navajo, and other languages reach non-English-speaking readers nationwide. Television shows are broadcast in non-English languages, and many videos are available for rental in other languages. The rise of the Internet has also made it easier to access newspapers and magazines in many parts of the world.

Readers actively negotiate their way through cultural texts such as magazines, consuming those that fulfill important personal needs. Thus, it is possible to be a consumer of various cultural texts that form a unique cultural configuration; that is, someone might read *Texas Monthly* and Spanish-language newspapers and magazines and watch *Will and Grace* and *CSI.* In this sense, not all popular culture texts are easily correlated to particular cultural groups. Think about the various television programs, movies, mass market paperbacks, and tabloids that flood the cultural landscape. The reasons that people enjoy some over others simply cannot easily be determined.

Resisting Popular Culture

At times, people actively seek out particular popular culture texts to consume. At other times, they resist cultural texts. People often resist particular forms of popular culture by refusing to engage in them. For example, some people feel the need to avoid television completely; some even decide not to own televisions. Some people refuse to go to movies that contain violence because they do not find pleasure in such films. These kinds of conscious decisions are often based on concerns about the cultural politics at work.

In a recent study on media consumption practices among members of the Church of Latter Day Saints (Mormons), there was significant resistance to Hollywood and television texts. Three media practices were identified in this study: "resistant readings of media texts that focus on the immoral nature of Hollywood and television personalities; a demarcation of the sanctity of the home and the media as an outside threat to their religiosity; and finally practices of program avoidance or resistance in some instances."[10] By resisting the messages of popular culture, their religious identity can be reaffirmed. For example, those who did watch some *Jerry Springer* shows felt the shows served as "a lens into the outside world of those who do not practice family values."[11] Some church members simply avoided certain shows once they were seen as threatening to their religious identity. One husband noted that he "walked to the kitchen and got a butcher knife, walked back to the TV and cut both the power and the cable cord."[12] In this way, he was able to eliminate threats to the home, while encouraging his wife to focus on her role as homemaker.

Resistance to popular culture can be related to a number of other identities; unlike members of the Church of Latter Day Saints, however, the motivation behind this resistance emerges more from how others might view their group. For example, CBS is considering a television show, the *Real Beverly Hillbillies,* which would bring a poor family to Beverly Hills to live in a mansion for a year. Set as a reality television show, this proposed show has drawn the criticism of many, including Teamsters, United Mine Workers, and the Louisiana State Senate.[13]

Surf's Up!

Should we "resist" certain texts by banning them, especially in schools? There are many reasons why people want to ban certain books. Some of these reasons are available at: http://www.booksatoz.com/censorship/banned.htm Have you read some of these books? How powerful are these books in influencing its readers?

While CBS has not yet decided to produce this reality television show, concerns about the stereotyping and images that would occur from the show have motivated resistance. People resist popular culture in many ways, and organizations have emerged to monitor media images and coverage. For example, MANAA (Media Action Network for Asian Americans) monitors anti-Asian images in the media and organizes resistance to them. GLAAD (Gay and Lesbian Alliance Against Defamation) serves a similar function by focusing on gay and lesbian media images. Both groups also praise positive and accurate depictions of their social identities. There are many other groups serving similar functions. Resistance, then, can happen on an individual level or a social level. You may choose not to watch a particular television show, or you may work with others to picket studios, boycott advertisers' products, or resist particular media images in more public ways.

REPRESENTING CULTURAL GROUPS

> A White student pointed out that his difficulty in answering questions about Latino culture was due to lack of knowledge. Growing up in an all-White town, he had never had any contact with Latinos. Based on what he knew from TV, he had negative feelings about their culture. This all changed when he came to college and had his own experiences. I thought this was interesting because I didn't think an all-White place existed in America.
>
> —*Adam*

As noted at the beginning of this chapter, people often are introduced to other cultures through the lens of popular culture. And these introductions can be quite intimate. For example, through movies, the audience sees and enters the private lives of people they do not know, in ways they never could as tourists.

Yet, we must also think about how these cultural groups are portrayed through that lens of popular culture. Not everyone sees the portrayal in the same way. For example, you may not think that the TV show *Judging Amy* represents quintessential U.S. American values and lifestyles. But some viewers may see it as their entree into the ways that European Americans live.

Because some groups are not portrayed as often in popular culture, it is easier to stereotype them. Conversely, some groups are portrayed so often in popular culture that it is difficult to stereotype them. For example, White Americans are portrayed as heroes and villains, as good people and bad people, as responsible and irresponsible, as hard working and lazy, as honest and dishonest.

To understand other cultures and groups, and their experiences, we can investigate their representations in popular culture. For example, U.S. Americans seldom learn about the Navajo code talkers, who played an important role in World War II. Serving as Marines during the war, the Navajo code talkers utilized the Navajo language to devise an unbreakable code. And by creating a GI Joe doll, called "Navajo GI Joe," the culture industry ensured that this history would not be forgotten. As Sam Billison, one of the Navajo code talkers,

Surf's Up!

Cultural critic bell hooks and other critical scholars often discuss the way media pathologize or use stereotyped images of African American men and women for profit. Stereotypes about certain groups can function and thrive, even in the minds of others who are marginalized in a culture. Have you heard of Ghettopoly? It's a game modeled after the family game Monopoly. But in Ghettopoly, the most sought-after property is not Boardwalk or Park Place—it's a peep show. Some of the board game pieces include an automatic weapon, a basketball, and marijuana, and instead of $200, game bonuses valued at $50 are picked up when a "playa" effectively gets neighbors addicted to crack cocaine. The goal is to make the most money through cheating, stealing, and fencing stolen properties. See the website created for the game at http://www.ghettopoly.com. The creator of the board game, a second-generation Taiwanese immigrant, was sued in 2003 by the parent company for Monopoly.

This woman is navigating her way through a dizzying array of popular culture choices. We make similar choices in everyday life. How might your choices reflect your cultural identity?

observed, "This will let people know about the code talkers. I think it's really going to put us on the map."[14] In this way, popular culture representations can increase a group's visibility in society.

Migrants' Perceptions of Mainstream Culture

Ethnographers and other scholars have crossed international and cultural boundaries to examine the influence of popular culture. In an early study, Elihu Katz and Tamar Liebes set up focus groups to see how different cultural groups viewed the TV show *Dallas:* "There were ten groups each of Israelis, Arabs, new immigrants to Israel from Russia, first and second generation immigrants from Morocco, and kibbutz members. Taking these groups as a microcosm of the worldwide audience of *Dallas*, we are comparing their readings of the program with [those of] ten groups of matched Americans in Los Angeles."[15]

Katz and Liebes found that the U.S. Americans in Los Angeles were much less likely to perceive *Dallas* as portraying actual life in the United States. By contrast, the Israelis, the Arabs, and the array of immigrants were much more inclined to believe that this television show was indeed all about life in the United States. Katz and Liebes note: "What seems clear from the analysis, even at this stage, is that the non-Americans consider the story more real than the Americans. The non-Americans have little doubt that the story is about 'America'; the Americans are less sure."[16] The results of this study are not surprising, but we should not overlook what we can learn about the intercultural communication process. We can see that these popular culture images are often influential in constructing particular ways of understanding cultural groups other than our own.

Another study that focused on immigrants to the United States found similar results.[17] Researchers asked female Korean immigrants why they preferred watching Korean TV shows (which they had to rent at the video store) to U.S. American TV shows. The women pointed out that, because of the cultural differences, the Korean TV shows were more appealing. Yet, as one respondent noted,

> I like to watch American programs. Actors and actresses are glamorous, and the pictures are sleek. But the ideas are still American. How many Korean women are that independent? And how many men commit incest? I think American programs are about American people. They are not the same as watching the Korean programs. But I watch them for fun. And I learn the American way of living by watching them.[18]

Here, both consumption of and resistance to U.S. American popular culture are evident. This woman uses U.S. American television to learn about the "American" way of living, but she prefers to watch Korean shows because they relate to her cultural identity.

The use of popular culture to learn about another culture should not be surprising. After all, many teachers encourage their students to use popular culture in this manner, not only to improve their language skills but also to help them learn many of the nuances of another culture. When Tom was first studying French, his French professor told the students that *Le dernier métro* (*The Last Metro*), a film by director François Truffaut, was playing in midtown Atlanta. The idea, of course, was to expose students to the French language as spoken by natives. But the film also served as a window to French culture and history, as it focused on the French Resistance in World War II and anti-Semitism in France.

Popular Culture and Stereotyping

> Intercultural communication still has a long way to go in this country. With so many different races being American, why do we still only picture white skin/blond hair/blue eyes as American?
> —*Cindy*

In what ways does reliance on popular culture create and reinforce stereotypes of different cultures? As noted at the outset of this chapter, neither Judith nor Tom

What Do You Think?
What kind of effects do video games have on people? Do violent video games lead to violence? What evidence would you need to be able to prove this link?

has had the opportunity to travel all over the world. Our knowledge about other places, even places we have visited, is largely influenced by popular culture. For people who do not travel and interact in relatively homogeneous social circles, the impact of popular culture may be even greater.

There are many familiar stereotypes of ethnic groups represented in the media. Scholar Jack Shaheen, who is of Lebanese descent, went in search of "real" Arabs after tiring of the way Lebanese and other Arabs were portrayed in the media—as oil billionaires, mad bombers, and sexy belly dancers. According to Shaheen, "Television tends to perpetuate four basic myths about Arabs: they are all fabulously wealthy; they are barbaric and uncultured; they are sex maniacs with a penchant for white slavery; and they revel in acts of terrorism."[19] Shaheen describes other common untruths—for example, that all Iranians are Arabs and that all Arabs are Muslims.

Communication scholar Lisa Flores describes the portrayal in television documentaries of Mexicans responding to natural disasters. According to Flores, news programs often show Mexicans as resilient, patient, faithful, and rather passive—and therefore as somehow acceptable. Yet we are also encouraged to feel pity for them; the inference is that they need White America's assistance to cope with these natural disasters. In turn, this feeds into the stereotype that Mexicans are not sufficiently hard-working, honest, or driven to become "Americans." In her study, Flores connects these images of Mexicans to portrayals of Mexican Americans as not quite U.S. American, "although the difficulty in becoming American is posited as not a lack of choice, but lack of ability."[20]

African American women also have been portrayed stereotypically on TV, especially in the 1950s and 1960s, when the roles they held were secondary—for example, as domestics. Scholar Bishetta Merritt also reminds us of the African American female characters who often appear as background scenery in prime-time TV: the person buying drugs, the homeless person on the sidewalk, the hotel lobby prostitute. Merritt points out that these women still project images, even if they aren't the focus.[21] Merritt explains:

> If the majority of black women the television audience is exposed to are homeless, drug-addicted, or maids, and if viewers have no contact with African American women other than through television, what choice do they have but to believe that all women of this ethnic background reflect this television image? . . . It is, therefore, important, as . . . the population of this country includes more and more people of color, that the television industry broaden the images of African American women to include their nuances and diversity.[22]

What about those ethnic groups that simply don't appear except as infrequent stereotypes: Native Americans and Asian Americans? How do these stereotypes influence intercultural interaction? Do people behave any differently if they don't hold stereotypes about people with whom they are interacting? Two communication researchers, Valerie Manusov and Radha Hegde, investigated these questions in a study in which they identified two groups of college students:

Pop Culture Spotlight

Although cultures are dynamic and heterogeneous, we often have very static images of what other cultures "look" like. Think of what is often called "ethnic costume"—the stereotypical kinds of things supposedly worn by people in other cultures. For instance, when you were a kid, did you think that Hawaiian girls wore grass skirts? That Dutch boys wore wooden shoes? That Native Americans wore feathers? That Fiji islanders wore loincloths? Or that Egyptians wore turbans?

those who had some preconceived ideas about India and those who didn't.[23] It turns out that the preconceived ideas were fairly positive. Manusov and Hegde then asked all of the students to interact, one at a time, with an international student from India who was part of the study. When the students with preconceptions talked with the Indian student, they interacted differently from those who had no expectations. Students from the former group relied less on small talk, covered more topics, and asked fewer questions within each topic. Overall, their conversations more closely resembled those between people who know each other. The students with the preconceptions also were more positive about the conversation.

What can we learn from this study? Apparently, having some information and positive expectations may lead to more in-depth conversations and positive outcomes than having no information. But what happens when negative stereotypes are present? It is possible that expectations are fulfilled in this case, too.

For example, in several studies at Princeton University, Whites interviewed both White and Black "job applicants" who were actually part of the study and were trained to behave consistently, no matter how interviewers acted toward them. The interviews were videotaped. The interviewers clearly behaved differently toward Blacks; their speech deteriorated, they made more grammatical errors, they spent less time asking questions, and they showed fewer "immediacy" behaviors—that is, they were less friendly and less outgoing. In a second study, interviewers were trained to be either "immediate" or "nonimmediate" as they interviewed White job applicants. A panel of judges watched the videotapes and agreed that those applicants interviewed by the nonimmediate interviewer performed less well and were more nervous. This suggests that the African American applicants in the first study never had a chance to show their qualifications to the best advantage. The interviewers were behaving in a way that would not have elicited a good performance had they not been confederates. Mark Snyder summarizes: "Considered together, the two investigations suggest that in interracial encounters, racial stereotypes may constrain behavior in ways to cause both blacks and whites to behave in accordance with those stereotypes."[24]

U.S. POPULAR CULTURE AND POWER

> My roommate Aaron and I took the two Japanese students to the Memorial Union to play pool. They seemed really excited and interested in all my questions or comments. . . . It was my belief that the Japanese people were very shy and quiet. However, these girls proved me wrong. They were somewhat shy, but most of the time they were laughing and having a good time. . . . They told me what kind of stereotypes they had about America. They told me that they thought everyone ate junk food and that there were a lot of criminals. I think most of these impressions are mainly due to the media portrayal of our country in Japan. I think most movies overly illustrate America's fast-paced life, which involves fast food.   —*Charlie*

Surf's Up!

What are the most popular movies of all time in America? Are they the same as the most popular in other countries? Visit the Internet Movie Database site (us.imdb.com/charts) and compare the U.S. and international all-time box office rankings.

One of the dynamics of intercultural communication that we have highlighted throughout this text is power. In considering popular culture, we need to think about not only the ways that people interpret and consume popular culture but also the ways that these popular culture texts represent particular groups in specific ways. If people largely view other cultural groups through the lens of popular culture, then we need to think about the power relations that are embedded in these popular culture dynamics.

Global Circulation of Images/Commodities

As noted previously, much of U.S. popular culture is circulated worldwide. For example, U.S.-made films are widely distributed by a culture industry that is backed by considerable financial resources. Some media scholars have noted that the U.S. film industry earns far more money outside the United States than from domestic box office sales.[25] This situation ensures that Hollywood will continue to market its films overseas and that it will have the financial resources to do so. For example, as of September 2, 2003, the blockbuster *The Matrix Reloaded* had

McDonald's has adapted to different cultures. For example, women in Dhahran, Saudi Arabia, must wait for their orders at the single women's counter. Cultural adaptation is an important phenomenon in the exportation of U.S. popular culture.

earned over $281 million in the United States and Canada but had earned nearly $454 million from the rest of the world.[26]

Many other U.S. media are widely available outside the United States, including television and newspapers. Cable News Network (CNN) is widely available around the world. MTV also broadcasts internationally. And the *International Herald Tribune*, published jointly by the *New York Times* and the *Washington Post*, is available in many parts of the world. The implications of the dominance by U.S. media and popular culture have yet to be determined, although you might imagine the consequences.

Recently, however, the emergence of Al Jazeera, the news channel based in Qatar, has begun to offer a different voice in international news. Given the recent focus on the Arabic-speaking world, Al Jazeera's perspective has taken a particularly significant place. As they describe themselves: "With more than 30 bureaus and dozens of correspondents covering the four corners of the world Aljazeera has given millions of people a refreshing new perspective on global events."[27] In late 2004, the French will launch a similar CNN-type news channel that is focused on providing an alternative view to the BBC, CNN, and Al Jazeera. Given the recent tensions between France and the United States over the invasion of Iraq, a French government official noted, "France may see things differently and we feel it is important that we get our message across."[28]

Popular Culture from Other Cultures

Although U.S. popular culture tends to dominate the world market, not all popular culture comes from the United States. The popularity of some contemporary culture is limited to particular cultures, while other forms of popular culture cross into a more international market. For example, the James Bond books and movies have roots in Britain, but the famous character has been exported to the United States. In their study of the James Bond phenomenon, scholars Tony Bennett and Janet Woollacott note that in the Bond film *License to Kill* "the threat to the dominance of white American male culture is removed not by a representative of that culture, and certainly not by a somewhat foppish English spy, but by the self-destruction of the forces ranged against it."[29] The appropriation of the British character into U.S. ideological and economic terrain complicates arguments about the dominance of U.S. popular culture products.

The popularity of Japanese animé or cartoons reflects another non-U.S. popular culture phenomenon. Animé clubs have emerged across the United States and around the world. The fascination with animé highlights the ability of non-U.S. popular culture to become popular internationally. Although many people think of animé as children's cartoons, "most animé tells sophisticated stories with complex characters aimed at adults."[30] Yet, "like so many cultural phenomena, animé is not just about anime itself, but about a subculture that's grown up enough to find some mainstream acceptance, but is often still misunderstood."[31] The way that Japanese popular culture is imported into the United States is reflected in the development of animé clubs, websites, meetings, and other social activities.

Pop Culture Spotlight

Did you like the last Kevin Costner movie? How about his last three? Do you think Leonardo DiCaprio is overrated? How about that John Travolta turkey *Battlefield Earth*? Stars are as important as they are because they help sell movies internationally. Can you name a non-U.S. or British movie star other than Jackie Chan?

What Do You Think?

Do movie ratings matter to you? How about television or music ratings? Why don't you think the ratings at movie theaters and record stores are enforced? What do you think would happen if they were?

Cultural Imperialism

It is difficult to measure the impact of the U.S. and Western media and popular culture on the rest of the world. But we do know that we cannot ignore this dynamic. The U.S. government in the 1920s believed that having American movies on foreign screens would boost the sales of U.S. goods. The U.S. government worked closely with the Hays Office (officially, the Motion Picture Producers and Distributors of America) to break into foreign markets, most notably in the United Kingdom.[32]

The discussions about **media imperialism** (domination or control through the media), **electronic colonialism** (domination or exploitation utilizing technological forms), and **cultural imperialism** (domination through the spread of cultural products), which began in the 1920s, continue today. Table 7.2 shows the top ten movies worldwide in 2002, but note how many of them are U.S.-made. The interrelationships among economics, nationalism, and culture make it difficult to determine how significant cultural imperialism might be. The issue of cultural imperialism is complex because the phenomenon of cultural imperialism is complex. In his survey of the cultural imperialism debates, scholar John Tomlinson identified five different ways of thinking about cultural imperialism: (1) as cultural domination, (2) as media imperialism, (3) as nationalist discourse, (4) as a critique of global capitalism, and (5) as a critique of modernity.[33] Tomlinson's analysis underscores the interrelatedness of issues of ethnicity, culture, and nationalism in the context of economics, technology, and capitalism. Because economic, technological, and financial resources are not equally distributed around the world, some ethnic, cultural, and national groups face more difficulty in maintaining their identities and traditions. To understand the concerns about cultural imperialism, therefore, it is necessary to consider the impact of U.S. American popular culture. There is no easy way to measure the impact of popular culture, but we should be sensitive to its influences on intercultural communication.

TABLE 7.2   Ten Top-Grossing Movies Worldwide in 2002

U.S. movies dominate the worldwide movie market. Here is a recent list of the top-grossing movies.

RANK	TITLE	RANK	TITLE
1	*Lord of the Rings: The Two Towers*	6	*Die Another Day*
2	*Harry Potter and The Chamber of Secrets*	7	*Signs*
3	*Spider-Man*	8	*Ice Age*
4	*Star Wars, Episode II: Attack of the Clones*	9	*My Big Fat Greek Wedding*
5	*Men in Black II*	10	*Minority Report*

Source: http://www.moviemarshal.com/boxworld2002.html

Sometimes the Western images are imported and welcomed by other countries. For example, the government of the Ivory Coast of West Africa has used foreign (mostly French) media to promote its image of a "new" Ivoirien cultural identity. The government purchased a satellite dish that permits it to broadcast 1,400 hours of French programming annually. But it has been criticized by many for borrowing too heavily from the Western media—for inviting cultural imperialism. One critic notes:

> While television, as mirror, sometimes reflects multiple Ivoirien cultures, the latter are expected to acquiesce to a singular national culture in the image of the Party, which is also synonymous with a Western cultural image. . . . The cultural priority is openness for the sake of modernization in the quest of the Ivoirien national identity.[34]

Many cultural groups around the world worry about the impact of cultural imperialism. The government of Quebec, for example, is very concerned about the effects of English-language media on French Canadian language and culture. The French have also expressed concern about the dominance of U.S. popular culture and its impact on French society. Yet the popularity of U.S. popular culture products, such as *Law & Order, 24* and Janet Jackson CDs and videos, outside the United States reinforces particular notions of romance, masculinity, friendship, and happiness and promotes often idealized images of where U.S. Americans live and what kinds of commodities they purchase.

Popular culture plays an enormous role in relations among nations worldwide. It is through popular culture that we try to understand the dynamics of other cultures and nations. Although these representations are problematic, we also rely on popular culture to understand many kinds of issues: the conflicts in Bosnia-Herzegovina and Kosovo; the murders of homeless children in Brazil; the rise of nationalism in Hawaii, Quebec, and Eritrea; the tensions between India and Pakistan. For many of us, the world exists through popular culture.

SUMMARY

In this chapter, we focused on popular culture, one of the primary modes of intercultural experience. The images produced by culture industries such as film and television enable us to "travel" to many places. We rely heavily on popular culture as a forum for the development of our ideas about other places. For example, many people who have never been to China or studied much about the Chinese economic system have very strong ideas about the country and its economy based on news reports, films, documentaries, and so on.

It is significant that much of our popular culture is dominated by U.S.-based cultural industries, considering how we use popular culture as a form of intercultural communication. Not all popular culture emerges from the United States, but the bulk of it does. And it contributes to a power dynamic—cultural imperialism—that affects intercultural communication everywhere.

Popular culture has four important characteristics: it is produced by culture industries; it is distinct from folk culture; it is ubiquitous; and it serves social

What Do You Think?

Some scholars argue that the Internet has become one of the most powerful tools of cultural imperialism to date. In an online journal article, Seongheol Kim notes: "Currently, 90% of traffic worldwide on the Internet is in English. . . . The Internet is anchored in the United States; the vast majority of World Wide Web sites are based in the U.S and are in English; most software used to navigate the Internet is in English; and search engines are mostly in English." (Refer to: http://interculturalrelations.com/v1i4Fall1998/f98kim.htm). What are the implications of this? (Source: Seongheol Kim, November 1, 1998, *The Edge: The E-Journal of Intercultural Relations*, Fall 1998, vol. 1, no 4. http://interculturalrelations.com/)

functions. Individuals and groups can determine the extent to which they are influenced by popular culture. That is, we may choose to consume or resist the messages of popular culture. Our cultural identities play a significant role as we navigate our way through popular culture. Popular culture also helps us understand other cultural groups. We tend to rely more heavily on media images of cultural groups we have little or no personal experience with, but stereotyping can be a problem here.

A great deal of popular culture is produced in the United States and circulated globally. The imbalance in the exchange of American popular culture and other popular culture texts has raised concerns about cultural imperialism.

BUILDING INTERCULTURAL SKILLS

1. Be a reflective consumer of popular culture. Be conscious of the decisions you make about which popular culture texts you choose. Think about why you choose certain television shows, magazines, and other cultural texts. Try reading magazines or watching films or TV shows that you normally would not to expand your intercultural communication repertoire.

2. Be aware of how popular culture influences the formation of your cultural identity and worldviews. Be conscious of how popular culture images create or reinforce your views about other places and other people, as well as yourself and your immediate environment.

3. Be aware of how media portrayal of different cultural groups might influence your intercultural interactions with those groups. How might others see you?

4. Think about how you might resist popular culture and when you should do so. Do you talk back to the TV when news is framed in a particular way? Do you notice who gets to speak and who is interviewed, as well as who is not allowed to speak?

5. Think about how you might be an advocate for those whose voices are not heard in popular culture. How might you help challenge imbalances in popular culture?

ACTIVITIES

1. *Popular culture:* Meet with other students in small groups, and answer the following questions:
   a. Which popular culture texts (magazines, TV shows, and so on) do you watch/buy, and why?
   b. Which popular culture texts do you not like and not watch/buy, and why? Discuss why we like certain products and not others. For example, do some products reinforce or support our worldviews? Do they empower us in some way? Enlighten us?

2. *Ethnic representation in popular culture:* Keep a log of your favorite TV shows for one week. Answer the following questions for each show, and discuss your answers in small groups.

a. How many different ethnic groups were portrayed?

b. What roles did members of these ethnic groups have?

c. What ethnic groups were represented in the major roles?

d. What ethnic groups were represented in the minor roles?

e. What ethnic groups were represented in the good-guy roles?

f. What ethnic groups were represented in the bad-guy roles?

g. What types of roles did women have?

h. What kinds of intercultural interactions occurred?

i. What were the outcomes?

j. How do the roles and interactions support or refute common stereotypes of the ethnic groups involved?

THE ONLINE LEARNING CENTER at www.mhhe.com/experiencing2 features self-quizzes, flashcards, and crossword puzzles based on the chapter's key terms and concepts.

**www.mhhe.com/
experiencing2**

ENDNOTES

1. Katz, E., & Liebes, T. (1987). Decoding *Dallas:* Notes from a cross-cultural study. In H. Newcomb (Ed.), *Television: The critical view* (4th ed.) (pp. 419–432). New York: Oxford University Press.

2. Brummett, B. (1994). *Rhetoric in popular culture.* New York: St. Martin's Press, p. 21.

3. Fiske, J. (1989). *Understanding popular culture.* New York: Routledge, p. 23.

4. Lipsitz, G. (1990). *Time passages: Collective memory and American popular culture.* Minneapolis: University of Minnesota Press, p. 140.

5. Lipsitz (1990), p. 159.

6. Newcomb, H., & Hirsch, P. M. (1987). Television as cultural forum. In Newcomb.

7. Dolby, N. (1999). Youth and the global popular: The politics and practices of race in South Africa. *European Journal of Cultural Studies, 2* (3), 296.

8. Poniewozik, J. (2003, February 17). Why reality TV is good for us. *Time,* p. 67.

9. Poniewozik, J. (2003, February 17), pp. 66–67.

10. Scott, D. (2003). Mormon "family values" versus television: An analysis of the discourse of Mormon couples regarding television and popular media culture. *Critical Studies in Media Communication, 20*(3), 325.

11. Scott (2003), p. 328.

12. Scott (2003), p. 324.

13. Pierce, S. D. (2003, August 1). Folks 'git mad' over 'Hillbillies.' (Salt Lake City) *Deseret News.* (online) (http://deseretnews.com/dn/view/0,1249,510043822,00.html)

14. G. I. Joe doll salutes Code Talkers. (2000, March 4). *The Arizona Republic,* p. E9.

15. Katz & Liebes (1987), pp. 419–432.

16. Katz & Liebes (1987), p. 421.

17. Lee, M., & Cho, C. H. (1990, January). Women watching together: An ethnographic study of Korean soap opera fans in the U.S. *Cultural Studies, 4*(1), 30–44.

18. Lee & Cho (1990), p. 43.

19. Shaheen, J. G. (1984). *The TV Arab.* Bowling Green, OH: Bowling Green State University Press, p. 4.

20. Flores, L. (1994). *Shifting visions: Intersections of rhetorical and Chicana feminist theory in the analysis of mass media.* Unpublished dissertation, University of Georgia, p. 16.

21. Merritt, B. D. (2000). Illusive reflections: African American women on primetime television. In A. González, M. Houston, & V. Chen (Eds.), *Our voices* (3rd ed.) (pp. 47–53). Los Angeles: Roxbury.

22. Merritt, B. D. (2000), p. 53.

23. Manusov, V., & Hegde, R. (1993). Communicative outcomes of stereotype-based expectancies: An observational study of cross-cultural dyads. *Communication Quarterly, 41,* 338–354.

24. Snyder, M. (1998). Self-fulfilling stereotypes. In P. Rothenburg (Ed.), *Race, class and gender in the United States* (4th ed.) (pp. 452–457). New York: St. Martin's Press.

25. Guback, T. (1969). *The international film industry: Western Europe and America since 1945.* Bloomington: Indiana University Press. See also Guback, T., & Varis, T. (1982). *Transnational communication and cultural industries.* Paris: Unesco.

26. Lee's Movie Info. (2003). The Matrix Reloaded. (http://www.leesmovieinfo.net/wbotitle .php?t=1929)

27. Aljazeera. (2003). About Aljazeera. (http://english.aljazeera.net/NR/exeres/5D7F956E-6B52 -46D9-8D17-448856D01CDB.htm)

28. Wilshire, K. (2003, March 30). Chirac demands France create a rival to CNN. (London) *Daily Telegraph.* (online) (http://www.telegraph.co.uk/news/main.jhtml?xml=/news/2003/03/30/ wchirc30.xml)

29. Bennett, T., & Woollacott, J. (1987). *Bond and beyond: The political career of a popular culture hero.* New York: Methuen, pp. 293–294.

30. Hung, M. (2001, August 2). Tooned into anime. *Houston Press.* (online) (http://www .houstonpress.com/issues/2001-08-02/feature.html/1/index.html)

31. Hung, M. (2001, August 2).

32. Nakayama, T. K., & Vachon, L. A. (1991). Imperialist victory in peacetime: State functions and the British cinema industry. *Current Research in Film, 5,* 161–174.

33. Tomlinson, J. (1991). *Cultural imperialism.* Baltimore: Johns Hopkins University Press, pp. 19–23.

34. Land, M. (1992). Ivoirien television, willing vector of cultural imperialism. *The Howard Journal of Communications, 4,* 25.

CHAPTER EIGHT

Culture, Communication, and Conflict

STUDY OBJECTIVES

After reading this chapter, you should be able to:

1. Identify and describe the characteristics of intercultural conflict.

2. Define interpersonal conflict and its characteristics.

3. Identify five different types of conflict.

4. List the basic principles of nonviolence.

5. Suggest some ways in which cultures differ in their views toward conflict.

6. Understand how people come by their conflict strategies.

7. Identify and describe four styles for dealing with intercultural conflict.

8. Discuss the relationship between ethnicity, gender, and conflict communication.

9. Define social movements.

10. Explain why it is important to understand the role of the social and historical contexts in intercultural conflicts.

11. Discuss some suggestions for dealing with intercultural conflicts.

KEY TERMS

accommodating style	intercultural conflict
conflict	interdependent
direct approach	intermediary
discussion style	mediation
dynamic style	pacifism
emotionally expressive style	religious conflict
engagement style	restraint style
incompatibility	social conflict
indirect approach	social movements

One thing we can be sure of is that conflict is unavoidable. Conflicts are happening all around the world, as they always have, and at many different levels. For example, conflicts can happen on the interpersonal level, which was the case for our student Joy, who described a recent conflict with her boyfriend. Joy is from a midwestern, third-generation Scotch-Irish family. Her boyfriend's family is first-generation Filipino. Cultural differences between the groups often cause conflict and misunderstanding. The most recent conflict occurred when Joy's family discovered that her step-grandmother was very sick with cancer. Joy described her boyfriend's reaction when she told him this news on the telephone:

> He really said nothing. His first reaction was "Oh," and then he went on with whatever he was doing at the time. I was shocked. I couldn't believe that he had been so insensitive to me and my family. I was furious, but he saw nothing wrong in what he had done. . . . We managed the conflict by arguing and talking . . . [and then] discussed what we were both angry about . . . and then agreed to try to be more aware of the differences we both have in regards to certain situations and to meet each other halfway, not just blame each other.

Conflict can also happen on a societal level. For example, environmentalists and developers may disagree on the importance of economic interests, as is the case in the Northwest United States. For many years, loggers and environmentalists have been at odds; the logging industries claim that logging is necessary to provide products, jobs, and economic growth. Environmentalists claim logging should be restricted or eliminated in places where it causes damage to mountains, rivers, and animal populations.[1]

Cultural conflicts can also occur on the international level. The recent disagreement between France and the United States over the invasion of Iraq led to some strong feelings on both sides of the Atlantic. In the United States, some school exchange trips involving French students were cancelled. A teacher in Philadelphia sent an e-mail to the French families to tell them the exchange was cancelled: "The main reason for this is that we do not feel that we can ensure a truly comfortable or hospitable stay for your students as the anti-French sentiment here in the U.S. is very strong."[2] The anti-French sentiment and the cutting of ties through an e-mail shocked "the French parents who decided to inform the American embassy and the Minister of Foreign Affairs."[3] The larger international conflict between the United States and France affects more everyday interactions between U.S. Americans and French, as in the case of these schoolchildren.

Conflict may also arise from mediated communication. U.S. television, film, and other media have dominated the world market for many years. Many people in other countries feel that this cultural dominance stunts their economic growth

What Do You Think?

Does counting to 10 work for you when you need to calm yourself? What about taking a deep breath? Have your parents or grandparents ever told you stories about the fist fights of their day? What methods do you use to solve conflicts in your everyday life?

Some conflicts are managed by mediators, who help disputants resolve their differences. Mediators may be used informally, as in auto accidents, or more formally, as when lawyers are consulted in divorce or real estate disputes.

and imposes U.S. cultural values, which has led to resentment and conflict.[4] Many Canadians, for example, believe that it has been difficult for their country to develop a distinct Canadian cultural identity since it is so heavily influenced by U.S. cultural products. But this resentment has lessened somewhat in recent years with the increasing number of Canadian celebrities who have contributed to U.S. popular culture—for example, Martin Short, Michael J. Fox, Mike Myers, Shania Twain, Dan Aykroyd, Jim Carrey, and Peter Jennings.

In this chapter, we identify characteristics of intercultural conflict, as well as different types of conflict and conflict styles. We also examine how cultural background can influence conflict management and discuss guidelines for engaging in intercultural conflict. Finally, we look at societal forces that influence intercultural conflict.

CHARACTERISTICS OF INTERCULTURAL CONFLICT

Conflict is usually defined as involving a perceived or real **incompatibility** of goals, values, expectations, processes, or outcomes between two or more **interdependent** individuals or groups.[5] A good example of intercultural conflict can be seen in the *maquiladoras*—sorting or assembly plants along the Mexican-U.S. border. Because Mexicans and U.S. Americans work alongside one another, intercultural conflict inevitably occurs.[6] For example, some Mexican managers think that the U.S. American managers are rude in their dealings with each other and with the workers. While both Mexican and U.S. American managers have common goals, they also have some different expectations and values, which

What Do You Think?

In the news, the conflicts between India and Pakistan, Serbia and Bosnia, Russia and Chechnya, and Israel and Palestine are described as ethnic conflicts or cultural conflicts. Can you name a war in history that was not an ethnic or cultural conflict? Has the United States ever been involved in a war that was not a cultural conflict?

leads to conflict. The Mexican managers expect the U.S. American managers to be more polite and to value harmony in their relationships. The U.S. American managers expect the Mexicans to be more direct and honest and to not worry so much about the "face" and feelings of other managers and workers. These conflicts have roots in the history of U.S.-Mexican relations, a history characterized by economic and military domination on the part of the United States and by hostility and resentment on the part of Mexico.

What are characteristics of **intercultural conflict?** How does intercultural conflict differ from other kinds of conflict? One unique characteristic is that intercultural conflicts tend to be more ambiguous than intracultural conflict. Other characteristics involve language issues and contradictory conflict styles.

Ambiguity

There is often a great deal of ambiguity in intercultural conflicts. We may be unsure of how to handle the conflict or of whether the conflict is seen in the same way by the other person. And the other person may not even think there is a conflict. In Joy's case, presented at the beginning of the chapter, she and her boyfriend both admitted the conflict; that was the first step in resolving it.

However, often when we encounter ambiguity, we quickly resort to our default style of handling conflict—the style we learned in our family. If your preferred way of handling conflict is to deal with it immediately but you are in a conflict with someone who prefers to avoid it, the conflict may become exacerbated as you both retreat to your preferred styles. Thus, the confronting person becomes increasingly confrontational, while the avoider retreats further.

Language Issues

The issues surrounding language may be important ones. Language can sometimes lead to intercultural conflict, and it can also be the primary vehicle for solving intercultural conflict. This was true for Jodi, a student of ours, who described a recent conflict she had with some fellow workers:

> I work in a restaurant where the kitchen employees are mostly of Mexican descent. Some of the men would make inappropriate comments in Spanish. I chose to ignore it, but my method of resolving the conflict was not beneficial. It just resulted in my feeling uncomfortable. Finally, I decided to take the initiative. I used my Spanish speaking skills to let the employees know I could understand them—somewhat. Then I decided to make an effort to greet them whenever I came into contact with them. I found that they are much more friendly. This was the best approach to take, and it yielded good results.

However, when you don't know the language well, it is very difficult to handle conflict effectively. At the same time some silence is not necessarily a bad thing. Sometimes it provides a "cooling off" period during which the participants can calm down and gather their thoughts. This was our student Dotty's experience with her host family in France. Initially, she was experiencing culture shock and was not getting along with her host "brother." So she told her host family to go out without her because she wasn't feeling well. She recalls: "I spent the afternoon and evening walking along the beach and exploring the forest. This allowed relations to continue, but it gave time to work things out. I felt good about the time out. It all turned out well, but it required some time and patience."

Contradictory Conflict Styles

Intercultural conflict also may be characterized by contradictory conflict styles. In the *maquiladoras*, the biggest difference between U.S. Americans and Mexicans seems to be in the way U.S. Americans express disagreement at management meetings. The Mexican managers tend to be more indirect and more polite in conflict situations, whereas the U.S. American managers prefer to confront conflict directly and openly. These very different styles in handling conflict cause problems in the workplace and sometimes lead to more conflict.

CONFLICT TYPES AND CONTEXTS

Perhaps if everyone agreed on the best way to view conflict, there would be less of it. The reality is that different approaches to conflict may result in more conflict. In this section, we identify five different types of conflict and some strategies for resolving them.

Types of Conflict

Common categories of conflict include affective conflict, conflict of interest, value conflict, cognitive conflict, and goal conflict.[7] Affective conflict occurs when individuals become aware that their feelings and emotions are incompatible. For example, suppose someone finds out that his or her romantic feelings for a close friend are not reciprocated. Their different levels of affection may lead to conflict.

A conflict of interest describes a situation in which people have incompatible preferences for a course of action or plan to pursue. For example, one student of ours described an ongoing conflict with an ex-girlfriend: "The conflicts always seem to be a jealousy issue or a controlling issue, where even though we are not going out anymore, both of us still try to control the other's life to some degree. You could probably say that this is a conflict of interest."

Value conflict, a more serious type, occurs when people have differing ideologies. For example, suppose that Ruben and Laura have been married for several months and are starting to argue frequently about their views on when to start their family and how to raise their children. Laura believes strongly that one parent should stay at home with the children when they are small, so she would like to wait until they have saved enough money and she can stop working for a

Surf's Up!

Kare Anderson has six tips for reducing workplace conflict that you've probably never heard before. Sidling? Not wearing plaid? Perfume? Check out her website to see why she thinks these tips can help people communicate better and reduce conflict (pertinent.com/pertinfo/business/kareCom3.html).

Nonviolent confrontation provides an opportunity for social change. People who protest peacefully can highlight injustices and lend credibility to social movements.

Surf's Up!

The way individuals handle conflict may have a lot to do with their personality in addition to their cultural background. Go to http://www.geocities.com/ptypes, and read about the Myers-Briggs personality types. Also note the link for the "passive aggressive" personality type, which some scholars note is related to behavior that provokes conflict.

few years. Ruben wants to have children immediately but does not want Laura to stop working; he thinks their children will do fine in day care. This situation illustrates value conflict.

Cognitive conflict describes a situation in which two or more people become aware that their thought processes or perceptions are in conflict. For example, suppose that Marissa and Derek argue frequently about whether Marissa's friend Bob is paying too much attention to her. Derek suspects that Bob wants to have sex with Marissa, but Marissa doesn't agree. Their different perceptions of the situation constitute cognitive conflict.

Goal conflict occurs when people disagree about a preferred outcome or end state. For example, suppose that Bob and Charles, who have been in a relationship for 10 years, have just bought a house. Bob wants to furnish the house slowly, making sure that money goes into the savings account for retirement. Charles wants to furnish the house immediately, using money from their savings. Their individual goals are in conflict with each other.

The Importance of Context

How we choose to manage conflict may depend on the particular context or situation. For example, we may choose to use discussion style when arguing with a close friend about serious relational issues in a quiet movie theater. By contrast, we may feel freer to use a more confrontational style at a political rally.

Nikki, a student with a part-time job at a restaurant, described an experience she had in serving a large group of German tourists. The tourists argued with her about the bill, claiming that they had been overcharged. Nikki explained that a 15 percent service charge had been added. The Germans thought that she had added the tip because they were tourists; they hadn't realized it was the policy when serving large groups. Nikki explained that she was much more conciliatory when dealing with this group in the restaurant than she would have been in a more social context. She thought the Germans were rude, but she practiced good listening skills and took a more problem-solving approach than she would have otherwise.

One of our students, Courtney, recounted a conflict she had when one of her friends made the college football team. She told him he had "natural talent," and he thought she was being racist because he was Black. Even though Courtney didn't mean to be racist, we can only understand the conflict within the historical context of White-Black relations in the United States; as he told her, he gets these kinds of comments a lot. Thus, the conflict context can be viewed in two ways: (1) in terms of the actual situation in which the conflict happens and (2) as a larger societal context. We'll discuss the larger societal context of conflict later in the chapter.

Info Bites

Active listening is a three-step process suggested by interpersonal communication scholars to help reduce conflict. It includes paraphrasing the other person's ideas, expressing understanding of them, and then asking questions about them. From an intercultural perspective, why would this process be helpful?

CULTURAL INFLUENCES ON CONFLICT MANAGEMENT

A key question is this: Is open conflict good or bad? That is, should conflict be welcomed because it provides opportunities to strengthen relationships? Or should it be avoided because it can only lead to problems for relationships and groups? Another key question is this: What is the best way to handle conflict when it arises? Should individuals talk about it directly, deal with it indirectly, or avoid it? Should emotions be part of the conflict resolution? Are expressions of emotions viewed as showing commitment to resolving the conflict at hand? Or is it better to be restrained and solve problems by rational logic rather than emotional expressiveness? Also consider the following questions: How do we learn how to deal with conflict? Who teaches us how to solve conflicts when they arise? How we answer all of these questions depends in large part on our cultural background and the way we were raised.

Family Influences

The ways in which people respond to conflict may be influenced by their cultural background. More specifically, most people deal with conflict in the way they learned while growing up—their default style. Conflict resolution strategies usually relate to how people manage their self-image in relationships. For example, they may prefer to preserve their own self-esteem rather than help the other person "save face." Or they may prefer to sacrifice their own self-esteem in order to preserve the relationship.

We tend to prefer a particular conflict style in our interactions for many reasons. A primary influence is our family background; some families prefer a particular conflict style, and children come to accept this style as normal. For example, the family may have settled conflict in a direct, confrontational manner, with the person having the strongest argument (or the biggest muscle) getting his or her way.

Sometimes people try very hard to reject the conflict styles they saw their parents using. For example, suppose that Maria's parents avoided open conflict and never discussed what was bothering them. Their children learned to avoid conflict and become very uncomfortable when people around them use a more expressive style of conflict management. Maria has vowed she will never deal with conflict that way with her own children and has tried very hard to use other ways of dealing with conflicts when they do arise in her family. It is important to realize that people deal with conflict in a variety of ways and may not have the same reasons for choosing a certain style.

Two Approaches to Conflict

There are at least two primary ways that you can approach conflict. You can be either direct or indirect, and you can be either emotionally expressive or restrained.[8] The way you approach conflict probably depends on your cultural background and the way you were raised. Let's look at each of these two dimensions more closely.

Direct and Indirect Conflict Approaches   This **direct/indirect approach** to conflict is similar to the direct/indirect language dimension we discussed in Chapter 5. There it was applied specifically to language use, whereas here it represents a broader conflict resolution approach. Some cultural groups think that conflict is fundamentally a good thing; these groups feel that it is best to approach conflict very directly, because working through conflicts constructively results in stronger, healthier, and more satisfying relationships. Similarly, groups that work through conflict can gain new information about members or about other groups, defuse more serious conflict, and increase group cohesiveness.[9]

People who take this approach concentrate on using very precise language. While they may not always feel comfortable with face-to-face conflict, they think that it's important to "say what's on your mind" in a conflict situation. The goal in this approach is to articulate the issues carefully and select the "best" solution based on an agreed-upon set of criteria.

However, many cultural groups view conflict as ultimately destructive for relationships. For example, many Asian cultures, reflecting the influence of Confucianism and Taoism, and some religious groups in the United States see conflict as disturbing the peace. For instance, most Amish think of conflict not as an opportunity for personal growth, but as a threat to interpersonal and community harmony. When conflict does arise, the strong spiritual value of **pacifism** dictates a nonresistant response—often avoidance or dealing with conflict very indirectly.[10]

What Do You Think?

War is a topic about which many individuals seem to disagree. But have you noticed how many films about war are released by Hollywood each year? Films like *Platoon* (1986), *Braveheart* (1995), *Saving Private Ryan* (1998), *Enemy at the Gates* (2001), *Behind Enemy Lines* (2001), *Black Hawk Down* (2002), and even *Gangs of New York* (2002), which highlights the interethnic conflicts that were raging in New York around the same time as the Civil War draft riots of 1863, all have done well at the box office. Do you think these films say anything about the social climate during the period of their release?

Also, these groups think that when members disagree they should adhere to the consensus of the group rather than engage in conflict. In fact, members who threaten group harmony may be sanctioned. One writer gives an example of a man from the Maori culture in New Zealand who was swearing and using inappropriate language in a public meeting:

> A woman went up to him, laying her hand on his arm and speaking softly. He shook her off and continued. The crowd now moved back from him as far as possible, and as if by general agreement, the listeners dropped their gaze to their toes until all he could see was the tops of their heads. The speaker slowed, faltered, was reduced to silence, and then sat down.[11]

These people tend to approach conflict rather indirectly. They concentrate on the meaning that is "outside" the verbal message and tend to be very careful to protect the "face" of the person with whom they disagree. They may emphasize vagueness and ambiguity in language and often rely on third parties to help resolve disagreements. The goal in this approach is to make sure that the relationship stays intact during the disagreement. For example, they may emphasize the past history of the disputants and try to build a deeper relationship that involves increased obligation toward each other.

Emotional Expressiveness/Restraint Conflict Style   A second broad approach to conflict concerns the role of emotion in conflict. People who value intense and overt displays of emotions during discussion of disagreement rely on the *emotionally expressive style*. They think it is better to show emotion during disagreement than to hide or suppress feelings; that is, they show emotion through expressive nonverbal behavior and vocalization. They also think that this outward display of emotions means that one really cares and is committed to resolving the conflict. In fact, one's credibility is based on the ability to be expressive.

On the other hand, people who believe in the **restraint style** think that disagreements are best discussed in an emotionally calm manner. For these people, it's important to control and internalize one's feelings during conflict and to avoid nonverbal emotion. They are uncomfortable with emotional expression and think that such expressions may hurt others. People who use this approach think that relationships are made stronger by keeping one's emotions in check and protecting the "face" or honor of the other person. Credibility is demonstrated by maintaining tight control over one's emotions.

These two approaches to conflict resolution reflect different underlying cultural values involving identity and preserving self-esteem. In the more individualistic approach that sees conflict as good, the concern is with individuals preserving their own dignity. The more communal approach espoused by both Amish and Asian cultures and by many other collectivist groups is more concerned with maintaining harmony in interpersonal relations and preserving the dignity of others. For example, in classic Chinese thought, social harmony is the goal of human society at all levels—individual, family, village, and nation.[12]

Pop Culture Spotlight

Martial arts are an integral part of Eastern traditions and history. Aikido, karate, or tae kwon do, for instance, are martial arts that seem to teach practitioners to respond to aggression in ways that avoid conflict or limit violence. Is that same message being translated through the media? Between video games and up-to-date Hollywood films, what kinds of images do we see of those who practice martial arts? Have those images changed over time? Compare films like *The Karate Kid* from the 1980s to more recent films like *Crouching Tiger Hidden Dragon* or *The Matrix*. What do these films tell us about the nature of conflict or about changes in our culture?

Intercultural Conflict Styles

It is possible to combine the four dimensions discussed and come up with four different conflict resolution styles that seem to be connected to various cultural groups: the discussion style, the engagement style, the accommodating style, and the dynamic style.[13]

The **discussion style** combines the direct and emotionally restrained dimensions and emphasizes a verbally direct approach for dealing with disagreements—to "say what you mean and mean what you say." People who use this style are comfortable expressing disagreements directly but prefer to be emotionally restrained. This style is often identified as the predominant style preferred by many White Americans, as well as Europeans, Australians, and New Zealanders. This approach is expressed by the Irish saying, "What is nearest the heart is nearest the mouth."

The **engagement style** emphasizes a verbally direct and confrontational approach to dealing with conflict. This style views intense verbal and nonverbal expression of emotion as demonstrating sincerity and willingness to engage intensely to resolve conflict. It has been linked to some African Americans and Southern Europeans (France, Greece, Italy, Spain), as well as to some people from Russia and the Middle East (Israel). This approach is captured in the Russian proverb, "After a storm, fair weather; after sorrow, joy."

The **accommodating style** emphasizes an indirect approach for dealing with conflict and a more emotionally restrained manner. People who use this style may be ambiguous and indirect in expressing their views, thinking that this is a way to ensure that the conflict "doesn't get out of control." This style is often preferred by American Indians, Latin Americans (Mexicans, Costa Ricans), and Asians. This style may best be expressed by the Swahili proverb, "Silence produces peace, and peace produces safety," or by the Chinese proverb, "The first to raise their voice loses the argument."

In this style, silence and avoidance may be used to manage conflict. For example, the Amish would prefer to lose face or money rather than escalate a conflict, and Amish children are instructed to turn the other cheek in any conflict situation, even if it means getting beat up by the neighborhood bully.

Individuals from these groups also use **intermediaries**—friends or colleagues who act on their behalf in dealing with conflict.[14] For example, a Taiwanese student at a U.S. university was offended by the People's Republic of China flag that her roommate displayed in their room. The Taiwanese student went to the international student advisor and asked him to talk to the U.S. American student about the flag. People who think that interpersonal conflict provides opportunities to strengthen relationships also use **mediation,** but mainly in formal settings. For instance, people retain lawyers to mediate disputes, hire real estate agents to negotiate commercial transactions, and engage counselors or therapists to resolve or manage interpersonal conflicts.

What are the basic principles of nonviolence applied to interpersonal relations? Actually, nonviolence is not the absence of conflict, and it is not a simple

Surf's Up!

What can the Quaker religion teach us about conflict resolution? Check out their website (mhnet. org/psyhelp/chap13/ chap13m.htm). One of their basic beliefs is pacifism. But then, how do they resolve conflicts, even potentially violent ones?

refusal to fight. Rather, it involves peacemaking—a difficult, and sometimes very risky, approach to interpersonal relationships. Individuals who take the peacemaking approach (1) strongly value the other person and encourage his or her growth, (2) attempt to de-escalate conflicts or keep them from escalating once they start, and (3) attempt to find creative negotiation to resolve conflicts when they arise.[15]

It is often difficult for people who are taught to use the discussion or engaging style to see the value in the accommodating style or in nonviolent approaches. They see indirectness and avoidance as a sign of weakness. However, millions of people view conflict as primarily "dysfunctional, interpersonally embarrassing, distressing and as a forum for potential humiliation and loss of face."[16] With this view of conflict, it makes much more sense to avoid direct confrontation and work toward saving face for the other person.

The **dynamic style** uses an indirect style of communicating along with a more emotionally intense expressiveness. People who use this style may use strong language, stories, metaphors, and use of third-party intermediaries. They are comfortable with more emotionally confrontational talk and view credibility of the other person grounded in their degree of emotional expressiveness. This style may be preferred by Arabs in the Middle East.

Cautions About Stereotyping   As with any generalization, however, it must be remembered that all conflict resolution styles can be found in any one cultural group, and while cultural groups tend to prefer one style over another, we must be careful not to stereotype. Also, these cultural differences may depend on a number of factors, including (1) whether regions have been historically homogenous and isolated from other cultures, (2) the influence of colonization, and (3) the immigration history of different cultural groups. For example, there is much more African influence in the Caribbean (compared to Central and Latin America), resulting in a more direct and emotionally expressive approach (engagement style) than in Mexico—which has maintained a more indirect and emotionally restrained approach (accommodation style). And there is a great variety of cultures within the African continent, accounting for tremendous variation in conflict resolution styles.[17]

Gender, Ethnicity, and Conflict

Our gender and ethnicity may influence how we handle conflict. Men and women in the United States seem to have different communication styles. These different ways of communicating sometimes lead to conflict and can influence how men and women handle conflict. One problem area involves what is known as "troubles talk." For example, women typically make sympathetic noises in response to what a friend says, whereas men may say nothing, which women interpret as indifference. Or women commiserate by talking about a similar situation they experienced, whereas men follow rules for conversational dominance and interpret this as stealing the stage. And in telling stories, men tend to be more linear, whereas women tend to give more details and offer tangential information, which men interpret as an inability to get to the point.[18]

Men and women also talk about relationships in different ways. Women may express more interest in the relationship process and may feel better simply discussing it. But men are more oriented toward problem solving and may see little point in discussing something if nothing is identified as needing fixing.[19]

How does ethnic background affect the way males and females deal with conflict? In one study, when African Americans, Asian Americans, White Americans, and Mexican Americans were asked to describe how they dealt with conflicts they had had with a close friend, they gave different kinds of answers.[20] African American males and females generally said they used a problem-solving approach. One respondent said, "I told him to stay in school and that I would help him study." Another explained, "We decided together how to solve the problem and deal with our friend."

White males and females generally seemed to focus on the importance of taking responsibility for their own behavior. Males mentioned the importance of being direct, using expressions like "getting things in the open" and "say right up front." Females talked about the importance of showing concern for the other person and the relationship and of maintaining situational flexibility. One woman explained, "She showed respect for my position and I showed respect for hers." By contrast, Asian Americans generally used more conflict-avoiding strategies than did White Americans.[21]

Mexican American males and females tended to differ in that males described the importance of talking to reach a mutual understanding. One man wanted to "make a better effort to explain"; another said that he and his partner "stuck to the problem until we solved it together." Females described several kinds of reinforcement of the relationship that were appropriate. In general, males and females in all groups described females as more compassionate and concerned for feelings, and males as more concerned with winning the conflict and being "right."

In any case, it is important to remember that, while ethnicity and gender may be related to ways of dealing with conflict, it is inappropriate and inaccurate to assume that any one person will behave in a particular way because of his or her ethnicity or gender.

Religion and Conflict

Religious differences also can be an important source of conflict. Religious beliefs are often a source of very strongly held views that can cause **religious conflict** with others who may not share those views. Recently, for example, Rev. Fred Phelps of Westboro Baptist Church in Kansas planned to mark the murder of Matthew Shepard in Wyoming with a granite monument in Casper. He "designed a granite monument with Shepard's face followed by these words chiseled in the stone: Matthew Shepard entered Hell October 12, 1998, at Age 21 In Defiance of God's Warning: 'Thou shalt not lie with mankind as with womankind; it is abomination.' (Leviticus 18:22)."

Many in Casper do not agree with Rev. Phelps's approach to marking the fifth anniversary of Shepard's murder. One resident of Casper noted, "I can't believe this is all happening here. Nobody hates anyone here." Yet, Rev. Phelps's "view of the Bible is hard and uncompromising. For the past five years he has made annual pilgrimages to Casper, Laramie and Fort Collins, Colo., to 'celebrate' Shepard's entry into Hell." While not all people read the Bible in the same way, religious differences can influence the way that people think about the murder of Matthew Shepard.[22]

A little farther west, in Utah, conflicts between Mormons and non-Mormons are not uncommon. The Salt Lake Tribune noted that "It is nothing new for protesters to loiter near the LDS Conference Center and Salt Lake Temple." Within a historical context, the anti-Mormon views of Latter-Day Saints (LDS) by other Christian groups is nothing new. Pressured to leave New York, Ohio, Missouri, and later Illinois before settling in Utah, Mormon history points to many anti-Mormon incidents, including the murder of the founder, Joseph Smith, in Illinois. The semiannual LDS General Conference in Salt Lake City continues to draw protesters, including "a small coterie of self-described Christian preachers." Some of their protests included displaying "in disrespectful and vulgar ways, some of the intimate, sacred temple garments worn by LDS women." This kind of conflict may provoke the LDS members into responding, which may escalate the conflict.[23]

Religious conflicts are not always nonviolent. Throughout European history, for example, the persecution of Jews often has been violent; recall, for instance, the atrocities of the Inquisition and the Holocaust. Religious conflicts between Catholics and Protestants also have been a mainstay of the conflict in Northern Ireland.

Value Differences and Conflict Styles

Another way of understanding cultural variations in intercultural conflict resolution is to look at how cultural values influence conflict management. Cultural values in individualistic societies differ from those in collectivist societies. Individualistic societies place greater importance on the individual than on groups like the family or professional work groups. Individualism is often cited as the most important European American value, as can be seen in the autonomy and independence encouraged in children. For example, children in the United States may be encouraged to leave home at age 18, and older parents often prefer to live on their own rather than with their children. By contrast, people from collectivist societies often live in extended families and value loyalty to groups.

These contrasting values may influence communication patterns. Thus, people from individualistic societies tend to be more concerned with preserving their own self-esteem during conflict, tend to be more direct in their communication, and tend to adopt more discussion conflict styles. By contrast, people from collectivist societies tend to be more concerned with maintaining group harmony and with preserving the other person's dignity during conflict. They

What Do You Think?

Two German philosophers, Hans-Georg Gadamer and Jurgen Habermas, have long debated exactly how people come to understand one another and avoid conflict. How do you think we learn to understand another person's "horizon"? Gadamer argues that it is through shared experience. Habermas thinks we can reason it out. From your experience, who do you think is right?

may take a less direct conversational approach and adopt accommodating and engaging conflict styles.[24]

How people choose to deal with conflict in any situation depends on the type of conflict and on their relationship with the other person. For example, in conflicts involving values and opinions, the Japanese may use the accommodating style more with acquaintances than with close friends. By contrast, they may use discussion conflict styles more with close friends than with acquaintances. In conflicts of interest, they may use a dominating style more with acquaintances than with close friends.[25] This suggests that, with people they don't know very well and with whom harmony is not as important, the Japanese use discussion or accommodating styles. However, with close friends, the way to maintain harmony is to work through the conflict using a discussion style.

MANAGING INTERCULTURAL CONFLICT

Productive Versus Destructive Conflict

Given all the variations in how people deal with conflicts, what happens when there is conflict in intercultural relationships? One option involves distinguishing between productive and destructive conflict in at least four ways.[26] First, in productive conflict, individuals or groups try to identify the specific problem; in destructive conflict, they make sweeping generalizations and have negative attitudes. For example, in an argument, one shouldn't say, "You never do the dishes," or "You always put me down in front of my friends." Rather, one should state the specific example of being put down: "Last evening when you criticized me in front of our friends, I felt bad."

Second, in productive conflict, individuals or groups focus on the original issue; in destructive conflict, they escalate the conflict from the original issues and anything in the relationship is open for reexamination. For example, guests on talk shows discussing extramarital affairs might start by citing a specific affair and then expand the conflict to include any number of prior arguments. The more productive approach would be to talk only about the specific affair.

Third, in productive conflict, individuals or groups direct the discussion toward cooperative problem solving ("How can we work this out?"); in destructive conflict, they try to seize power and use threats, coercion, and deception ("Either you do what I want, or . . .").

Finally, in productive conflict, individuals or groups value leadership that stresses mutually satisfactory outcomes; in destructive conflict, they polarize behind single-minded and militant leadership. In many political conflicts, such as those in the Middle East, people seem to have fallen into this trap, with leaders unwilling to work toward mutually satisfactory outcomes.

Competitive Versus Cooperative Conflict

As you can see, the general theme in destructive conflict is competitive escalation. Conflict often spirals into long-term negativity, with the conflicting parties establishing a self-perpetuating, mutually confirming expectation. As one writer

Surf's Up!

Are you good at dealing with conflict? How would you know? Do other people come to you for advice on their conflicts? And even if they do, are you sure you are good at resolving your own conflicts? Find out with the Conflict Resolution Questionnaire (www. qvctc.commnet.edu/ classes/conflict/questnr. html).

The "Truth and Reconciliation" hearings in South Africa were founded on a notion of forgiving—but not forgetting. The hearings provided a forum for South Africans to recount and admit to the injustices and violence of apartheid and move toward national healing.

notes, "Each is treating the other badly because it feels that the other deserves to be treated badly because the other treats it badly and so on."[27]

How can individuals and groups promote cooperative communication in conflict situations? According to Morton Deutsch, the general tone of a relationship will promote certain processes and acts.[28] For example, a competitive atmosphere will promote coercion, deception, suspicion, rigidity, and poor communication; a cooperative atmosphere will promote perceived similarity, trust, flexibility, and open communication. The key here is that this atmosphere needs to be established in the beginning stages of the relationship or group interaction. It is much more difficult to turn a competitive relationship into a cooperative one once the conflict has started to escalate. Our colleague Moira remembered a potential conflict during her first week at a new job and how she tried a cooperative approach:

> One of the staff members, Florence, seemed very cool to me. All the other staff members welcomed me to the organization; Florence never said a word. Then we had a misunderstanding about a project we were working on together, and it looked as if things could escalate into a big conflict. I decided that I really didn't want to get off on the wrong foot with her. So I took a deep breath, took a step back, and tried to get things off on a better foot. She had remarked that she was worried about her son, who was having problems in school. I had found a tutor for my son, who also had problems. So I decided to share this with her. We found that we had a lot in common. I found that she wasn't aware that she was being cool; she was just worried about a lot of family problems. We got the work thing cleared

up, and we're actually pretty good friends now. I'm really glad I didn't let things escalate.

Exploration is essential in developing a cooperative atmosphere. Exploration may be done in various ways in different cultures, but it has several basic steps: (1) The issue is put on hold, (2) both parties explore other options, or (3) they delegate the problem to a third party. Blaming is suspended, so it's possible to come up with new ideas or positions. "If all conflicting parties are committed to the process, there is a sense of joint ownership of the recommended solution. . . . [M]oving toward enemies as if they were friends exerts a paradoxical force on them and can bring transcendence."[29]

UNDERSTANDING CONFLICT AND SOCIETY

To fully understand intercultural conflict, we need to look beyond individuals who may be in conflict. Many intercultural conflicts can be better understood by looking at the social, economic, historical, and political forces.

Social and Economic Forces

Social conflict results from unequal or unjust social relationships between groups. Consider, for example, the social conflict in northern Wisconsin between many Whites and Native Americans over fishing rights. Much of the media attention focused only on the intercultural conflicts between particular individuals, but these individual conflicts were only the tip of the iceberg.[30] The economy in this part of Wisconsin is heavily dependent on tourism and fishing. Many Whites accused the Anishinabe (Chippewa) of overfishing, causing an economic downturn in the area and leading to uneasy social relationships. A treaty signed in 1837 had given the Anishinabe year-round fishing rights in exchange for the northern third of Wisconsin. Recognizing these social, economic, and historical contexts is necessary to understanding the current conflict.

Historical and political forces also are sources of conflict. Many international conflicts have arisen over border disputes. For example, Argentina and the United Kingdom both claimed the Malvinas (or Falkland) Islands in the South Atlantic, which led to a short war in 1982. Disputes between France and Germany over the Alsace-Lorraine region lasted much longer—from about 1871 to 1945. Similar disputes have arisen between Japan and Russia over islands north of Japan. The historical reasons for such conflicts help us understand the claims of both sides.

Some conflict may be due to political or cultural differences, but other conflicts occur during **social movements,** in which individuals work together to bring about social change. These individuals often use confrontation as a strategy to highlight the injustices of the system. So, for example, when African American students in Greensboro, North Carolina, sat down at Whites-only lunch counters in the 1960s, they were pointing out the injustices of segregation. Although the students were nonviolent, their actions drew a violent reaction that, for many people, legitimized the claims of injustice. Similarly, the women's suffrage movement in the United States was not an individual effort, but a mass effort to win the right to vote. Indeed, many contemporary social movements involve conflicts, including movements against racism, sexism, and homophobia; movements to protect animal rights, the environment, free speech, and civil rights; and so on. College campuses are likely locations for much activism.

There is, of course, no comprehensive list of existing social movements. They can arise and fall apart, depending on the opposition they provoke, the media attention they attract, and the strategies they use. To stimulate social change, social movements need confrontation to highlight whatever perceived injustice is being done and to open the way for social change to halt the continuation of this injustice.

Confrontation, then, can be seen as an opportunity for social change. In arguing for a nonviolent approach to working for change, Dr. Martin Luther King, Jr., had this to say:

> Nonviolent resistance is not a method for cowards; it does resist. . . . [It] does not seek to defeat or humiliate the opponent, but to win his friendship and understanding. The nonviolent resister must often express his protest through noncooperation or boycotts, but he realizes that these are not ends themselves; they are merely means to awaken a sense of moral shame in the opponent.[31]

Info Bites

Did you know *conflict* comes from the Latin word *conflictus*, which means to strike together? What images come to mind when you think of what it means to "strike together"? (Source: http://www.hyperdictionary.com)

Although nonviolence is not the only form of confrontation employed by social movements, it has a long history—from Mahatma Gandhi's struggle for India to gain independence from Britain, to the civil rights struggle in the United States, to the struggle against apartheid in South Africa. And images of the violent confrontations with nonviolent protesters tended to legitimize the social movements and delegitimize the existing social system. For example, the televised images of police dogs attacking schoolchildren and riot squads turning fire hoses on protesters in Birmingham, Alabama, in the 1950s and 1960s swung public sentiment in favor of the civil rights movement.

Some social movements have also used violent forms of confrontation. Groups such as Action Directe in France, the Irish Republican Army, the environmental group Earth First!, and independence movements in Corsica, Algeria, Kosovo, and Chechnya have all been accused of using violence, which tends to result in their being labeled as terrorists rather than simply protesters. Even the suggestion of violence can be threatening to people. For example, in 1964, Malcolm X spoke in favor of civil rights: "The question tonight, as I understand it, is 'The Negro Revolt and Where Do We Go from Here?' or 'What Next?' In my little humble way of understanding it, it points toward either the ballot or the bullet."[32] Malcolm X's rhetoric terrified many U.S. Americans, who then refused to give legitimacy to his movement. To understand communication practices such as these, it is important to study the social context in which the movement operated.

Many conflicts are fueled by economic problems, which often find their expression in terms of cultural differences. Many people find it easier to explain economic troubles by pointing to cultural differences or by blaming cultural

Figure 8.1   Hot spot of conflict in 2002. There are currently 29 countries that have conflicts. Conflicts are not unusual, but common around the world. For details, see http://fas.org/man/dod-101/ops/war/index.html

Source: http://www.ploughshares.ca/imagesarticles/ACR03/Armedconflicts2002.pdf

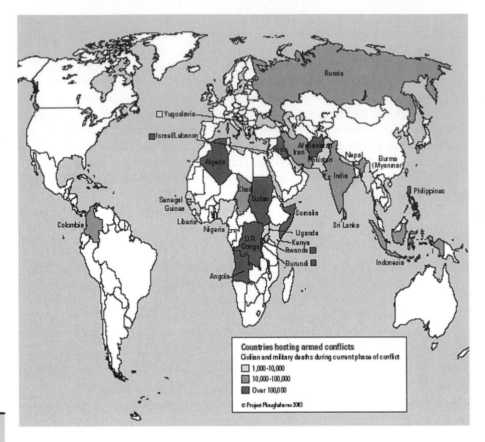

Countries hosting armed conflicts
Civilian and military deaths during current phase of conflict
☐ 1,000–10,000
▨ 10,000–100,000
▪ Over 100,000

© Project Ploughshares 2003

Pop Culture Spotlight

Of the four most popular professional sports in the United States—baseball, football, basketball, and hockey—which one do you think promotes the most open interpersonal conflict in general—among players, and between players and referees or umpires? Why? Which promotes the least? Why? Which have the best and worst cultures for solving conflicts once they begin?

groups. For example, in the United States, we hear many arguments about limiting immigration, with the focus largely on non-European immigrants. Concerns about illegal immigrants from Mexico far overshadow concerns about illegal immigrants from, say, Ireland. Discussions about the contributions made by different immigrant groups, for some reason, do not usually include European immigrants. For instance, in comparing the median household income of U.S. Americans of various backgrounds, one economist makes this point: "We rarely hear media pundits pondering aloud why the Irish lag so far behind the Greeks in median income, and why all four Scandinavian nationalities fall in the bottom half of the European roster. . . . But it has been deemed best not to accentuate distinctions, and rather to reserve remarks of that sort for members of another race."[33] U.S. Americans of French ancestry and of Dutch ancestry earn less than those who trace their ancestry to the Philippines, India, Lebanon, China, Thailand, Greece, Italy, Poland, and many other countries. French and Dutch Americans also are at the bottom of the ranks of European immigrants, and yet we do not hear calls for halting immigration from France and the Netherlands.

We might also ask who benefits from this finger pointing. It is possible that blaming immigrants, people of color, and Jews for economic problems in the

United States keeps the actual culprits out of the limelight. The fact is that people of color and Jews don't make most of the decisions that affect people's jobs and economic well-being. It is actually the wealthy—mostly White and Christian—who are responsible for closing factories and moving them to "cheaper" parts of the country or abroad. They are also the ones responsible for busting unions, blocking increases in the minimum wage, and decreasing health care and other benefits. They do this to increase their own profits. Blaming immigrants, illegal workers, welfare mothers, the poor, or members of other less powerful groups actually diverts our attention from the people who wield the power and own the wealth.[34]

As the economic contexts change, we see more cultural conflict taking place. In the former East Germany, for example, there are now many more racially motivated attacks as the residents attempt to rebuild their economy. Scapegoating, stereotyping, and hate mongering that lead to conflict are often due to perceived economic threats and competition.

Historical and Political Forces

Although as children we may have learned that "Sticks and stones may break my bones, but names will never hurt me," we know that derogatory words can be a source of many intercultural conflicts. Many derogatory words gain power from their historical usage and the legacy of oppression that they reference. As noted in Chapter 3, much of our identity has historical roots. It is only through understanding the past that we can understand what it means to be a member of a particular cultural group. For example, understanding the history of Ireland helps us understand the meaning of Irish identity.

Sometimes identities are constructed in opposition to or in conflict with other identities. When people identify themselves as members of particular cultural groups, they are marking their difference from others. These differences, when infused with historical antagonism, can lead to future conflicts. Consider, for example, the modern-day conflicts in Bosnia-Herzegovina. They did not emerge from interpersonal conflicts among the current inhabitants; rather, in large part, they represent reenactments of centuries-old conflicts between cultural groups. The same is true for conflicts in the Middle East between Arabs and Jews. The contemporary participants are caught in a historical web pitting cultural identities against one another. In fact, these dynamics are at work all around the world. Historical antagonisms become part of cultural identities and cultural practices that place people in positions of conflict. Whether in the Middle East, Northern Ireland, Rwanda, Uganda, Nigeria, Sri Lanka, East Timor, Kosovo, or Chechnya, we can see these historical antagonisms lead to various forms of conflict.

Another controversy that reflects the importance of politics and history in understanding conflict occurs in Arizona. An historical marker outside the small town of Campe Verde refers to Fort Verde as "protecting settlers against 'hostile' Indians." A park ranger, who is not American Indian, was incensed by the sign, saying it was derogatory toward Native Americans, and she had the sign

Pakistani Prime Minister Zafarullah Jamali welcomes Indian Prime Minister Atal Behari Vahpayee to a summit in Islamabad on January 5, 2004. Conflicts between India and Pakistan can only be understood in terms of regional history and British colonialism. This conflict is not an interpersonal one between these two leaders, as they are caught in a historical web that positions their two nations against each other. Recent talks have raised optimism about peace in the region.

taken down. Now the town of Camp Verde is up in arms. The local Historical Society has collected 400 signatures demanding that the marker be returned to its site on Main Street with the words "hostile Indians" intact. A book sold in Camp Verde bookstores describing local history refers repeatedly to "hostile Indians," "renegades," "marauding Apaches," and "wily thieves."

One of the local Yavapai-Apache tribe members said, "If our elders were invited to share their stories of the inhuman cruelties perpetrated on their families by U.S. military forces, only the hardest of hearts could come away with a dry eye." Many Yavapa and Apaches from the Verde Valley area died as a result of frontier wars and during a 180-mile forced relocation walk.

Apparently the offending sign was removed during the 1980s because of similar complaints, but it was put up again two years later. Here is a conflict, ostensibly over several words, and yet these several words have provoked sustained conflict in this town over generations, understood only by knowledge of the history of the settling of the western United States.[35]

When people witness conflict, they often assume that it is caused by personal issues between individuals. When we reduce conflict to the level of interpersonal interaction, we lose sight of the larger social and political forces that contextualize these conflicts. People are in conflicts for reasons that extend far beyond personal communication styles.

SUMMARY

In this chapter, we identified several characteristics of intercultural conflict: ambiguity, language issues, and contradictory conflict styles. There are different types of conflict relating to interests, values, and goals, and to cognitive and affective factors. There are also different conflict styles, including discussion style which is direct and emotionally restrained, the engagement style which is direct and confrontational, the accommodating style which is indirect and emotionally restrained, and the dynamic style which is indirect and emotionally intense. Some cultural groups use intermediaries to resolve conflict.

We also outlined two very different cultural approaches to conflict: conflict as productive versus conflict as destructive. In most U.S. contexts, conflict is seen as ultimately positive, offering opportunities for personal growth. In contrast, many Asian cultures and some ethnic groups within the United States view conflict as ultimately destructive and harmful to relationships. Gender and ethnicity can influence conflict style preferences. For example, people from individualistic cultures may tend to use discussion style, whereas people from collectivist cultures may prefer the accommodating or dynamic style. However, the type of conflict and the relationship of the disputants also influence these tendencies.

Finally, we highlighted productive versus destructive and cooperative versus competitive approaches to conflict and discussed the importance of social, economic, historical, and political forces in understanding conflict and society. Conflicts arise against the backdrop of existing social movements—for example, in reaction to racism, sexism, and homophobia. Some social movements use nonviolent means of dealing with these conflicts; others confront conflict with violence.

BUILDING INTERCULTURAL SKILLS

1. Stay centered and do not polarize. This means moving beyond traditional stereotypes and either-or thinking. It is important, though difficult, to avoid explaining the other person's motives as simple while seeing your own as complex. Try to see both sides, and be open to a third, centered perspective

What Do You Think?

The following riddle is bound to be a good discussion starter: Although there are many who protest and discourage war, there are yet others who think war or conflict is an integral part of how we establish who "we" are. In constructing the difference between "us" and "them," if we make "them" us and "us" them, then where would "we" be?

that may bring a new synthesis into view.[36] It's OK to get angry, but it's important to move past the anger—to refrain from acting out feelings.

2. Maintain contact. This does not mean that you have to stay in the conflict situation. Sometimes we need to walk away for a while. However, do not cut off the relationship. Attempt a dialogue rather than isolating yourself from or fighting with your opponent. Unlike normal conversation, dialogue is slow, careful, full of feeling, respectful, and attentive.[37] Dialogue offers an important opportunity for coming to a richer understanding of your own intercultural conflicts and experiences.

3. Recognize the existence of different styles. Conflict is often exacerbated because of the unwillingness of partners to recognize style differences, which often have cultural origins. Failure to recognize cultural differences can lead to negative evaluations of partners.

4. Identify your preferred style. Although we may change our way of dealing with conflict, based on the situation and the type of conflict, most of us tend to use the same style in most situations. It is also important to recognize which conflict styles "push your conflict button." Some styles are more or less compatible, and it's important to know which styles are congruent with your own.

5. Be creative and expand your repertoire. If a particular way of dealing with conflict is not working, be willing to try a different style. In most intercultural communication, adaptability and flexibility serve us well, and conflict communication is no exception. This means that there is no so-called objective way to deal with conflict. Recognizing this condition may promote conflict resolution.

6. Recognize the importance of context. It is important to understand that larger social, political, and historical contexts give meaning to many types of conflict. Conflict arises for many reasons, and it would be misleading to think that all conflict can be understood solely within the interpersonal context. And once you understand the contexts that frame the conflict, whether cultural, social, historical, or political, you will be in a better position to conceive of possibilities for resolution.

7. Be willing to forgive. This means letting go of—not forgetting—feelings of revenge.[38] This may be particularly useful in intercultural conflict.[39]

ACTIVITY

Cultures in conflict: In groups of four, select two countries or cultural groups that are currently or have historically been in conflict. Divide each group of four into pairs, and have each pair research the conflict from the perspective of one of the two cultural groups. Using library and community resources, including interviews with cultural members, outline the major issues and arguments of the assigned culture. Explore the role of cultural values, political contexts, and historical contexts in the conflict. Be prepared to present an oral or written report of your research.

THE ONLINE LEARNING CENTER at www.mhhe.com/experiencing2 features self-quizzes, flashcards, and crossword puzzles based on the chapter's key terms and concepts.

www.mhhe.com/ experiencing2

ENDNOTES

1. Hymon, S. (2003, January 14). Firm's logging degrades rivers, increases floods, state study says. *Los Angeles Times*, p. B7.
2. Woodall, M. (2003, June 11). E-mail galls French school. *The Philadelphia Inquirer* (online) (http://www.philly.com/mld/inquirer/living/education/6059080.htm)
3. Dupont, T. (2003, June 3). Des lycéens de Carcassonne victims de la francophobie américaine. *Transfert* (Paris). (http://www.transfert.net/a8904) [« Le collectif de parents français a décidé d'avertir l'ambassade américaine à Paris et le ministère des Affaires étrangères »])
4. Delgado, F. (2002). Mass-mediated communication and intercultural conflict. In J. N. Martin, T. K. Nakayama, & L. A. Flores (Eds.), *Readings in intercultural communication* (2nd ed.) (pp. 351–359). Boston: McGraw-Hill.
5. See Hocker, J. L., & Wilmot, W. W. (2000). *Interpersonal conflict* (6th ed.). New York: McGraw-Hill; Cupach, W. R., & Canary, D. J. (1997). *Competence in interpersonal conflict*. New York: McGraw-Hill.
6. Lindsley, S. L., & Braithwaite, C. A. (1996). You should "wear a mask": Facework norms in cultural and intercultural conflict in *maquiladoras*. *International Journal of Intercultural Relations, 20*, 199–225.
7. Cole, M. (1996). *Interpersonal conflict communication in Japanese cultural contexts*. Unpublished dissertation, Arizona State University, Tempe.
8. Hammer, M. R. (under review). The Intercultural Conflict Style Inventory: A conceptual framework and measure of intercultural conflict approaches. *Mediation Quarterly*.
9. Filley, A. C. (1975). *Interpersonal conflict resolution*. Glenview, IL: Scott, Foresman.
10. Kraybill, D. (1989). *The riddle of Amish culture*. Baltimore: Johns Hopkins University Press.
11. Augsburger, D. (1992). *Conflict mediation across cultures*. Louisville, KY: Westminster/John Knox Press, p. 80.
12. Ting-Toomey, S., & Oetzel, J. G. (2002). Cross cultural face concerns and conflict styles: Current status and future directions. In W. B. Gundykunst & B. Mody. *Handbook of international and intercultural communication* (2nd ed.) (pp. 143–165). Thousand Oaks, CA: Sage. See also Ting-Toomey, S. (Ed.). (1994). *The challenge of facework: Cross cultural and interpersonal issues*. Albany: State University of New York Press.
13. Hammer, R. (2003). The Intercultural Conflict Style Inventory: Individual profile and interpretive guide. N. Potomac, MD: Hammer Consulting Group, LLC. *Conflict Resolution Quarterly*.
14. Ting-Toomey, S., Yee-Jung, K. K, Shapiro, R. B., Garcia, W., Wright, T. J., & Oetzel, J. G. (2000). Ethnic/cultural identity salience and conflict styles in four U.S. ethnic groups. *International Journal of Intercultural Relations, 24*, 47–81.
15. Hocker, J. L., & Wilmot, W. W. (1991). *Interpersonal conflict* (3rd ed.). Dubuque, IA: Brown.
16. Kim, M-S. (2002). *Non-western perspectives on human communication*. Thousand Oaks, CA: Sage, p. 63.
17. Hammer, M. R. *Intercultural Conflict Style Inventory, Facilitators Manual*. Hammer Consulting Group, L. L. C., 267 Kentlands Boulevard, PMB 705, N. Potomac, MD 20878.
18. Tannen, D. (1986). *That's not what I meant! How conversational style makes or breaks relationships*. New York: Ballantine Books. See also Tannen, D. (1990). *You just don't understand: Women and men in conversation*. New York: Morrow.
19. Wood, J. T. (1994). *Gendered lives: Communication, gender, and culture*. Belmont, CA: Wadsworth.
20. Collier, M. J. (1991). Conflict competence within African, Mexican, and Anglo American friendships. In S. Ting-Toomey & F. Korzenny (Eds.), *Cross-cultural interpersonal communication* (pp. 132–154). Newbury Park, CA: Sage.
21. Ting-Toomey et al. (2000), pp. 47–81.

22. Kelly, D. (2003, October 12). Pastor's salute to gay's killing troubles city. *The Arizona Republic*, p. A10.

23. The other cheek. (2003, October 19). *The Salt Lake Tribune*, p. AA1.

24. Ting-Toomey, S., Gao, G., Trubisky, P., Yang, Z., Kim, H. S., Lin, S. L., & Nishida, T. (1991). Culture, face, maintenance and styles of handling interpersonal conflicts: A study in five cultures. *International Journal of Conflict Management, 2,* 275–296; Ting-Toomey, S. (1997). Intercultural conflict competence. In Cupach & Canary, pp. 120–147. See also Trubisky, P., Ting-Toomey, S., & Lin, S. L. (1991).The influence of individualism-collectivism and self monitoring on conflict styles. *International Journal of Intercultural Relations, 15,* 65–84; Nadler, L. B., Nadler, M. K., & Broome, B. J. (1985). Culture and the management of conflict situations. In W. B. Gudykunst, L. Stewart, & S. Ting-Toomey (Eds.), *Communication culture, and organizational processes* (pp. 77–96). Beverly Hills, CA: Sage.

25. Cole (1996).

26. Augsburger (1992), p. 47.

27. Deutsch, M. (1987). A theoretical perspective on conflict and conflict resolution. In D. Sandole & I. Sandole-Staroste (Eds.), *Conflict management and problem solving.* New York: New York University Press, p. 41.

28. Deutsch, M. (1973). *The resolution of conflict: Constructive and destructive processes.* New Haven, CT: Yale University Press.

29. Hocker & Wilmot (1991), p. 191.

30. Hall, B. "J." (1994). Understanding intercultural conflict through kernel images and rhetorical visions. *The International Journal of Conflict Management, 5*(1), 62–86.

31. King, M. L., Jr. (1984). Pilgrimage in nonviolence. In J. C. Albert & S. E. Albert (Eds.), *The sixties papers: Documents of a rebellious decade* (pp. 108–112). New York: Praeger. (Original work published in 1958).

32. X, Malcolm. (1984). The ballot or the bullet. In Albert & Albert, pp. 126–132. (Original work published in 1965.)

33. Hacker, A. (1997). *Money: Who has how much and why.* New York: Scribner, p. 158.

34. Kivel, P. (1996). *Uprooting racism: How White people can work for racial justice.* Gabriola Islands, British Columbia: New Society, pp. 50–51.

35. Shaffer, M. (2003, September 15). History or derogatory? Sign riles Camp Verde. *Arizona Republic,* B1.

36. Augsburger (1992), p. 66.

37. See Hocker & Wilmot (1998), p. 266.

38. Lulofs, R. S. (1994). *Conflict: From theory to action.* Scottsdale, AZ: Gorsuch Scarisbrick.

39. Augsburger (1992), p. 66.

CHAPTER NINE

Intercultural Relationships in Everyday Life

STUDY OBJECTIVES

After reading this chapter you should be able to:

1. Identify and describe the benefits and challenges of intercultural relationships.
2. Understand the role that similarities and differences play in intercultural relationships.
3. Identify cultural differences in relational communication.
4. Identify and describe issues in intercultural friendships, intercultural romantic relationships, and gay relationships.
5. Describe how computer mediated communication (CMC) can both facilitate and hinder intercultural relationships.
6. Understand how society influences intercultural relationships.

KEY TERMS

complementarity
compromise style
consensus style
friendship
gay relationships
intercultural dating
intercultural relationships

intimacy
obliteration style
physical attraction
romantic relationships
similarity principle
submission style

A student of ours named Erich worked on campus at the Memorial Union, where most of his coworkers were from India. This multicultural working environment raised several interesting issues for Erich:

> One thing I realized was the fact that similarity played a big role in the integration of the Indian students. After sitting down and talking, difficult at first, we realized that we were all university students, working together, and this opened up lines of communication and sped up the integration process. After one semester, we were all integrated and had a new batch of students show up. This time we knew how to help them and ourselves feel more comfortable.

Another student, Susie, and the guy she was dating were both raised in the southwestern United States, but their cultural backgrounds differed. Susie had a middle-class Mexican cultural background that was very family-oriented. Her parents were always involved in and showed great concern for all her decisions in life. As she explained it, "With a Mexican father of three girls, it was a very protective environment." Her boyfriend had been raised in a working-class suburb by an Asian mother and German father who were not as intimately involved in his activities. Thus, school and education were his highest priority. According to Susie,

> The relationship experiences were very interesting as we both learned about our cultural traits and norms. I enjoyed learning about and understanding his environment even as he began to experience and understand the environment I was raised in. It was a continuous learning process for both of us.

Think about your friends, classmates, and coworkers, all of whom may differ from you in terms of age, physical ability, ethnicity, religion, class, or sexual orientation. How did you get to know them? Perhaps in the workplace, as Erich did, or perhaps in a romantic relationship, as Susie did. Do your intercultural relationships differ from those that are characterized by cultural similarity? How do intercultural relationships form? What are some strategies you can use to build better intercultural relationships—at school, at work, and at play?

In this chapter, we explore the benefits and challenges of intercultural relationships. We then discuss different kinds of intercultural relationships, including friendships and romantic relationships. We also examine the role society plays in intercultural relationships. Finally, we talk about strategies to build solid intercultural relationships and alliances.

Surf's Up!

Intercultural communication is so important economically that companies like America at Work train people to work in intercultural issues. On its website, it says that "The market and the workforce are changing, and today's successful businesses are recognizing the value of employees who can reach emerging communities and provide a new, dynamic edge to the company in competition" (www.americaatwork. com/). Visit the website to see what specific skills are needed in today's multicultural workplace.

BENEFITS OF INTERCULTURAL RELATIONSHIPS

Most people have a variety of **intercultural relationships** that span differences in age, physical ability, gender, ethnicity, class, religion, race, and nationality. Take Maria, for example, a student who works part-time in a resort as a bartender. Her coworkers are ethnically diverse—Latinos, Whites, and African Americans. The clientele is international—Europeans, Asians, and South Americans who come to the resort to play golf and relax. One of her good friends is an older woman, Linda, a neighbor who is disabled with severe emphysema. Maria and Linda watch TV and fix meals together. Maria's Black friend Shawna is dating Jurgen, an international student from Germany, and all three enjoy rollerblading and hiking together. Maria's family is Catholic, but her sister married Jay, who is Jewish. Maria's parents had difficulty accepting Jay at first, but eventually they became more accepting, especially after the grandchildren were born.

As this example shows, intercultural relationships can encompass many kinds of cultural differences and offer many rewards and opportunities. The key to these relationships is often an interesting balance of differences and similarities. While Maria's friends are diverse, she has many things in common with each one—rollerblading with Shawna and Jurgen, watching TV and preparing gourmet meals with Linda, building ties with her sister's family. Through all these relationships, Maria and her friends and acquaintances learn about each other's different worlds.

The benefits of such relationships include (1) learning about the world, (2) breaking stereotypes, and (3) acquiring new skills. In intercultural relationships, we often learn specific information about unfamiliar cultural patterns and language. For example, Annelise, a graduate student who lived in Guatemala, explained that she learned a new way of looking at time, that "meeting at 9 o'clock" might mean 9:30 or 10:00, not because someone forgot or wasn't "on time," but because there was a completely different definition for "9:00." She also learned a different language than the Spanish she had learned in the university setting.

We may also learn more about what it really means to belong to a different culture. For example, recall how Susie learned something about what it meant to grow up in a different class and ethnic environment through her relationship with her boyfriend. A romance or close intercultural friendship may be a way to bring abstractions like "culture" or "race" to life.[1]

Or we may learn something about history. Another one of our students, Jennifer, told us how she learned more about the Holocaust from her Jewish friends and about the "Middle Passage" from her African American friends. This is a kind of "relational learning," learning that comes from a particular relationship but generalizes to other contexts. So, while Jennifer learned something specific about Jewish and African American history, she also learned the importance of different ethnic histories and is now more curious to learn about the histories of other ethnic groups. Relational learning is often much more compelling than knowledge gained from books.

Info Bites

There are magazines devoted to exploring issues of intercultural and interracial relationships, including *New People, Interracial Classified, Small World,* and *Interrace Magazine.* Based on your study of intercultural communication, what kinds of issues do you think these magazines should address?

Relationships often are formed because of proximity. That is, we are attracted to people who live near us and who work, study, and worship with us. How many friends do you have who are culturally different from you?

Intercultural relationships also can help break stereotypes. Another student, Andy, told us he used to think that Mexicans were lazy. He formed this opinion from media images, discussions with friends, and political speeches about immigration in the Southwest. However, when he met and made friends with immigrants from rural Mexico, his opinion changed. He saw that the everyday life of his friends was anything but easy. They had family responsibilities and sometimes worked two jobs to make ends meet.

We also often learn how to do new things in intercultural relationships. For example, through her friendships with students in the United States and abroad, Judith has learned to make paella (a Spanish dish) and *nopalitos con puerca* (a cactus-and-pork stew), to play bridge in French, and to downhill ski. Through intercultural relationships, newcomers to the society can acquire important skills. Andy's immigrant friends often asked him for help with unfamiliar tasks like buying car insurance or shopping at supermarkets. And when Tom first moved to France, his new French friends helped him navigate the university cafeteria.

In short, intercultural communication can lead to a sense of connection with others and can establish a lifelong pattern of communicating to bridge differences. For example, yet another student, Jessica, recounts how an encounter with an international exchange student led to a lifetime interest in intercultural relations. It all began when she was a freshman in high school:

> My best friend's older sister had just gotten back from Germany and brought home an exchange student. My one memory of my first encounter with Edith, the exchange student, happened at breakfast one morning after a sleep-over party. We were going to make waffles, and Edith didn't know what waffles were. I loved explaining them to her and telling her about different syrups and then learning about the different foods she ate in Germany. It was so fun to talk to her.

Three years later, Jessica went on the same exchange program to New Zealand:

> What an amazing experience. Not only did I get to stay with a family that had three girls, one my age, but I also learned about the Maoris, the first people to inhabit New Zealand. I developed a lifelong relationship with my host family and relished learning the difference and similarities between our cultures. I have fond memories of sitting up late at night drinking tea, not coffee, with my New Zealand mother. We would talk for hours. This was a powerful learning experience.

This led to still more intercultural experiences and relationships:

> My exchange sister came home with me, and the other seventeen delegates in the program also brought their exchange sisters or brothers home from all over the world. Talk about a salad mix of cultures. We took various trips for six weeks. It was so exhilarating.
>
>   Although my experiences have for the most part been overseas, I feel they have opened a window for me. My worldview has gone from just me to phenomenally huge. I see things from other people's point of view; I actually try to see things in a different light. I have my experiences with people from other cultures to thank.

What Do You Think?

The Friendship Force website says, "You are cordially invited to join The Friendship Force to form new friendships with interesting people and thereby help promote peace throughout the world." Are intercultural friendships the key to world peace?

CHALLENGES IN INTERCULTURAL RELATIONSHIPS

Differences in Communication Styles, Values, and Perceptions

Intercultural relationships are unique in several ways and present particular challenges. First, intercultural relationships, by definition, are often characterized by cultural differences in communication styles, values, and perceptions. These dissimilarities probably are most noticeable in the early stages of the relationship, before people get to know each other on a more personal, individual level. However, once some commonality is established, these cultural differences may have less effect because all relationships become more individualized as they move to more intimate stages. For example, when Agusia first met Angelina in a class project, all they knew about each other was that Angelina was a Latina and that Agusia grew up in Poland. But as they got to know each other, they found out they both had small daughters, were active in their Catholic churches, and were social work majors. And as they got to be good friends and learned about what they shared and how they differed, the cultural differences became less important.

As Angelina and Agusia found out, there is an interplay of both differences and similarities in intercultural relationships. The differences are a given, and the challenge often is to discover and build on the similarities. These similarities may consist of common interests and activities, common beliefs, or common goals.

Negative Stereotypes

Surf's Up!

Read the essay about bicultural identity (members.tripod.com/ maya_ilusion/bicultural/ personal.htm). This essay argues that "one interesting fact to point out is that there is probably no one on this earth today who is of completely pure blood. We are all in a sense of mixed descent." This is even more the case when you factor in ethnicity. How many different cultural backgrounds are you a product of?

A second challenge in intercultural relationships is negative stereotyping. As discussed in Chapter 2, stereotypes are a way of categorizing and processing information, but they are particularly detrimental when they are negative and held rigidly. Sometimes it takes work to get individual information, information that can counteract the stereotype.

An African American professor describes the beliefs and stereotypes about White people passed along to her in her family: (1) White people are often violent and treacherous; (2) White people probably have some kind of inferiority complex, which drives them to continually "put down" Blacks and anyone else who is not White; (3) White men are usually arrogant; (4) White women are lazy; and (5) there are some good White people, but they are the exception.[2] More important, she goes on to describe how she did not let these stereotypes become a "prison" that determined how she felt about herself or all White people. And because of her open-mindedness, her beliefs changed and her reliance on stereotypes decreased. She learned that race was not a predictor of intelligence, but that income and opportunity were. She learned that all people, regardless of color, deserve to be treated with dignity and respect. And she made definite choices about how to relate to others and about the importance of having a variety of friends, not just African Americans.

Anxiety

A third challenge in intercultural relationships involves overcoming the increased anxiety commonly found in the early stages of the relationship. (Some anxiety always exists in the early stages of any relationship.) This anxiety stems from fears about possible negative consequences of our actions. We may be afraid that we will look stupid or will offend someone because we're unfamiliar with that person's language or culture. For example, our student Sam has a lot of friends who speak Spanish at home, and he has studied Spanish for five years in high school and college. But when he visits with his friends' families, he's often anxious about speaking Spanish with them. He's afraid he'll say something stupid or reveal his ignorance in some way.

Differences of age are not usually cause for discomfort, but relationships that span differences in physical ability, class, or race may engender more anxiety. Caterina described for us the last meeting of an interracial discussion group.

> We really did make great connections and friendships in our time together, based on intelligence and honor. It was great to see that some of the girls who initially spoke of their discomfort around others who are different from them spoke out and informed us they were not as scared anymore. They gave up their fear and took a great step forward, one that I hope they will remember always.

As this statement suggests, people face a kind of "hurdle" in developing intercultural relationships, and once they pass that hurdle, it's much easier to develop other intercultural relationships.[3]

The level of anxiety may be even higher if people have negative expectations based on previous interactions or on stereotypes.[4] For example, some White and African American students seem to have more difficulty discussing intercultural issues with each other than they do with international students, perhaps because of negative stereotypes held by both groups. By contrast, intercultural interactions in which there are few negative expectations and no history of negative contact probably have less anxiety associated with them. For example, one student tells of traveling to New Zealand as an 18-year-old on a sports team. He had no negative preconceptions about New Zealanders and no real language barrier. While he experienced a little anxiety at the beginning, he quickly found similarity with people he met, and it was "truly an unforgettable experience."

Affirming Another Person's Cultural Identity

A fourth challenge in intercultural relationships is affirming the other person's cultural identity. This means that we need to not only recognize that the other person might have different beliefs, perceptions, and attitudes, but also that we accept those characteristics as an important part of the other's identity.[5]

However, this is often difficult, especially for majority group individuals. There is often a tendency for members of the majority culture to assume their attitudes, beliefs, and behaviors are the norm and that the minority member should adapt to them.[6] For example, a college student, Andrea, had a good friend Sherry who is Filipino and tended to have a collectivistic approach to friendship. When the two friends went to Europe, Sherry had a last-minute emergency and needed to borrow $600 from Andrea. From Sherry's perspective, lending money was a natural thing for friends to do and was not that unusual. But Andrea had a tough time getting over the fact that Sherry took it so matter of factly, did not thank Andrea profusely, and did not repay it immediately. This aspect of Sherry's identity was a difficult thing for Andrea to accept and is still a barrier in their friendship.

The Need for Explanations

Finally, intercultural relationships often present the challenge of having to explain things. Intercultural relationships can be more work than in-group relationships and can require more "care and feeding" than do those relationships between people who are very similar. A lot of the work has to do with explaining—explaining to themselves, to each other, and to their respective communities.[7]

First, in some way, consciously or unconsciously, we ask ourselves what it means to be friends with someone who is not like us. Do we become friends out of necessity, or for our job, or because everyone around us is different in some way? Do we become friends because we want to gain an entree into this group for personal benefit or because we feel guilty?

Second, we explain things to each other. This process of mutual clarification is one of the healthiest characteristics of intercultural relationships. Judith recalls her Algerian friends explaining that they really thought their sisters and mothers were treated better in some ways than women are treated in the United States. For example, they explained that no woman would be expected to raise children by herself in Algeria, as is commonly practiced in the United States. They felt sorry for single mothers in the United States who often struggle on their own to raise children. Judith grew to understand that situations can be viewed in very different ways and to realize that others can interpret things very differently.

People who cross cultural boundaries and form close relationships with individuals who are, say, much older or of a different ethnicity often have to explain this to their respective communities. For example, in the film *Naturally Native*, three Native American sisters have different views on being Indian. The oldest sister, Karen, doesn't understand why her youngest sister can't be more Indian, why she wants to go outside her group to find friends, and why being Indian isn't more important to her.

Note that usually the biggest obstacles to boundary-crossing friendships come not from minority communities but from majority communities. This is because those in the majority, such as Whites, have the most to gain by maintaining social inequality and are less likely to initiate boundary-crossing friendships. By contrast, minority groups have more to gain. Developing intercultural relationships can help them survive and succeed, particularly economically and professionally.

In intercultural relationships, individuals recognize and respect the differences. In these relationships, we often have to remind ourselves that we can never know exactly what it is to walk in another person's shoes. Furthermore, those in the majority group tend to know less about those in minority groups than vice versa. As one of our White students told us, thanks to intercultural relationships with other students, she "was able to hear several examples of true stories of discrimination that Hispanic people go through on a daily basis. I never really thought any of that existed anymore. I don't know why, but their stories really

Intercultural relationships present both opportunities for and challenges to communication. They can also reflect an interesting balance of similarities and differences. In what ways might these young women be similar, and in what ways might they be different?

impacted me, and made me much more aware of the hardships that minorities have to go through. It was a real learning opportunity." Overall, intercultural friendships, while challenging, add a special richness to our lives. To be successful, they require "mutual respect, acceptance, tolerance for the faux pas and the occasional closed door, open discussion and patient mutual education; all this gives.crossing friendships—when they work at all—a special kind of depth."[8]

FOUNDATIONS OF INTERCULTURAL RELATIONSHIPS

How do we come to know people who are different from ourselves? Some relationships develop simply because of circumstances—for example, when students work together on a course project. Some relationships develop because people come into contact with each other on a frequent basis—for example, neighbors in dorms or apartments. Others develop because of a strong **physical attraction** or because of similar interests, attitudes, or personality traits. And sometimes relationships develop between dissimilar people simply because they are different. Paradoxically, there seems to be some truth to both "Birds of a feather flock together" and "Opposites attract."

Similarities and Differences

An awareness of the importance of both similarities and differences is at the heart of understanding intercultural relationships. According to the **similarity principle,** we tend to be attracted to people whom we perceive to hold attitudes similar to ours in terms of politics, religion, personality, and so on.[9] And there is evidence that this principle holds for many cultural groups.[10] Finding people who agree with our own beliefs confirms those beliefs. After all, if we like ourselves, we should like others who share our views. Thus, individuals may explicitly seek partners who hold the same beliefs and values due to deep spiritual, moral, or religious convictions. For example, our student Christine, who is Greek Orthodox, has decided that she'll seek a marriage partner who shares her religious beliefs and values. Also, if we're friends with people who are like us, we can better predict their behavior than if they are different from us.

In addition, the similarity principle seems to reinforce itself. Not only do we like people we think are similar to us, but we also may think that people we like are more similar to us than they actually are. Similarity is based not on whether people actually are similar, but on the perceived (though not necessarily real) recognition or discovery of a similar trait. This process of discovery is crucial in developing relationships. In fact, when people think they're similar, they have higher expectations about future interactions.[11]

But we may also seek out people who have different personality traits and therefore provide balance, or **complementarity,** in the relationship. For example, an introverted individual may seek a more outgoing partner, or a spendthrift may be attracted to an individual who is more careful with money.

Some individuals are attracted to people simply because they have different cultural backgrounds. Intercultural relationships present intriguing opportunities to have new experiences and to learn new ways of looking at the world. And whether (and when) we seek out people who are different or similar to ourselves may be due partly to our own experiences. For example, when Judith was in college, she wanted to socialize with international students because she was intrigued by their backgrounds and experiences. Growing up, Judith had had little opportunity to be with people who were different from her. By contrast, Tom sought out other Asian Americans when he was in college because he had had little prior opportunity to be around Asian Americans.

U.S. Americans tend to accept some relationships of complementarity more than others. For example, it's more acceptable to date international students than to date across class lines. So, intercultural relationships are characterized by both

TABLE 9.1 Some Interesting Cultural Variables in Relationships

Brazil: To be invited to a Brazilian's home is an honor. Guests are expected to stay for many hours rather than stop for a brief visit.

China: Face-saving is extremely important in China. Chinese always avoid embarrassing situations and help one another save face and retain self-respect.

France: When French greet people, they tend to be formal. Titles such as Monsieur, Madame, and Mademoiselle are often used. If they know the person, they may give the traditional kiss by the cheek/air.

Spain: The Spanish often invite guests to their home out of courtesy. One should wait until the host insists to accept the invitation.

Germany: Germans tend to be formal. They do not use first names unless they know the person very well.

Egypt: Always use titles such as Doctor or Professor to address people.

Kenya: The Kenyan socialize at the end of the meal, not before the meal.

Greece: Avoid overpraising any item in a Greek home because the host may feel obligated to present it as a gift later.

Source: M. Mancini. (2003). *Selling destinations: Geography for the travel professional*, 4th ed. Clifton Park, NY: Thomson/Delmar Learning.

What Do You Think?

How would (or did) your family respond to your being in an intercultural romantic relationship? If you are the product of an intercultural relationship, do you think that would make your family more or less accepting?

similarities and differences. Although we may be attracted initially by differences, some common ground or similarity must be established if the relationship is to develop, flourish, and be mutually satisfying over time.[12]

Cultural Differences in Relationships

Friendships   How are **friendships**—personal, nonromantic relationships with culture-specific overtones—formed? What are the characteristics of a friend? How do these notions vary across cultures? For some people, a friend is someone to see or talk with occasionally and someone to socialize with—go to lunch or a movie, discuss interests, and maybe share problems. These casual friendships may not last if one person moves away. But other people view friendship much more seriously. For these people, friendships take a long time to develop, include many obligations (perhaps lending money or doing favors), and last a lifetime. Some differences in relationship expectations can be seen in Table 9.1.

The term *friend* may have different meanings for different cultural groups. For example, in the United States, the term applies to many different kinds of relationships. In contrast, in India and in many other countries, the concept is defined more narrowly. Shyam, a student from India, described the difference between friendship in the United States and friendship in India:

[Americans] try to have a lot of friends; they don't meet the same people again and again all the time. . . . In India close friends are together most of the time, day after day after day hanging out together. My impression is, Americans probably don't do that; they try to meet different people.[13]

What most people in the world consider simply a friend is what U.S. Americans would consider a "close friend." A German student explained that in Germany one can hardly call somebody a friend even if he or she has known that person for over a year. Only if one has a "special emotional relationship" can he or she view that person as a friend.[14] For most U.S. Americans, the special emotional relationship would be reserved for a close friend.

Europeans are often amazed at the openness and informality of Americans and how quickly they can form friendships. In contrast, Europeans are not so quick to invite people into their home and do not necessarily introduce their friends to other friends. While in America, a friend of a friend is practically your own friend, Europeans see friendship as much more of an exclusive club.[15]

The upshot is that Americans often come across as forward, intrusive, and overbearing. They sometime embarrass their European acquaintances by their openness and by how quickly they reveal things about themselves. As one Polish man visiting the United States observed:

> I discover I am learning many intimate details of the personal lives of the people I have just met. I find myself a bit embarrassed, but I doubt that they are. They become my friends so quickly, and as quickly they begin to share their problems with me. . . . In America, when one meets someone, he or she immediately becomes a friend.[16]

It's possible that this American informality and openness may drive Europeans to be even more reserved and distant. It might be better for Americans to give their European acquaintances more time to open up and initiate intimacy, and they should be careful not to interpret European reserve as lack of warmth.

Sometimes this openness and informality can be interpreted negatively. For example, international students in the United States often remark that U.S. American students seem superficial. That is, they welcome interactions with strangers and share information of a superficial nature—for example, when chatting at a party. When some international students experience these types of interactions, they assume that they have become "close" friends. But then they discover that the U.S. American students consider them to be merely acquaintances. A student from Singapore described her relationships with American students:

> I learned in the first couple months that people are warm yet cold. For example, I would find people saying "Hi" to me when I'm walking on campus or asking me how I am doing. It used to make me feel slighted that even as I made my greeting back to them, they are already a mile away. Then when real interaction occurs, for example, in class, somehow I sense that people tend to be very superficial and false. Yet they disclose a lot of information, for example, talking about personal relationships, which I wasn't comfortable with. I used to think that because of such self-disclosure, you

would share a special relationship with the other person, but it's not so because the same person who was telling you about her personal relationship yesterday has no idea who you are today. Now I have learned to not be offended or feel slighted by such incidents.

The differences in the openness and informality of Americans compared to Europeans may have something to do with the different histories and geography. Early Americans had to reach out to people they didn't know, whether they wanted to or not; when people move to a new place, they don't have the luxury of keeping distant. For Europeans, whose populations are much denser and who have a history of invasions and wars from close neighbors, a certain caution and formality seems understandable.[17]

There are also both similarities and differences between Japanese and U.S. American students with regard to friendships.[18] In general, young people in both countries seem to be attracted to people who are similar to them in some way, and they use the same words to describe characteristics of a friend: trust, respect, understanding, and sincerity. However, they give these characteristics different priority. For Japanese students, togetherness, trust, and warmth are the top characteristics; for U.S. American students, understanding, respect, and sincerity are most important. These preferences may reflect different cultural values: The Japanese value relational harmony and collectivism, whereas the U.S. Americans value honesty and individuality. For many U.S. Americans, relationships are based on and strengthened by honesty, even if the truth sometimes hurts.

Hispanic, Asian American, African American, and Anglo American students hold similar notions about two important characteristics of close friendship: trust and acceptance. However, whereas Latino, Asian American, and African American students report that it takes, on average, about a year to develop a close friendship, Anglo Americans report that it takes only a few months. And each group may emphasize a slightly different aspect of friendship. For example, Latinos/as emphasize relational support; Asian Americans emphasize a caring, positive exchange of ideas; African Americans emphasize respect and acceptance; and Anglo Americans emphasize recognizing the needs of individuals.[19]

Romantic Relationships   There are also similarities and differences in how **romantic relationships** are viewed in different cultures. In general, most cultures stress the importance of some degree of openness, involvement, shared nonverbal meanings, and relationship assessment in romantic relationships. However, there are some differences. In general, U.S. American students emphasize the importance of physical attraction, passion, love, and autonomy, reflecting a more individualistic orientation. Thus, togetherness is important as long as it doesn't interfere too much with one's own freedom. Practicing openness, talking things out, and retaining a strong sense of self are strategies for maintaining a healthy intimate relationship.

But many other cultural groups emphasize the acceptance of the potential partner by family members as more important than romantic or passionate love,

Pop Culture Spotlight

Have you seen either the movie or the television show *The Odd Couple?* How does the friendship between Felix, the neat freak, and Oscar, the slob, resemble an intercultural friendship?

Intercultural relationships can provide a window into different ways of living and thinking. They can also lead to a sense of connection with others and help establish a lifelong pattern of communication across differences.

reflecting a more collectivist orientation.[20] For example, our student Mark described the experience of meeting his fiancée Elea's Greek American parents for the first time:

> It was the inevitable "meeting the parents" that posed the greatest conflict in this relationship. At home, they spoke Greek, ate only Greek food, went to a Greek Orthodox church, and lived under traditional, conservative, old-country rules. In this meeting, what ended up causing difficulties for me was a cultural handicap in interpreting their messages. I could listen politely and answer respectfully, yet I could not understand their stories and how they related to me. I sensed they were probing for some key to my values and integrity. They asked questions about my intentions toward their daughter, my goals in life, and my family's background. I sensed that there were "right" and "wrong" answers, and I grew anxious without their cultural answer key.

Mark went on to say that he was still learning about their culture and values: "Years into this relationship, I am continually developing a sense of the values, philosophies, and methods that drive the culture, the questions and the stories of my parents-in-law."

The U.S. American emphasis on individual autonomy in relationships can be problematic. Trying to balance the needs of two "separate" individuals is not easy, and extreme individualism makes it difficult for either partner to justify sacrificing or giving more than he or she is receiving. All this leads to fundamental conflicts as partners try to reconcile the need for personal freedom with marital obligations. In fact, one study indicated that people with extremely individualistic orientations may experience less love, care, trust, and physical attraction with their partners in romantic relationships. These problems are less common in more collectively oriented societies.[21]

Gay Relationships   We have far more information about heterosexual friendships and romantic relationships than about **gay relationships,** or same-sex romantic relationships. But we know that homosexuality has existed in every society and in every era. And while we in the United States tend to have fairly rigid categories ("heterosexual," "bisexual," "homosexual," and so on), cross cultural and historical studies show a great deal of variety in how intimate human relations are carried on. For example, although sexual relations among the ancient Greeks occurred between persons of the same gender, there is no evidence that they were systematically differentiated from others or made into a uniform category. For another example, traditional Mojave Indians recognize gay individuals as being unique, "two spirit persons." A special ceremony in late childhood marks a transition into the third-gender role. The child is then recognized as a "two spirit" person, usually accepted by the parents who supported him. This acceptance of homosexuality was the product of a long cultural history that involved myth and ceremonial initiation.[22]

In many cultures, people engage in activities that would be considered homosexual in contemporary United States, but are not regarded as such in their culture. They may regard themselves as "straights" or just "human beings" who on occasion participate in gay encounters. They simply might be unwilling to identify themselves with a category term such as homosexual.

Gay relationships may be intracultural or intercultural. Although there are many similarities between gay and straight relationships, they also differ in several ways. For example, same-sex friendship relationships may be viewed differently by gay and straight males in the United States. Typically, U.S. American males are socialized toward less self-expression and emotional **intimacy,** or closeness. Most heterosexual men turn to women for emotional support; often, a wife or female romantic partner, rather than a same-sex friend, is the major source of emotional support.

This was not always the case in the United States. And in many countries today, male friendships are similar to romantic love relationships in that men feel

Pop Culture Spotlight

In the film *A Bronx Tale*, an Italian American boy and an African American girl fall in love. Although their communities have a history of violent interactions, the young lovers still try to see each other. But as the boy becomes more deeply involved in his community's gang, learning the ropes and getting to know the people, he pulls back from the relationship. How do your intercultural relationships affect your connections with your own culture?

free to reveal to their male friends their deepest feelings and may show physical affection by holding hands. In this instance, same-sex friendships and romantic love relationships may involve expectations of undying loyalty, devotion, and intense emotional gratification.[23] This seems to be true for men in gay relationships; they tend to seek emotional support from same-sex friendships.[24] But this does not seem to apply for straight women and lesbians. That is, both gay and straight women seek intimate friendships with women more than with men.

The role of sexuality also may differ in heterosexual relationships and in gay friendships. In heterosexual relationships, friendship and sexual involvement typically are mutually exclusive; the "sex thing" always seems to "get in the way." Friendships between straight men and women can be ambiguous because of the "sex thing." This ambiguity does not hold in gay relationships. Gay friendships often start with sexual attraction and involvement but persist even after sexual involvement is terminated.

Close friendships may be more important for gay people than for straight people. Gay people often suffer discrimination and hostility from the straight world.[25] In addition, they often have strained relationships with their families. For these reasons, the social support they receive from friends in the gay community can play a special role. Sometimes friends fill in as family, as one young man explained:

> Friends become part of my extended family. A lot of us are estranged from our families because we're gay and our parents don't understand or don't want to understand. That's a separation there. I can't talk to them about my relationships. I don't go to them; I've finally learned my lesson: family is out. Now I've got a close circle of good friends that I can sit and talk to about anything. I learned to do without the family.[26]

In the United States, there is little legal recognition of permanent gay relationships, even though some mayors have proposed and issued marriage licenses to same-sex couples. The federal government passed the "Defense of Marriage" Act, which allows states to avoid recognizing such marriages in other states. These political and legal actions influence how gay and lesbian relationships develop and how they are terminated in the United States. When straight people end marriage relationships, there is often a delay, due to family and social pressures, religious beliefs, custody battles, and so on. However, some gay relationships probably terminate much more quickly, because they are not subject to these pressures. This also may mean that, even though they are shorter-lived, gay relationships are happier and more mutually productive.[27]

Some countries, however, do recognize same-sex relationships and so create a different environment for gay and lesbian relationships. Belgium, the Netherlands, and Canada recognize gay marriages.[28] Several other European countries give same-sex couples at least some of the same rights as married heterosexual couples. For example, in France, the Civil Solidarity Pact allows same-sex couples to register their union and gain inheritance, housing, and social welfare rights.[29] Germany and Australia grant similar rights; in addition, foreign part-

Info Bites

There has been a move to amend the U.S. Constitution to define marriage as only between a man and a woman. Do you think this is going to lead to greater or lesser acceptance of gay relationships in the United States? Should gay couples have the same rights as straight couples?

ners there are eligible for a permanent residence permit.[30] Regardless of one's position on the desirability of gay and lesbian marriage, it is important to understand how society can influence same-sex relationships.

RELATIONSHIPS ACROSS DIFFERENCES

Communicating in Intercultural Relationships

Intercultural relationships among people from different cultures may be similar to intracultural relationships in many ways. But some unique themes related to issues of competence, similarity, involvement, and turning points can guide our thinking about communicating in these relationships.[31]

Competence   It is important to have language skills in intercultural interactions. Even when people speak the same language, they sometimes have language difficulties that can prevent the relationship from flourishing. There are four levels of intercultural communication competence: (1) unconscious incompetence, (2) conscious incompetence, (3) conscious competence, and (4) unconscious competence.[32]

Unconscious incompetence reflects a "be yourself" approach in which an individual is not conscious of cultural differences and does not see a need to act in any particular way. Sometimes this works. However, being ourselves works best in interactions with people who are very similar to us. In intercultural contexts, being ourselves often means that we're not very effective and we don't realize our ineptness. For example, a few years ago, high-ranking government officials from Rwanda visited an American university to participate in an agricultural project. The Americans dressed informally for the meeting and did not pay attention to the seating arrangement. In Rwanda, however, the seating arrangements in meetings indicate rank and are very important. Thus, the Rwandans were insulted by what they perceived to be rudeness on the part of the Americans, although they said nothing. The Americans, by "being themselves" and being oblivious to Rwandan cultural preferences, were unconsciously incompetent.

At the level of conscious incompetence, we realize that things may not be going very well in the interaction, but we're not sure why. Most of us have experienced intercultural interactions in which we felt that something wasn't quite right but we couldn't figure out what it was. For example, in the movie *Gung Ho*, Michael Keaton's character, trying to save a failing auto plant in the Midwest, travels to Japan to try to interest Japanese businessmen in a joint venture. He shows up late to the meeting, speaks informally, and makes jokes. The businessmen do not respond, sitting with stony expressions on their faces. Keaton's character realizes things aren't going well, but he doesn't recognize that he is insulting them by being so informal.

As instructors of intercultural communication, we teach at a conscious, intentional level. Our instruction focuses on analytic thinking and learning. This describes the level of conscious competence. Reaching this level is a necessary

Surf's Up!
Erving Goffman argues that we present ourselves in terms of social roles, much like the roles an actor plays. We have different roles for different situations, and Goffman says that trying to keep them straight involves "impression management." Go to this website to learn more about Goffman's ideas (soc-pc1.cudenver.edu/sociology/introsoc/topics/UnitNotes/week04.html). Do you ever have trouble keeping your different roles straight?

Sharing a common goal or working on a common task, as these workers are doing, can help facilitate intercultural relationships. Sometimes intercultural alliances are formed when people share common interests, beliefs, and goals.

Surf's Up!

Look at the history of the multicultural people called "coloureds" in South Africa (www.grmi. org/~jhanna/obj08. htm). Their existence is the result of a great many intercultural connections, not all of which were made with the best of intentions. How intercultural is your family background?

part of the process of becoming a competent communicator. However, reaching this level is necessary but not sufficient.

Unconscious competence is the level at which communication goes smoothly but is not a conscious process. You've probably heard of marathon runners "hitting the wall," or reaching the seeming limits of their endurance, and then, inexplicably, continuing to run past this point. Communication at the level of unconscious competence is like this. We cannot reach this level by consciously trying; rather, we achieve it when the analytic (conscious, rational) and holistic (unconscious, intuitive) parts of our brains are functioning together. When we concentrate too hard or get too analytic, things don't always go easier.

You've also probably had the experience of trying unsuccessfully to recall something, letting go of it, and then remembering it as soon as you're thinking about something else. This is what unconscious competence involves—being well prepared cognitively and attitudinally, but knowing when to "let go" and rely on your holistic cognitive processing.

Similarity While dissimilarity may account for an initial attraction between two people, it is very important to find and develop some similarity that transcends the cultural differences. For example, shared religious beliefs can help establish common bonds, as can shared interests in sports or other activities, or similar physical appearances, lifestyles, or attitudes.[33] When our student Jaclyn was 15, her family hosted a student from France for the summer. She automatically assumed that they wouldn't have anything in common and that the French student would be "uncool." However, Jaclyn was wrong, and they got to be good friends: "It turned out that we both liked the same music and the same groups. We both learned a lot about each other and each other's cultures. I even decided to start learning French. To this day we keep in touch through e-mail."

Involvement All relationships take time to develop, but it is especially important to make time in intercultural relationships. This is one aspect of involvement. Intimacy of interaction is another element of involvement, as are shared friendship networks. Sharing the same friends is often more important for international students than the host country students because they have left their friends behind. Our student Dotty recalled introducing her friend Sung Rim to her other friends:

> I actually felt a little nervous about introducing my friends to her. I wasn't sure how well they would communicate with her. It was fine, though, and I think she felt at ease. She mostly just listened to the conversation. I could tell she was listening and trying to understand. We would try to talk slower so she could feel comfortable to participate and we made some plans to get together after finals. I would like to continue to really get to know her.

Turning Points There are often significant events that relate to perceived changes in the relationship—turning points that move the relationship forward or backward. For example, asking a friend to do a favor or to share an activity might be a turning point. And if the other person refuses, the relationship may not develop beyond that point. Likewise, self-disclosure may reveal similarities and move a relationship to a new level. For example, in conversation, two professors found that they had similar ideas about communicating and teaching in the classroom. They also discovered that they both came from working-class families and that religion played a strong role in their childhood. But a turning point in their relationship came when one professor revealed that she was gay. Her friend recalled, "As a heterosexual I had never before given much thought to sexual orientation or gays 'coming out of the closet.' Thanks to Anna, I have become far more sensitive and enlightened."[34]

The process of dealing with differences, becoming involved by finding similarities, and moving beyond prejudice was summed up by a U.S. American student talking about her relationship with a Singaporean friend:

> We just had different expectations, different attitudes in the beginning, but at the end we were so close that we didn't have to talk about it. . . . After we erased all prejudices, that we thought the other person has to be different, after we erased that by talking, we just understood each other.[35]

Intercultural Dating

Intercultural dating involves the pursuit of an intercultural romantic relationship. Why do some people date interculturally and others not? The reasons people give for dating within and outside their own ethnic group are very similar: They are attracted to the other person, physically and/or sexually. However, the reasons people give for not dating someone within or outside their own ethnic group are often very different. One reason given for not dating someone within the ethnic group is lack of attraction; reasons given for not dating outside the ethnic group include not having an opportunity and not having thought about it.[36]

These different responses may reflect the social and political structure of American society. That is, most people, by the time they reach adolescence, have been taught that it is better to date within one's ethnic and racial group; and they probably have very little opportunity to date interethnically. One student, Nathan, described how his best friend in junior high school was Native American and that everyone got along. But things changed when they got to high school, even though there was more diversity:

> Everyone still got along, but there was much more separation. There were groups of friends that hung out before classes, but the groups were racially separated. I specifically remember a couple of friends that I had in Junior High that no longer wanted to hang out. Instead, they chose to make new friends because we were of different color. It was never stated blatantly, but it was understood.

In general, what kind of people engage in intercultural dating? Not surprisingly, young people who date interculturally tend to have experience with diversity in general; they have grown up in diverse neighborhoods, have diverse acquaintance and friendship networks, and their family members also date interculturally.[37]

Another characteristic of those who date interculturally might have to do with the development of cultural identity. Recall in Chapter 4 that we talked about the different stages that majority and minority individuals go through in developing their cultural identity. Young people who are in stages characterized by weak ethnic identity are more likely to date outside their ethnic group than those at stages with secure or strong ethnic identity. This might be explained by the fact that young people with very strong ethnic identity tend to see potential outgroup dating partners with greater social distance and less trust and receptivity.[38]

Families often pass on negative attitudes about interracial friendships or romances to their children.[39] Sara, a White student, described how her parents would not give her permission to date her African American friend: "They explained their decision by telling me that it was okay to be friends with him, but he could not be my boyfriend because they did not want me to bring a biracial child into the world."

Intercultural Marriage

There has been a steady increase in the number of intercultural marriages over the past 20 years, and the opposition to such marriages seems to be in a continuing decline, so much so that one scholar refers to it as a "love revolution."[40] However, not all intercultural marriages are accepted. While there seems to be little opposition to a German American marrying an Italian American, there is still some resistance to interreligious marriages. Some Jewish, Christian, and Muslim parents object to their children marrying outside their faith. However, the real division seems to lie in crossing racial lines. While the most recent U.S. census shows that indeed interracial marriages are on the increase, having risen from 0.4 percent of the total in 1960 to almost 2 percent of all intermarriages, there is still a great deal of resistance to interracial marriages.[41]

What are the major concerns of couples who marry interculturally? Their concerns, like those of dating couples, often involve dealing with pressures from their families and from society.

As one of our students told us:

> I have experienced many cultural misunderstanding because I grew up Catholic and have converted to the church of Jesus Christ of Latter-Day Saints. When I was married in the temple, this caused a lot of conflict because that meant my parents could not attend the ceremony. We resolved the conflict by seriously limiting those of the LDS faith who attended the ceremony and by holding a ring ceremony in which we exchanged rings which we did not do inside the temple. Compromise and sensitivity continues to be an important part of our lives.

In addition, they face the issue of raising children. Sometimes these concerns are closely related. Although many couples are concerned with raising children and dealing with family pressures, those in intercultural marriages must deal with these issues to a greater extent. They are more likely to disagree about how to raise the children and to encounter opposition and resistance from their families about the marriage. They are also more likely to have problems related to values, eating and drinking habits, gender roles, attitudes regarding time, religion, place of residence, stress, and ethnocentrism.[42]

Of course, every husband and wife develop their own idiosyncratic way of relating to each other, but intercultural marriage poses consistent challenges. Most couples have their own systems for working out the power balance in their relationships, for deciding who gives and who takes. There are four common styles of interaction in intercultural marriages: submission, compromise, obliteration, and consensus. Couples may adopt different styles depending on the context.

The **submission style,** the most common style, occurs when one partner accepts the culture of the other partner, abandoning or denying his or her own. The submission may occur only in public; in their private life, the relationship may be more balanced. But this style rarely works in the long run. People cannot erase their core cultural background, even though they may try.

What Do You Think?

Are interreligious relationships intercultural relationships? Are they easier or harder to develop than interracial relationships? Does it depend on how important religious faith is to the people involved?

There are many different definitions and meanings related to marriage relationships. For example, gay marriages are very controversial in the United States, but they are legally recognized in other countries such as Netherlands, Belgium and parts of Canada.

With the **compromise style,** each partner gives up some parts of his or her culturally bound habits and beliefs to accommodate the other. Although this may seem fair, it really means that both people sacrifice important aspects of their life. For example, the Christian who gives up celebrating Christmas for the sake of a Jewish spouse may eventually come to resent the sacrifice.

With the **obliteration style,** both partners deal with differences by attempting to erase their individual cultures. They may form a new culture, with new beliefs and habits, especially if they live in a country that is home to neither of them. In fact, this might seem to be the only way for couples whose backgrounds are completely unreconcilable to survive. However, because it's difficult to be completely cut off from one's own cultural background, obliteration is not a particularly good long-term solution.

The style that is the most desirable, not surprisingly, is the **consensus style,** one based on agreement and negotiation. It is related to compromise in that both partners give and take, but it is not a tradeoff. It is a win-win proposition. Consensus may incorporate elements of the other models. Thus, on occasion, one spouse might temporarily "submit" to the other's culture. One of our Navajo students described how she adapts somewhat to her husband's more traditional culture when his mother comes to visit by letting his mother cook breakfast.

> I am half-native American and half Irish. Though I was raised on the reservation, I attended school intown and was taught to try to adapt to the "outside" world. Because of this I was often accused of trying too hard to "be white."
>
> I never realized how drastic these differences were until after I got married. My husband, who is full native American grew up on an isolated reservation and in a home where his mother woke up at 6 each morning to make breakfast for the family.
>
> My husband got used to me not doing this and seemed ok with it, but the first time his parents came to visit, boy did I hear about it! His mom was so upset with me. We explained my point of view to her but it didn't really help. Whenever she comes over now, she gets up early and makes breakfast. . . .

True consensus requires flexibility and negotiation.

Couples who are considering permanent intercultural relationships should prepare carefully for the commitment by living together, spending extended time with the partner's family, learning the partner's language, studying the partner's religion, and learning the partner's cuisine. For example, a student named Vicki dated and eventually married Hassan, a graduate student from Morocco. Before marrying, they spent time in Morocco with his family; Vicki even lived with his family for six months while Hassan was still in the States. They knew it was important for her to get to know his family and cultural background, as he had learned about her and the American culture. Couples who marry interculturally should also consider legal issues like citizenship, children's citizenship, finances and taxation, ownership of property, women's rights, divorce, and issues regarding death.

Internet Relationships

Do intercultural relationships develop differently on the Internet? Computer mediated communication (CMC) is playing an increasing role in our lives, so it also needs to be considered when thinking about intercultural relationships. One might argue that there are aspects of CMC that are both helpful and a hindrance in intercultural relationships.

There are at least three ways that CMC is beneficial. For one, the Internet gives us the opportunity to communicate and develop relationships with people who are very different from us. We can communicate with people in other countries as easily as talking to our next-door neighbor. This presents exciting

Surf's Up!

The Intercultural E.-Mail Classroom Connections website (www.iecc.org) is a central gathering point for intercultural student pen pals. When this book was written, there were over 1,400 college-age subscribers from 58 countries and over 3,200 from 57 countries at the K-12 level. Why do you think so many young people participate in programs like these?

possibilities. As one of our students told us, "I can't even imagine our society without the Internet . . . This summer I studied in Spain and I came to fully appreciate the convenience . . . It is amazing how easy it is to connect to other people, even when you are thousands and thousands of miles away."

A second way that CMC facilitates intercultural communication lies in the fact that it filters out much of the information that we base first impressions on—physical attractiveness, gender, age, and race. While we may find it helpful to have information about people's characteristics, this information also sometimes causes prejudice and discrimination. When we communicate through e-mail or on discussion boards, we have no idea (unless someone chooses to tell us) about the writer's appearance, including height, race, gender, or age. So our interactions may be freer of the tendency to stereotype or discriminate against someone based on those physical characteristics.

Because of the relative anonymity of CMC, it is easier for the writer to disclose personal information and base conversation on similarities instead of physical attraction; therefore, CMC friendships sometimes develop more quickly and more intensely.[43]

However, there are also aspects of CMC that make intercultural communication more difficult. CMC filters out nonverbal cues (facial expressions, gestures, and so on) that help us interpret the tone of what the writer is saying (using sarcasm, jokes, and so on). This filtering can present many possibilities for misunderstanding in an intercultural communication situation, particularly if one speaker is writing in a language that is not his or her first language.[44] For example, Dalila, an Egyptian college student, thought that her American e-mail "pen pal" Jenna was often stilted in her messages and didn't really respond when Dalila would make small jokes or poke fun at herself. She eventually realized that this was probably because Jenna was focusing more on the content of her messages, trying to write in correct Arabic and couldn't really get all the nuances of Dalila's humor.

In addition to misunderstanding due to lack of nonverbal cues, intercultural CMC can also lead to misunderstandings based on different contexts and forms for Internet usage. For example, in some countries people are charged by the minute for their Internet use, so their messages might naturally be shorter and to the point, leading some U.S. Americans to conclude that they are abrupt or rude.

SOCIETY AND INTERCULTURAL RELATIONSHIPS

Finally, it is important to consider how society views and influences interpersonal relationships. Why do some people marry outside their racial or ethnic group more than others? For example, 50 percent of Native Americans marry outside their racial group, while only 25 percent of Asians do.[45] Of course, people marry outside their group for love. But in a racist society, one could argue, this "love" cannot be free from societal thinking. Therefore, these relationships can never be equal, because the partners will always be seen by themselves and by society as unequal.

For example, the official 2000 Census shows that Black men are 2.8 times more likely to marry outside their racial group—predominantly to White women—than Black women. And Asian women are 2.4 times more likely to marry outside their group, predominantly to White men.[46]

These statistics reflect a great deal of frustration for African American women and Asian American men. The statistics also beg the question of why this is the case. Why do so few African American women and Asian men marry outside of their racial group? One answer might be that society, the media, and individuals reinforce a negative image of both groups.

One young Taiwanese American who attended a dinner/discussion event, "Mating and Dating in the Asian American Community," said, "we're at the bottom of the pile, right along with black women." Lakshmi Chaudhry, an Indian American who attended the dinner, recounts:

> The rage among the men in that room was palpable as they spoke of a lifetime of sexual invisibility in a culture that constructs them as either effeminate or repulsive. . . . The sexual marketplace is a minefield for people of color. Our choice of bed partners is defined by a racial hierarchy that places Anglos squarely at the top. They determine who's hot and who's not. . . . Asian men, unfortunately don't cut it.[47]

And we can see how Hollywood movies reinforce this negative image by consistently pairing Asian women with Anglo men rather than Asian men. For example, in *Shanghai Knights*, actress Fann Wong is paired up with Owen Wilson instead of Jackie Chan, who is conveniently cast as her brother. As Chaudhry describes it, "Hollywood's message is unmistakable: No women for the Asian guy." Asian women have a better shot at connecting with Anglos, but it comes at a price. They are often stereotyped as exotic and expected to be deferring and serve White men. One of our Japanese graduate students recounted her experience in dating a White American:

> Everything went fine at the beginning. My English was not good, so he would help me with different things, and I thought that he was very nice and good to me. . . . When I didn't speak English well, he had the control in our relationship and he could manipulate information around me, for example, if his friends said something he didn't want me to understand, he didn't translate it for me and kept it secret from me. Also, I was being more dependent on him first, because I was new to the culture and I didn't speak English well. So it was easy for him to control me and our relationship. But it didn't continue that long, soon he started losing his power in our relationship as I started understanding better, and he started feeling threatened. . . . after I started understanding English and American culture more, I gained more power and he lost his power. When we were fighting, we were actually negotiating our power relation, and when it changed so

significantly that the relationship was no longer worth it for either of us, our relationship was over.

Chaudhry summed up his feelings on the issue:

> A chirpy white woman I once met at an airport lounge said to me, 'I don't care about race when it comes to dating. It's all about chemistry.' Smug in her liberal credentials, she didn't understand that color-blind attraction is a racial privilege. Even as an increasing number of folks of color find love and companionship outside our community, it's a luxury we simply can't afford. . . . in a world still defined by racial division, there is no such thing as just plain old chemistry.

It is important to consider intercultural relationships within the society in which they develop. Because of societal pressures, interracial couples especially find that they have to develop strategies for dealing with the outside world. If they have internalized the negative images of the other group, they may feel like they're "sleeping with the enemy" or feel cut off from their own ethnic group. They may develop ways of ignoring those who see every problem as racial, and they may turn to each other for support and strength—seeing their home as a refuge from an often hostile society.[48]

What kinds of persecution might intercultural relationships encounter? What social institutions might discourage such relationships? Think, for example, how much more difficult it would be to have an interracial relationship if such marriages were illegal, if you attended racially segregated educational institutions, if your church leaders preached against it, or if your family discouraged it.[49] Some of these no longer apply, of course. For example, public schools no longer can segregate students based on race. But social restrictions continue to exist that discourage the development of intercultural relationships.

SUMMARY

In this chapter, we discussed intercultural communication in relationships with people who are both similar to and different from ourselves. Through intercultural relationships, we can acquire specific and general knowledge beyond our local communities, break stereotypes, and acquire new skills. But developing relationships with people who are different from ourselves requires us to deal with differences in communication styles, values, and perceptions; to avoid the tendency to stereotype; to cope with the anxiety that sometimes accompanies these relationships; to try to confirm the other's cultural identity; and to explain to ourselves and others.

We also discussed the foundations of intercultural relationships and the cultural variations in how relationships develop. Two principles—similarities and differences—seem to operate for most people in most cultures, in that individuals are simultaneously drawn to the similarities and the differences of other people. Gay relationships are similar in many ways to heterosexual relationships, but they differ in some aspects. In gay relationships, friendship and sexual involvement are not mutually exclusive, as they tend to be for heterosexuals. Gay men seem to seek more emotional support from same-sex friends than heterosexual men do. Friendships may play a special role in gay relationships because the individuals often experience strained relationships with their families.

Finally, we described how communication in intercultural relationships involves issues of competence, involvement, and similarity and hinges on turning points. Intercultural dating and marriage, particularly in the United States, are still not very common and are often disapproved of by family and society. Computer mediated communication can both facilitate and hinder intercultural relationships. Society can influence our relationships in important ways, helping or hindering us in exploring and developing intercultural relationships.

BUILDING INTERCULTURAL SKILLS

1. Be aware of the complexities of communicating across cultures and of power issues. The goal is to find a way in which we can work toward unity based on "conscious coalition, of affinity, of political kinship," in which we all win.[50]

   Intercultural friends recognize and try to understand how ethnic, gender, and class differences lead to power differentials, and to manage these power issues. They also recognize that history is seen as more or less important by those who are more and those who are less powerful. Finally, they value differences and affirm others as members of culturally different groups.

2. Recognize the value of building coalitions. Coalitions can develop from the multiple identities of gender, sexual orientation, race, physical ability, region, religion, age, social class, and so on. Become involved in whatever way you can in your immediate spheres—of friendships and activities—and cultivate emotional interdependence with others.

3. Look to role models for how to be an effective agent of change. Perhaps you can find these role models in the lives of those around you or in literature or those who have gone before us. And be aware that it's easy to get overwhelmed and feel a sense of despair or powerlessness in working to improve things. Identify your strengths, and use them. Thus, if you're a parent, talk to your children about intercultural issues and building bridges and coalitions between cultural groups. If you have a job, talk to your coworkers. If you are an extrovert, use your people skills to gather others together for dialogues on cross-cultural awareness and understanding. If you are an employer, identify who is missing from your workforce. What are you doing about it?

ACTIVITY

1. *Intercultural relationships:* Think about all your friends, and make a list of those to whom you feel close. Identify any friends on the list who are from other cultures. Then answer the following questions, and discuss your answers with other class members.

a. Do people generally have more friends from their own culture or from other cultures? Why?

b. What are some of the benefits of forming intercultural friendships?

c. In what ways are intercultural friendships different from or similar to friendships with people from the same culture?

d. What are some reasons people might have for not forming intercultural friendships?

www.mhhe.com/
experiencing2

THE ONLINE LEARNING CENTER at www.mhhe.com/experiencing2 features self-quizzes, flashcards, and crossword puzzles based on the chapter's key terms and concepts.

ENDNOTES

1. Brislin, R. W. (1983). The benefits of close intercultural relationships. In S. H. Irvine & J. W. Berry (Eds.), *Human assessment and cultural factors* (pp. 521–538). New York: Plenum.
2. James, N. C. (2004). When Miss America was always White. In A. González, M. Houston, & V. Chen (Eds.), *Our voices: Essays in culture, ethnicity and communication* (4th ed.) (pp. 61–65). Los Angeles: Roxbury.
3. Brislin (1983), pp. 521–538.
4. Stephan, W. G. (1999). *Reducing prejudice and stereotyping in schools.* New York: Teachers College Press.
5. Collier, M. J., & Bornman, E. (1999). Core symbols in South African intercultural friendships. *International Journal of Intercultural Relations, 23,* 133–156.
6. Chen, L. (2002). Communication in intercultural relationships. In W. B. Gudykunst & B. Mody (Eds.), *Handbook of international and intercultural communication* (2nd ed.) (pp. 241–257). Thousand Oaks, CA: Sage.
7. Pogrebin, L. C. (1992). The same and different: Crossing boundaries of color, culture, sexual preference, disability, and age. In W. B. Gudykunst & Y. Y. Kim (Eds.), *Readings on communicating with strangers* (pp. 318–336). New York: McGraw-Hill.
8. Pogrebin (1992), p. 318.
9. Byrne, D. (1971). *The attraction paradigm.* New York: Academic Press. See also Byrne, D., & Blaylock, B. (1963). Similarity and assumed similarity of attitudes between husbands and wives. *Journal of Abnormal and Social Psychology, 67,* 636–640.
10. Osbeck, L. M., & Moghaddam, F. M. (1997). Similarity and attraction among majority and minority groups in a multicultural context. *International Journal of Intercultural Relations, 21,* 113–123. See also Tan, D., & Singh, R. (1995). Attitudes and attraction. *Personality and Social Psychology Bulletin, 21,* 975–986.
11. Duck, S., & Barnes, M. K. (1992). Disagreeing about agreement: Reconciling differences about similarity. *Communication Monographs, 59,* 199–208. See also LaGaipa, J. J. (1987). Friendship expectations. In R. Burnett, P. McGee, & D. Clarke (Eds.), *Accounting for relationships* (pp. 134–157). London: Methuen.
12. Hatfield, E., & Rapson, R. L. (1992). Similarity and attraction in close relationships. *Communication Monographs, 59,* 209–212.
13. Gareis, E. (1995). *Intercultural friendship: A qualitative study.* Lanham, MD: University Press of America, p. 96.
14. Gareis (1995), p. 128.
15. Storti, C. (2001). *Old world, new world: Bridging cultural differences: Britain, France, Germany and the U.S.* Yarmouth, ME: Intercultural Press.

16. Storti (2001), p. 68
17. Storti (2001).
18. Barnlund, D. S. (1989). *Communication styles of Japanese and Americans: Images and reality*. Belmont, CA: Wadsworth.
19. Collier, M. J. (1991). Conflict competence within African, Mexican and Anglo American friendships. In S. Ting-Toomey & F. Korzenny (Eds.), *Cross cultural interpersonal communication* (pp. 132–154). Newbury Park, CA: Sage. See also Collier, M. J. (1996). Communication competence problematics in ethnic friendships. *Communication Monographs, 63,* 314–346.
20. Gao, G. (1991). Stability of romantic relationships in China and the United States. In Ting-Toomey & Korzenny, pp. 99–115. See also Sprecher, S., Aron, A., Hatfield, E., Cortese, A., Potapova, E., & Levitskaya, A. (1994). Love: American style, Russian style, and Japanese style. *Personal Relationships, 1,* 349–369.
21. Dion, K. K., & Dion, K. L. (1991). Psychological individualism and romantic love. *Journal of Social Behavior and Personality, 6,* 17–33. See also Dion, K. K., & Dion, K. L. (1993). Individualistic and collectivistic perspectives on gender and the cultural context of love and intimacy. *Journal of Social Issues, 49,* 53–59.
22. Herdt, G. (1997). *Same sex, different cultures: Exploring gay and lesbian lives*. Boulder, CO: Westview Press.
23. Hammond, D., & Jablow, A. (1987). Gilgamesh and the Sundance Kid: The myth of male friendship. In H. Brod (Ed.), *The making of masculinities: The new men's studies* (pp. 241–258). Boston: Allen & Unwin.
24. Nardi, P. (1999). *Gay men's friendships: Invincible communities*. Thousand Oaks, CA: Sage.
25. Nakayama, T. K. (1998). Communication of heterosexism. In M. L. Hecht (Ed.), *Communication of prejudice* (pp. 112–121). Thousand Oaks, CA: Sage.
26. Nardi, P. M. (1992). That's what friends are for: Friends as family in the gay and lesbian community. In K. Plummer (Ed.), *Modern homosexualities: Fragments of lesbian and gay experience* (pp. 108–120). New York: Routledge.
27. Patterson, C. (2000). Family relationships of lesbians and gay men. *Journal of Marriage and the Family, 62,* 1052–69.
28. BBC news. (2003, June 17). Canada pushes gay marriages. (http://news.bbc.co.uk/1/hi/world/americas/2999270.stm). See also Cohen, T. (2003, June 12). Court supports gay marriages. *Concord Monitor* (online). (http://www.concordmonitor.com/stories/front2003/061203canadasame_2003.shtml)
29. ABC News Online. (1999, October 14). France grants equal legal rights to gay couples. Australian Broadcasting Corporation. (www.abc.net.au)
30. Cole, D. (2001, July 31). Germany opens door to gay marriage. *Agence Presse* (online). (www.gfn.com/archives/story.phtml?sid-9975). See also Hart, J. (1992). A cocktail of alarm. Same-sex couples and migration to Australia, 1985–1990. In K. Plummer (Ed.), *Modern homosexualities: Fragments of lesbian and gay experience* (pp. 121–133). New York: Routledge.
31. Sudweeks, S., Gudykunst, W. B., Ting-Toomey, S., & Nishida, T. (1990). Developmental themes in Japanese–North American relationships. *International Journal of Intercultural Relations, 14,* 207–233.
32. Howell, W. S. (1982). *The empathic communicator*. Belmont, CA: Wadsworth.
33. Graham, M. A., Moeai, J., & Shizuru, L. S. (1985). Intercultural marriages: An intrareligious perspective. *International Journal of Intercultural Relations, 9,* 427–434.
34. Allen, B. J. (2004). Sapphire and Sappho: Allies in authenticity. In A. González, M. Houston, & V. Chen (Eds.), *Our voices: Essays in culture, ethnicity and communication* (4th ed.) (pp. 198–202). Los Angeles: Roxbury.
35. Quoted in Gareis (1995), p. 136.
36. Martin, J. N., Bradford, L. J., Drzewiecka, J. A., & Chitgopekar, A. S. (2003). Intercultural dating patterns among young white U.S. Americans: Have they changed in the past 20 years? *The Howard Journal of Communications, 14,* 53–73.
37. Martin, J. N., Bradford, L. J., Drzewiecka, J. A., & Chitgopekar, A. S. (2003).

38. Chen, L. (2002). Communication in intercultural relationships. In W. B. Gudykunst & B. Mody (Eds.), *Handbook of international and intercultural communication* (2nd ed.) (pp. 241–257). Thousand Oaks, CA: Sage.

39. Harris, T. M., & Kalbfleisch, P. J. (2000). Interracial dating: The implications of race for initiating a romantic relationship. *The Howard Journal of Communications, 11,* 49–64.

40. Root, M. P. P. (2001). *Love's revolution: Interracial marriage.* Philadelphia: Temple University Press.

41. Lind, M. (2003, June 16). Far from heaven. *The Nation* (online), (http://www.thenation.com/doc.mhtml?i=20030616&s=lind)

42. Romano, D. (1997). *Intercultural marriage: Promises and pitfalls* (2nd ed.). Yarmouth, ME: Intercultural Press.

43. McKenna, K. Y. A., Green, A. S., & Gleason, M. E. J. (2002). Relationship formation on the Internet: What's the big attraction? *Journal of Social Issues, 58,* 9–31.

44. Olaniran, B. A. (2001). The effects of computer-mediated communication on transculturalism. In V. H. Milhouse, M. K. Asante, & P. O. Nwosu (Eds.), *Transcultural realities* (pp. 83–105). Thousand Oaks, CA: Sage.

45. Lind, M. (2003, June 16).

46. Lee, B. (June/July 2003). The reality of interracial marriages. *The Multiracial Activist* (online). (http://www.multiracial.com/readers/lee.html)

47. Chaudhry, L. (2003, February 3). Chemistry isn't color-blind. *AlterNet.org.* (http://www.alternet.org/story.html?StoryID=15090)

48. Foeman, A., & Nance, T. (2002). Building new cultures, reframing old images: Success strategies of interracial couples. *The Howard Journal of Communications, 13,* 237–249.

49. Kivel, P. (1996). *Uprooting racism: How White people can work for racial justice.* Gabriola Island, British Columbia: New Society, pp. 204–205.

50. Kivel, P. (1996).

CHAPTER TEN

Intercultural Communication in Tourism Contexts

CHAPTER OUTLINE

STUDY OBJECTIVES

After reading this chapter you should be able to:

1. Describe variations in host attitudes toward tourists.
2. Identify and describe characteristics of tourist-host encounters.
3. Describe ways in which tourists can learn about the cultures they visit.
4. Understand the various communication challenges that tourists encounter.
5. Identify cross-cultural differences in social norms and expectations encountered by tourists.
6. Understand the role culture shock might play in a tourism experience.
7. Describe the language challenges that tourists might face.
8. Understand how social and political contexts influence tourism encounters.

KEY TERMS

boundary maintenance
eco-tourism
host
resistance

retreatism
revitalization
tourist

What Do You Think?

"Have passport—will travel," is a statement sometimes uttered in jest. According to U.S. State Department statistics, during the 2003 fiscal year, over 7 million Americans were issued valid U.S. passports (see http://travel.state.gov/ passport_statistics.html). Still, many charge that the United States is a very insular society, as Americans generally know very little about countries outside of their own and have limited travel experiences. Try doing a quick survey of classmates or close friends or family. How much have they traveled abroad? How many of the people you know have passports? Ask yourself the same questions. If possible, discuss your findings in class.

Since the beginning of time, humans have been traveling in ever-widening patterns about the earth. From the days of early explorers, who traveled on foot and by boat, to modern roamers, who travel by car and plane, there has been an increase in travel and tourism. In fact, according to the World Travel and Tourism Council, travel and tourism is the world's largest industry, accounting for nearly 200 million jobs and over 10 percent of world GDP—billions of dollars. In 2002 alone, there were more than 700 million international travelers.[1] By 2010, this industry is expected to generate $8 trillion of economic activity and 328 million jobs.[2]

Almost all of us have been tourists or will be someday. Being a tourist may involve travel to another region of the United States, like a visit to Disneyland or a trip to the Amana colonies in Iowa, or an international trip like those described by Sarah and Jeanine. It may involve a bus trip in Europe, visiting seven countries in seven days, or an **eco-tourism** cruise to remote areas in Australia or Indonesia that emphasizes appreciation for and conservation of the environment. Table 10.1 shows the top ten world tourist destinations in 2002. In any case, tourism contexts provide rich opportunities for intercultural encounters.

These encounters may be positive, as was our student Sarah's experience when she traveled to Italy with her senior class. She gained a great appreciation for the art and history of Italy and an admiration for the bilingual Italians she met. It was the first time she had been out of the country and didn't know what to expect:

> I remember getting off the plane and being in awe of my surroundings. During our two-week stay, we traveled to Rome, Venice, Assisi, and the Padua. I learned a lot about the Italian culture during those two weeks,

TABLE 10.1 The Top Ten World Tourist Destinations in 2002

Tourists travel around the world. Are these destinations top on your list? Are there places left off of this list that you would like to visit? How do tourists pick destinations?

1. France	6. United Kingdom
2. Spain	7. Canada
3. United States	8. Mexico
4. Italy	9. Austria
5. China	10. Germany

Source: World Tourism Organization (http://www.world-tourism.org/market_research/facts/highlights/Highlights.pdf)

Some cultural groups desire only limited contact with the outside world, often restricted to business transactions. This is the case for many Mennonites and Amish. Here, a Mennonite girl sells cheese in Chihuahua, Mexico.

but the one thing that stood out in my mind was that most of the Italians we met spoke English, while hardly any of us could speak Italian.

In contrast to Sarah's experience, some tourist encounters are tinged with resentment and power differentials, as in Jeanine's experience. She told us that on numerous occasions during a vacation in Mexico, she saw American tourists being rude and demanding to the Mexican staff at the hotel, not even trying to disguise the fact that they felt superior to the Mexicans. She also noticed that when the Mexican staff were treated badly by the U.S. Americans, they would pretend to not speak English and would play 'dumb' for the hotel guests who were rude and demanding. "Watching interactions like these would amuse me because most of the staff spoke quite fluent English to my mother and me."

All of this has implications for intercultural communication. What are typical intercultural encounters in tourist contexts? How do cultural differences influence communication in these contexts? How do societal structures influence tourist encounters? How do politics and economic events impact tourist encounters? How can communication be improved in these contexts? These are some of the questions we'll be tackling in this chapter. First, we describe some tourist experiences that lead to particular kinds of host-tourist interaction. Then we discuss the communication challenges in tourist contexts and some of the societal impacts of tourism. Finally, we look at some skills that can help us communicate better in tourist contexts.

Surf's Up!

What is the difference between packing for a short trip to a tourist destination and packing for travel that lasts a lifetime? Packing and unpacking is a powerful metaphor that stands out in preparing for intercultural experiences. What do you pack when you are going just "out of town"? What do you pack if you are staying for a long time? What do you pack if you are not coming back? Read "...Zzip," a short personal narrative that re-defines the politics of packing (http://future.state.gov/future/where/stories/transition/zip.html). In one instance, the author writes, "I'm cramming souvenirs and pictures into my bag in an effort to pack my identity." Reflect on this narrative. Compare it to your own story or sense of travel.

INTERCULTURAL COMMUNICATION AND TOURISM

Several different groups come into contact in tourism contexts—the tourists themselves, businesses/service providers in the host culture, and members of the host culture community. First, there are the **tourists**—the visitors to another region. Tourists may have different motivations for visiting. For example, history buffs might travel to Gettysburg, Pennsylvania, as a way to experience what they've read in history books. Culture-seekers who are fascinated by different ways of life might enjoy socializing and meeting new people, or they may want to seek out their own ethnic and cultural roots. Tourists could include religious pilgrims or people simply seeking recreation or adventure. A recent type of traveler is the ecotourist who wishes to see and protect endangered species of flora or fauna. Finally, status-seekers are those tourists who want to travel to the most expensive and exotic locations.[3] Tourists also come from a variety of socioeconomic backgrounds, from the college student backpacker on a limited budget to the status-seeker who travels first class. Second, there are the businesses/service providers. These are the people who serve in the tourist industry—hotel workers, tour guides, waiters, and so on. And finally, there is the **host,** or residents of the tourist region, and the host community may have varying attitudes toward the tourists.

Attitudes of Hosts Toward Tourists

Coping with tourists can be a complex process for people in host countries. The attitudes of residents may range from retreatism, to resistance, to boundary maintenance, to revitalization and adoption.[4] Some communities that are not enthusiastic about tourism may simply practice **retreatism,** or avoiding contact with tourists. This may occur especially in places where the economy has become dependent on tourism but the community feels invaded by tourists. The downside of tourism can include crowded streets, transportation, and shops. High demand during tourist season results in high prices of food and other items and can lead to overcharging of locals and tourists alike. Scarce resources like water and sanitation systems may come under pressure, and tourists may unknowingly insult local sensibilities. For example, locals in small Mediterranean villages are often shocked and feel violated by the scantily clad tourists who walk the streets of their conservative villages or go topless on their beaches. Or in one village in Greece, residents were appalled at visitors sleeping in their churches. "They went there with their sleeping bags, they used this holy place for camping. Now we keep all the churches locked during the summer and the keys are kept by a neighbor."[5]

This sense of invasion may result in locals finding ways to keep their everyday life hidden from the eyes of the tourists. They may go so far as to change the language or the dates of community events to ensure that these events are for locals only. For example, locals in Sardinia were advised to use the term *Sagra* rather than *Fiesta* in advertising their village festivals since fewer non-Italians would recognize the term *Sagra*. On the Greek island of Skyros, locals wait until the tourist buses leave the annual feast of their Saints before they celebrate the "real feast." They can then relax, eat, drink, and sing together, away from the curious eyes of the tourists.

Another example of retreatism happens in a small village in Norway, where residents complain that tourists feel free to walk into their yards and peer into their "quaint" houses. And in Malta, a local family discovered two German tourists peering into their home. This curious couple, who came to the village with a tour, simply opened the glass inner door and walked into the family's brightly lit front room. To cope with this and to protect their privacy, the family felt like they had to close the wooden outer door that was previously always left open.[6]

Similar situations occur when U.S. tourists visit American Indian reservations. Judith has attended the Navajo Nation Annual Fair in Window Rock, Arizona, several times and was surprised to see tourists pointing their video cameras directly in the faces of the Navajo dancers while they were dancing. When people feel so invaded, they may resort to forms of **resistance** to tourist intrusions. Resistance may take fairly passive forms like grumbling and gossiping about tourists or denigrating stereotypes about difficult tourists. For example, stereotypes about arrogant Germans, complaining Dutch, and stingy Swedes abound in many Mediterranean tourist locales.

Resistance can also include more assertive forms, as in our earlier example of the Mexican staff pretending not to speak English to rude tourists or in harassment of female tourists. Making fun and using ridicule are also forms of resistance, as in this encounter between a tourist and an American Indian:

> A lady was examining the silver balls on a squash blossom necklace. She turned to Cippy Crazyhorse and in a slow, overemphasized fashion intended for someone who does not really understand English she asked "Are these hollow?" Cippy promptly replied "Hello" and warmly shook her hand. Again the lady asked "Are they hollow" pronouncing the words even more theatrically this time. Cippy cheerily responded with another "Hello." This went on a few more times, by which time everyone around was laughing, until eventually the lady herself saw the joke.[7]

When locals feel pushed beyond their limit by tourism, they may even resort to organized protest or even violence. For example, when locals on Skyros, a small Greek island, first encountered topless tourists sunbathing, they were appalled, called the police, and eventually designated one beach that would be used by topless tourists. Sometimes reactions can be even more dramatic and violent. In one incident, a French tourist was stoned to death by the villagers of San Juan

What Do You Think?

James Clifford, in the essay "Traveling Cultures" (in *Cultural Studies*, Routledge, 1992), argues that when we travel we are involved in many more relationships than we might think—with maids, bellhops, guides, and so on. If you have traveled to other countries for vacations, what different kinds of people did you depend on that you were perhaps unaware of?

Chamula in Chiapas, Mexico, for photographing their carnival. And in another case, a furious Navajo man shot out the tires of a tourist's car when the tourist barged into his hogan to photograph his family eating there.[8]

Boundary maintenance to regulate the interaction between hosts and tourists is a common response among certain cultures within the United States, like the Amish, Hutterites, or Mennonites, that do not really desire a lot of interaction with tourists. The Amish in these communities may interact with tourists on a limited level, but they maintain a distance from outsiders and often will turn their backs to cameras. They take no pictures themselves and do not appreciate anyone photographing them. They base their objection on the second commandment in the Bible (Exodus 20:12: "Thou shalt not make unto thee any graven image . . ."). They learn to ignore or endure the tourists' gaze and the insulting photography, and to go on with their lives.[9]

In Lancaster County, Pennsylvania, where many Amish and Mennonites live, there are many commercial simulated cultural experiences, like "Amish Village" or "Amish Farm and Home," in which actors play Amish characters and educate tourists about Amish culture. In this way, a boundary is retained between the real Amish and the tourists. However, this boundary is breaking down somewhat as many Amish feel forced to leave their community. Due to escalating land values caused by development, many young Amish can no longer afford to buy or work farms when they marry and so cannot continue the tradition of Amish farming communities. Therefore, many Amish are leaving the Lancaster area and relocating where land is cheaper. Those who stay depend more and more on tourism and interact more directly with tourists—turning their homes into bed and breakfast inns and selling quilts, crafts, and Amish food.

A final response of host to tourists is **revitalization** and adoption. Some communities have been revitalized economically by embracing tourism—like colonial Williamsburg and many towns in New England that feature colonial architecture. Communities may decide to actively invest money to draw tourists or may be more passive, accepting the tourism but maintaining boundaries. Some communities wholeheartedly embrace tourism and welcome interaction with tourists, accepting tourism as part of their social and cultural fabric. For example, towns like Tombstone, Arizona, and seasonal beach and ski towns capitalize on tourism.

By marketing their culture, local residents sometimes rediscover their own history and traditions and begin to realize their own worth. They may establish museums for tourists, and they learn about their own traditions. Or they may set up heritage parks, festivals, and handcraft markets that lead to preservation of the local culture. In some poor areas with declining populations, tourism can have the effect of revitalizing the area and halting the depopulation.

However, residents often do not share equally in the profits from revitalization and marketing of culture. In poor areas, the tourism potential is often first discovered and initiated by outsiders, who reap most of the profits, as is the case in Hawaii:

What Do You Think?

You may have heard of the "pushy American" stereotype: tourists who ignore local customs, do not bother to learn the local language but expect English to be spoken everywhere, and loudly complain at the slightest provocation. Do you think that most U.S. American travelers are really like this? Why or why not?

[T]ourism has only brought the same kinds of low paying menial, dead-end jobs that have always been the lot of local workers. The setting of a luxury hotel may be worlds away from the sugar plantation, but in terms of the degradation and oppression of human labor, it is probably a good deal worse.[10]

Of course, there can be a variety of responses within the same community. There may be some residents who prefer to retreat and limit their interaction with tourists, while others may embrace tourism and welcome the visitors. This can cause conflicts in communication among community members.

Characteristics of Tourist-Host Encounters

Whatever the attitude of the host community toward the tourists, most intercultural contact between host and tourist is very limited. These interactions are transitory, have time constraints, lack spontaneity, and are unbalanced.[11] For example, consider our student Robin's experience in Spain:

> I was traveling from Barcelona to Madrid and stopped in a small town to get some lunch. There seemed to be few English-speaking people in this area. This was a problem when I was ordering food in a restaurant. The menu was written in Spanish, of course, of which I know none. To make things more difficult, they didn't have any items I recognized, such as tacos. I told the waiter to bring me anything, which he understood, and I gave him $10. I let the waiter decide what I ate. It was good, and I would definitely eat it again.

As Robin's experience illustrates, most tourism encounters, by definition, are short-term and transitory. Tourists rarely stay in one place for long and often have very little interaction with people in the host country. In fact, one writer observes that tourists on tour buses rolling through a country are really watching a silent movie, with the tour guide supplying the soundtrack.[12] This means that most contact between tourists and hosts or service providers will be quite brief, as in the preceding example. Many encounters are simply business exchanges—a service is provided, and money is exchanged. So these brief, superficial interactions are predictable and ritualistic.

As Robin's experience also illustrates, most tourist-host encounters are limited by time considerations. Even on vacation, many tourists are pressed for time and really don't have the time to engage in long interactions. There is also a lack of spontaneity in tourist-host encounters and a lack of opportunities for tourists to engage in genuine social interactions with local people.

The final characteristic of tourist-host communication is the unbalanced nature of the interaction. That is, tourists, hosts, and service providers often have different socioeconomic backgrounds, with the tourists more economically and socially privileged than those with whom they interact.

Pop Culture Spotlight

Have you ever noticed that places featured in Hollywood motion pictures often become popular tourist destinations? Consider the film *Thelma and Louise*. Remember the cliff scene at the end? It has drawn thousand of tourists to the National Park in Utah where the scene was originally shot. The State of Iowa owes much to movies like *The Bridges of Madison County* and *Field of Dreams*. Is tourism spawned by movie madness?

Interactions between tourists and members of the host culture often are superficial and transitory. Taking videos and photos during a bus tour, as this tourist is doing, is a common tourist practice; however, interacting with U.S. Americans would reveal far more about U.S. culture.

Given these characteristics, when is contact between locals and tourists likely to result in more positive feelings and good communication between hosts and tourists? And when is the outcome more likely to be negative? As you might expect, when tourists are friendly and respectful and demonstrate interest in a country and culture (beyond an interest in the beaches and recreational sites), local residents perceive tourists to be more like guests, develop pride in their culture, and are more likely to welcome interaction with tourists. Also, when tourists take opportunities for more extensive interaction with locals, there is the possibility of mutual understanding and even lasting friendships.

On the other hand, when tourists visit historically unfriendly places (like U.S. Americans visiting the Middle East), have little prior knowledge of the culture, and have only superficial encounters with hosts, outcomes of tourist-host encounters are likely to result in negative attitudes and reinforced stereotypes. Negative outcomes are also more likely where there are major differences in religious or cultural values (for example, Western tourists in Muslim countries who violate norms of female modesty or prohibition of alcohol). In addition, economic differences can also lead to negative outcomes, as when rich tourists to developing countries display little regard for their hosts. This can lead to resentment and unwillingness to communicate on the part of hosts, and tourists then learn less about the host culture than they might have otherwise.[13]

Cultural Learning and Tourism

Some tourist-host encounters do go beyond the superficial confines of the tourist role. This may happen unexpectedly when sharing food, holding a long conversation, or simply participating in a meaningful slice of the local culture. A Canadian student described just such an incident:

> One of my best experiences occurred in Antilles, France, where we met a young Dutch couple. They were interested in getting to know us because we were Canadians. They were going to Monte Carlo the next day and asked us to go along. We squeezed into a tiny convertible Renault and spent a marvelous day visiting and learning about the country. Between Dutch, French, and English we managed to understand one another. It was a fantastic experience to get to know them.[14]

And one can learn something about the local culture even in a short time. As an Australian traveler writes: "My impression of England is that everywhere people seemed to be valued for their own sake rather than from a materialistic, functional point of view. There seemed to be less sex role differentiation than in Australia."[15]

COMMUNICATION CHALLENGES IN TOURISM CONTEXTS

Social Norms and Expectations

There are many cultural norms that have implications for intercultural communication between tourists and hosts. Some of the most relevant are norms about public social behavior, shopping, and communication style.

Comportment on the Street   As we saw in Chapter 6, norms regarding nonverbal behavior vary dramatically from culture to culture. And expectations about comportment in the street are no exception, ranging from very informal, as in the United States, to more formal, as in many countries. Sometimes the norms are related to religious beliefs and traditions, as with Muslims, Amish, and others whose religion dictates one's appearance.

Cultural norms also dictate how people interact with each other in public. In some cultures, strangers are expected to greet each other and interact in the

What Do You Think?

Tourists are often faced with many challenges they don't anticipate in traveling for pleasure. Attitudes about family, religion, and sexual orientation seem to be most relevant in tourist intercultural encounters. Anti-gay protests about the presence of gay and lesbian tourists in Jamaica, the Cayman Islands, and the Bahamas have been reported in the news. Read up on details about one such instance in early 1998, when gay passengers aboard a cruise ship that docked at Nassau in the Bahamas were met with protest signs warning them that they were unwelcome (http://www.cnn.com/TRAVEL/NEWS/9804/14/bahamas.gay/).

streets. For example, in Egypt and many North African countries, there is a great deal of interaction in the streets, with shopkeepers greeting everyone and children interacting with strangers, especially tourists. In the United States, strangers may interact in some public contexts, such as in a line at a checkout counter, on an airplane, or at a sporting event. And people may smile at strangers. However, in some countries, such as those in Europe, there is much less smiling at strangers. And in Japan, there is very little interaction, verbal or nonverbal, among strangers in public.[16]

Of course, the type of interaction that occurs in public depends on many things, including the size of the town and cultural expectations for male-female interaction. Our student Shannon described an experience she had when she and her mother were visiting Mexico:

> As we were walking along the streets, window shopping, several groups of men were whistling and shouting things at us. We were both extremely offended. As we were eating lunch, we asked our waiter about this. We wanted to know if they were being rude or making fun of us. He informed us that it was actually a compliment. The way we reacted was not productive, and we realized that we were just not accustomed to this.

This same kind of interaction is expected in many other cultures that value open appreciation of (mainly) women's appearance. French women comment that they feel invisible in the United States, that no one notices them, unlike in France, where appreciation is expressed more openly.

Shopping   Communication norms involved in shopping also vary from culture to culture. One shopping norm has to do with touching merchandise. In the United States, shoppers are expected to touch the merchandise and try on clothing before making a purchase. However, in many cultures, one does not touch merchandise and tries on clothing only if one is almost certain to buy. Our student Caterina found this out in Italy:

> I was in a boutique, a very formal setting, and I began to pick up some shirts, unfold them, look in the mirror, then refold and move on. This was not "proper" behavior, and a saleswoman came up to me and explained in a harsh tone to not touch the merchandise, but to tell her or another woman and they would put it in a fitting room. In the end, I felt as though I found out something important about the culture.

A second shopping norm has to do with bargaining. Expectations about bargaining also vary from culture to culture. In most transactions in the United States, for example, the price for the merchandise is set and is not negotiated. However, in many countries, shoppers are expected to bargain; through the act of bargaining, people are connected. Some tourists find this very challenging and, given the differences in resources between tourist and host, confusing. Should one enter into the bargaining process as part of adapting to local customs,

Many tourist groups depend on a tour guide while exploring unfamiliar lands. The tour guide becomes the "culture broker" for the group, interpreting the language, history, and cultural traditions of the host country.

or should one simply pay the stated price, given the fact that the tourist often has more resources? A student visiting Mexico described this dilemma after she was approached by street vendors who seemed tired of what they were doing: "Their voices are weary of the effort to persuade. I feel uncomfortable and out of place in this environment. The uneasiness and suspicions concerning business relationships vie with my feelings about humanity. This lingers on with me and I am left confused."[17] We feel uncomfortable with our First World status only when we are confronted with another's poverty, which highlights the economic disparity between tourists and hosts.

Culture Shock

As we discussed in Chapter 4, being in new cultural contexts can often lead to culture shock and feelings of disorientation. Of course, sometimes tourists have so little contact with the host culture that there is little opportunity for culture shock. The degree of culture shock may also depend on how different the host culture is from the tourist's home culture. For example, when our student Jordan visited Canada with his grandparents, he experienced very little culture shock, because the language was the same (they visited English-speaking areas of Canada). And he actually experienced very little culture shock when he visited Austria with his church choir. The little sightseeing he did was by bus with other members of the choir and with an English-speaking tour guide. The group ate all its meals together and stayed in the same hotel. So he actually had very few intercultural encounters.

What Do You Think?

Are there times when and places where travel is not appropriate? In the 1980s and 1990s, Caribbean cruise ships usually stopped in Haiti, where tour buses frequently were chased by legions of impoverished children for whom a dollar would have been a small fortune. Laos has a newly emergent tourist industry, and backpackers can find a hotel room and a day's worth of food for under a dollar. Aren't these two sides of the same coin?

By contrast, when he visited Vietnam with his father, who had been there during the war, he experienced quite a big culture shock: "It was so hot, I couldn't understand a word that was said, and the food was strange. I thought it would be easier, since I had already been abroad before, but it was hard." Indeed, the physiological aspects of traveling can be troublesome for tourists. On short-term trips, one's body doesn't have the time to adjust to new climate conditions or new foods or eating customs. And feeling fatigued or under the weather often can affect communication with others.

Keep in mind that it is the tourist who is experiencing the culture shock; the problem is not the culture itself. However, tourists who experience culture shock often take it out on the host community. For example, they may get angry with waiters for not serving food fast enough, or complain about the smells or sights, or take a prejudicial or patronizing attitude toward the local culture. This behavior also presents a challenge for members of the host culture. When presented with rude behavior, is difficult for them to remember that the tourist who is complaining about the service actually may be expressing general frustration, may be suffering from culture shock, or may simply be fatigued.

And perhaps it is not just the tourist who experiences culture shock, for the host population can suffer the same shock. The encounters might be stressful for both because both tourist and host are being confronted with new values and behaviors and uncertainty. They are both required to accommodate, to some extent, the other group. Both hosts and tourists probably experience more shock when they have limited previous intercultural experience.[18]

Some tourist experiences represent a prepackaged version of national or regional history, such as this re-enactment of an 18th-century colonial farm scene in Yorktown Victory Center in Virginia. But who decides how this history is to be presented? How might the scene be different if presented from the viewpoint of Indians who lived in Virginia at that time?

Language Challenges

Language is often a problem for tourists. One cannot learn all the languages of cultures where one might visit in a lifetime, and it can be frustrating not to be able to understand what is being said. It is often part of culture shock. As our student Laura explained:

> When I went to Hermosillo, I definitely felt a huge dose of culture shock. I remember trying to talk to my host sister through the use of Spanish-English dictionaries and a bit of sign language. This experience was very tough. I remember trying to act friendly and saying "hello" to several Mexican students. They would look at me like I was crazy and often offer no response. I felt very stupid when I couldn't understand what people were saying while speaking Spanish.

The expectations of various host cultures regarding language also may differ. Sometimes tourists are expected to get along using the host language, but other cultures provide more language assistance for travelers. Our student April was 16 when she took a trip to France with a group from her high school, while a group of French students visited her hometown. It was not exactly an exchange program because they weren't touring each other's schools or community, but there would be one dinner with prominent townspeople in their respective communities. She recalled the experience:

> The first day we arrived, everyone spoke in English. We got to our hotel, and everything there had English writing. Since none of us spoke fluent French, an English speaker accompanied us, happily translating for us. I thought it was a wonderful trip.

However, when she got back home, she discovered that the French students had had quite a different experience:

> They were expected to know English, so nobody from my school district bothered to get an interpreter. They had to rely on the fluent English speakers of their own group to do even the most simple things like ride the bus. At the dinner my town hosted, the English-speaking French students had to interrupt their meal to translate to the other students. I am sure when they returned they could not have had many good things to say about my town.

SOCIAL AND POLITICAL CONTEXTS OF TOURISM

We also need to consider the social and political impacts on tourism. As the events of 9/11 attested, political events can impact the tourism industry dramatically. As one tourism expert declared, "that four plane crashes could possibly not only trigger a decline in tourism, but hasten the end of some very large

Surf's Up!

Today's traveler has a lot more to think about when deciding to travel for business or pleasure. Safety is becoming a major concern for anyone planning a trip overseas. Check out the U.S. State Department website, which publishes detailed safety protocols and tip sheets designed to assist travelers in facing issues of security abroad (http://travel.state.gov/asafetripabroad.html). The site also includes links to safety advisories for specific countries. It might be interesting to look at the link "Tips for Travelers to the Middle East and North Africa." In thinking of the social and political contexts of tourism, how might you compare these tips to, for example, tips for avoiding buying phony souvenirs? What do these bits of information tell us about the importance of intercultural communication in today's world?

companies and even possibly be the deciding factor in turning an economic downturn into a global recession is beyond most people's thinking."[19] This terrorist act had far-reaching effects, including decline in profits for airline, hotels, and other parts of the tourism industry; increases in security; and a fear of flying for many people. And the events did not just affect the United States; there was also a global downturn in international travel.

At the same time, there were some areas of tourism that were not affected. Backpackers, for example, continued to travel and vacation, and some destinations suffered less than others. China and other countries in Asia, for instance, remained fairly strong until another set of attacks in Bali, the Philippines, and Thailand.[20]

The tourism industry was also hugely affected by the outbreak of SARS (Severe Acute Respiratory Syndrome) in the Spring of 2003. Almost 10,000 cases of this deadly disease were reported in 29 countries. Most of these cases were in Asia, which cut business in the tourism industry in Asia by 40 percent—just at a time when Asia drew more visitors than North and South America for the first time in history. Asian airlines canceled more than 1,150 weekly flights in May.[21]

After SARS and the Iraq War seemed under control and travel confidence was gradually restored, it was further dented by terrorist attacks in Riyadh, Casablanca, Jakarta, and Mumbai. "However these had far less impact than expected as the public seems to have grown accustomed to living in an unsafe world," said WTO Chief of Market Intelligence and Promotion, Augusto Huéscar.[22]

While the travel industry concentrates primarily on the economic impacts of the industry, we should also explore the many implications for intercultural communication. These political, health, and economic events can lead to an atmosphere of fear of each other and fear of traveling to certain areas of the world, which can lead to a lack of opportunity for understanding and empathy for others.

SUMMARY

In this chapter, we addressed the intercultural communication issues that are relevant in tourist contexts. It's important to learn more about communication aspects of cross-cultural tourism encounters, especially given the increase in travel and the enormous amount of money spent on tourism each year.

We also described the various types of host attitudes toward tourists. Host communities may resist tourist encounters, retreat from them, maintain some boundaries, or actively seek them out. Tourist-host encounters often are superficial, brief, and ritualistic.

We identified some of the communication challenges in these encounters, including differing social norms, culture shock on the part of the tourist, and language issues. Finally, we explored some of the social and political impacts on tourism like 9/11 and the SARS outbreak in Asia.

BUILDING INTERCULTURAL SKILLS

1. Gather knowledge about the culture that you would like to visit, even if you would be there for only a short time. Having some information about the places you are visiting communicates respect for the local culture and customs.

2. Learn a few words of the language—again, even if you visit for only a short time. Locals tend to respect the traveler who tries to communicate something in the local language. At least learn how to say "Please" and "Thank you."

3. Learn something about the local customs that may affect your communication. What are the local religious holidays? For example, Ramadhan, celebrated in many Muslim countries, falls on different days each year and is a time of fasting by day and feasting at night. In many Muslim countries, it is considered very impolite to eat in public during the day. Learn something about the social norms for public dress, behavior, and comportment.

4. Observe. Perhaps this is the primary skill to practice, especially for many Americans who are used to acting or speaking first when presented with ambiguous or unfamiliar situations. There's a piece of advice for travelers to Africa that could apply anywhere: "Keep quiet. Listen and observe behavior before offering an opinion."[23] As a Swahili proverb says, "Travel with open eyes and you will become a scholar."[24] This underscores the importance of observation before speaking. If you're not sure of appropriate behavior, observe others.

5. Practice staying flexible and tolerating ambiguity. In traveling, the cardinal rule is to be flexible. You often don't know exactly how things are going to turn out. Your communication in encounters with local people and service providers will always be more effective and enjoyable if you remain flexible.

ACTIVITIES

1. *Tourist websites:* Go to various tourist websites (for example, www.visit.hawaii .org or www.visitmississippi.org or www.state.nj.us/travel). Analyze these sites for cultural aspects of their marketing strategies. For example, which cultural groups are they targeting? How many and which languages are available on these websites?

2. *Newspaper travel sections:* Go to the travel section in a Sunday newspaper. Read some of the travel advice or articles about other places. What kind of cultural information is presented? Who is the intended audience of the articles? How are the host communities portrayed? As welcoming tourists? As retreating from tourists? As maintaining boundaries?

www.mhhe.com/
experiencing2

THE ONLINE LEARNING CENTER at www.mhhe.com/experiencing2 features self-quizzes, flashcards, and crossword puzzles based on the chapter's key terms and concepts.

ENDNOTES

1. Gee, C. Y., & Fayos-Sola, E. (Eds). (1997). *International tourism: A global perspective.* Madrid, Spain: World Tourism Organization. See also http://www.hoteljobresource.com/menu/article8011.html, http://www.world-tourism.org/newsroom/Releases/2003/jan/numbers2002.htm.

2. Goeldner, C. R., & Brent Ritchie, J. R. (2002). *Tourism: Principles, practices, philosophies* (9th ed.). New York: Wiley.

3. Mancini, M. (2004). *Selling destinations: Geography for the travel professional* (4th ed.). New York: Delmar Learning.

4. Boissevain, J. (1996). Introduction. In J. Boissevain (Ed.), *Coping with tourists: European reactions to mass tourism* (pp. 1–26). Providence, RI: Berghahn Books.

5. Zarkia, C. (1996). Philoxenia receiving tourists—but not guests—on a Greek island. In J. Boissevain (Ed.), *Coping with tourists: European reactions to mass tourism* (pp. 143–173). Providence, RI: Berghahn Books, p. 167.

6. Boissevain (1996), p. 8.

7. Boissevain, p. 15.

8. Boissevain, p. 21.

9. Denlinger, M. (1993). *Real people: Amish and Mennonites in Lancaster County, Pennsylvania.* Scottdale, PA: Herald Press.

10. Kent, N. (1977). A new kind of sugar. In B. R. Finney & K. A. Watson (Eds.), *A new kind of sugar: Tourism in the Pacific.* Santa Cruz, CA: Center for South Pacific Studies, p. 182.

11. Reisinger, Y., & Turner, L. W. (2003). *Cross-cultural behavior in tourism.* Oxford: Butterworth Heinemann.

12. Leclerc, D., assistant professor, Department of Recreation, Management, and Tourism, Arizona State University.

13. Reisinger & Turner (2003).

14. Pearce, P. L. (1982). *The social psychology of tourist behavior.* New York: Pergamon Press, p. 127.

15. Pearce (1982), p. 134.

16. See Hall, E. T., & Hall, M. R. (1990). *Understanding cultural differences.* Yarmouth, ME: Intercultural Press. See also Barnlund, D. C. (1989). *Communication styles of Japanese and Americans: Images and reality.* Belmont, CA: Wadsworth.

17. From a student journal compiled by Jackson, R. M. (1992). *In Mexico: The autobiography of a program abroad.* Queretaro, Mexico: Comcen Ediciones, p. 73.

18. Reisinger & Turner (2003), p. 159.

19. Butler, R. (2002). Editorial. *Tourism and Hospitality Research, 3,* 197–198.

20. Atkins, B., Chew, J. K. S., Gschwind, D., & Parker, A. (2003). The impact of terrorism on tourism and hospitality business: An online debate by experts in the field. *Tourism and Hospitality Research, 4,* 264–267.

21. Monaghan, G., & Ryan, D. (2003, May 18). Tourism industry hopes SARS ends soon. Detroit Free Press (online). (http://www.freep.com/features/travel/sars18_20030518.htm)

22. World Tourism Organization (29 October 2003). News release. (http://www.world-tourism.org/newsroom/Releases/2003/october/barometer.htm)

23. Richmond, Y., & Gestrin, P. (1998). *Into Africa: Intercultural insights.* Yarmouth, ME: Intercultural Press, p. 227.

24. Richmond & Gestrin (1998), p. 227.

CHAPTER ELEVEN

Intercultural Communication and Business

STUDY OBJECTIVES

After reading this chapter you should be able to:

1. Describe how demographic changes influence intercultural communication in business contexts.

2. Identify and describe the role of power in intercultural business contexts.

3. Identify the primary work-related values.

4. Discuss how work-related values influence intercultural business encounters.

5. Discuss the role of language and communication style in intercultural business.

6. Give example of how rules for business etiquette vary from culture to culture.

7. Understand how diversity, prejudice, and discrimination play out in various domestic and global business contexts.

8. Describe the impact of social and political events on business encounters.

KEY TERMS

affirmative action (AA)
Americans with Disabilities
  Act (ADA)
collectivist

equal employment
  opportunity (EEO)
multinational

It is possible that for many people, particularly in the United States, the workplace presents the most opportunities for intercultural encounters. Indeed, the business context presents many opportunities and challenges for intercultural communication. Often the challenges are introduced by language differences. One of our students works in a bilingual (Spanish/English) company that recently changed health care providers. As a result, the many benefits changes (physician networks, benefits, copays, and so on) had to be communicated accurately to both English- and Spanish-speaking employees. Our student recounted the frustration of trying to ensure that all technical terms were communicated properly in both languages.

Sometimes cultural differences surface in the form of lack of knowledge and stereotyping, as Kaori, one of our graduate students, experienced when she worked for a Japanese American boss at a small company in the United States. Her boss was born and raised in United States and never lived in Japan.

> One day, we had very important clients from Japan. As we got seated around the table, my boss offered them beer. Yes, beer, during the business meeting! They politely declined his offer, but he insisted that we had beer, saying he knows that Japanese people drink alcohol when they do business. I had no idea where he got that information from, but the Japanese businessmen didn't want beer, so we did not drink during the meeting. . . .

Many of us actually have experience in dealing with cultural differences in a business context—perhaps from working in a restaurant with a multicultural kitchen and wait staff, or perhaps in a business that exports or communicates frequently with overseas clients and consumers. In this chapter, we address intercultural communication issues that arise in both domestic and international cultural settings.

THE DOMESTIC AND GLOBAL ECONOMY

Domestic Growth

As we noted in Chapter 1, there is increasing demographic diversity in the United States, and so the workforce is becoming increasingly diverse as well. The new workers will be younger, more likely to be female, and more ethnically diverse than the current workforce, which is only 30 percent White male and 41 percent minority. About one-fourth of the new workers likely will be Hispanic or Asian, and 50 percent are expected to be women.[1]

In addition, the market is more diverse; at the turn of the century, Asian Americans, Blacks, and Hispanic Americans saw their annual purchasing power exceed their 1990 level by 95 percent, to total more than $1,200 billion. In

What Do You Think?

With the booming stock market of the 1990s came the rise of international mutual funds. Mutual funds, which buy blocks of stock or shares in a company, are run by managers who research the best companies to buy. Some managers simply use computer programs to help choose their stocks. Others visit companies to see what's going on. With international business, which kind of manager would you prefer?

the past five years, Asian American buying power increased by 124 percent, Hispanic by 118 percent, African American by 86 percent, and Native American by 81 percent—all growing faster than White buying power.[2]

Businesses are also starting to realize the enormous buying power of people with disabilities. For example, improved advertising images and improved access to advertising by deaf people led to changes in consumer behavior. When closed captioning became widely available to deaf television viewers in 1980, 73 percent of deaf people switched to a brand that had television ad captioning. This is an important statistic, for according to government estimates, at least 23 million Americans have hearing impairments. Recent U.S. Census figures show that one-fifth of the U.S. population has some form of disability; with these numbers, advertisers are starting to understand how important it is to tap into that market.[3]

Women also have more buying power today than ever before, and as a group, they influence 80 percent of all vehicle purchases in the United States. In 2003, women spent about $55 billion of the $100 billion spent in the U.S. consumer electronics market. In fact, they initiate nearly 75 percent of electronics purchases on their own or with a spouse.[4] This increasing diversification in both the workplace and the consumer market has tremendous implications for intercultural communication.

Global Growth

The global markets are expanding as well, and multinational companies play an increasingly important role in brick-and-mortar as well as Internet business. Table 11.1 shows the top ten importer and exporter countries in 2003. As a leading economist recently observed, "of the world's 100 largest economies, 51 are now corporations, only 49 are nation states." She continues, "The sales of General Motors and Ford are greater than the GDP of the whole of Sub-Saharan Africa, and Wal-Mart, the U.S. supermarket retailer, now has a turnover higher than the revenues of most of the states of Eastern Europe."[5] In addition, one might think of the tremendous impact of transnational advertising. In 2000, transnational advertising agencies conducted business worth $235 billion— larger than the GNPs of several countries. In earlier times, companies used mostly local advertising or a combination of local and standardized advertising. With increased globalization and the popularity of global brands like Nike and Coca-Cola, one might speculate that even more standardization might be the way of the future.[6]

Some people fear that this increased standardization might negatively impact local cultural values. The glamour business, which includes the sale of clothing, cosmetics, fragrances, and toiletries, is a good example. Critics suggest that much of the advertising in this business promotes dissatisfaction over body images among women. They argue that the standardized global advertising— particularly in print magazines—promotes mostly Western notions of beauty. And these images are having an impact all over the world. Indian women, for

TABLE 11.1 The Top 10 Importer/Exporter Countries to the United States in 2003

International trade is very important to the U.S. economy. Note the countries to which the United States exports most of its goods and the countries from which it imports most of its goods.

Exports to:	Imports from:
1. Canada	1. China
2. Mexico	2. Mexico
3. Japan	3. Japan
4. United Kingdom	4. Germany
5. Germany	5. United Kingdom
6. China	6. South Korea
7. South Korea	7. Taiwan
8. Netherlands	8. France
9. France	9. Malaysia
10. Taiwan	10. Ireland

Source: Adapted from data obtained from http://www.ita.doc.gov/td/industry/otea/usftd/Country.xls.

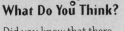

What Do You Think?

Did you know that there is a movement in certain parts of Africa, Asia, the Caribbean, and the United Kingdom to ban skin-whitening products? These products (often referred to as bleaching creams) are sometimes used to cover or clear away age or liver spots in North American cultures. However, in places like Japan, Thailand, and China, where pale skin is a symbol of beauty, there is a history of using substances like licorice and aloe vera to lighten the skin. In Africa and the Caribbean, many Black women attempt to lighten their skin to improve status, thinking that they appear less threatening or more attractive to the opposite sex. (SOURCE: A. Holloway (2003, March 31). *Canadian Business, 76* 72.)

example, are buying $1.5 billion worth of beauty products. One executive in India said, "the Indian woman no longer compares herself to other Indians. She uses the international concept of beauty."[7]

A lot of debate exists about the pros and cons of the rampant globalization that is now occurring. However, one thing is certain: we have to agree with the authors of *Workforce 2020:* "The rest of the world matters to a degree that it never did in the past. We can no longer say anything sensible about the prospects for American workers if we consider only the U.S. economy. . . . Fast-growing Asian and Latin American economies present us with both opportunities and challenges."[8] The international market has become especially attractive as communication and transportation costs have plummeted; in the case of the Internet, the communication costs are almost zero. And in both domestic and international settings, intercultural encounters occur.

POWER ISSUES IN INTERCULTURAL BUSINESS ENCOUNTERS

Intercultural communication occurs in many different types of business settings, including domestic contexts with multicultural workforces and international contexts. Intercultural communication also can occur in encounters with superiors, subordinates, and peers, and with customers and clients. For example, Francine, a student of ours, described an intercultural encounter with the manager, who happened to be from Syria, of the health club where she worked: "He was very rude and disrespectful to me. He humiliated me in front of other members and refused to give me any information in order to contact the corporate office." She described how she tried to resolve the conflict, but she felt very dominated by the manager. She speculated that the root of the conflict might lie in cultural differences in communication style. He had a very forceful, expressive way of speaking, and she interpreted this very negatively, although it may have been perfectly appropriate conduct in his culture.

Communication across power divides can be very difficult, particularly when there is a cultural difference in how power is viewed or how power distance, as explained in Chapter 2, is expressed. Cultural groups that believe in high power distance feel that an organization functions best when differences in power are clearly marked. That is, bosses act like bosses and workers act like workers, and there is no confusion about which is which. This may have been the case with Francine's boss; he was perhaps emphasizing the power differential between himself and Francine.

By contrast, cultural groups that believe in low power distance (as in most U.S. contexts) feel that power differences, though very real, should be minimized and that an egalitarian view is best. An example of a misunderstanding due to cultural differences in views on power distance is the interaction between two employees of a French business—Tom, an American, and Claudine, a French worker:

Tom: I think we'll need to hire two part-time people to help us plan the conference.

Claudine: Yes. We're running out of time, and this conference has to go well.

Tom: I could speak to human resources today.

Claudine: Did you already mention this to Mr. Marceau?

Tom: The chief? I didn't want to bother him with this. He's busy getting ready for that sales meeting. Besides, it's your division. He'll agree to anything you say.

Claudine: Yes, I'm sure he'll approve.

Tom: Good. Then I'll call human resources this afternoon.

Here, Tom has a somewhat looser approach to power than Claudine by assuming that it is most important to get things done and not "bow and scrape" to a superior. He also assumes that people who have power officially designated to them are free to exercise this power without further consultation. Both of these assumptions are wrong in the French context and in many other countries as well. Tom's assumption that Claudine can make this hiring decision is inaccurate, and he also misinterprets when Claudine says she's sure the boss will approve. What she really means is that she's sure he'll approve when she asks him and to take any action prior to this would be inappropriate and discourteous. This is not to say that French workers meekly comply with all decisions by superiors—there

Info Bites

In Taiwan and Hong Kong, Chinese businesspeople will shake hands or exchange bows with a U.S. American visitor, but if you bow you must get it right. Keep your feet together. Let superiors rise first. If you are an inferior, bow lower. How many ways can you think of that someone might "incorrectly" shake hands in a business context?

is often tension where workers are constantly on the lookout to thwart their power-wielding bosses.[9]

COMMUNICATION CHALLENGES IN BUSINESS CONTEXTS

Communication challenges in business contexts can reflect cultural differences in work-related values, language issues, communication styles, and business etiquette, as well as issues related to diversity, prejudice, and discrimination.

Work-Related Values

Individualism Versus Collectivism   One of the value differences that affects intercultural communication in business contexts is the distinction between individualism and collectivism. As discussed in Chapter 2, many cultures (such as most U.S. cultures) are individualistic, while others (such as many cultures in Asia and in Central and South America) are **collectivist**—that is, they place more importance on the individual in relation to groups. How does this difference play out in work situations?

Surf's Up!

Look at the Introduction to Cross Cultural Training website (www.expat.or.id/ business/crosscultural training.html). It discusses some of the frustrations of American businesspeople who come to Indonesia. That there is such an interest today in cross-cultural training indicates how difficult it is to assimilate to a new culture, even when big money and big business are on the line.

In countries with individualistic views, workers are expected to perform certain functions with clearly defined responsibilities; a clear boundary exists between their job and another person's job. In collectivist countries like Japan, the opposite is true. That is, Japanese organizations do not necessarily define the precise job responsibilities assigned to each individual; rather, it's the job of a work unit, a section, or a department.[10] The same is true for many Latin American and southern European cultures, in which people are much more apt to help one another out at work and to see less rigid lines between tasks. These cultural differences in values can present challenges to workers and management. For example, Roberto, a manager from Colombia, has a high collectivist work and communication style. He encourages his subordinates to fill in for each other when they can, he tries to preserve the harmony of the work team, and he is careful not to criticize workers in front of their peers. He prefers to talk with them one on one in private or to communicate through a third person if there is a conflict situation. This style sometimes clashes with that of other managers, who have a more individualistic orientation. They think he is too lenient with his staff and sticks up for them too much.

There are some cultural groups, like the Greeks, for whom individualism in the workplace may be even more developed than in the United States. Thus, most Greeks strongly prefer not to work for a large company. About half the labor force is self-employed, and 90% of businesses have fewer than 10 employees. And Greeks are not accustomed to working in teams—unless the team happens to be the family. Indeed, the concept of family often extends to the workplace. As one observer noted, "Greek managers sometimes use the term *nikokyris* to describe their job, which means that they see themselves as the head of the family, the one who takes care of family matters."[11]

Working on projects in groups is very common in business settings. Although this diverse office staff may have more cultural gaps to work through than a more homogeneous group, the potential benefits of diverse viewpoints are significant. What do the nonverbal cues and the seating arrangements tell you about this group?

Work and Material Gain   Most Americans think that hard work is a virtue that will eventually pay off. To the people of many other cultures, however, work is a necessary burden. Australians, for example, admire the "bludger"—the person who appears to work hard while actually doing little.[12] Most Mexicans consider work a necessary evil, needed to earn enough money to live and, if possible, to have enough left over to enjoy the really important things in life: family and friends.[13] And some Europeans share the Mexican attitude toward work. An Italian air force officer gave his impressions of Germans:

> He liked Germany, but found the Germans very *lineare*, meaning direct, purposeful and efficient. *"Lineare"* is not a compliment. It characterizes a one-dimensional person, while Italians feel it is important to develop the whole person, not just the work side. I said I thought the Americans were probably just as bad as the Germans, but he shook his head and grinned. "Worse," he said, "much worse."[14]

Cultural groups that see work as having a low priority believe that, because work is necessary and takes up most of the daylight hours, ways should be found to make it more agreeable by creating a convivial workplace.

Pop Culture Spotlight

In the 1980s, many Americans feared the growing economic power of Japan. Movies like *Gung Ho* reflected this fear. In that movie, a U.S. auto factory was bought by a Japanese firm. The main conflict in the film was between the new bosses, who tried to instill a Japanese work ethic in the employees, and the workers, who sided with prankster Michael Keaton. Do you think the fear of Japan's economic power has shifted to other countries, such as China?

Cultural norms regarding space and privacy in business contexts vary from culture to culture. How might this office space be set up differently if it were in the United States?

The different attitudes toward work can lead to intercultural communication conflicts in the workplace. This was the case when U.S. Americans, Japanese, and Saudi Arabians worked together on a major project in Tokyo. As one writer observed,

> When the American and Saudi managers went to Japan to meet with the Japanese engineers, the cross-cultural problems between the Saudis and Japanese were instant, dramatic and chronic. The Saudis stood too close, made intense eye contact and touched the Japanese. On top of that, the Saudis were enjoying Tokyo's sights. Their leisurely approach clashed with the Japanese work ethic—the Japanese concluded they weren't serious about the project. The tension escalated until Americans became the buffers between the Saudis and Japanese.[15]

Related to attitudes toward work is the variation in views toward business in general. Not everyone sees business as an academic subject. For example, the British don't quite accept that business is something a person would actually study the way one has to study subjects such as biology or statistics. According to the British, business is not a real field or profession, and one simply needs a few months to get the hang of it. While this has begun to change in the era of globalization, it is still an attitude held by some, particularly the upper class who were taught that there is something vulgar about wealth. In 1996, while there were 80,000 MBAs graduating in the United States, Oxford awarded its first MBA degrees ever—to 49 graduates. As further evidence of this attitude toward business, the Oxford University administrators rejected a controversial $34 million gift from a Saudi businessman to build a school of business.[16]

Quality Versus Efficiency

Another conflict in work-related values is based on the relative value placed on quality versus efficiency and practicality. For most Americans, efficiency and getting the job done for the lowest cost are the ultimate goals. However, people in many different cultures hold different views. For example, French are more interested in designing. There is a notion among the French that in business one should not worry so much about whether a product is competitive as long as it is well designed. They feel that if the product is well designed and elegant, it will be competitive.

Germans insist on quality, both as producers and consumers. Quality may come at a high price, but the German view is that people will pay for the best quality and that as a worker it's important to do the best job on principle. In German and American work settings, conflict can arise when Americans would rather produce something expediently than elegantly (or exquisitely).

These differences in priorities can lead to intercultural conflict. For example, Pam (an American) and Andre (a Frenchman) argue about whether to redesign an existing product or get it to market sooner in order to beat their competition. Andre insists that it is worth taking the time to make a sleeker, more elegant design. Pam appeals to profit motive, timeliness, and competence—not persuasive arguments in Andre's world.

One might explain these U.S. business values partly by the fact that the United States is a young country and that we have less appreciation for history and time. We feel pressured by time, because we don't think we have much of it. Whereas for European businesses, five years is not long, many European businesses routinely plan 10 and 20 years ahead. Also, U.S. Americans historically have placed more emphasis on the practical aspects of products. In the history of the European settlers, things had to be done expediently, and there was little time to tinker with perfection.[17]

Task Versus Relationship Priority   A related value has to do with whether the highest priority is placed on relationships or on task completion. In most work contexts in the United States, the most important thing is to accomplish the task. It is not necessary to really like the people one works with. However, in many cultures, work gets done because of relationships. This can cause much frustration in multicultural work settings.

For example, as one of the top salesmen at his U.S. firm, Tom was asked to head up a presentation to a Latin American company. He arrived, ready to explain his objectives to the marketing rep sent to meet him at the airport. But the rep was continually changing the subject and asking personal questions about his family and his interests.

[Tom] was informed that the meeting was arranged for several days later and his hosts hoped that he would be able to relax a little first and recover from his journey, perhaps see some sights and enjoy their hospitality. . . . During the next few days, Tom noticed that though they had said they

Pop Culture Spotlight

Attitudes about the workplace vary from culture to culture and can vary even more from city to city or business to business. But sometimes it is possible to see how workplace experiences overlap within a culture, as many Americans seemed to empathize with the characters in the 1999 movie *Office Space*. The protagonists in the film confront the sometimes dull routines of U.S. corporate culture and parody the plight of workers whose 8-to-5 workday often consists of monotonous tasks they are forced to complete within the limits of a small office cubicle. One of the movie's biggest moments is when the major characters beat a malfunctioning fax machine to death out of frustration. The film is often seen as a metaphor for working class lives.

wanted to discuss details of his presentation, they seemed to spend an inordinate amount of time on inconsequentials. This began to annoy Tom as he thought that the deal could have been closed several days earlier.[18]

This was a classic case of culture clash. Tom's top priority was to accomplish the task; his counterparts' top priority was to establish a good relationship so that the work could get accomplished. These different priorities also show up in the multicultural workplaces of the United States. Some people work better if they have a good relationship; others merely want to get the task done. Our student Karla observed this in her job:

> Currently, I work in a restaurant with many people who are from Mexico. After working with them, I have come to realize that they have very different attitudes about work from what I am used to. While teamwork is always stressed at my job, these workers actually do look out for the best interests of one another. It is a great learning experience for me to work side by side with them and to learn about their work ethics.

Language Issues

Language issues can come into play in various ways in business contexts. One of our students, Robert, who worked for a cellular telephone company, described a language problem he experienced one day when he had two customers who spoke only Spanish:

> What I understood was that their cell phone was not working. I couldn't tell the exact problem because they didn't speak English. We both became very upset, since neither of us spoke the language of the other. I ended up having to get our Spanish customer service rep on the phone to help bridge the communication gap between the two of us. This was definitely productive, because we were able to figure out the problem and resolve the situation with little hassle from that point on. I was glad in the end that I could help, but was also very frustrated because I needed outside help. It was a very uneasy feeling: to stand face to face with someone and have no idea what they are talking about and not being able to communicate with them.

And in overseas contexts or in multinational corporations, most people do not speak English. In fact, outside of the major cities and in most offices, the average staff member does not speak English. Thus, increasingly, international business travelers have to deal with a medley of languages.

And the same can be true in domestic business situations. With the growing cultural diversity in the workplace comes linguistic diversity. To make working with a multilinguistic workforce easier, don't assume that, just because people are speaking a language other than English, they are talking about you. This may be a common reaction when those around us are speaking a language we don't understand, but it's egocentric and erroneous. Generally, people speak the language

In Québec, French is given priority over English, yet many businesses operate in both languages. In the U.S., there are many places that have attempted to institute "English-Only" policies. Why might businesses find it advantageous to conduct their businesses in many languages, rather than English only?

they feel most comfortable with. Laura, one of our students, experienced this first-hand:

> When I was working in a restaurant, I was constantly hearing my name being spoken in Spanish conversations. It was very frustrating to have people talking about me when I had no clue what they were saying. Finally, I was standing next to a friend who speaks both English and Spanish, and I heard my name again in conversation. When I asked my friend why people were always talking about me, he gave me a blank look. I told him one of the staff had just said my name. He laughed and said, "No, no, they said '*La hora*'" (per hour). We both had a good laugh, and now I know that wages, not me, are a popular subject.

A second suggestion in working with a multilinguistic workforce is to speak simple, but not simpleminded, English. A nonnative speaker will be able to understand language that is spoken slowly and that includes no big words. For example, use "letter" instead of "communication," and "soon" instead of "momentarily," and "pay" instead of "compensation." In addition, try to avoid slang and jargon, don't crowd too much into one sentence, and pause between sentences. And always pronounce words clearly—for example, "Did you eat yet?" and not "Djeet yet?" Finally, don't be condescending, and don't raise your voice.[19]

Another potential language issue involves communication between deaf and hearing people. For example, Linda, a sales associate, is deaf in one ear. When customers ask her for assistance, she may not hear them, and they sometimes interpret her behavior negatively.

Interactions between bosses and subordinates vary from culture to culture. While the norms for boss-subordinate interactions are relatively informal in the United States, direct eye contact is required. By contrast, in many countries and cultures, hierarchy and formality are more important than in the United States.

Communication Styles

Several elements of communication style, as introduced in Chapter 5, are especially relevant in business contexts. These include indirect versus direct and honesty versus harmony.

Indirect Versus Direct Exchange of information is important in many work settings, especially when a problem exists and information is needed to solve it. People with a direct communication style simply ask for information from the appropriate person. However, a person with an indirect style might not feel comfortable giving the information, particularly when a problem exists and there is a need to save face. How do you obtain information when no one is speaking up? One way is to watch how others who are respected get information from one another and how they get it from you. Observe how subordinates, supervisors, and colleagues give and obtain information, since the approach may vary with an individual's status or relationship.[20]

In general, to have good intercultural business communication, people need to slow down and "sneak up" on information. Many Europeans don't get right to the point. For example, even at a business meeting in a restaurant, the French want to enjoy their dinner. Africans, too, are suspicious of U.S. American directness. In fact, in African business settings, intermediaries often are used to smooth business dealings. One foreign worker was puzzled when a Kenyan coworker complained to him at length about the behavior of someone outside the office. At first, the foreigner couldn't understand why his colleague was complaining so much about an outsider's behavior, but he eventually realized that the Kenyan was trying to explain indirectly what he should be doing.[21]

Honesty Versus Harmony   Honesty is not always the best policy in intercultural business contexts, as noted in Chapter 5; form and social harmony may be more highly valued. For example,

> Koreans take considerable care not to disturb one's *kibun*, the sense of harmony or "wellness," in a person. They will hold back or delay or "adjust" bad news to avoid upsetting a person's *kibun*. This is not considered dishonest; the *kibun* takes priority over accuracy. It is rare for anyone to give bad news in the morning. No matter how urgent the matter may appear, the news is likely to be given in the afternoon, so the recipient can recover his *kibun* at home.[22]

As one experienced businessman said, "Everywhere you go, except in Europe and Australia, people will tell you what they think you want to hear." This means that if you ask people for directions and they don't know the way, they will give you directions anyway simply to make you happy. Thus, in these contexts, you need to ask questions in such a way that the other person can't really figure out what you want to hear. Even better, you need to engage the other person in a conversation such that the information you need simply "falls out."

There are also cultural variations in how truth is defined. In many businesses in Asia, there are a number of behaviors that would be considered acceptable everyday practices, whereas in the United States they would be regarded as deceptive, perhaps even unethical. For example, Japanese refiners signed a contract to buy sugar from Australia for $160 a ton, and when world prices dropped, they refused to pay. The Australians thought that "a deal is a deal." The Japanese, much more context-sensitive, thought that the changing circumstances allowed for changes in agreement.[23]

Business Etiquette

Business etiquette varies from culture to culture and is related to the differences in values and communication styles discussed previously. In general, most cultural groups tend to be more formal in business contexts than Americans are. For instance, most Europeans greet each other formally with a verbal greeting and a

Pop Culture Spotlight

In the James Bond movie *Goldeneye* and the Val Kilmer movie *The Saint,* we see an image of Russian businesspeople that is common in television and movies today: The people who run the businesses are either tied to organized crime or are themselves criminals. How do you think Russians or other countries' people conceptualize U.S. American businesspeople?

Business is now a global phenomenon, as the presence of this UPS truck in Germany suggests. This expansion increasingly requires a workforce that is skilled in intercultural communication and management.

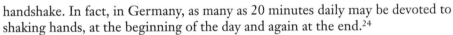

Info Bites

We like to have a simple set of rules to follow in an intercultural business encounter, but sometimes we can't take the easy road. Singapore is such a mix of cultures, ethnicities, and religions that *The Complete Idiot's Guide to Cultural Etiquette* admits that no one set of rules governs proper business etiquette. Would the same be true in the United States?

handshake. In fact, in Germany, as many as 20 minutes daily may be devoted to shaking hands, at the beginning of the day and again at the end.[24]

Similarly, Latin Americans attach great importance to courtesy. A well-mannered person is described as *muy educado* in Mexico, and a prescribed set of behaviors is expected in business settings, including ritual handshaking with and greeting of staff members each morning. The same is true in many African countries. There, high-level officials and business executives expect to be treated with the solemnity and respect due their position. Protocol must be observed; in many countries, at official dinners, no one eats or drinks until the higher-ranking people do, and no one leaves before the highest-ranking guests do so.

In general, when conducting business in most cultures, one should be very careful to avoid excessive familiarity, especially in initial meetings; this means no slouching, putting one's feet up on a desk, or lounging in general.[25] This emphasis on formality can extend to language use. For example, the formal form of "you" (*Usted*) is always used in business contexts in Spanish-speaking Central and South America, except with personal friends. And it is considered proper to address a person by his or her title.[26] The French also do not like informality, the use of first names, or anything that smacks of familiarity or lack of respect. In particular, they "object to hearty backslapping, joking or teasing behavior, or any kind of phony chumminess."[27] This is also true in business settings in Francophone Africa, where language is more formal and flowery, and titles are necessary—for example, *Monsieur Ministre* or *Conseiller*, or *Monsieur le Directeur* or *Monsieur le Président*.

Etiquette is a traditional value that pervades French society, and business etiquette is symbolized by properly engraved business cards, giving a professional title and academic credentials. But the Japanese may have perfected business card etiquette. When people present cards to a Japanese business professional, they hold the card with both hands so that the other person can read it, and then bow and give their name. If they are presenting cards to several people, they start with the highest ranking. Similarly, in the People's Republic of China, when people receive someone else's card, they should use both hands, bowing and thanking the person for the opportunity to meet him or her. It is considered rude to put the card away immediately.[28] Business cards also are important in most African business settings, and the more elaborate the better; the fancy cards indicate that you want to stay in touch.[29]

Diversity, Prejudice, and Discrimination

You may never have the occasion to hand out business cards in a multinational context overseas, but you still may have to address issues of diversity in the U.S. workplace. It may be interesting to identify cultural differences in workplace communication styles and values, but the real challenge is knowing how to work with these differences in a productive way. Unfortunately, not all differences are seen as "equal," and certain communication styles often are viewed negatively and can lead to prejudice and discrimination.

As discussed in Chapter 5, the language and communication style of those holding the most power is often the desired form of communication, and business contexts are no exception. Until recently, in most U.S. organizations, there was one dominant culture with a corresponding style of communication—White, Anglo Germanic, mostly Protestant, and male. In terms of communication and values, this means it was individualistic and emphasized directness, honesty over harmony, and task completion over relationship building. Individuals who held other values and used different communication styles often didn't fit in—or worse, were not hired or promoted.

In a classic book on management written in 1938, Chester Barnard observed that the key function of the business executive was the ability to get along and "fit in" with others in the workplace. A requirement for fitting in with others, according to Barnard, was shared "education, experience, age, sex, race, nationality, faith, politics, and very specific personal traits as manners, speech, personal appearance, etc."[30] Unfortunately, these traits are sometimes still required for those who want to succeed in the workplace, which can make it difficult for women, minorities, and international workers who do not possess these attributes. The resulting discrimination and prejudice have led, among other things, to diversity training and **affirmative action** policies—statutes that direct companies to hire a certain percentage of women and minorities.

Some minorities and women are grateful for the emphasis on diversity and the implementation of affirmative action policies. Our colleague Marie, for example, had this to say:

Pop Culture Spotlight

American comedienne and popular culture icon Whoopi Goldberg stars in the 2003 NBC sitcom *Whoopi*. The comedy takes place in a New York hotel owned by Goldberg's character, Mavis Rae, who is a former one-hit-wonder diva and songstress. Intercultural themes run throughout the comedy, and the show seems to critique cultural stereotypes using the workplace as a backdrop. For example we see Courtney (Wren T. Brown), Mavis' struggling attorney brother, who accepts her offer to set up his office in the hotel but spouts conservative politics opposing Mavis' liberal attitudes. But Courtney brings along Rita (Elizabeth Regen)—his White American girlfriend, who dresses, talks, and acts like a stereotypical African American woman. All characters critique common stereotypes we would normally associate with their race, ethnicity, or gender.

I know that the only reason the company hired me for my first job was that I am a woman. I was the first woman in the department, and they were under a lot of pressure to hire me. And they should have been under pressure, and they were right to hire me. I was qualified for the job, but they wouldn't have given me the chance if it weren't for AAP. In my next job, I was also an affirmative action hire, because the company needed more women at senior levels. I also realize that I, along with other White women, have actually benefited more than women of color have from AAP.

But other women and minorities, while grateful for a chance to compete, are troubled by the question of whether they are viewed as having been given advantages. Anna, a successful businesswoman, observes:

I have worked in corporate America for 11 years. In my current management position, I am responsible for promotions and staffing in two departments. We were deciding promotional moves when the director asked where we were in terms of affirmative action for a particular department. I was floored. Though I was aware of what affirmative action was and why it existed, it was my first experience in seeing how it could affect people positively or negatively. We had ranked potential candidates based on productivity and results. This was a tough experience in that I started to doubt my own self-worth. Even though I have won awards and received recognition for my accomplishments, I still had to wonder if that was truly the only variable in their decision to promote me.

For many people, affirmative action is troublesome. Although affirmative action policies began as a way to address past discrimination, the focus now is on reverse discrimination, with majority members claiming that they are being disadvantaged by affirmative action.[31] Anna describes her struggles in dealing with affirmative action issues in her position as manager:

It is a thorny issue for people in positions of power also, particularly for minorities. I am now in a position to train employees whom I see as potential management candidates. I have struggled with how to balance this idea of affirmative action when picking my candidates. I don't want to be perceived as someone who gives special privileges to minorities. And I don't want to be perceived as a minority who ignores affirmative action policies. When it comes to intercultural communication, whether you are from a minority or dominant culture, you will encounter such issues. In this time of my life, I only want to try to make a difference.

Companies have many reasons for addressing affirmative action and diversity issues.[32] There may be moral grounds—a need to address the long history of racism, sexism, and conflictual intergroup relations in the United States. There may be a feeling that it is the responsibility of those who have benefited from this historical pattern to begin to "level the playing field." However, more often it is legal and social pressures—in the form of **equal employment opportunity (EEO)** laws, affirmative action (AA), and the **Americans with Disabilities Act**—that cause companies to address affirmative action issues. For example, the ADA requires employers to make "reasonable" accommodations for employees and potential employees with disabilities. It also requires that public accommodations, buildings, transportation, and telecommunications be accessible to people with disabilities, as when Wal-Mart, the world's largest retailer, was sued in California for gender discrimination. The class action lawsuit may finally come to involve 500,000 women workers—the largest sex discrimination suit ever. Those who brought the lawsuit contended that women have not been given equal job assignments and that their career opportunities have not been the same as for men. They also felt that there has been inequality in training and compensation.[33]

Finally, companies may address issues of multiculturalism and diversity because they think it will have an impact on their bottom line—profit. And this does seem to be the case. A number of studies show that companies that value, encourage, and ultimately include the full contributions of all members of society have a much better chance of succeeding—and profiting.[34]

SOCIAL AND POLITICAL CONTEXTS OF BUSINESS

It is important to consider the social and political contexts of business and to think about how social and political events can affect business encounters. For example, the terrorist acts of 9/11 had a tremendous effect on business encounters both domestically and internationally. This event triggered loss of confidence and a downturn in the stock market, and many travel-related businesses lost money and were forced to lay off workers. Social events like the SARS medical scare in the summer of 2003 also had a tremendous impact on business. Companies cancelled business trips and conventions in Asia and Canada. Again, this had a ripple effect, and many businesses outside of travel and tourism were impacted.

These and other recent events impact intercultural encounters. There are lost opportunities for contact, fear of contact, and suspicion about people from the Middle East and Asia. After 9/11, there were also many examples of discrimination and prejudice toward Middle Easterners. For example, after 9/11, people who simply appeared to be Middle Eastern were sometimes denied boarding on airplanes or were refused service in businesses. During the SARS scare, some people refused to interact with or sit close to people who appeared to be from Asia. Business declined in Chinatown, and incidents of harassment were reported.[35] Thus, it is important to remember that each intercultural encounter occurs in a social and political context that goes beyond the few individuals involved.

What Do You Think?

Mirroring the protests at the World Trade Organization meeting in Seattle in early 2000, demonstrators from around the United States and other parts of the Americas made their voices heard in November 2003 in Miami, Florida. They raised placards, marched, held press conferences, and many were arrested as they confronted city police and state troopers. But some were students from American universities and men and women representing labor movements in places like Canada. Their protests focused on issues such as sweatshops in Mexico, animal rights, and the rights of blue-collar workers. What do you think about the arguments of either side in these debates?

SUMMARY

In this chapter, we looked at some of the communication issues in intercultural business settings. Intercultural communication is becoming increasingly important in business due to increasing domestic diversity and the expansion of global markets.

We also described the various kinds of intercultural encounters that occur in various business settings. Intercultural encounters can occur between subordinates and superiors or among peers. Power differentials often complicate intercultural work encounters.

Finally, we addressed several communication challenges in business contexts: cultural differences in work-related values and communication style, in language use, and in norms of business etiquette. These cultural differences can lead to prejudice and discrimination if only one dominant style is accepted in an organization.

BUILDING INTERCULTURAL SKILLS

1. Try to identify the ways in which your workplace is diverse. Are there differences in race, ethnicity, gender, age, and physical ability? Are there different values and communication styles that accompany this diversity?

2. Try to identify the different cultural values in your workplace. What are the dominant values that are expressed in your workplace? Are these similar to those values you were raised with? Or are they in conflict with your own values? Or in conflict with values of other employees? Are there communication style differences in your workplace?

3. If you are dealing with a multilingual workforce, remember to practice good language skills: Speak slowly, use everyday language, and avoid jargon. Also try paraphrasing.

4. Be flexible; try to see other people's point of view. Practice being patient. Sometimes a diverse workplace requires more empathy and understanding than a monocultural setting, and this takes time to achieve.

5. Be an advocate for people who are not being treated fairly in the workplace. Are the legal standards (EEO and ADA laws) being met?

ACTIVITIES

1. *Newsworthy businesses:* Watch the news for international coverage of business events. What kinds of businesses are newsworthy? What kinds of business events are considered important? Which countries' economies are considered most interesting? Are we more interested in learning about business etiquette in England or Japan than in Kenya or Egypt?

2. *Business media:* Look at business magazines such as *Wall Street Week* or *Forbes.* How much focus is there on diversity issues in American businesses? How much of the coverage is on the dominant culture values and communication

style? How many stories are there about women and minorities in the business world?

3. *State websites:* Look at a state website (such as www.yesvirginia.org). Analyze the site for cultural benefits for locating in Virginia. To which cultural groups are the appeals pitched? Is any attention given to attracting a diverse workforce?

THE ONLINE LEARNING CENTER at www.mhhe.com/experiencing2 features self-quizzes, flashcards, and crossword puzzles based on the chapter's key terms and concepts.

www.mhhe.com/
experiencing2

ENDNOTES

1. From Ameristats (http://www.prb.org/AmeristatTemplate.cfm?Section=RaceandEthnicity&template=/ContentManagement/ContentDisplay.cfm&ContentID=7884). See also Brewer, C. A., & Suchan, T. A. (2001). *Mapping Census 2000: The geography of U.S. diversity* (U.S. Census Bureau, Census Special Reports, Series CENSR/01-1). Washington, DC: U.S. Government Printing Office.

2. Humphreys, J. M. (2000). Buying power at the beginning of a new century. *Georgia Business and Economic Conditions, 60,* 1–23.

3. Haller, B. (2001, February 18). Disability and advertising. *The Baltimore Sun* (online). (http://www.towson.edu/-bhalle/dis-advert.html).

4. Palmer, I. L. (2000, August 21). Why women love sport-utility vehicles (http://4wheeldrive.about.com/gi/dynamic/offsite.htm?site=http://www.edmunds.com/news/feature/general/42997/article.html). See also Jones, C. (2003, January 11). Electronics experts tout power of women consumers. *Reviewjournal.com* (http://www.reviewjournal.com/lvrj_home/2003/Jan-11-Sat-2003/business/20453578.html).

5. Hertz, N. (2002). *The silent takeover: Global capitalism and the death of democracy.* Free press. Quoted by Rob van Tulder, R. (no date provided). The power of core companies. *European Business Forum* (online). (http://www.ebfonline.com/at_forum/at_forum.asp?id=289&linked=288).

6. Viswanath, K., & Zeng, L. B. (2002). Transnational advertising. In W. B. Gudykunst & B. Mody (Eds.), Handbook of international and intercultural communication (2nd ed.) (pp. 359–379). Thousand Oaks, CA: Sage.

7. Quoted in Viswanath & Zeng (2002), p. 373.

8. Judy, R. W., & D'Amico, C. (1997). *Workforce 2020.* Indianapolis: Hudson Institute. See also Kikoski, J. F., & Kikoski, C. K. (1999). *Reflexive communication in the cultural diverse workplace.* Westport, CT: Praeger, p. 3.

9. Storti, C. (2001). *Old world, new world: Bridging cultural differences: Britain, France, Germany and the U.S.* Yarmouth, ME: Intercultural Press, pp. 102–116.

10. Fatahi, K. (1996). *International management: A cross-cultural and functional perspective.* Upper Saddle River, NJ: Prentice-Hall.

11. Broome, B. J. (1996). *Exploring the Greek mosaic: A guide to intercultural communication in Greece.* Yarmouth, ME: Intercultural Press, p. 86.

12. Fatahi (1996), p. 168.

13. Kras, E. S. (1989). *Management in two cultures: Bridging the gap between U.S. and Mexican managers.* Yarmouth, ME: Intercultural Press, p. 46.

14. Copeland, L., & Griggs, L. (1985). *Going international: How to make friends and deal effectively in the global marketplace.* New York: Random House, p. 13.

15. Copeland & Griggs (1985), p. 112.

16. Storti (2001).

17. Storti (2001).
18. Brislin, R. W., Cushner, K., Cherrie, C., & Yong, H. (1986). *Intercultural interactions: A practical guide.* Beverly Hills, CA: Sage, p. 154.
19. Brislin et al. (1986), p. 105.
20. Brislin et al. (1986), p. 101.
21. Richmond, Y., & Gestrin, P. (1988). *Into Africa; Intercultural insights.* Yarmouth, ME: Intercultural Press, p. 129.
22. Copeland & Griggs (1985), p. 105.
23. Begley, S. (2003, March 28). Science Journal: East-West differences challenge assumptions about human thinking. *Wall Street Journal* (Europe) A5. See also Kim, M-S. (2002). *Nonwestern perspectives on human communication.* Thousand Oaks, CA: Sage.
24. Hall, E. T., & Hall, M. R. (1990). *Understanding cultural differences.* Yarmouth, ME: Intercultural Press, p. 64.
25. Richmond & Gestrin (1998), p. 134.
26. Kras (1989), p. 36.
27. Hall & Hall (1990), p. 116.
28. Business card etiquette. (1998). *International business resources on the WWW.* Michigan State University Center for International Business Education and Research (ciber.bus.msu,edu/busres/channel/businesscard.html).
29. Richmond & Gestrin (1998), p. 132.
30. Barnard, C. (1938). *The functions of an executive.* Cambridge, MA: Harvard University Press, p. 224. Quoted in Kikoski & Kikoski (1997), p. 14.
31. Little, B. E., Murry, W. D., & Winbush, J. C. (1998). Perceptions of workplace Affirmative Action Plans. *Group and Organization Management, 23*(1), 27–47.
32. Ferdman, B. M., & Brody, S. E. (1996). Models of diversity training. In D. Landis & R. Bhagat (Eds.), *Handbook of intercultural training* (2nd ed.) (pp. 282–305). Thousand Oaks, CA: Sage.
33. Daniels, C. (2002, July 21). Women vs Wal-Mart. *Fortune, 148,* 79.
34. Hayles, R. (1996). What do racism and sexual harassment cost your business? *Cultural Diversity at Work, 9,* 1.
35. SARS and Accusations of Discrimination. Wikipedia. (http://en.wikipedia.org/wiki/SARS_and_accusations_of_racial_discrimination)

Intercultural Communication and Education

STUDY OBJECTIVES

After reading this chapter, you should be able to:

1. Understand the role of culture in setting educational goals. Note how colonization influences educational goals and curricula. Explain how colonization might influence study-abroad programs.

2. Understand the ways that different cultural groups were educated and the purposes of those different experiences. Be able to identify the educational goals of Indian schools, historically Black colleges and universities, and women's colleges.

3. Explain how different cultural role expectations can influence classroom communication. Note that different cultures may use different grading systems.

4. Explain how power differences can influence communication in educational contexts.

5. Describe the complexities of affirmative action and reverse discrimination.

6. Understand how cultural identities are formed in the educational process.

7. Be able to describe some social issues that arise in education.

KEY TERMS

Afrocentric	international students
colonial educational system	learning styles
Eurocentric	reverse discrimination
grading system	study-abroad programs
HBCUs	teaching styles

Surf's Up!

Howard University is one of the more famous traditionally Black universities. Look over its website (www.howard.edu/), especially the "Howard Experience" and "Howard Past" sections. Why do Black students choose to attend Howard?

Education is an important context for intercultural communication, as students and teachers come from a variety of cultural backgrounds and bring a variety of expectations to the classroom. Educational institutions may be structured differently within different cultures, but they remain one of the most important social institutions for advancement in any society. If educators and students communicate in ways that are not sensitive to cultural differences in the educational institution, these same institutions may end up reproducing the social inequality of U.S. society. As noted in the report *Workforce 2020*, "The disparity between whites and minorities in college attendance is actually increasing."[1] Despite the reduction in barriers to college admissions based upon race, minority enrollments are decreasing. Improved intercultural communication practices can only help alleviate this problem. Further, many students are **international students,** meaning that they come to the United States or go abroad to study. In this chapter, we explore intercultural communication issues in the educational context.

EDUCATIONAL GOALS

What is the purpose of education? As noted previously, education is widely perceived to be an important avenue for advancement in society. After all, if you cannot read or write, it is difficult to succeed in this society. Yet, beyond the basic skills of reading, writing, and arithmetic, we need to think about the educational goals that various cultures establish. For example, what kinds of knowledge does an Italian need to acquire to succeed in Italian society? What kinds of things should a South Korean student study to prosper in South Korean society? How might these things differ from what U.S. American students need to study to advance in their society?

There is no universal curriculum that all students follow. Thus, clearly, it's more important for Brazilians to know the history of Brazil than it is for Indonesians. Not surprisingly, educational goals for different cultural groups are largely driven by members' need to know about themselves and their society. For example, students in France study French geography and learn that "La Manche" separates France from Britain; students in Britain study their island's geography and learn that the "English Channel" separates Britain from France. We are all taught to look at the world through our own culture's framework. Thus, in the United States, we call that body of water the "English Channel," just as the British do, because of our common language and historical ties. And our education necessarily frames our worldviews and our particular ways of knowing.

Education, however, is not driven simply by the desire to teach and learn about ourselves. In colonial contexts, for example, the colonial power often imposed its own educational goals and system upon the colonized. In so doing, this

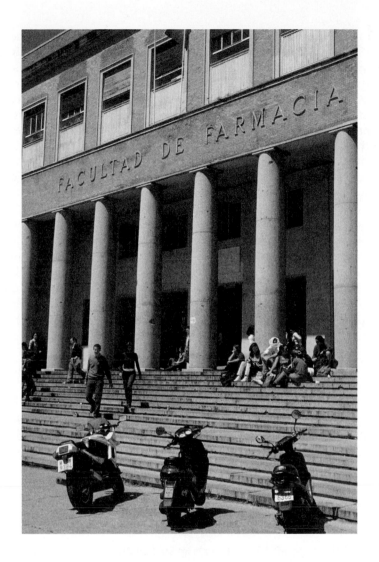

Many universities attract students from all over the world and so are common sites for intercultural interaction. Thus, many U.S. American students study abroad, just as many international students come to the United States to study. Cultural differences can impact what happens in the classroom.

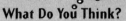

What Do You Think?

The May 2000 issue of *Spectra*, the professional publication of the National Communication Association, ran an advertisement for a teaching job at Sultan Qaboos University in Oman. The ad promised "tax-free salaries . . . paid travel, free and good housing . . . and end-of-contract gratuity." Assuming you had the credentials, would you take the job? Why or why not?

colonial educational system served educational goals that differed from what the colonized might have valued. Thus, "in colonial and neocolonial historical situations, a hierarchy of cultural importance and value is imposed by the colonising power, both on the conquered indigenous societies, and on the white agents of colonial oppression themselves."[2] Within educational institutions, this meant that students were expected to study Bach, Beethoven, and Debussy rather than their own culture's music; to read Chaucer, Shakespeare, and Milton instead of their native literature; and so on. This displacement of educational goals had a tremendous impact upon the ways that these former colonial societies were formed. The path to success involved embracing and understanding the colonizer's culture, history, literature, and society rather than the native one.

You might be surprised to learn that your educational experience reflects America's colonial legacy. Despite the popular claim that we are a multicultural society with immigrants from all over the world, we tend to value European writers, artists, and histories more than, say, Asian writers, artists, and histories. For example, you learned more about the medieval period than the Heian period. The United States began as 13 colonies, and the reverberations of this colonial history persist in our educational goals today—to the benefit of some people and the detriment of others.

STUDYING ABROAD

Surf's Up!

What kinds of things are you supposed to learn when studying abroad? What kinds of activities do you think you would participate in? Check out a program for study abroad in Kenya by entering "Kenya" at the search page www.istc.umn.edu/study/search.html. How does it differ from what you would expect of a study-abroad program?

We encounter cultural differences in education in a variety of contexts. While you may be most familiar with the traditional U.S. classroom setting, this is not the only educational context. Many students become "international students" by studying in another country. You may have encountered international students in your classes, and you may know American students who have gone abroad to study and to experience another culture. In fact, many universities offer **study-abroad programs** to give their students international experiences. However, study abroad opportunities are not equally available or taken advantage of by all students. Most are White, as shown in Table 12.1. Because the cultural norms in different educational settings vary widely, international students engage directly in issues relevant to intercultural communication.

History plays an important role in these students' experiences, as do the educational systems they enter. Many students from former European colonies study at institutions in the former colonizing nation. For example, Indonesian students may study in the Netherlands, Indian students may study in Britain, and Lebanese students may study in France. Belgians sometimes point out that the second largest Congolese city is Louvain-la-Neuve, where the Francophone (French-speaking) Université Catholique de Louvain is located. When Tom

TABLE 12.1 Ethnicity of U.S. Students Who Studied Abroad from 1998-1999

Although race/ethnicity is not a requirement for studying abroad, why do you think that White Americans and Asian Americans study abroad at higher rates than their demographic proportion of U.S. society? Why are other groups at lower rates?

Caucasian/White	85%	110,359
Hispanic American	5.2%	6,692
Asian American	4.4%	5,681
African American	3.3%	4,330
Multiracial	1.2%	1,524
Native American	0.9%	1,184

Source: http://www.daad.org/pdf/Study%20Abroad%20Market.pdf

asked students from the Congo why they came to Belgium, which once colonized the Congo, to study, they pointed out that the Belgian educational system is structured similarly to their own and that they learn French in school. Therefore, they can move easily between institutions in the two nations. Because of the history of Belgium's colonization of the Congo, these intercultural connections remain vibrant. Notably, fewer students from the Congo attend the Katholieke Universiteit Leuven in Belgium; this university is located across the Belgian linguistic border in Leuven, where Flemish, not French, is spoken. Again, history is very important in understanding intercultural relations and intercultural communication.

CULTURALLY SPECIFIC EDUCATION

Also relevant to intercultural communication is the historical rise and development of educational institutions geared toward various cultural groups. For example, the Morrill Act of 1890 established what are today known as **HBCUs,** or historically Black colleges and universities. Alabama State, Delaware State, South Carolina State, Tennessee State, Grambling State, and Howard are all examples of HBCUs. Debates over the purpose of these educational institutions reflect the cultural attitudes inherent in education. For example, rather than being routes for empowering African Americans, some critics charged, these educational institutions focused on creating subservient Black workers in a White-dominated society. A century ago, for example, the famous Black educator

Pop Culture Spotlight

Have you seen the movie *Drumline* starring Nick Cannon, Orlando Jones, and Zoe Saldana? It's a film about a young drummer from Harlem, Devon Miles (Nick Cannon), who is uniquely talented but struggles to overcome his pride in order to understand the importance of community in "the line." But this story is not simply about the struggles in one young man's life. The backdrop of the film highlights the uniqueness of the Black college experience.

MONROE SCHOOL
Topeka Kansas March 3 1949

KINDERGARTEN
Miss Doris Pittman
Miss Olita Burnette
Practice Teacher

This photo of the segregated Monroe School in Topeka, Kansas, was taken in 1949. In 1954, in *Brown v. Board of Education of Topeka,* the Supreme Court declared such segregation to be unconstitutional. How do you think integration changes the educational process? As you look around your classroom, how integrated is your educational experience?

Booker T. Washington pushed for the study of industrial arts and vocation training, as "no race can prosper till it learns that there is as much dignity in tilling a field as in writing a poem."[3] After all, one writer noted, "Black colleges, which in many cases were little more than secondary schools, received unequal funding from state or, under land-grant provisions, federal sources."[4] And this inequality only served to perpetuate the historical inequality between Whites and Blacks—a sad legacy that persists to this day.

Other educational institutions were established for White women, such as Mississippi University for Women and Texas Women's University, and for Native Americans, such as the College of the Menominee and Diné College. The White women's colleges were established for reasons quite different from those for establishing the Native American colleges. But in each case, education was intimately related to a specific culture and served different purposes for different students. In the same sense, your own cultural identity is reflected in your educational choices and experiences.

Not all of these colleges and universities have retained their original missions, yet many continue to draw the students for whom they were originally established. Following a U.S. Supreme Court decision, Mississippi University for Women, the "first public college for women in America,"[5] changed its policies to admit women and men. Today, MUW's mission statement reflects its traditional emphasis: "MUW is dedicated to the liberal arts and to professional education for all students, with an emphasis on academic and leadership preparation for women."[6]

The educational experiences of minority and majority students in these institutions are not necessarily the same as those of students in institutions that were initially established for White males, such as Georgia Tech. Georgia Tech has long since departed from its original charter as the university's website boasts: "Women students were admitted in 1952, and in 1961 Georgia Tech became the first university in the Deep South to admit African American students without a court order."[7] The student experiences at these different kinds of institutions reflect these different histories, different student composition, and different social contexts, as well as institutional goals.

There are many other kinds of educational institutions that no longer exist but whose reverberations are still felt. For example, "Indian schools" were established to assimilate Native American children to White American society by educating them off reservation in boarding schools. In Phoenix today, there is a main artery called "Indian School Road," along which the Phoenix Indian School once sat. In writing about an Indian school in Oklahoma, K. Tsianina Lomawaima tells us that "although Chilocco was closed in 1980, it persists as a social reality today in many communities across Oklahoma,"[8] in that many alumni continue to gather regularly. Indeed, because in these schools "acculturation and assimilation into the dominant White society remained the explicit goal of policy and practice,"[9] it is hardly surprising that the education that these students received after being separated from their families and communities "had a tremendous impact on language use and retention, religious conservatism and conver-

TABLE 12.2 Nations Sending the Most Students to the United States to Study

Many students come to the United States to study. The following list ranks nations sending the most students to the United States.

RANK	COUNTRY OF ORIGIN	2000/01	2001/02	2000/01– 2001/02 PERCENTAGE CHANGE	PERCENTAGE OF U.S. FOREIGN STUDENT TOTAL
1	India	54,664	66,836	22.3	11.5
2	China	59,939	63,211	5.5	10.8
3	Republic of Korea	45,685	49,046	7.4	8.4
4	Japan	46,497	46,810	0.7	8.0
5	Taiwan	28,566	28,930	1.3	5.0
6	Canada	25,279	26,514	4.9	4.5
7	Mexico	10,670	12,518	17.3	2.1
8	Turkey	10,983	12,091	10.1	2.1
9	Indonesia	11,625	11,614	−0.1	2.0
10	Thailand	11,187	11,606	3.7	2.0

Source: http://opendoors.iienetwork.org/?p=25184

sion, attitudes toward education and feelings of self-esteem, to name but a few influences."[10]

The effects of education reverberate across generations, because once languages, customs, traditions, and religions are lost it is difficult, if not impossible, for subsequent generations to recover them. Education is very influential in maintaining or irreparably altering various cultural communities.

INTERCULTURAL COMMUNICATION IN EDUCATIONAL SETTINGS

Much of our communication behavior in the classroom is not interpreted in the way we intend it by people from different cultural backgrounds. Education is deeply embedded in culture, and our expectations for the educational process are a part of our culture. The roles that we enact in the classroom are very much a part of the cultural influences on education. Let's look at how these roles can differ.

Roles for Teachers and Students

When Tom taught at a Francophone university in Belgium, another professor gave him a helpful cultural tip: "In Belgium, students don't answer the professor's questions, even if they know the answer. In the United States, American

Info Bites

It wasn't until 1934 that discussions of Native American culture were permitted in schools sponsored by the Bureau of Indian Affairs. Previously, the policy of the federal government had been "full assimilation and eradication of Indian culture." (SOURCE: www. oiep.bia.edu/)

What Do You Think?

When we talk about intercultural experiences in the classroom, the focus is often on American teachers abroad or American teachers with foreign students in a domestic context. But how much do you hear about foreign teachers in the United States? A 1999 article in the *San Francisco Chronicle* noted how the Immigration and Naturalization Service (now the Bureau of Citizenship and Immigration Services) set in place a policy that would issue a maximum of 50 work visas each year to foreign teachers, as part of a "global educators outreach program." At the time, the Chicago school system (the third largest in the nation) had about 400 vacancies. What kinds of issues do foreign teachers face in U.S. school systems? What values do they bring from their own cultures, and how do those values affect the dynamics of the classroom? (Source: *San Francisco Chronicle*, December 24, 1999, p. A-3)

students answer the professor's questions, even if they don't know the answer." This cultural generalization was helpful to Tom as he navigated the role of professor in this different context. Although he did ask questions throughout the term, the lack of discussion in the classroom was understandable. Because he was concerned about imposing his own cultural framework on the Belgian students, Tom did not push them to participate in discussions, nor did he demand that they answer his questions. As the term progressed, some of the students began to speak more in class, even as Tom felt that he was moving toward more of a lecture format. The classroom became a site for negotiation of these cultural differences.

These kinds of cultural differences can create confusion in the classroom for students and teachers. Note the following example from the Netherlands:

> When Setiyo Hadi Waluyo came from his native Indonesia to study at Wageningen Agricultural University here, he was shocked by what he saw. Time and again a professor would ask a question, a student would answer, and the professor would say, "You're absolutely right!"
>
> "I felt: What's going on here?" recalls Mr. Waluyo. "The students know more than the professors?" [11]

The culture clash over **learning styles** (the different ways that students learn in different cultures) and **teaching styles** (the styles that instructors use to teach) are common as students increasingly travel to study in other cultures. Often we are unaware of our cultural assumptions about education until we are confronted with different ways of learning. Think about the assumptions you have concerning how your instructors should behave. Perhaps you think that instructors should set time aside in class for discussion of the material, or that students should be allowed to say what they think about the readings, or that grading should be done "on a curve." In many universities, for example, students are assigned books to read before the end of the term and take one exam at the end of the term, rather than getting a structured reading list and assignments along the way.

Grading and Power

As in any other social setting, the classroom is embedded with cultural expectations about power relations. While there may always be a power difference in the communication between instructors and students, this difference can be greater or lesser in various cultures. In the United States, for example, the relationships between instructor and students tend to be less formal than in other cultures. Michael, a student of ours, recalled the following intercultural conflict, which reflects this power difference:

> While on a study-abroad program in Malaysia, I received what I thought was an unfair grade on a paper. As I discussed my unhappiness in his office, the teacher became increasingly angry that I was commenting about his grading in his office. In the heat of the argument, I was threatening to re-

port him to the school's governing board, and he was threatening to get me kicked out of the school! Obviously, this conflict spiraled way out of control. . . . Several red flags were telling me that intercultural differences were at play. . . . In his culture, students are disrespectful when they question teachers' decisions. In my culture, questions show that you are paying attention. I chose to explain my actions to the teacher, and we were able to put out the fire. We refocused on communication behaviors and ended in a win/win situation: I got a better grade, and he received more respect.

Michael's experience highlights the role that culture plays in the educational process. The relationship between instructor and student is not uniform around the world. Michael's decision to discuss these cultural differences openly with his instructor in Malaysia was helpful in resolving this situation. Cultural differences often cause intercultural conflicts simply because the individuals involved fail to confront those differences.

Notions of "fair" and "unfair" are culturally embedded as well. Our grading system is far from universal. Different cultures use different ways of evaluating student work. When Tom taught in Francophone Belgium, he was familiar with the grading system, as it is the same grading system used in French universities, where the highest grade (which is almost never given) is 20. In most U.S. colleges and universities, the highest grade, which is expected to be given to a number of students in every class, is an A.

Admissions, Affirmative Action, and Standardized Tests

Debates over university admissions are not new. Because university resources are expensive and limited, admissions to universities are competitive. The University of Bristol in the United Kingdom faces such competition, receiving "about 39,000 applicants for 3,300 undergraduate places each year."[12] The high costs of university education eventually led to the closing of the Université de Kinshasa in the Congo.[13]

Because of the economic importance of university degrees, admissions are important in empowering and disempowering cultural groups. Thus, many people struggled to break down barriers to university admissions that were based on nonacademic factors such as race. The University of Tennessee reflects many of these tensions, as "Black undergraduates were not admitted until 1961; the first black faculty member was appointed in 1964."[14] Those explicit barriers to admission have long been dismantled. Today, universities do not deny admission based on race. Arizona State University has a nondiscrimination statement that, in part, says, "Discrimination is prohibited on the basis of race, color, religion, national origin, citizenship, sex, sexual orientation, age, disability, and special disabled veteran, other protected veteran, newly separated veteran, or Vietnam era veteran status."[15]

In order to overcome some of the historical as well as contemporary reasons that have led to student bodies that do not reflect the demographic profiles of

What Do You Think?

Many U.S. American students who think about studying abroad want to go to England or Ireland or find a place where they can either stay with a family who speaks English or live in a dormitory with other U.S. American students. Other students who go to places where they are forced to learn a new language might claim that their experience was better. If you had only one opportunity to study abroad, which kind of experience do you think would be the most valuable?

society at large, the Civil Rights movement led to the establishment of affirmative action policies. These policies encouraged institutions to act affirmatively to ensure a more representative student body. As a part of this movement, questions were raised about the ability of institutions to measure "merit," particularly on standardized tests. How do we know who is more qualified to be admitted? Recently questions have been raised about the ways that equal opportunity is thwarted by privileging children of alumni in the admissions process. Given the historical barriers that prevented some cultural groups from attending some colleges and universities, how might the children of alumni not reflect society at large?

Across the Atlantic, the prestigious *Institut d'études politiques* in Paris has established what some have called a French affirmative-action program and what the French refer to as *zone d'éducation prioritaire*, or ZEP. Students from disadvantaged backgrounds are "offered counseling, special courses, and visits to Sciences Po's campus."[16] This way of acting affirmatively has recently withstood a court challenge. The court did not question the principle of the program but has instructed the institution to modify and to clarify some of its regulations. According to government commissioner Jean-Pierre Demouveaux, however, there was no opposition from the court to creating "a path for access to high school students from socially disadvantaged backgrounds."[17] The principle behind ZEP is to integrate all sectors of society into French society.

More recently, concern over admissions policies also have shifted to the admissions criteria themselves and the ways that they favor some cultural groups over others in admissions. The emergence of the notion of **reverse discrimination,** or policies that disadvantage Whites and/or males, has become a rhetorical strategy to argue for more spaces for those dominant groups. The University of Michigan recently won a Supreme Court battle to include race as one of many factors in its admissions decisions. The university has posted a website that explains the two related court cases and their current admissions policies at http://www.umich.edu/~urel/admissions/.

Other universities also face similar concerns. The University of Utah recently has come under scrutiny for the admissions practices of its medical school. The dean of the medical school noted that there is a misperception "that white male applicants experience reverse discrimination, despite the fact that the medical school is 87 percent white and 65 percent male."[18] Yet Utah's "controversy, which isn't nearly over and done, stems from accusations by some state legislators of 'reverse discrimination' at the medical school against 'white, Mormon males.'"[19] Similar concerns about reverse discrimination have arisen at other universities as well.

Part of the criteria in U.S. undergraduate admissions may include the SAT. In developing the "new SAT," some groups will likely benefit over others:

> Girls tend to outperform boys on writing exams, so their overall scores could benefit from the addition of the new writing section. Boys usually score higher on the math section, but the new exam will contain fewer of

the abstract-reasoning items at which they excel. The elimination of analogies may exacerbate the black-white SAT score gap, since the gap is somewhat smaller on the analogy section than on the test as a whole.[20]

Concern over the value of trying to predict academic success led the president of the University of California to recommend that the SAT no longer be used in admissions to its eight undergraduate campuses. In announcing his recommendation, he noted that "minorities are concerned about the fact that, on average, their children score lower than white and Asian American students." While there may be a myriad of reasons for this disparity in scores, he also noted that the "strength of American society has been its belief that actual achievement should be what matters most. Students should be judged on the basis of what they have made of the opportunities available to them."[21] While changes to the SAT may help mitigate some of the problems with the test, it still remains notoriously difficult to predict academic success.

COMMUNICATION, EDUCATION, AND CULTURAL IDENTITY

> A Navajo student shared a cultural myth/experience that people from her tribe are all familiar with. Apparently, people in her tribe have encountered "beings" called skin chasers. They are beings that have the face of a human but the body of an animal. They appear in the evening, but not to everyone. She received feedback from her teacher, who said in so many words that it couldn't be true. The Navajo student was really upset that [the teacher] could pass judgment and in her eyes ridicule something that was so sacred to her tribe and cultural background.—Mona

Mona's story strikes at the heart of the debates over cultural identity, education, and the role of communication in reinforcing or challenging identities. Education itself is an important context for socialization and empowerment. Education professor Ann Locke Davidson observes:

> Education is popularly conceptualized as one factor integral to achieving the economic parity and geographic dispersal presumed basic to integrating diverse citizens into American society. Yet, while it is clear that education improves individual chances for social mobility, it is equally apparent that schools work less well for impoverished African American and Latino school children.[22]

Similarly, Mona's story about her Navajo friend demonstrates the alienation that students from other cultures may experience in the classroom.

We often like to think that education provides equal opportunities for all students, but inequities in the paths that students follow reflect differing patterns of treatment. These experiences are powerful forces in the shaping of their

This photo of a classroom at the Carlisle Indian Industrial School in Carlisle, Pennsylvania, was taken around 1902. Carlisle was one of many "Indian schools" that attempted to "civilize" their students by eradicating tribal identities, languages, and religions. What ramifications might this educational process have for contemporary Native Americans?

identities, and students are very attuned to these forces. One Mexican American high school student, Sonia, notes about her White teachers:

> It's probably in the way they look at you, the way they talk, . . . like when they talk about the people who are going to drop out. And then Mr. Kula, when he's talking about teenage pregnancy or something like that, he turns around and looked at us. It's like, he tries to look around the whole room so we won't notice, but like he mostly tries to get it through our heads. . . . Sometimes I think he's prejudiced.[23]

Sonia, like other students, develops her identity within this educational context. Because her experience is shared by other students who are also of Mexican descent, it is a shared cultural experience that shapes a cultural identity. It is not simply an individual identity.

Even teachers who are not overtly racist may not have received the kind of education necessary to incorporate materials into the curriculum that reflect the diversity of their students. Nor have they been able to develop this curriculum. Education professor Henry Giroux tells us that, "despite the growing diversity of students in both public schools and higher education, there are few examples of curriculum sensitivity to the multiplicity of economic, social and cultural factors bearing on a student's educational life."[24]

Think about your own education. How much did you learn about the history of other cultural groups in the United States or elsewhere? How much literature did you read that was written by authors from a range of cultural backgrounds? How much art and music were you exposed to that came from non-Western cultures?

SOCIAL ISSUES AND EDUCATION

As noted previously, the development of educational institutions, as well as the educational process itself, is deeply embedded in any culture. As students and instructors meet in the classroom, cultural differences can lead to misunderstandings in communication. There is, of course, no way to escape the history of education and the ways this history has created cultural expectations about what should happen in the educational process. Nor is this a call to find a way to escape education. After all, you are pursuing education in an educational institution, and as authors of this book, we also have a role in the educational institution. In any case, there are some social issues that we should consider as they bear upon intercultural communication.

First, it is important to recognize that the educational process reflects cultural power. The things we study (and do not study), the way we communicate in the classroom, the relationships between students and instructors—all involve issues of power. How do we determine what gets studied and what does not in various courses? Whose communication style sets the tone in the classroom? Why are interactions between students and instructors always embedded in a hierarchical relationship? The answers to these questions all have to do with power issues, and it is important to recognize that everyone's culture is not treated the same in the curriculum.

Second, it is important to recognize that the structure of educational institutions, as opposed to the people in them, often plays a significant role in the way that power functions. Thus, we need to understand how the educational system empowers some over others—and how this happens because of the way the system is set up. For example, some colleges require history or literature courses, but the history and literature that they teach might be **Eurocentric,** focusing on European or Western views of history and literature. By taking a Eurocentric approach, these courses reinforce a particular worldview that challenges some student identities more than others. As noted earlier in the book, we are often taught the history of our state or nation. Clearly, however, this approach to education can create barriers to intercultural communication.

One response to this problem is to teach **Afrocentric** history,[25] which centers on the African rather than the European experience and exposes African American students to an entirely different view of the world and their place in it.

What Do You Think?

Since the 1980s, spurred by the writings of people like E. D. Hirsch, Alan Bloom, and William Bennett, conservatives have increasingly stressed the importance of teaching Western civilization classes. These efforts are in response to the attempt to broaden the curriculum to include the histories of other cultures. If you've taken a Western civilization class, what did you think of it? What did it teach you?

Thanksgiving is an important U.S. holiday. The educational process is important in instilling a sense of the significance of this holiday. Thanksgiving is not seen as a "White" holiday in the way that Kwanzaa, Lunar New Year, and other holidays are seen as ethnically specific. Why do you think it is important for us to view Thanksgiving as a national holiday instead of a holiday for Whites?

Of course, as sociologist James Loewen notes, "To be sure, the answer to Eurocentric textbooks is not one-sided Afrocentric history, the kind that has Africans inventing everything good and whites inventing slavery and oppression."[26] These curriculum innovations are vital to the self-esteem, cultural identity, and empowerment of all students, but schools don't seem to know how to teach in ways that are more inclusive and that are fair to all cultural groups. As James Loewen says about U.S. history, "Students will start learning history when they see the point of doing so, when it seems interesting and important to them, and when they believe history might relate to their lives and futures. Students will start finding history interesting when their teachers and textbooks stop lying to them."[27]

Finally, as education professor William Tierney suggests, "Our colleges and universities need to be noisier—in the sense that honest dialogue that confronts differences is good. To be sure, we must not drown out other voices. . . . We must work harder at developing dialogues of respect."[28] To accomplish this, we must be willing to point out cultural differences that are creating problems in the educational process. Only by talking about these differences and the reasons for them can we begin to change the educational process. We have to create an environment in which cultural differences are assumed to exist and are discussed. We need to move away from an environment in which culture is assumed to be irrelevant since everyone shares the same culture.

SUMMARY

In this chapter, we looked at some of the challenges that cultural differences bring to the educational process. Because education is a process of socialization and enculturation, it is relevant to intercultural communication. Different cultures have differing educational goals. The curricula in some nations do not reflect their own cultures, but instead focus on the European cultures of their former colonizers. And some culturally specific educational institutions may have different educational goals from other institutions. Both teachers and students enact cultural roles in the educational setting. Even grading is cultural, in that all educational systems do not use the same grading system. And varying admissions policies, sometimes discriminatory, have important historical and contemporary implications for intercultural relations. Standardized tests, part of the admission procedures, have sometimes contained implicit cultural biases.

We also examined the ways that communication in education can influence the cultural identities and self-esteem of students. Some instructors may knowingly or unknowingly communicate their cultural biases in the classroom. Finally, the issue of Eurocentric versus Afrocentric approaches to history and the need for more dialogue in the classroom highlight the social relevance of education.

BUILDING INTERCULTURAL SKILLS

1. Be more sensitive to the ways that your educational curriculum reinforces or challenges your culture and cultural identity. Think about how it might not function in the same way for other students. How is the education you receive targeted toward the majority of students at your college? How is bias reflected in the history you are taught, the literature you are assigned, the music and art you experience, and the social issues you study?

2. Be aware of the cultural nature of the expectations you have for educational roles. If you sense that someone is not acting as a "student" should or as an "instructor" should, how much of this feeling is due to cultural differences?

ACTIVITIES

1. *Maps and worldviews:* Look at a map of the world. Unless you are looking at a "Peter's Projection" map, you will notice that the equator is not in the middle of the map, even if it does run around the middle of the world. Why is the equator not in the middle of the map, and what kinds of worldview might this map be projecting?

2. *Culture and the curriculum:* Find an old college catalogue from your school or another one. Look for courses that were taught then but that are less important or nonexistent today. Were there courses in home economics? Who were these for? What assumptions did such courses make about socialization? How about industrial arts? What languages were taught then, and which ones are taught today? What cultural needs did education fulfill?

www.mhhe.com/experiencing2

THE ONLINE LEARNING CENTER at www.mhhe.com/experiencing2 features self-quizzes, flashcards, and crossword puzzles based on the chapter's key terms and concepts.

ENDNOTES

1. Judy, R. W., & D'Amico, C. (1997). *Workforce 2020: Work and workers in the 21st century.* Indianapolis: Hudson Institute, p. 116.
2. Docker, J. (1995). The neocolonial assumption in university teaching of English. In B. Ashcroft, G. Griffiths, & H. Tiffin (Eds.), *The post-colonial studies reader* (pp. 443–446). New York: Routledge.
3. Washington, B. T. (1971). The Atlanta Exposition address, September 1895. In A. Meier et al. (Eds.), *Black protest thought in the twentieth century* (2nd ed.) (pp. 3–8). Indianapolis: Bobbs-Merrill, p. 5.
4. Goodenow, R. K. (1989). Education, Black. In C. R. Wilson & W. Ferris (Eds.), *Encyclopedia of southern culture* (Vol. 1). New York: Anchor Books, p. 253.
5. Mississippi University for Women. History. (http://www.muw.edu/misc/history.htm)
6. Mississippi University for Women. Mission. (http://www.muw.edu/misc/mission.htm)
7. Georgia Institute of Technology. About Tech. (http://www.gatech.edu/about-tech/history-traditions.html)
8. Lomawaima, K. T. (1994). *They called it Prairie Light: The story of Chilocco Indian School.* Lincoln: University of Nebraska Press, p. 160.
9. Lomawaima (1994), p. 3.
10. Lomawaima (1994), p. xv.
11. Burton, B. (2000, February 25). Preventing culture clashes: Learning styles, food, and dorm life challenge foreign students in Holland. *The Chronicle of Higher Education*, p. A56.
12. BBC News. (2003, February 26). Bristol denies admissions bias. (http://news.bbc.co.uk/2/hi/uk_news/education/2798507.stm)
13. Juakali, K. (2001, December 19). L'Université de Kinshasa ferme ses portes. *Afrik.com.* (www.afrik.com/article3775.html)
14. University of Tennessee. Brief historical sketch of the University of Tennessee. (http://web.utk.edu/~mklein/brfhist.html)
15. Arizona State University. Equal Employment Opportunity/Affirmative Action Policy. (http://www.eoaa.asu.edu/Pres%20EOAA%20policy%20statement.html)
16. Bollag, B. (2003, November 7). French court upholds landmark program of affirmative action in college admissions. *The Chronicle of Higher Education* (online). (http://chronicle.com/prm/daily/2003/11/2003110703n.htm)
17. Laronche, M. (2003, November 7). Sciences-Po condamné à revoir la méthode de ses conventions ZEP. *Le Monde* (online). (http://www.lemonde.fr/web/recherche_articleweb/1, 13-0, 36-341087,0.html?query=sciences+po&query2=&booleen=et&num_page=1&auteur=&dans=dansarticle&periode=30&ordre=pertinence&G_NBARCHIVES=796331&nbpages=2&artparpage=10&nb_art=11)
18. Betz, L. (Summer 2002). True admissions. *Continuum Magazine* (online). (http://www.alumni.utah.edu/continuum/summer02/andfinally.htm)
19. Keller, R. H., & Keller, D. R. (2003, October 19). Machen's bane: Just who gets into medical school at the U? *The Salt Lake Tribune*, AA7.
20. Cloud, J. (2003, October 27). Inside the new SAT. *Time*, 49–50.
21. Atkinson, R. C. (2001, February 18). Standardized tests and access to American universities. Robert H. Atwell Distinguished Lecture. 83rd Annual Meeting of the American Council on Education. Washington, DC. (http://www.ucop.edu/pres/comments/satspch.html)
22. Davidson, A. L. (1996). *Making and molding identity in schools: Student narratives on race, gender, and academic empowerment.* Albany: State University of New York, p. 22.

23. Davidson (1996), p. 128.

24. Giroux, H. A. (1996). Is there a place for cultural studies in colleges of education? In H. A. Giroux, C. Lankshear, P. McLaren, & M. Peters (Eds.), *Counternarratives: Cultural studies and critical pedagogies in postmodern spaces.* New York: Routledge, p. 50.

25. Loewen, J. W. (1995). *Lies my teacher told me: Everything your America history textbook got wrong.* New York: Touchstone, p. 302.

26. Loewen (1995), p. 302.

27. Loewen (1995), p. 311.

28. Tierney, W. G. (1997). *Academic outlaws: Queer theory and cultural studies in the academy.* Thousand Oaks, CA: Sage.

CHAPTER THIRTEEN

Intercultural Communication and Health Care

STUDY OBJECTIVES

After reading this chapter you should be able to:

1. Understand the importance of communication in health care delivery. Describe some of the ways that communication can be overlooked and how this might impact the delivery of medical services.

2. Explain some of the intercultural barriers to effective health care. Explain the ways that some cultural groups have been or continue to be treated in the health care system. Describe how prejudicial attitudes can influence health care delivery.

3. Explain how religious or spiritual beliefs may be important in effective health care delivery. Describe some of the ways that health care professionals can deal with religious and spiritual beliefs. Discuss the ethical implications of some of the ways that health care professionals deal with religious or spiritual beliefs.

4. Explain how power differences can influence health communication.

5. Identify the four frameworks that physicians might use in communicating about a patient's health.

6. Describe the role of ethics committees. Describe some of the complex issues to be dealt with in making ethical health care decisions.

KEY TERMS

AIDS
alternative medicine
benevolent deception
contractual honesty
ethics committees
euthanasia
health care professionals
HIV
medical jargon

medical terminology
prejudicial ideologies
religious history
religious freedom
strict paternalism
Tuskegee Syphilis
    Project
unmitigated honesty

What you have learned about intercultural communication has important applications in the health communication context. As the U.S. population ages and new medical technologies are developed, health care will become even more significant in our lives. Health care has also become increasingly controversial as more and more managed care corporations have entered the market. Within this changing context, as the U.S. population becomes increasingly diverse, U.S. Americans are beginning to seek out health care from a variety of sources—from traditional Western practitioners to more "exotic" Eastern practices.

In this chapter, we discuss some of the reasons communication about health has become more important and some of the ways you might navigate this communication context. Not only patients, but **health care professionals**—including physicians, nurses, physical and occupational therapists, and medical technicians—can come from a variety of cultural backgrounds. Intercultural communication and misunderstandings in health communication arise daily in this context.

THE IMPORTANCE OF COMMUNICATION IN HEALTH CARE

Intercultural communication is increasingly relevant in the health communication context for a number of reasons. First, as our population becomes increasingly diverse, complexities arise in communicating about health issues. Not only are health care professionals communicating with people from differing cultural backgrounds, but these same patients are communicating with nurses, doctors, and other health care professionals from differing cultural backgrounds. Table 13.1 shows some of the diversity of cultural backgrounds of U.S. physicians. And in some cultures, there may be certain stigmas associated with communicating about health issues, making it difficult to discuss these concerns. For example, in some cultures, subjects such as mental illness, AIDS, sexually transmitted diseases, impotence, and abortion are not easily broached.

Second, health care professionals and patients may not realize the importance of communication. This oversight may seem incidental to medical training and treatment, but the reality is, much medical practice, particularly diagnosis, relies heavily on patient communication. In many ways, this shortcoming in health care reflects a Western cultural phenomenon, "due partly to the belief that the biomedical model of health care—the predominant model in Western societies—is based on a range of predominantly physical procedures (physical examination, physical manipulation, injections, etc.) rather than communication between two parties."[1] In other words, Western physicians tend to rely heavily

TABLE 13.1 Home Countries of Foreign Doctors

About 23% of all physicians in the United States were educated abroad. Here is a list of the top ten countries that send physicians to the United States. How might intercultural communication be important here?

1. India—19.5%	6. Dominican Republic—2.5%
2. Pakistan—11.9%	7. Syria—2.5%
3. Philippines—8.8%	8. United Kingdom—2.4%
4. Ex-USSR—3.1%	9. Germany—2.3%
5. Egypt—2.6%	10. Mexico—1.8%

Source: http://www.mdgreencard.com/situation.html

Surf's Up!

Did you know that you can major in health communication? The Emerson-Tufts website (www.emerson.edu/acadepts/cs/healthcom/hcmajor.html) describes its program in this way: "Effective health communication is the art and technique of crafting messages, informing, influencing and motivating institutional and public audiences about important health issues." In a culturally diverse setting, how might health communication reach these goals?

on physical symptoms to evaluate illness, rather than communicating with patients about what they are experiencing.

However, good communication is crucial to quality health care. Health care providers ask questions to diagnose problems, to help patients understand the treatment, and so on. And patients come to health professionals to seek treatment and ask questions. But even native English speakers complain about the use of **medical jargon**—potentially confusing or difficult-to-understand medical terminology—by physicians. In trying to understand more about a patient's family history, doctors commonly ask a number of questions about the health of family members. In the following example, the use of jargon results in miscommunication:

DOCTOR: Have you ever had a history of cardiac arrest in your family?

PATIENT: We never had no trouble with the police.[2]

While the term "cardiac arrest" may not seem like medical jargon to the physician or to you, the patient clearly did not understand it. The dialogue continues:

DOCTOR: How about varicose veins?

PATIENT: Well, I have veins, but I don't know if they're close or not.[3]

If English speakers have trouble with common medical terms, health care professionals need to be especially careful using these terms. For those patients who are communicating in a second language, **medical terminology**—scientific language used by doctors to describe specific medical conditions—can be particularly confusing. And when cultural misunderstandings arise, it can lead to inadequate treatment.

Health care providers and patients alike may operate out of an ethnocentric framework without realizing it. Assumptions about health care often have cultural roots. Consider the following example: Setsuko, a Japanese woman now living in the United States, had to spend several months in the hospital for a chronic illness. She became extremely depressed, to the point of feeling suicidal. When-

Patients and health care providers come from a variety of cultural backgrounds with differing assumptions about health care and the proper roles of doctors and nurses. These cultural differences can influence the health care patients receive. Health care providers need to be sensitive to these cultural differences in providing health services.

ever the staff would ask her how she was doing, Setsuko would answer that she was fine. Based on this lack of communication, the nursing and medical staff were unaware of her depression for weeks. It was not until she began to exhibit physical signs of depression that she was offered a psychiatric consultation. The problem was that Setsuko was culturally conditioned to be a good patient by not making a fuss or drawing attention to herself or embarrassing her family with complaints about being depressed, so she always reported that she was fine. Although the psychiatrist tried to explain that in this context a "good patient" was expected to discuss and report any and all problems or symptoms, Setsuko still had to work to redefine her cultural role as a good patient in order to receive better health care. In this case, both the health care providers and the patient struggled to negotiate a more effective communication framework to ensure better treatment.

Third, treating patients is not always a matter of communication between the physician and the patient. While one-to-one communication generally works well in Western cultures, which are more oriented to individualism, other cultures may focus more on the family's role in health care. Thus, communication between the physician and the patient is only one element in the communication process. Unfortunately, most health communication research has limited itself to the physician-patient relationship. Laurel Northouse, a nursing professor, and Peter Northouse, a communication professor, note: "This lack of systematic study of professional-family interaction is symptomatic of the lack of importance that health professionals have traditionally attributed to this relationship in health care."[4]

This cultural bias in thinking about the role of the family in health care can lead to problems. Consider the case of the Samoan man hospitalized with a gunshot wound. Throughout the day, more and more family members gathered in the waiting room. Because there were so many extended family members, hospital personnel asked them to wait in the main lobby. The family members became increasingly irate because they wanted to see the patient as a large group, but the hospital had a policy of only three visitors at a time. Tensions between the family and the staff continued to escalate until a hospital administrator, sensitive to cultural differences, made a special exception and allowed large groups of family members to visit the patient.

Families, of course, can provide very important support to a patient as she or he recovers. Their role is even more important after the patient returns home. But this means that the family must receive adequate information about the patient's condition. In turn, this means that health care professionals must be sensitive to cultural differences and must adapt their communication accordingly.

INTERCULTURAL BARRIERS TO EFFECTIVE HEALTH CARE

In Chapter 3, we discussed the importance of history in intercultural communication. Let's look at some of these historical dynamics as they influence health care today. This is important because the history of medicine guides how different cultural communities may relate to health care.

Historical Treatments of Cultural Groups

First, historically, widespread ideologies about different cultures have fostered differential treatment for some groups, especially racial and ethnic minorities, by medical professionals. As sociologist Chris Shilling writes, "Historically, the negative construction of black bodies has made them targets for a variety of moral panics surrounding health and disease."[5] In the past, medical conclusions about alleged racial difference have justified a number of deplorable social practices, from slavery, to colonization, to immigration restrictions.[6]

This differential treatment has caused some cultural groups to be justifiably suspicious of contemporary health care. For example, the infamous **Tuskegee Syphilis Project,** conducted by the U.S. Public Health Service on unsuspecting African Americans in Tuskegee, Alabama, over a 40-year period, spurred some of these concerns.[7] In this study, Black patients who sought out medical care for syphilis were instead given placebos (sugar pills), but were not told that they were part of a study, simply to establish an experimental control group. The purpose of the study was to explore how syphilis spreads in a patient's body and how it spreads in a population. Periodic reports were published in medical journals, but the Centers for Disease Control received only one letter from a physician raising ethical concerns. The study was finally halted, not by the medical community, but only after a public denouncement by Senator Edward Kennedy in Con-

AIDS protests shed light on the ways that resources for medical services and for medical research are unequally distributed. It is important to recognize how cultural attitudes influence the medical community. By bringing medical issues into the public arena, cultural differences can be confronted and resolved.

gress. Unfortunately, it's hardly surprising that such a study was not conducted on wealthy White Americans in Beverly Hills.

The Tuskegee Syphilis Project, among other studies and projects, has reinforced suspicion about the medical community from many marginalized communities. The rise of **AIDS** (acquired immune deficiency syndrome) and **HIV** (human immunodeficiency virus) in the late 20th century provoked new fears among gays and minorities that the medical community would again provide differential treatment. As Jeffrey Levi, an AIDS and health policy consultant, argues:

> Homophobia was not introduced into the health-care system only with the AIDS epidemic. Rather, its long-standing legacy of discrimination and exclusion has resulted in the creation of a separate health-care system within the gay community, a health-care system that responded to this new crisis immediately, saving countless gay lives—and heterosexual lives as well—while the government-sponsored system floundered, unable to find the will or the funds to operate.[8]

The slow response to the AIDS epidemic by the federal government has been widely discussed and critiqued.[9] In his analysis of public discourses about AIDS, Larry Gross, a communication professor, concludes that "AIDS thus taught two lessons. First, a disease that strikes gay people (and people of color, and drug users, and poor people) will not receive adequate attention. Second, people will begin to pay attention when famous and important people are involved."[10] Thus, the HIV/AIDS epidemic highlighted the traditional lack of trust between the health care system and minority communities.

Surf's Up!

Read about President Clinton's apology for the Tuskegee Project (www. chron.com/content/ chronicle/page1/97/05/ 17/clinton.2-0.html) This kind of research is likely to make minority populations suspicious of doctors and the medical system. Do you think Clinton's apology is intended for the medical community or the minority communities? How might his message be read by different audiences, and how might this influence the health care system?

These Hong Kong residents are riding a fairly empty MTR train on April 12, 2003. Their masks point to concerns about Severe Acute Respiratory Syndrome (SARS). Hong Kong announced April 12th that three more people had died and another 49 had been infected with SARS. How might prejudicial attitudes affect how health care workers interact with people from Hong Kong or other SARS-infected areas?

Prejudicial Ideologies

Second, **prejudicial ideologies**—sets of ideas based on stereotypes—about various cultural groups affect both health care professionals and patients. These attitudes can present significant barriers to intercultural communication. Consider the following case: A social worker in one of the nursing units was recording information on a patient's chart when she overheard staff members discussing a patient who had recently been admitted to the unit. They were not certain if the patient was Chinese, Taiwanese, or Vietnamese. The head nurse called the supervisor of international services, who helped clarify that the patient was Taiwanese and so needed a Taiwanese-speaking interpreter. As they continued to discuss the patient, one staff member said, "So she doesn't speak any English at all? How does she get along in this country if she can't speak English?" Another staff member responded, "She doesn't need to get along here. They are all on welfare."[11] Given our concern with the kinds of health care received by members of nonmainstream cultural groups, these comments take on even more significance than simply being prejudicial. Such attitudes may influence the quality of health care that patients receive. And health care professionals are hardly immune to prejudice. Attending nursing school or medical school does not purge feelings of homophobia, racism, sexism, and other kinds of prejudice.

Patients, too, often enter the health care system with prejudicial attitudes. Tom's brother-in-law, for example, a physician in North Carolina, often encounters patients who prefer not to be treated by doctors who are "Yankees." He is frequently asked, "Where are you from?" which suggests that regional differences remain barriers. Because he is from California, these patients consent to his treatment; after all, he is not a "damn Yankee." Regional identities can influence whether people trust medical professionals.

Because of this mistrust, many people prefer to obtain a significant amount of their medical information from their own communities. For example, in the case of AIDS, many gay men turned to the gay community for information on the latest experimental drugs and treatments. In the South, some low-income Whites believe that Prozac is addicting despite scientific evidence to the contrary. However, because Prozac is seen as addictive within this community, patients often refuse to take the drug when it is prescribed. The point here is that people may turn to their own communities out of mistrust of medical professionals. Sometimes these communities can provide significant alternative health care, as in the case of gay men and AIDS; other communities, however, can provide misinformation.

Because of this mistrust, people also sometimes turn to **alternative medicine**—health care provided outside the traditional Western medical system—to find cures for their ailments. For some people, this means a return to their traditional cultural medicinal practices, such as herbal remedies. For others, it means seeking out medical practices that are part of cultural traditions other than their own or new treatments altogether, such as acupuncture. During the earlier stages of the AIDS epidemic, for example, many patients sought out treatments outside the mainstream health care system.

RELIGION AND HEALTH CARE

Even when they are not facing serious illness or death, many people turn to religion or spirituality to help them try to understand the complexities of life.[12] When they are ill, however, some people are driven to seek answers to questions that science cannot always answer. While some people turn to spiritual healing, others prefer to combine their spiritual beliefs with traditional medical care. Sometimes spirituality and/or religion can be helpful in the healing process; other times, it may be helpful in facing death.

What Do You Think?

On January 28, 2003, in his State of the Union address, President George W. Bush announced a commitment of $15 billion to fight HIV and AIDS in parts of Africa and the Caribbean. With the help of such big names as Oprah and her Angel Network and Dublin-born rock star Bono, as well as increased media attention from programs like the HBO documentary *Pandemic: Facing AIDS,* international outreach is increasing. But can money and aid also change cultural values and people's attitudes toward the disease?

What Do You Think?

Should hospitals provide interpreters for their patients who do not speak English? For all languages or only a few? If you were vacationing in, say, Italy and had to go to the hospital, would you expect someone at the hospital to speak English? What about Mongolia, which gets very few English-speaking tourists?

The role of religion and spirituality in health care is still a controversial topic, but today "more than half of the med schools in the country" offer courses in religion and spirituality, "up from just three a decade ago."[13] Yet the role of religion and spirituality in health care raises a number of issues about ethical ways to approach the topic of incorporating health practices into existing beliefs and helping patients avoid any pressure they may feel about their beliefs. It is also important for health care professionals to avoid imposing their beliefs on patients. One example of such an error is when a "doctor told his patient that 'if she was right with God, she wouldn't be depressed.'"[14] Needless to say, health care professionals should not assume that all patients share their beliefs, as people around the world hold a wide range of spiritual views.

Yet, accommodating for religious differences can be an important part of effective health care. Consider the following example:

> Dr. Susan Strangl, a family-medicine doctor at UCLA [had] a Muslim patient who needed medication, but was observing Ramadan and couldn't drink or eat during the day. After taking a **religious history**—routine for all hospitalized patients at UCLA—Strangl chose a once-a-day medication that could be taken after sundown. "If we hadn't talked about it, I would have written him a prescription for four times a day and he would not have taken it," she says.[15]

While religious and spiritual beliefs vary widely, Drs. Koenig, McCullough, and Larson attempted to survey the studies available in this area and compiled the *Handbook of Religion and Health Care*. Our understanding of the role of religion and spirituality in health still leaves us with many unanswered questions, but they do recommend seven specific strategies for physicians and other health care professionals in dealing with patients:[16]

- Take a religious history.
- Support or encourage religious beliefs.
- Ensure access to religious resources.
- Respect visits by clergy.
- View chaplains as part of the health care team.
- Be ready to step in when clergy are unavailable.
- Use advanced spiritual interventions cautiously.

Some of these suggestions may be difficult for health care professionals to follow, particularly when they are followers of different religions, hold different spiritual beliefs, or are atheists or agnostics. Patients also may not want to discuss such topics. One physician, "Dr. Jim Martin, head of the American Academy of Family Physicians, teaches residents to take spiritual histories, but 'if a patient flinches, we don't go there.' And if a patient says faith or spiritual beliefs are not important, 'we check that box and move on.'"[17]

Some physicians, however, argue against some of the previously suggested guidelines. For example, Dr. Richard P. Sloan of the Columbia-Presbyterian Medical Center cautions against praying with patients: "It confuses the relationship. It may encourage patients to think a prayer is going to somehow improve their well-being. It certainly will improve their spiritual well-being but there's no evidence it's going to improve their health." His biggest concern about health care professionals engaging in religious issues is "Manipulation of **religious freedom.** Restriction of religious freedom. Invasion of privacy. And causing harm. It's bad enough to be sick, it's worse still to be gravely ill, but to add to that the burden of remorse and guilt for some supposed failure of religious devotion is unconscionable."[18] While some health care professionals may believe that spiritual beliefs or religious beliefs can help patients be healthier, Dr. Sloan notes, "The question is if religion is demonstrably efficacious, if it really influences longevity, morbidity and mortality, and the quality of life, why don't the insurance companies get in on it?"[19] The point here is that there is no easy list of ways to deal with cultural differences and religious differences in health care. Issues of ethics, however, should always be at the forefront of considerations. Communication about these issues can be key to unraveling the ethical issues at hand.

Many health care professionals may not be aware of the diversity of religious and spiritual beliefs around the world. How can studying religious and cultural differences be helpful to health care professionals? How can health care professionals communicate respect for others religious or spiritual beliefs without compromising their own beliefs? How assertive should patients be about asking health care professionals to accommodate their religious or spiritual beliefs? Health care professionals should also be aware that some patients may fear getting inferior care if they do not share the dominant religious beliefs. How might patients and health care professionals assure each other in this context? All of these questions are at the forefront of the debate about the role of religious or spiritual beliefs in health care.

POWER IN COMMUNICATION ABOUT HEALTH CARE

There is often an imbalance of power in health communication situations. We examined the role of power in Chapter 2, but let's take a look at how it might function in communication in the health care context.

Imbalances of Power in Health Communication

Communication between physician and patient is often marked by an imbalance in power with regard to medical knowledge and access to treatment. Patients, for example, may not have access to drugs without a written prescription from a physician. In order to get that prescription, the patient must rely on the physician, who has the power to prescribe drugs. Physicians in HMOs (health maintenance

Surf's Up!

Do you hate HMOs? Most U.S. Americans seem to. There are complaints about poor coverage and bad decisions, but when you look at the complaints in the Ten Commandments for HMOs website (www.healthcare-disclose.com/), every one of the complaints is about communication.

Physician-patient communication reflects the power imbalance built into the health care structure in the United States. Physicians' power over patients includes medical knowledge and access to treatment, prescriptions, and tests.

What Do You Think?

Before children played "doctor" or "nurse," perhaps they played "healer." The ways in which people care for the sick and dying in society have varied across cultures and throughout history. The doctors of western society today attribute many remedies to the cultural healers of yesterday. So, why is it that contemporary science seems to want to divorce itself from folk or ancient traditions?

organizations), which are increasingly common in the United States, can elect to refer or not refer patients to specialists. Physicians have power over patients in other ways as well. For example, they can recommend certain treatments (and not others), order medical tests, and otherwise determine what kind of treatment the patient receives.

This power imbalance is built into the health care structure in the United States, but physician-patient communication also reflects these power differences. For example, if Judith goes to see a physician for the first time, the physician may introduce herself by saying, "Hi Judith, my name is Doctor Tyndall." What would happen if Judith were to respond, "Hi Lisa, my name is Doctor Martin"? Some physicians would be amused, but others would be irritated by the perceived effort to challenge the power imbalance.

Note also the potential confusion of patients when they meet Dr. Tyndall. Who is Dr. Tyndall? Is she an intern? A staff physician? What role does she play in providing health care? And how many other health care professionals will the patient see today? Because patients may encounter many health care workers in a single day, cultural differences in communication may be exacerbated. The process of negotiating cultural differences may be especially difficult for the patient because each communication interaction may be brief.

Health Care as a Business

It is important to remember that the health care industry in the United States is a huge business. The implications for patients have been the subject of heated public debates over the allocation of health care resources. One controversial issue is whether HMOs ration health care resources; obtaining such resources often is not easy or automatic.

The continuing rapid rise in health care costs in the United States does not appear to have any easy answers. The Arizona Republic recently reported on the rapid rise in the past year: "Nationally, employees' premium contributions are now 22.3 percent, up from 20.5 percent in 2002, according to Hewitt Associates, a national consulting firm. In Phoenix, the news is even worse. In 2003, the cost to cover employees increased 19 percent on average, one of the highest increases in the country."[20] These rising costs are leading employers to shift more of the costs to the employee, as well as considering other more innovative ideas. If health care costs continue to skyrocket, what will happen to the availability of health care resources?

Patients from countries where health care is provided by the government may be confused by the private health care system in the United States. U.S. Americans, too, can become lost in the maze of rules and regulations governing the access to specialists and special treatments. Because there is a power imbalance at work here, patients need to recognize that HMOs are businesses. It may not be enough simply to ask for many medical services, particularly higher-priced treatments.

For example, Didier, a French patient who needed extensive occupational therapy after an accident, did not understand why the number of occupational therapy hours was so limited, especially after his physician told him he would need much more therapy before returning to work. It was only after Didier realized that his HMO was a business that he began to pester the HMO for more hours; in France, this service is provided by the government. Eventually, the HMO consented to more therapy. But Didier believes that it was only after the cost associated with his relentless pestering threatened to exceed the cost of the therapy that the HMO consented to the additional therapy. Thus, patients have to realize that they are the objects of a cost-benefit analysis and that they have to insist on getting access to health care resources.

Intercultural Ethics and Health Issues

What are the ethics of health care communication? In the physician-patient relationship, the physician has far more information than the patient, and the ethics are complicated, particularly in intercultural situations. With regard to communication ethics in health care, physicians can give information about the patient's health within four general frameworks: (1) strict paternalism, (2) benevolent deception, (3) contractual honesty, and (4) unmitigated honesty.[21]

Strict paternalism reflects a physician's decision to provide misinformation to the patient when the physician believes it is in the best interests of the patient. If a patient has terminal cancer, for example, the physician may not feel it would be helpful to tell the patient that he or she has high blood pressure as well. **Benevolent deception** occurs when the physician chooses to communicate only a part of a patient's diagnosis. For example, a patient might be told that she or he

Surf's Up!

Colonialism and powers established by historic conquests seem to play a role in conflicts between traditional beliefs about health and contemporary science. Read the article "Christianity, African Religion and African Medicine" by Gordon L. Chavunduka at http://www.wcc-coe.org/wcc/what/interreligious/cd33-02.html. How can training in intercultural communication help solve the conflict between Christian ideology and African religious beliefs and medicine?

Terri Schiavo is shown here with her mother Mary. Her case is an ongoing case. See if you can find out the latest developments in this case. If you are disabled, should your spouse have more legal rights than your parents to make decisions about remaining on life support? What cultural and ethical values does this reflect?

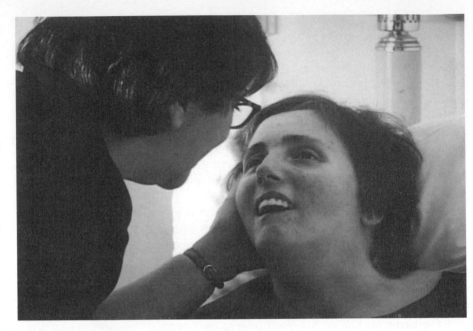

Pop Culture Spotlight

Films about lawyers taking on big corporations for health violations, like *Erin Brockovich, The Rainmaker,* and *A Civil Action,* have been popular. In *The Rainmaker,* an underdog attorney takes on an insurance company that denied cancer treatment to a terminally ill boy. Given the number of jokes about how much we hate lawyers, it is almost as if HMOs are so bad that they make even lawyers look good. Does our communication about our health now have to go through legal channels to be heard?

has cancer and that treatments are available, but not be told that the prognosis is very poor. **Contractual honesty** refers to the practice of telling the patient only what she or he wants to hear or to know. For example, if a patient says, "I only want to hear about the treatments available to me, but not my chances of survival," a physician may choose to follow the patient's wishes. Finally, **unmitigated honesty** refers to when a physician chooses to communicate the entire diagnosis to a patient. Some health care professionals prefer this communication route as a protection against lawsuits. However, some patients are put off by the bluntness of this approach. For instance, if a physician told a patient that some very expensive and painful treatments were available but the patient probably wouldn't survive anyway, that patient might be justifiably upset.

The fear of malpractice suits guides many decisions related to ethics. Sometimes health care organizations use **ethics committees**—often staffed by health care professionals, religious leaders, and social workers—to help make decisions about ethics.[22] In the intercultural context, these decisions can be complex. In some cultures, the family is intimately involved in the health care and medical treatment of its members. In other cultures, medical information is confidential and is given only to the patient, unless he or she is incapacitated or incapable of understanding. Knowing the appropriate way to communicate with patient and family is not easy. For example, some patients may not want their families involved in their care if they have a miscarriage, are suffering from colon-rectal cancer, or are depressed. And many medical procedures are very controversial, even among members of the same culture.

Think about the recent case of Terri Schiavo who suffered brain damage in 1990 and is dependent on a feeding tube. Her legal guardian is her husband, Michael Schiavo, who has asked the courts to withdraw the feeding tube and allow his wife to die. After six years of court battles, "The life-and-death disagreement reached a crescendo when a court order allowed the removal of Terri Schiavo's feeding tube on Oct. 15. She went without food and water for six days, until the Florida Legislature intervened and gave Gov. Jeb Bush the power to have the tube reinserted."[23] Her case has highlighted disagreements between right-to-die and right-to-life groups, particularly as she did not leave any written instructions about her wishes. Michael Schiavo plans additional legal action, and this matter has not yet been settled. What is the right thing to do in this case? Why?

In some religious systems, **euthanasia,** which involves ending the life of a terminally ill patient, is seen as suicide and therefore is unacceptable. In other religions, euthanasia is acceptable for terminally ill patients. Key issues include how much control a patient should have in this situation, how much power a physician should have if his or her ethical framework differs from the patient's, and how much power the state should have in making laws preventing or permitting euthanasia.

Surf's Up!

Find out more about the Terri Schiavo case by going to http://www.usatoday.com/news/graphics/righttodie/flash.htm, which allows you to hear audio recordings of arguments on either side of the debate. After listening to questions and answers from different points of view, how would you decide? How do religion and politics seem to influence each position?

SUMMARY

In this chapter, we examined a number of issues relevant to intercultural communication and health care. Intercultural communication is becoming more important in health care as the population becomes more culturally diverse. Communication is vitally important to the functioning of health services, and this communication is not simply between patient and physician.

We also looked at barriers to effective health care. The history of differential medical treatment and medical studies has created mistrust among some cultural groups. The Tuskegee Syphilis Project and the AIDS epidemic are two examples of how and why groups can come to mistrust the health care system. Many health care providers and patients also hold prejudicial ideologies that can create barriers to effective treatment and to the provision of health care resources. In addition, religious beliefs can also present communication and health care challenges.

Finally, we turned to the issue of power in health communication. There is an imbalance of power between physician and patient, as well as an imbalance of power between patients and the health maintenance organizations. Four ethical approaches to health issues are strict paternalism, benevolent deception, contractual honesty, and unmitigated honesty.

BUILDING INTERCULTURAL SKILLS

1. Reflect on the history of your own family and traditional health care. Do you have many family members who are health care professionals? Did you grow up going to the doctor frequently? How much trust do you have in physicians?

2. Think about how you communicate to others in health care situations. As a patient, do you realize the importance of your communication to the physician or nurse in the diagnosis and treatments you receive? How might you better communicate your health situation to health care professionals? What kinds of cultural attitudes about various health issues do you hold that could be barriers to more effective communication? For example, have you been raised to be ashamed to ask questions about certain parts of your body?

3. Think about how health care professionals communicate with you. If you have a serious illness that may require much interaction with a physician, for example, is this someone whom you can trust?

4. Think about how health care professionals might encourage more open communication from patients so that they can receive better health care.

ACTIVITIES

1. *The media and health care:* Watch the news media for coverage of health issues as they relate to the most affected cultural groups. For example, is AIDS still framed as a "gay disease"? Is the hanta virus portrayed as a Navajo illness? In what ways does the conflation of the cultural group with the disease create misunderstandings?

2. *Communication about health care:* Talk to a health care professional about his or her experiences with cultural differences in communication. What were the main problems in the communication process? What suggestions might you make to avoid these problems in the future?

www.mhhe.com/
experiencing2

THE ONLINE LEARNING CENTER at www.mhhe.com/experiencing2 features self-quizzes, flashcards, and crossword puzzles based on the chapter's key terms and concepts.

ENDNOTES

1. Pauwels, A. (1995). *Cross-cultural communication in the health sciences.* South Melbourne, Australia: Macmillan Education Australia, p. 3.
2. Pauwels (1995), p. 94.
3. Pauwels (1995), pp. 94–95.
4. Northouse, L. L., & Northouse, P. G. (1998). *Health communication: Strategies for health professionals.* Stamford, CT: Appleton & Lange, p. 103.
5. Shilling, C. (1993). *The body and social theory.* Newbury Park, CA: Sage, p. 58.
6. See, for example, Gilman, S. L. (1985). *Difference and pathology: Stereotypes of sexuality, race and madness.* Ithaca, NY: Cornell University Press; Gilman, S. L. (1988). *Disease and representation: Images of illness from madness to AIDS.* Ithaca, NY: Cornell University Press; Harding, S. G. (Ed.). (1993). *The "racial" economy of science: Toward a democratic future.* Bloomington: Indiana University Press; Harding, S. G. (1998). *Is science multicultural? Postcolonialism, feminisms, and epistemologies.* Bloomington: Indiana University Press; Mondimore, F. M. (1996). *A natural history of homosexuality.* Baltimore: Johns Hopkins University Press; Stoler, A. L. (1995). *Race and the education of desire.* Durham, NC: Duke University Press.

7. Solomon, M. (1985). The rhetoric of dehumanization: An analysis of medical reports of the Tuskegee Syphilis Project. *Western Journal of Speech Communication, 49*, 233–247.

8. Levi, J. (1992). Homophobia and AIDS public policy. In W. J. Blumenfeld (Ed.), *Homophobia: How we all pay the price* (pp. 217–232). Boston: Beacon Press, p. 217.

9. For some of these discussions, see, for example, Patton, C. (1990). *Inventing AIDS.* New York: Routledge; Patton, C. (1996). *Fatal advice: How safe-sex education went wrong.* Durham, NC: Duke University Press; Shilts, R. (1987). *And the band played on: Politics, people and the AIDS epidemic.* New York: St. Martin's Press.

10. Gross, L. (1993). *Contested closets: The politics and ethics of outing.* Minneapolis: University of Minnesota Press, p. 34.

11. Northouse & Northouse (1998), pp. 288–289.

12. Aldridge, D. (2000). *Spirituality, healing and medicine: Return to the silence.* Philadelphia: Jessica Kingsley Publishers.

13. Kalb, C. (2003, November 10). Faith & healing. *Newsweek*, p. 44.

14. Kalb, C. (2003, November 10), p. 55–56.

15. Kalb, C. (2003, November 10), p. 54.

16. Koenig, H. G., McCullough, M. E., & Larson, D. B. (2001). *Handbook of religion and health.* Oxford: Oxford University Press.

17. Kalb, C. (2003, November 10), p. 54.

18. Sloan, R. P. (2003, November 10). 'Religion is a private matter.' Interview with C. Kalb. *Newsweek*, p. 50.

19. Sloan, R. P. (2000, January/February). Religion, spirituality and medicine. *Freethought Today* (online). (http://www.ffrf.org/fttoday/jan_feb00/sloan.html)

20. Snyder, J. (2003, November 2). Ouch! Many feel pain of health care costs. *The Arizona Republic*, p. A1.

21. Pauwels (1995), p. 272.

22. Kreps, G. L., & Kunimoto, E. N. (1994). *Effective communication in multicultural health care settings.* Thousand Oaks, CA: Sage, pp. 67–69.

23. Gray, C. (2003, October 28). On TV, Michael Schiavo displays anger, resolve. *The Philadelphia Inquirer* (online). (http://www.philly.com/mld/inquirer/news/local/states/pennsylvania/counties/montgomery_county/7118945.htm)

Glossary

accommodating style Emphasizes an indirect approach for dealing with conflict and a more emotionally restrained manner.

adaptors Gestures related to managing our emotions.

affirmative action (AA) Statutes that attempt to stop discrimination by encouraging the hiring of minorities and women.

Afrocentric An orientation toward African or African American cultural standards, including beliefs and values, as the criteria for interpreting behaviors and attitudes.

age identity The identification with the cultural conventions of how we should act, look, and behave according to our age.

AIDS Acquired immune deficiency syndrome; a disease caused by a virus, HIV, transmitted through sexual or blood contact, that attacks the immune system. (See **HIV**.)

alternative medicine A medical approach that goes against the norms of the medical establishment. It can incorporate holistic medicine, spirituality, and/or non-Western wellness philosophies.

Americans with Disabilities Act (ADA) A law requiring that places of business make "reasonable" accommodations for employees with physical disabilities.

assimilatable The degree of participation in a type of cultural adaptation in which an individual gives up his or her own cultural heritage and adopts the mainstream cultural identity. (See **cultural adaptation**.)

benevolent deception Withholding information from a patient, ostensibly for his or her own good.

bilingual Able to speak two languages fluently or at least competently.

bilingualism The ability to speak two languages.

boundary maintenance The regulation of interaction between hosts and tourists.

class identity A sense of belonging to a group that shares similar economic, occupational, or social status.

class structure The economic organization of income levels in a society; the structure that defines upper, middle, lower, and other social classes.

cocultural group Nondominant cultural groups that exist in a national culture—for example, African American or Chinese American.

code switching Changing from one language or communication style to another.

collectivism The tendency to focus on the goals, needs, and views of the ingroup rather than individuals' own goals, needs, and views. (Compare with **individualist**.)

colonial education system Schools established by colonial powers in colonized regions. They often forbade the use of native languages and discussion of native cultures.

colonial histories The histories that legitimate international invasions and annexations.

communication A symbolic process whereby reality is produced, maintained, repaired, and transformed.

communication style The metamessage that contextualizes how listeners are expected to accept and interpret verbal messages.

complementarity A principle of relational attraction suggesting that sometimes we are attracted to people who are different from us.

compromise style A style of interaction for an intercultural couple in which both partners give up some part of their own cultural habits and beliefs to minimize cross-cultural differences. (Compare with **consensus style, obliteration style,** and **submission style**.)

conflict The interference between two or more interdependent individuals or groups of people who perceive incompatible goals, values, or expectations in attaining those ends.

consensus style A style of interaction for an intercultural couple in which partners deal with cross-cultural differences by negotiating their relationship. (Compare with **compromise style, obliteration style,** and **submission style**.)

constructive identity An identity that is actively negotiated from various cultures in contact and that often creates feelings of a new multicultural identity.

contact cultures Cultural groups in which people tend to stand close together and touch frequently when they interact—for example, cultural groups in South America, the Middle East, and southern Europe. (See **noncontact cultures.**)

context The physical or social situation in which communication occurs.

contractual honesty Telling a patient only what he or she wants to know.

core symbols The fundamental beliefs that are shared by the members of a cultural group. Labels, a category of core symbols, are names or markers used to classify individual, social, or cultural groups.

cross-cultural trainers Trainers who teach people to become familiar with other cultural norms and to improve their interactions with people of different domestic and international cultures.

cultural contact When two or more cultures come together, sometimes on an individual basis, but often through larger social migrations, wars, and other displacements.

cultural group histories The history of each cultural group within a nation that includes, for example, the history of where the group originated, why the people migrated, and how they came to develop and maintain their cultural traits.

cultural identities Who we are as influenced by the cultures to which we belong.

cultural imperialism Domination through the spread of cultural products.

cultural space The particular configuration of the communication that constructs meanings of various places.

cultural texts Cultural artifacts (magazines, TV programs, movies, and so on) that convey cultural norms, values, and beliefs.

culture Learned patterns of behavior and attitudes shared by a group of people.

culture industries Industries that produce and sell popular culture as commodities.

culture shock A relatively short-term feeling of disorientation and discomfort due to the lack of familiar cues in the environment.

deception The act of making someone believe what is not true.

demographics The characteristics of a population, especially as classified by age, sex, and income.

diaspora A massive migration, often caused by war or famine or persecution, that results in the dispersal of a unified group.

diasporic histories The histories of the ways in which international cultural groups were created through transnational migrations, slavery, religious crusades, or other historical forces.

direct approach Emphasizes that conflict is fundamentally a good thing and should be approached head on.

discrimination Behaviors resulting from stereotypes or prejudice that cause some people to be denied equal participation or rights based on cultural group membership (such as race).

discussion style Combines the direct and emotionally restrained dimensions and emphasizes a verbally direct approach for dealing with disagreements.

dynamic style Uses an indirect style of communicating along with a more emotionally intense expressiveness.

eco-tourism Tourism of sites of environmental or natural interest.

electronic colonialism Domination or exploitation utilizing technological forms.

emblems Gestures that have a specific verbal translation.

emotionally expressive style Conflict style where intense and overt displays of emotions are valued during discussion of disagreements.

encapsulated identity An identity that is torn between different cultural identities and that often creates feelings of ambiguity.

enclaves Regions that are surrounded by another country's territory; cultural minority groups that live within a larger cultural group's territory.

engagement style Emphasizes a verbally direct and confrontational approach to dealing with conflict.

equal employment opportunity (EEO) Laws against discrimination in the workplace.

equivalency An issue in translation, the condition of being equal in meaning, value, quantity, and so on.

ethics Principles of conduct that help govern behaviors of individuals and groups.

ethics committees Groups that provide guidance in making health care decisions; usually composed of health care professionals, administrators, lawyers, social workers, members of the religious community, and patient representatives.

ethnic histories The histories of ethnic groups.

ethnic identity A set of ideas about one's own ethnic group membership; a sense of belonging to a particular group and knowing something about the shared experience of the group.

ethnocentrism An orientation toward one's own ethnic group; often a tendency to elevate one's own culture above others.

Eurocentric The assumption of the centrality or superiority of European culture.

euthanasia The ending of the life of a terminally ill patient.

eye contact A nonverbal code that communicates meanings about respect and status and often regulates turn taking during interactions.

facial expressions Facial gestures that convey emotions and attitudes.

family histories The body of knowledge shared by family members and the customs, rituals, and stories passed from one generation to another within a family.

friendship A personal, nonromantic relationship that has culture-specific definitions.

gay relationships Same-sex romantic relationships.

gender histories The histories of how cultural conventions of men and women are created, maintained, and/or altered.

gender identity The identification with the cultural notions of masculinity and femininity and what it means to be a man or a woman.

gestures Nonverbal communication involving hand and arm movements.

globalization The increasing tendency toward international connections in media, business, and culture.

global nomads People who grow up in many different cultural contexts because their parents relocated.

global village A term coined by Marshall McLuhan in the 1960s that refers to a world in which communication technology links people from remote parts of the world.

grand narrative A unified history and view of humankind.

HBCUs Historically black colleges and universities.

health care professionals Physicians, nurses, and all the other medical staff with whom patients in the health care system come into contact.

heterogeneity Consisting of different or dissimilar elements.

hidden histories The histories that are hidden from or forgotten by the mainstream representations of past events.

high-context communication A style of communication in which much of the information is contained in the contexts and nonverbal cues rather than expressed explicitly in words. (Compare with **low-context communication.**)

high culture The cultural activities that are considered elite, including opera, ballet, and symphony. (Compare with **low culture** and **popular culture.**)

HIV Human immunodeficiency virus. (See **AIDS.**)

home The immediate cultural context for our upbringing; where we have lived.

homo narrans A term used to describe the story-telling tendencies of human beings.

host Residents of a tourist region.

hyphenated Americans Americans who identify not only with being American citizens but also with being members of ethnic groups.

identity The concept of who we are. Characteristics of identity may be understood differently depending on the perspectives that people take (for example, social psychological, communication, or critical perspectives).

illustrators Gestures that go along with and refer to speech.

immigration Movement to a new country, region, or environment to settle more or less permanently.

improvised performance A way of thinking about intercultural interaction in which two people are making up a performance as they go along.

incompatibility A state of incongruity in goals, values, or expectations between two or more individuals.

indirect approach Emphasizes that conflict should be avoided.

individualism The tendency to emphasize individual identities, beliefs, needs, goals, and views rather than those of the group. (Compare with **collectivism.**)

intellectual histories Written histories that focus on the development of ideas.

intercultural communication The interaction between people from different cultural backgrounds.

intercultural conflict The perceived or real incompatibility of goals, values, or expectations between two parties from different cultures.

intercultural dating The pursuit of a romantic intercultural relationship.

intercultural relationships Relationships that are formed between individuals from different cultures.

interdependent A state of mutual influence; the action or behavior of one individual affecting the other person in a relationship.

intermediary In a formal setting, a professional third party, such as a lawyer, real estate agent, or counselor, who intervenes when two parties are in conflict. Informal intermediaries may be friends or colleagues who intervene.

international students Students attending high school or college in another country. (See **study-abroad programs.**)

interpersonal allies People, often friends, who work for better interpersonal and intergroup relations.

interpretation The process of verbally expressing what is said or written in another language.

intimacy The extent of emotional closeness.

labels Terms used to refer to people's identities.

language A means of communication using shared symbols.

language acquisition The process of learning language.

language policies Laws or customs that determine which language will be spoken when and where.

learning styles The different ways students learn in different cultures.

low-context communication A style of communication in which much of the information is conveyed in words rather than in nonverbal cues and contexts. (Compare with **high-context communication.**)

low culture The non-elite activities seen as the opposite of high culture (for example, movies, rock music, and talk shows). In the past, low culture was considered unworthy of serious study. With the rise of cultural studies, however, the activities that are associated with low culture have become important representations of everyday human lives. (Compare with **high culture.** See also **popular culture.**)

macrocontexts The political, social, and historical situations, backgrounds, and environments that influence communication.

majority identity development The development of a sense of belonging to a dominant group.

maquiladoras Assembly plants or factories (mainly of U.S. companies) established on the U.S.-Mexico border and using mainly Mexican labor.

masculinity/femininity value A cultural variability dimension that concerns the degree of being feminine—valuing fluid gender roles, quality of life, service, relationships, and interdependence—and the degree of being masculine—emphasizing distinctive gender roles, ambition, materialism, and independence.

media imperialism Domination or control through media.

mediation The act of resolving conflict by having someone intervene between two parties.

medical jargon Medical terminology, especially that which is confusing or difficult for the layperson to understand.

medical terminology A set of scientific words and phrases used by doctors to precisely describe illness.

melting pot A metaphor that assumes that immigrants and cultural minorities will be assimilated into the U.S. majority culture, losing their original cultures.

migrating When an individual leaves the primary cultural context in which he or she was raised and moves to a new cultural context for an extended period of time. (See also **immigrant** and **sojourner.**)

minority identity development The development of a sense of belonging to a nondominant group.

mobility The state of moving from place to place.

monochronic An orientation to time that assumes it is linear and is a commodity that can be lost or gained.

multicultural identity A sense of in-betweenness that develops as a result of frequent or multiple cultural border crossings.

multilingual The ability to speak more than two languages fluently or at least competently.

multinational Companies that have operations in two or more nations.

multiracial and multicultural people People whose heritage draws from more than one racial or cultural group.

national history A body of knowledge based on past events that influenced a country's development.

national identity National citizenship.

neighborhood Living area defined by its cultural identity, especially an ethnic or racial one.

noncontact cultures Cultural groups in which people tend to maintain more space and touch less often than people do in contact cultures. Great Britain and Japan tend to have noncontact cultures. (See **contact cultures.**)

nonverbal codes Systems for understanding the meanings of nonverbal behavior, including personal space, eye contact, facial expressions, gestures, time orientation, and silence.

nonverbal communication Communication through means other than language—for example, facial expressions and clothing.

obliteration style A style of interaction for an intercultural couple in which both partners attempt to erase their individual cultures in dealing with cultural differences. (Compare with **compromise style, consensus style,** and **submission style.**)

pacifism Opposition to the use of force under any circumstances.

perception The process by which we select, organize, and interpret external and internal stimuli to create our view of the world.

personal identity A person's notions of self.

personal space The immediate area around a person, invasion of which may provoke discomfort or offense.

phonology The study of speech sounds.

physical ability identity A knowledge of self based on characteristics related to the body, either more permanent or temporary—for example, sight, hearing, and weight.

physical attraction Sexual desire based on the appearance of another.

political histories Written histories that focus on political events.

polychronic An orientation to time that sees it as circular and more holistic.

popular culture A new name for low culture; referring to those systems or artifacts that most people share and that most people know about, including television, music, videos, and popular magazines.

postcolonialism An intellectual, political, and cultural movement that calls for the independence of once colonized states and also liberation from colonialist ways of thinking.

power A state of differential levels of societal and structural privilege.

power distance A cultural variability dimension that concerns the extent to which people accept an unequal distribution of power.

pragmatics The study of how meaning is constructed in relation to receivers and how language is actually used in particular contexts in language communities.

prejudice An attitude (usually negative) toward a cultural group based on little or no evidence.

prejudicial ideologies Sets of ideas that rely on stereotypes.

racial and ethnic identity Identifying with a particular racial or ethnic group. Although in the past racial groups were classified on the basis of biological characteristics, most scientists now recognize that race is constructed in fluid social and historical contexts.

racial histories The histories of nonmainstream racial groups.

reader profiles Portrayals of readership demographics prepared by magazines.

regionalism Loyalty to a particular region that holds significant cultural meaning for that person.

regulators Gestures used to guide the flow of a conversation, especially for turn taking.

relational messages Messages (verbal and nonverbal) that express how we feel about others.

relativist position The view that the particular language we speak, especially the structure of the language, shapes our perception of reality and cultural patterns. (Compare with **nominalist position** and **qualified relativist position**.)

religious conflicts Conflicts that arise from strongly held views and religious beliefs.

religious freedom The ability to practice one's religion without fear; a concern among health care professionals who worry about engaging in religious issues.

religious histories Bodies of knowledge containing the items of faith and that faith's prescriptions for action that have been important for a cultural group.

religious identity A sense of belonging to a religious group.

resistance Avoiding intrusions; may take fairly passive forms or more assertive forms.

restraint style Conflict style where disagreements are best discussed in an emotionally calm manner.

retreatism The avoidance of tourists by hosts.

revitalization The economic benefits associated with tourism in certain areas.

romantic relationships Intimate relationships that comprise love, involvement, sharing, openness, connectedness, and so on.

self-awareness Related to intercultural communication competence; the quality of knowing how you are perceived as a communicator, as well as your strengths and weaknesses.

self-reflexivity A process of learning to understand ourselves and our own position in society.

semantics The study of words and meanings.

sexual orientation histories The historical experiences of gays and lesbians.

silence The absence of verbal messages.

similarity principle A principle of relational attraction suggesting that we tend to be attracted to people whom we perceive to be similar to ourselves.

social conflict Conflict that arises from unequal or unjust social relationships between groups.

social histories Written histories that focus on everyday life experiences of various groups in the past.

social movements Organized activities in which individuals work together to bring about social change.

social positions The places from which we speak that are socially constructed and thus embedded with assumptions about gender, race, class, age, social roles, sexuality, and so on.

social roles Roles we enact that are learned in a culture—for example, mother, big brother, and community leader.

socioeconomic class histories Bodies of knowledge relating to a group's relationship to social class and economic forces.

source text The original language text of a translation. (See also **target text.**)

status The relative position an individual holds in social or organizational settings.

stereotypes Widely held beliefs about a group of people.

stereotyping The use of stereotypes.

strict paternalism A physician's provision of misinformation for the supposed benefit of the patient.

study-abroad programs University-sponsored programs that give course credit for study in other countries.

submission style A style of interaction for an intercultural couple in which one partner yields to the other partner's cultural patterns, abandoning or denying his or her own culture. (Compare with **compromise style, consensus style,** and **obliteration style.**)

syntactics The study of the structure, or grammar, of a language.

target text The new language text into which the original language text is translated. (See also **source text.**)

teaching styles The different ways teachers teach in different cultures.

third culture style A new communication style that results from two people trying to adapt to each other's styles.

tourists Visitors to another country or region.

translation The process of producing a written text that refers to something said or written in another language.

traveling The changing of cultural spaces through locomotion.

Tuskegee Syphilis Project A government-sponsored study of syphilis in which treatment of the disease was withheld from African American males for the purpose of establishing an experimental control group.

U-curve theory A theory of cultural adaptation positing that migrants go through fairly predictable phases (excitement/anticipation, shock/disorientation, and adaptation) in adapting to a new cultural situation.

uncertainty avoidance A cultural variability dimension that concerns the extent to which uncertainty, ambiguity, and deviant ideas and behaviors are avoided.

universalist position An ethical approach that emphasizes the similarity of beliefs across cultures—for example, killing within the group or treason.

unmitigated honesty A physician's communication of the entirety of a medical diagnosis to a patient.

values A system for viewing certain ideas as more important than others.

Whiteness The associations having to do with the identities of White people.

worldview Underlying assumptions about the nature of reality and human behavior.

Photo Credits

Index